Institute for Early Christianity
in the Graeco-Roman World,
Cambridge

FIRST-CENTURY CHRISTIANS
IN THE GRAECO-ROMAN WORLD

Andrew D. Clarke
Series Editor

Seek the Welfare of the City:
Christians as Benefactors and Citizens
Bruce W. Winter

Serve the Community of the Church:
Christians as Leaders and Ministers
Andrew D. Clarke

Solicit the Progress of the Gospel:
Christians as Partners and Stewards
G. Walter Hansen and Simon J. Gathercole

Secure the Well-Being of the Family:
Christians as Householders and Servants
Bruce W. Winter, Andrew D. Clarke and Gerald W. Peterman

Strengthen the Fellowship of Believers:
Christians as Élites and Havenots
David W. J. Gill

Strive for the Faith of the Gospel:
Christians as Public Speakers and Apologists
Philip H. Kern

FIRST-CENTURY CHRISTIANS IN THE GRAECO-ROMAN WORLD

Serve the Community of the Church

Christians as Leaders and Ministers

by

Andrew D. Clarke

WILLIAM B. EERDMANS PUBLISHING COMPANY
GRAND RAPIDS, MICHIGAN / CAMBRIDGE, U.K.

© 2000 Wm. B. Eerdmans Publishing Company
255 Jefferson Ave. S.E., Grand Rapids, Michigan 49503 /
P.O. Box 163, Cambridge CB3 9PU U.K.

Printed in the United States of America

06 05 04 03 02 01 00   7 6 5 4 3 2 1

Library of Congress Cataloging-in-Publication Data

Clarke, Andrew D.
Serve the community of the church : Christians as leaders
and ministers / by Andrew D. Clarke.
p.   cm. — (First-century Christians in the Graeco-Roman world)
Includes bibliographical references and index.
ISBN 0-8028-4182-1 (pbk. : alk. paper)
1. Leadership — Religious aspect — Christianity — History of
doctrines — Early church, ca. 30-600.   2. Christian leadership —
History of doctrines — Early church, ca. 30-600.   3. Church history
— Primitive and early church, ca. 30-600.   I. Title.   II. Series.
BR195.L42 C53 2000
270.1 — dc21   99-046841

TABLE OF CONTENTS

PREFACE

This book reflects a deep-seated fascination over the last ten years with the nature of leadership in the Christian community, most especially as it was variously taught by Paul and practised in the congregations of the first century. This interest inevitably overflows into consideration of church organization in the modern era and I am grateful for the interactions I have had with many individuals in the churches of which I have been a member over these years.

The bulk of the writing of this project took place during a period of research leave in 1998 when I was able to benefit from the excellent resources available to me at Tyndale House Biblical Research Library, Cambridge. I would like to register my thanks to the Department of Divinity with Religious Studies and the Faculty of Arts and Divinity at the University of Aberdeen for granting me the time away from teaching duties. Additionally, I would like to thank warmly Sir Kirby Laing who generously provided a grant towards the expenses of the research trip. Of no less importance, the hospitality of Dr and Mrs Peter Smethurst during this period considerably enhanced my stay in Cambridge.

A number of colleagues and friends have read sections of the work and have offered helpful insight which has been incorporated into the text. In particular I would like to thank Dr Bruce Winter, Professors Howard Marshall and Francis Watson, Dr Helen Bond, the New Testament postgraduate seminar at the University of Aberdeen, and my father.

Most especial gratitude is extended to my family, and in particular my wife, Jane, who stoically tolerated the disruption to family life during my time in Cambridge.

Aberdeen

CHAPTER 1

INTRODUCTION

I. The Social Context of the New Testament

In his foundational textbook, *The Birth of the New Testament*,[1] Professor Moule addressed a number of questions concerning the self-awareness of the early church: 'What were the early Christians concerned about? How did they live? What were the problems that lay heavy upon them?'[2] Scholars have long been aware that the early church stood in the wake of centuries of Jewish and Greek philosophical and theological traditions. The first Christian believers continually sought to discover and express their own identity in relation to both these heritages.[3] During the first century there was, however, another context which dominated the lives of Jews, Greeks and Christians.

During the first century, Jewish communities, especially in the diaspora, were struggling to redefine their identity in relation to the

---

[1]C.F.D. Moule, *The Birth of the New Testament* (3rd ed.; Harper's New Testament Commentaries; San Francisco: Harper & Row, 1982).

[2]This is Stephen Neill's analysis in S. Neill, *The Interpretation of the New Testament, 1861-1986* (2nd ed.; Oxford: Oxford University Press, 1988) 275; but see C.F.D. Moule, *The Birth of the New Testament*, 45.

[3]We see a similar struggle very clearly in first-century Egypt where Jewish scholars sought to interpret their own tradition in the light of the dominant Greek ideas of the time.

complex and multi-cultural world of the emerging early Roman
empire. Should they pursue assimilation with the surrounding social
context or should they maintain their distinctiveness and cultural
isolation?[4] Greek communities in the east of the empire, also with
centuries of proud history, were at the same time endeavouring to
lose neither their ancient religious customs nor their tried and tested
systems of government. In many cases, however, they could only do
so by redefining these cherished customs in relation to the new,
dominant power in the west.

The Robert Wilken argued in the 1970s that 'we have an inflated
view of the history of early Christianity'.[5] By this he meant that New
Testament scholars, while focusing on early Christianity, occluded
the broader social framework of which it was a particularly small
part. In recent years New Testament scholars have returned to
studying these precious texts within the much broader social context
of the early Roman empire. It is also significant that many ancient
historians have developed an increasing awareness of the value of the
New Testament documents in informing the increasingly emerging
picture of Graeco-Roman social history in the first century.[6] It must
not be overlooked, therefore, that, like the contemporary Jewish and
Greek communities, the first Christians were also struggling to
establish an identity within this complex and multi-cultural world of
the early Roman empire. They were subject to the same powerful
social, political and religious forces. The series in which this
monograph is published recognizes that the early Christians were
'members of households, possibly associations, and certainly cities in
the first-century Graeco-Roman world before they embraced the
preaching of the gospel'. This context inevitably provided for them a
range of 'challenges, difficulties, and necessary adjustments'.

The Graeco-Roman world of the mid-first century A.D. was the
multi-cultural context which surrounded the first Christians and
within which they endeavoured to express their faith. Both Jewish

---

[4]On this see the recent volume of essays, L.V. Rutgers, *The Hidden Heritage of
Diaspora Judaism* (Contributions to Biblical Exegesis and Theology, 20; Leuven:
Peeters, 1998).

[5]R.L. Wilken, 'Collegia, Philosophical Schools, and Theology', in S. Benko & J.J.
O'Rourke (eds.), *Pagan Rome and the Early Christians* (Bloomington: Indiana
University Press, 1984) 269.

[6]In recent scholarly work, New Testament texts are now frequently cited by
ancient historians as primary sources alongside Jewish and pagan literature
which together fill out our picture of the social world of the first century A.D.

and Gentile Christians, living in the urban centres of the Roman empire, were deeply integrated into the social, cultural and economic fabric of that society before they had encountered the Christian gospel. Theirs was not a 'Christian' world, but they lived within a wider society as a distinct minority.[7] This raises many fascinating questions for the social historian, answers to which are beyond the reach of exclusively theological interrogation of the New Testament texts.[8] How were these Christians to engage with their surrounding cultural context? What model of organization were these Christian communities to adopt? And what would have been their perception of the nature and practice of leadership? Early Christianity was an urban phenomenon,[9] and the models of leadership and structures of organization which were most accessible to them were those of the Graeco-Roman cities, the Roman colonies, the ubiquitous smaller guilds and associations of which some Christians would have been members, the family and household networks within which both citizens and non-citizens lived, and the Jewish synagogues by then established throughout Palestine and the diaspora.

This study will compare both the theory and practice of leadership in each of these areas of first-century society. Paul visited, and founded Christian communities in, a number of different urban communities. In the first century A.D., these can be helpfully divided into two main types: the Graeco-Roman cities and the Roman colonies. Consideration will first be given to the ancient Greek city as it survived into the Roman empire, and in particular to the rôle of the civic popular assembly, or ἐκκλησία, the contexts and ways in which its leaders exercised power, and the place of religion within this civic sphere. Secondly, we shall look at the civic constitutions and the profiles of leading figures in the specifically Roman colonies and cities throughout the empire during the first century A.D. Here we shall also reflect on how the imperial cult was a tool of social cohesion. Almost all early Christians will have been affected by one

---

[7]H. Moxnes, '"He saw that the City was full of Idols" (Acts 17:16): Visualizing the World of the First Christians', in D. Hellholm, H. Moxnes & T.K. Seim (eds.), *Mighty Minorities?: Minorities in Early Christianity — Positions and Strategies: Essays in Honour of Jacob Jervell on his 70th birthday, 21 May 1995* (Oslo: Scandinavian University Press, 1995) 107, points out that this is reflected in the notable lack of early archaeological evidence of Christian buildings or works of art.

[8]H. Moxnes, '"He saw that the City was full of Idols" (Acts 17:16)', 109.

[9]*Cf.* the widely influential volume, W.A. Meeks, *The First Urban Christians: the Social World of the Apostle Paul* (New Haven: Yale University Press, 1983).

or another of these models of local civic government, either in respect to the privileges given to them as citizens, the entertainments regularly provided for its wider population, or the public practice of civic religion.

Where leadership within the civic context was almost exclusively the domain of the élites in Graeco-Roman society, there were also a number of contexts in which poorer members of society could exercise both power and influence. The voluntary associations, professional guilds and trade unions were highly popular in the early empire. For the most part they had highly developed constitutions with an established pattern of selecting and appointing leading officials. Many of these groups included non-citizen or slave members who earned positions of leadership within this limited context. The Roman family or household was a further context in which leadership was exercised or experienced by both rich and poor, citizen and non-citizen, slave and free. The late Republic and early Roman empire was a period in which the traditional family was under considerable pressure. The first emperors established a programme of legislation seeking to restore family values. We shall look at these values and the dominant place of the father within this institution.

Finally, consideration will be given to the function and organization of the Jewish synagogue, widely spread throughout the empire in the first century A.D. Epigraphic evidence uncovered and analysed in recent decades has enabled scholars to reconsider the previously widely-accepted view of life and leadership within these communities. We shall, in particular, consider who were the leading figures within these Jewish communities and on what grounds they rose to prominence.

It will become clear that there were significant aspects of leadership which were consistent across each of these contexts. Once these common denominators are identified we shall be in a better position to assess how a Christian in the first century might have broadly conceived of the nature of leadership and the rôle of leaders in the surrounding social context of the Graeco-Roman world. This perspective can then provide a context to inform our reading of the New Testament texts and enable us to reflect on the extent to which these models of community organization and leadership may have influenced the first-century Christians as they sought to define the parameters and distinctives of their own communities.

In the course of correspondence with a number of these communities, Paul endeavours to lay some important parameters for leadership which he considers appropriate to the new Christian context. Some of these are defined in express contrast to the patterns of leadership widely practised in Graeco-Roman society and occasionally also in the early Christian communities.

II. Mind the Gap

One of the major problems facing the interpreter of first-century sources, not least the texts which comprise the New Testament, is the hermeneutical gap which inevitably exists between the languages and beliefs of today's society and those of the distant Graeco-Roman world.[10] The insidious hazard lies in the confident, but often unconsidered, assumptions which today's readers can sometimes make about context and meaning without due recourse to an appropriate means of transposing across the intervening historical and cultural divides. Lester Grabbe notes with regard to scholarly discussion of the origins of the synagogue, for example (but this could so easily apply to many areas of New Testament research):

> Unfortunately, the assumptions are so strong that questions of data and matters of historical evidence often seem to make little headway against the tide of tradition. They are confounded by that most persistent and hardy of species — the impregnable defence of 'what everyone knows,' the incontrovertible argument of 'what must have been.' This results in the use of the flimsiest of evidence to support sweeping conclusions, not to mention standard reconstructions which go on paragraph after paragraph without reference to a piece of primary data. Alternatively, discussions mix data from various periods and geographical areas without any discussion of the methodological problems for doing so.[11]

Recent decades have witnessed a significant wealth of archaeological finds. Much epigraphical, papyrological, numismatic

---

[10]Cf. the challenging article by S.E. Alcock, 'Minding the Gap in Hellenistic and Roman Greece', in S.E. Alcock & R. Osborne (eds.), *Placing the Gods: Sanctuaries and Sacred Space in Ancient Greece* (Oxford: Clarendon Press, 1994) 247-61.

[11]L.L. Grabbe, 'Synagogues in Pre-70 Palestine: a Reassessment', in D. Urman & P.V.M. Flesher (eds.), *Ancient Synagogues: Historical Analysis and Archaeological Discovery* (Studia post-Biblica, 47; 2 vols.; Leiden: E.J. Brill, 1995) 17.

and other ancient non-literary evidence has been unearthed, catalogued and evaluated. These resources are now beginning to influence long-established scholarly opinions and are kindling a renewed interest in the social location of Greek, Roman, Jewish and Christian communities in the first century A.D. Careful reading of both literary and non-literary primary source material highlights the extent of the hermeneutical gap across the centuries and the degree to which many of the 'assured results' of scholarly opinion need to be reassessed.

One important area which highlights the width of the hermeneutical gap is the way in which people from the first-century Graeco-Roman world regarded the relationship between the religious and secular aspects of their culture. Although deriving from the Latin words *religio* and *saeculum*, the meanings of these modern terms have become considerably distanced from their etymological antecedents. John Richardson reminds the interpreter of ancient sources that:

> such communality of language, by creating a sense of familiarity in the mind of a modern observer of the Roman empire, may hinder a proper understanding of antiquity, because the importance of the afterlife of these words and symbols tends to obscure the nature of the contexts from which they originated.[12]

In actuality neither of these modern categories, the religious or the secular, would have been especially meaningful to a Greek or Roman citizen of the first century.[13] As terms widely used today, they may nonetheless prove useful in our present task of transposing across the intervening centuries precisely because they can serve to highlight the incongruity of these terms in that ancient society. Over the next five chapters the structures and ethos of a number of specific institutions will be considered. It will be seen that although the focus of each of these institutions might be regarded, from our perspective, as secular, political or social, there was an all-important and inseparable 'religious' context which embraced both the ethos and business of each of these establishments.

---

[12]J.S. Richardson, '*Imperium Romanum*: Empire and the Language of Power', *Journal of Roman Studies* 81 (1991) 1.

[13]*Cf.* M. Beard, J. North & S. Price, *Religions of Rome: a History* (Cambridge: Cambridge University Press, 1998) 216-17, for an assessment of the term *religio* in the early empire.

Relationships within Graeco-Roman society clearly operated within a framework dominated by distinctions of honour and status. From our knowledge of ancient literary sources, we expect to see this very clearly in the civic context dominated by the élites and their preoccupation with patronage. The magistrates and priests were largely honorific posts, earned not through skill or training, but on the grounds of wealth and social standing. What is equally the case, but rather more unexpected, is that personal influence also operated within other contexts in a similar way, even among the comparatively poorer members of society. The epigraphic and papyrological evidence demonstrates to us, for example, that a similar honour system was at work in the guilds or associations which were more often the preserve of slaves or freedmen. It operated even at the familial level between master and freedman or between father and son. On closer inspection we may be surprised to find that personal influence also operated along the same lines in the so-called 'religious' context of the Jewish synagogues and communities. As Jon Lendon argues:

> In the Roman world personal influence could be mobilized for the cheap purchase of a farm, for the return of a loan, for a roof over a traveller's head far from home, for a post in the army, or even for the capture of a runaway, book-stealing slave; it pervaded the whole sphere of action.[14]

We shall see, therefore, a remarkable consistency across the different echelons of society. The religious was inseparable from the secular, and social status was the ubiquitous measure of all personal relationships and interactions. At what points, however, did Christianity either challenge or incorporate these conceptions? This will be the focus of the second section of the volume.

---

[14]J.E. Lendon, *Empire of Honour: the Art of Government in the Roman World* (Oxford: Clarendon Press, 1997) 30.

PART ONE

LEADERSHIP IN
GRAECO-ROMAN SOCIETY

CHAPTER 2

LEADERSHIP IN THE GRAECO-ROMAN CITY

I. Introduction

In the preface to his book, *The Greek City from Alexander to Justinian*, the ancient historian, Professor A.H.M. Jones, chose to define the Greek city to include 'not only cities Greek by origin and blood, but any community organized on the Greek model and using Greek for its official language'.[1] This 'Greek model' of civic organization enjoyed its heyday during the Hellenistic age and became widespread in those Near Eastern lands which had been conquered during the campaigns of Alexander the Great. For the most part, later domination from Rome did not impose on these ancient cities fundamentally new *structures* of administration, although the autonomy which they had previously enjoyed as independent city-states became a thing of their glorious past.[2] A new ethos was introduced, however, which ensured that the implementation of local

---

[1]A.H.M. Jones, *The Greek City from Alexander to Justinian* (Oxford: Oxford University Press, 1966) v.

[2]S.E. Alcock, *Graecia Capta: the Landscapes of Roman Greece* (Cambridge: Cambridge University Press, 1993) 1-3, 18-19; and W.A. Meeks, *The Moral World of the First Christians* (Library of Early Christianity, 6; Philadelphia: Westminster Press, 1986) 20, 31.

11

government in these Graeco-Roman cities remained supportive of those central policies emanating from the imperial capital and further reinforced the dominance of the wealthier elements in society.[3]

Many of the Graeco-Roman cities which Paul visited while travelling in the eastern provinces of the Roman empire were, thus, founded on the ancient Greek civic constitution and had been forced into modifying this in the light of the new political régime — for example, Athens, Ephesus, Samothrace, Neapolis, Amphipolis, Troas, Miletus and Thessalonica. In a number of these cities, by the mid-first century A.D., some of the earliest Christian communities had been established. Those believers who lived in such urban municipalities would consequently have been familiar with the modified Greek model of civic administration. This civic context will have played an important part in informing their perception of the nature of successful civic leadership in the new political climate.

In this chapter we shall reflect on the constitutional structures and ethos of these Graeco-Roman cities in the Roman East. We shall then examine what type of people occupied leading positions in the city and what characterized their rôles. Although we would expect the focus of local government administration to be secular or political, we shall see that there was also an all-important 'religious' context which embraced the ethos, business and leadership of these urban communities.

From New Testament times the word 'church' (ἐκκλησία) has been associated with the gathering of Christians. Although in later times it has more often been applied in the narrower sense of the *building* in which Christians customarily gather, its original application was rather to the *people* as they constituted that gathering.[4] Whereas the English word 'church', the Scots word 'kirk' and the German word 'Kirche' probably derive from the Greek κυριακός, meaning 'belonging to the Lord (κύριος)', a number of other English words associated with 'church', for example 'ecclesiastical' and 'ecclesiology', share a common etymology with the Greek word ἐκκλησία. It is interesting to note, however, that this

[3]*Cf.* the recent collection of papers considering the Romanization of Greek cities, with specific regard to Athens, in M.C. Hoff & S.I. Rotroff (eds.), *The Romanization of Athens: Proceedings of an International Conference held at Lincoln, Nebraska (April 1996)* (Oxbow Monograph, 94; Oxford: Oxbow Books, 1997); and S.E. Alcock, *Graecia Capta*, 215.
[4]*Cf.*, for example, Mt 18:17; Acts 5:11; Rom 16:16; 1 Cor 1:2.

Greek word had a more obviously political connotation well before it was adopted by Christians in the first century, and in these secular contexts the term is widely translated 'assembly'.[5] It is to this political assembly that we now turn.

II. The Political Structures of the Graeco-Roman City

Dating as far back as the sixth century B.C. ἐκκλησία was the official term for the lawful democratic assembly of the Greek self-governing city-state (πόλις). This assembly traditionally comprised two bodies. Of these two, the smaller was called 'the council' (βουλή), and the larger, incorporating all of the adult male citizens of the city, was described simply as 'the people' (δῆμος). It was a fundamental characteristic of the traditional Greek city and its associated surrounding territory that all citizens (πολῖται) enjoyed equal voting rights in civic affairs, and this was achieved through direct access to the combined popular assembly.[6] Citizenship was generally only accorded to the offspring of citizens, and inevitably was viewed as a highly prized status. Foreigners and newcomers, even if resident in the Greek city, did not share the same political privileges. The importance of this citizen group in civic affairs is reflected in Thucydides' statement, 'for the men are the city (ἄνδρες γὰρ πόλις)',[7]

---

[5]For a conceptual association between the ἐκκλησία of the New Testament and the ἐκκλησία of the Septuagint see W. Horbury, 'Septuagintal and New Testament Conceptions of the Church', in M. Bockmuehl & M.B. Thompson (eds.), *A Vision for the Church: Studies in Early Christian Ecclesiology in Honour of J.P.M. Sweet* (Edinburgh: T. & T. Clark, 1997) 1-17; and J.Y. Campbell, 'The Origin and Meaning of the Christian Use of the Word Εκκλησία', in J.Y. Campbell, *Three New Testament Studies* (Leiden: E.J. Brill, 1965) 41-54, who questions continuity between the Old Testament and Christian uses. For discussion of how ἐκκλησία would have been viewed in its secular sense during the first century, see B.W. Winter, 'The Problem with "Church" for the Early Church', in D. Peterson & J. Pryor (eds.), *In the Fullness of Time: Biblical Studies in Honour of Archbishop Donald Robinson* (Lancer Books; Homebush West: Anzea, 1992) 203-17. See also the ironic (in the present context) statement of R. Garland, 'Priests and Power in Classical Athens', in M. Beard & J. North (eds.), *Pagan Priests: Religion and Power in the Ancient World* (London: Duckworth, 1990) 75, 'there was no "Church" to the Athenian "State" — just the *dêmos*'.

[6]Demosthenes, *Third Philippic* 3, observes that whilst the Athenians esteemed freedom of speech, they permitted neither slaves nor foreigners to participate in the city's political deliberations.

[7]Thucydides 7.77.7.

and one of the benefits of this universal citizen franchise was that it
engendered considerable loyalty to one's city.[8]

As autonomous, self-governing city-states, the particular ways
in which government was implemented differed from location to
location and from period to period. This inevitably makes precise
description of the situation in a given city often difficult to achieve.
The varied availability of extant sources from these different periods
further limits how explicitly the picture can be presented. It is
possible, however, to draw some useful generalizations which will
helpfully inform our understanding of the ways in which many
people from the first century will have broadly conceived of the term
ἐκκλησία in its primary technical sense of a political assembly.

The chief example, and widely conceived as the ideal, of this
form of government is to be found in the Athenian democracy of the
fourth century B.C. The use of the term ἐκκλησία persisted, however,
in political contexts throughout the first century A.D. We repeatedly
come across the term not only in those ancient textbooks and fictional
works which continued to be studied during the first century A.D.,[9]
but it also appears in numerous inscriptions and decrees generated
during the first century which clearly demonstrate its continued
contemporary usage in many of the local civic constitutions in the
eastern provinces of the Roman empire.[10] In addition to these non-
literary sources, we can find further evidence of its currency in a
number of first-century literary sources.[11] One further literary source
of particular importance for us is the book of Acts which records a
significant occasion when ἐκκλησία is used with reference to both an
impromptu and an official gathering of the popular civic assembly in
the city of Ephesus.[12] While the devotion of Christians in the
surrounding region had begun to affect adversely the economy of

---

[8]S. Mitchell, *Anatolia: Land, Men, and Gods in Asia Minor* (2 vols.; Oxford:
Clarendon Press, 1993) I.206-207.

[9]R. Wallace & W. Williams, *The Three Worlds of Paul of Tarsus* (London:
Routledge, 1998) 96.

[10]*Cf.* P.J. Rhodes, *The Athenian Boule* (Oxford: Oxford University Press, 1985) 87,
222.

[11]*Cf.*, for example, Dio Chrysostom, *Orationes* 31; 34; 40; 43; Plutarch, *Moralia* 798-
99; 813D; 815C-D.

[12]Acts 19:32, 39-40. *Cf.* J.Y. Campbell, 'The Origin and Meaning of the Christian
Use of the Word Ἐκκλησία', 43; also J. Murphy O'Connor, 'Galatians 4:13-14 and
the Recipients of "Galatians"', *Revue Biblique* 105 (1998) 202-207, who suggests
that ἐκκλησία may be being used ironically in its 'secular' sense in Gal 4.

some of the local businesses, the silversmiths, who otherwise benefited directly from the local cult of Artemis, reacted strongly and dragged some of Paul's fellow-workers before the citizen body. The townclerk (γραμματεύς), however, urged the citizens not to act too hastily, but, if they felt it so necessary, they should present their formal complaint at an official meeting of the civic assembly (ἐν τῇ ἐννόμῳ ἐκκλησίᾳ).

In the Greek cities, this combined assembly of councillors and citizens conventionally provided the ultimate executive power. It was the assembly which deliberated over and passed decrees and resolutions affecting all aspects of the life of that city. This government by a council (βουλή) together with the body of citizen people (δῆμος) came to be conceived as democracy.[13]

The civic council (βουλή) of a Greek city, the smaller of the two constitutional bodies which comprised the combined popular assembly, frequently consisted of some 500 annually elected members.[14] These men were necessarily over thirty years old and had demonstrated conduct appropriate to such a prominent public appointment.[15] In Archaic Greece, the composition of the council had been largely aristocratic, but, in later Classical Greece, membership was less restricted. It is widely assumed, however, that the majority derived from the propertied classes since the poorer members of the population may have found the commitment of time together with the related loss of income from being away from their main

[13]Demosthenes, *Apollodorus against Neaera* 88, '... the civic body (δῆμος) of Athens, ... has supreme authority over all things in the state, and it is in its power to do whatsoever it pleases'; Aristotle, *Politica* 1298a.11, 'For all the citizens to be members of the deliberative body and to decide all these matters is a mark of a popular government (δημοτικόν), for the common people (δῆμος) seek for equality of this nature'; Pseudo-Xenophon, *Athenaion Politeia* 1.4, 'For the poor, the popular, and the base, inasmuch as they are well off and the likes of them are numerous, will increase the democracy (δημοκρατία); but if the wealthy, good men are well off, the men of the people (δημοτικοί) create a strong opposition to themselves'. 'Democracy' should be understood in terms of 'direct democracy', rather than the 'representative democracy' which is characteristic of many modern democratic governments; cf. M.H. Hansen, *The Athenian Assembly: in the Age of Demosthenes* (Oxford: Blackwell, 1987) 5; and J.S. Richardson, 'Imperium Romanum: Empire and the Language of Power', *Journal of Roman Studies* 81 (1991) 1.
[14]P.J. Rhodes, *The Athenian Boule*, 1.
[15]Xenophon, *Memorabilia* 1.2.35, 'he is not permitted to sit in the Council, because as yet he lacks wisdom. You shall not converse with anyone who is under thirty'. Cf. also P.J. Rhodes, *The Athenian Boule*, 1-2.

employment too sacrificial. By the first century A.D. this body had
gained considerably greater powers and prestige, and coveted
membership of this élite was often restricted to those who met a
stringent property qualification.[16]

It was usual that a citizen would be permitted to serve on the
council only once, although instances, and even periods, when a
subsequent term of office was admissible are recorded.[17] The council
convened daily to conduct the affairs of the city-state,[18] and its main
task was to prepare an agenda and make recommendations which
could be presented to the regular meetings of the combined
assembly.[19] It was normal that all decrees which became ratified by
the assembly had received prior deliberation by the council,[20]
although it was accepted that this body of 500 men would also
exercise a limited executive power to make a number of minor
decisions.

Although the 'people' (δῆμος) stood collectively for the whole
male citizen population of a city-state, in practice both time and
distance prevented significant proportions of the eligible population
from attending, and thereby exercising their voting rights at the
regular assemblies.[21] It is this larger body which lay at the heart of
the democratic principle, and there are numerous instances in the
primary sources when δῆμος is used interchangeably with ἐκκλησία.

---

[16]C.P. Jones, *The Roman World of Dio Chrysostom* (Loeb Classical Monographs;
London: Harvard University Press, 1978) 96. *Cf.* also S. Mitchell, *Anatolia*, I.201,
'The city councils ... enjoyed increasing prominence in the Roman period,
usurped the role of the people's assembly, and offered a defining criterion of city
status itself ... The people's assembly itself was reduced to a mere cipher'.

[17]P.J. Rhodes, *The Athenian Boule*, 3.

[18]P.J. Rhodes, *The Athenian Boule*, 30.

[19]Aristotle, *Athenaion Politeia* 43.3.

[20]*Cf.* Demosthenes, *On the Embassy* 185, 'first the Council (βουλή) must be
informed, and must adopt a provisional resolution — and even that not at any
time, but only after written notice given to marshals and embassies; then the
Council must convene an Assembly (ἐκκλησία), but only on a statutory date'; see
also P.J. Rhodes, *The Athenian Boule*, 52-55.

[21]Thucydides 8.72.1, 'there were five thousand, not four hundred only,
concerned; although, what with their expeditions and employments abroad, the
Athenians had never yet assembled to discuss a question important enough to
bring five thousand of them together'. There was the inducement of small
payments for those attending the assembly; *cf.* E.A. Judge, *The Social Pattern of
Christian Groups in the First Century: some Prolegomena to the Study of New
Testament Ideas of Social Obligation* (London: Tyndale Press, 1960) 19.

The combined assembly may have convened as many as forty times per year.[22] A significant quorum was needed in order either to ratify decisions,[23] or to elect the city's magistrates and officials.[24] Ratification was normally signalled by a show of hands.[25] Those decrees which were passed by the assembly were then published in accordance with a strictly worded protocol.[26] The standardized formula, recorded in many inscriptions both from Athens and elsewhere, is reflected in the following general pattern:

> Resolved by the council (βουλή) and the people (δῆμος), in the presidency (πρυτανεία) of the tribe ..., when ... was secretary and when ... was chairman, ... said:

Although all male citizens were enfranchised, the right to speak in an assembly was restricted to those who had attained the age of twenty.[27] In the more oligarchic climate of the Roman empire, the right to speak may well also have become the earned prerogative of the wealthy. It was they, after all, who were more likely to command the attention of the people.[28] Significantly, the politically active members of the assembly were normally the orators (ῥήτορες) and magistrates (στρατηγοί).[29] The former were people who volunteered to make speeches in the assembly, and would have been especially trained in the skills of rhetoric;[30] the latter were elected magistrates of

---

[22]Cf. Aristotle, *Athenaion Politeia* 43.3.

[23]Cf. Demosthenes, *Apollodorus against Neaera* 89.

[24]M.H. Hansen, *The Athenian Assembly*, 44-46.

[25]M.H. Hansen, *The Athenian Assembly*, 41-44.

[26]Cf. in particular examples in P.J. Rhodes & D.M. Lewis, *The Decrees of the Greek States* (Oxford: Clarendon Press, 1997).

[27]Xenophon, *Memorabilia* 3.6.1.

[28]C.P. Jones, *The Roman World of Dio Chrysostom*, 97.

[29]Cf. Aeschines, *The Speech on the Embassy* 74; *Against Ctesiphon* 55; and M.H. Hansen, *The Athenian Assembly*, 50-70.

[30]Aeschines, *Against Timarchus* 35, lists strict guidelines for speechmakers in the assembly: 'If any public man, speaking in the senate or in the assembly of the people, shall not speak on the subject which is before the house, or shall fail to speak on each proposition separately, or shall speak twice on the same subject in one day, or if he shall speak abusively or slanderously, or shall interrupt the proceedings, or in the midst of the deliberations shall get up and speak on anything that is not in order, or shall shout approval, or shall lay hands on the presiding officer, on adjournment of the assembly or the senate the board of presidents is authorized to report his name to the collectors, with a fine of not more than 50 drachmas for each offence. But if he be deserving of heavier

the city (often with military responsibilities). The trained orators would, in delivering their speech, be subject to both applause and heckling from the assembly. At the hands of a critical audience in the assembly, one could see the individual popularity of these leaders wax and wane in proportion to the public's often fickle response to their speeches. Aware of this dynamic, Plutarch offers helpful advice to those speakers in the popular assembly who are faced with an unappreciative audience.[31]

In the later Hellenistic period, political influence returned once again to be largely the prerogative of an advantaged few — a situation which was further reinforced under Roman domination when the cause of those who were outspokenly pro-Roman was most openly promoted.[32] Notwithstanding this, it would seem to be the case even during the so-called more 'democratic' periods that members of the council assumed an air of élitism which might give the lie to true democracy. Such an impression is depicted in a dramatic way in Aristophanes' comedy The Acharnians, which, although fictional, must have reflected a recognizable satire of reality.[33] In the opening scene, Aristophanes portrays the day scheduled for the public assembly. The meeting place, the Pnyx, is initially deserted. In the central market place there is no sense of urgency, and the citizens need to be cajoled into gathering for the assembly. Eventually, but not until midday, the presiding officials (πρυτάνεις) begin to arrive. They are caricatured by their jostling for position, each seeking pride of place on the front bench. The onlooker could be excused for thinking that they were more concerned with these trappings of honour than with the far weightier business which concerned the fragile peace of the city. Similarly we read Dio Chrysostom's perception, in his speech to the citizens of Nicomedia, that leadership was the prerogative of the wealthy:

---

penalty, they shall impose a fine of not more than 50 drachmas, and refer the case to the senate or to the next meeting of the assembly'.

[31]Plutarch, Moralia 796C-F; 814A; 815A; and Dio Chrysostom, Orationes 7.24-63, records a riotous assembly in Euboea, cited in J. Reynolds, 'Cities', in D.C. Braund (ed.), The Administration of the Roman Empire (241 B.C. – A.D. 193) (Exeter Studies in History, 18; Exeter: University of Exeter, 1988) 27.

[32]J.L. O'Neil, The Origins and Development of Ancient Greek Democracy (Greek Studies; Lanham: Rowman & Littlefield, 1995) 114-19.

[33]Aristophanes, Acharnenses 19-42.

all cities, or rather the great cities, need not only the men of wealth, both to finance the public spectacles and liberally to provide such customary expenses, and flatterers to afford pleasure by their demagogic clap-trap ...[34]

Thus, for the inhabitants of first-century, Graeco-Roman cities, the term ἐκκλησία conjured powerful, political associations. This was first and foremost a civic assembly in the proud tradition of Classical Greek democracy, at which the citizen populace had a theoretical right of expression, but where in practice the wealthy held dominant sway.

III. The Religious Structures of the Graeco-Roman City

Although strange to modern Western minds, the ancient world conceived of no clear separation between the secular and religious spheres.[35] 'Religion in Rome should be seen not as an independent force, but as an integral part of the system, sharing in its political-social character and in the changes which it underwent.'[36] We see this no less in the Greek city-state which 'anchored, legitimated, and mediated all religious activity'.[37]

Each Graeco-Roman city prospered or declined under the perceived patronage or guardianship of its gods or goddesses. As a consequence of this, it will be appreciated that many of the most important structures of civic life were expressly directed towards the

---

[34]Dio Chrysostom, *Orationes* 38.2.

[35]See the discussion on page 6 above. *Cf.* also P. Schmitt-Pantel, 'Collective Activities and the Political in the Greek City', in O. Murray and S. Price (eds.), *The Greek City: From Homer to Alexander* (Oxford: Clarendon Press, 1990) 200. P. Cartledge writes in his Introduction to the English translation of L. Bruit Zaidman & P. Schmitt Pantel, *Religion in the Ancient Greek City* (Cambridge: Cambridge University Press, 1995) xv, 'the proper context for evaluating Classical Greek religion is not the individual immortal soul ... but rather the city, the peculiar civic corporation that the Greeks labelled *polis*'. A. Wardman, *Religion and Statecraft among the Romans* (London: Granada, 1982) assesses how Roman religion changed in relation to the changing political scene from the third century B.C. to the fourth century A.D.

[36]J.A. North, 'Religion and Politics, from Republic to Principate', *Journal of Roman Studies* 76 (1986) 258.

[37]C. Sourvinou-Inwood, 'What is *Polis* Religion?', in O. Murray and S. Price (eds.), *The Greek City: From Homer to Alexander* (Oxford: Clarendon Press, 1990) 297.

promotion and honouring of the city's favoured deities.[38] We can see
the effect of this dynamic still present in the mid-first century A.D. by
looking once again at the Ephesian incident recorded in Acts 19.
Demetrius, the silversmith who feared for the ongoing economic
prosperity of his trade, expressed his anxieties to his fellow craftsmen
in terms also of the potential loss of favour in the eyes of their patron
goddess Artemis. At the heart of his warning was the belief that
actions which might arouse the displeasure of Artemis could have
disastrous implications for personal, civic and regional prosperity:
'there is danger not only that this trade of ours may come into
disrepute but also that the temple of the great goddess Artemis may
count for nothing, and that she may even be deposed from her
magnificence, she whom all Asia and the world worship'.[39] The
judicious response of the townclerk is to reassure the citizens that
these Christians are not offending their patron goddess, and, in any
case, her position is assured.[40]

The closeness of this association between the religious and the
political becomes particularly visible when walking around the
elaborate city centres of the Graeco-Roman cities.[41] The juxtaposition
of religious and political buildings and monuments cannot escape
notice.[42] One first-century writer describes vividly the extent to
which the religious sphere was evident in the city of Athens when he
reports that 'the city was full of idols'.[43] The importance of this
religious dimension in civic politics would have been no less
apparent to a visitor to the Roman colony of Corinth,[44] or to the

---

[38]D.R. Edwards, *Religion and Power: Pagans, Jews, and Christians in the Greek East*
(Oxford: Oxford University Press, 1996) 149.

[39]Acts 19:27.

[40]Acts 19:35-37.

[41]This was no less the case in the rural areas; *cf.* S.E. Alcock, 'Minding the Gap in
Hellenistic and Roman Greece', in S.E. Alcock & R. Osborne (eds.), *Placing the
Gods: Sanctuaries and Sacred Space in Ancient Greece* (Oxford: Clarendon Press,
1994) 247.

[42]L. Bruit Zaidman & P. Schmitt Pantel, *Religion in the Ancient Greek City*, 96-97.

[43]Acts 17:16. *Cf.* especially H. Moxnes, '"He saw that the City was full of Idols"
(Acts 17:16): Visualizing the World of the First Christians', in D. Hellholm, H.
Moxnes & T.K. Seim (eds.), *Mighty Minorities?: Minorities in Early Christianity —
Positions and Strategies: Essays in Honour of Jacob Jervell on his 70th Birthday, 21 May
1995* (Oslo: Scandinavian University Press, 1995) 119-23.

[44]C.K. Williams, 'The Refounding of Corinth: Some Roman Religious Attitudes',
in S. Macready & F.H. Thompson (eds.), *Roman Architecture in the Greek World*

imperial capital itself. Livy describes Rome as a city 'founded by the auspices and augury; there is not a corner of it that is not full of our cults and our gods; our regular rituals have not only their appointed places, but also their appointed times'.[45]

This belief that the gods influenced and directed the affairs of people and the fortunes of cities was deep-seated in the ancient world and governed not only their thinking but also the ways in which they conducted their most important affairs. It should not seem unexpected, therefore, that the civic calendar was dominated with numerous sacred days and festivals.[46] Furthermore, not only occasions of civic importance but also more mundane business was marked by religious ceremony. The meetings of both the council and the combined assembly were consequently conducted within a prominent religious ambiance. Their gatherings were announced by a herald and marked by a number of cultic practices:[47] prayers were offered,[48] curses were recited against speakers who might

---

(Occasional Paper, Society of Antiquaries of London, New Series, 10; London: Thames and Hudson, 1987) 26-37.

[45]Livy, *History of Rome* 5.52.2, writing in the late first century B.C.; cited in M. Beard, J. North & S. Price, *Religions of Rome: a History* (Cambridge: Cambridge University Press, 1998) 168.

[46]M.I. Finley, *Authority and Legitimacy in the Classical City-State* (Offprint from Kongelige Danske Videnskabernes Selskab Historisk- filosofiske Meddelelser 50:3, 1982; Copenhagen: Munksgaard, 1982) 21; and H.H. Scullard, *Festivals and Ceremonies of the Roman Republic* (London: Thames & Hudson, 1981).

[47]P.J. Rhodes, *The Athenian Boule*, 31-32, 36-37. *Cf.* also Lysias, *Against Andocides* 33: 'he attends meetings of the Council, and takes part in debates on sacrifices, processions, prayers and oracles. Yet, in allowing yourselves to be influenced by this man, what gods can you expect to be gratifying? For do not suppose, gentlemen of the jury, that, if you wish to forget the things that he has done, the gods will forget them also'.

[48]*Cf.* Dinarchus, *Against Aristogiton* 14, 'The law demands that the herald shall first pray, amid dead silence, before he surrenders to you the task of deliberating on public affairs'; Demosthenes, *De corona* 1, 'Let me begin, men of Athens, by beseeching all the Powers of Heaven that in this trial I may find in Athenian hearts such benevolence towards me as I have ever cherished for the city and the people of Athens. My next prayer is for you, and for your conscience and honour. May the gods so inspire you that the temper with which you listen to my words shall be guided, not by my adversary'; Demosthenes, *On the Embassy* 70, 'To show you that this man is already accursed by you, and that religion and piety forbid you to acquit one who has been guilty of such falsehoods — recite the curse. Take and read it from the statute: here it is. *Prayer* — This imprecation, men of Athens, is pronounced, as the law directs, by the marshal on your behalf at every meeting of the Assembly, and again before the Council at all their

maliciously wish to mislead the people,[49] and a purificatory sacrifice of a piglet was ordinarily conducted at the start of business of the gathered assembly.[50] Aeschines, from the fourth century B.C., details the following dramatic protocol:

> ... the lawgiver ... turned to the question of the proper manner of conducting our deliberations concerning the most important matters, when we are met in public assembly (συλλεγομένους ἡμᾶς εἰς τὰς ἐκκλησίας). ... And how does he command the presiding officers to proceed? After the purifying sacrifice has been carried round and the herald has offered the traditional prayers, the presiding officers are commanded to declare to be next in order the

---

sessions'; Plutarch, *Pericles* 8.4, 'The truth is, however, that even Pericles, with all his gifts, was cautious in his discourse, so that whenever he came forward to speak he prayed to the gods that there might not escape him unawares a single word which was unsuited to the matter under discussion'; Aristophanes, *Thesmophoriazusae* 295-311, includes the following prayer and curses at the outset of his parody of an assembly of women: 'Silence! Silence! Pray to the Thesmophorae, Demeter and Cora; pray to Plutus, Calligenia, Curotrophus, the Earth, Hermes and the Graces, that all may happen for the best at this gathering (ἐκκλησία), both for the greatest advantage of Athens and for our own personal happiness! ... Address these prayers to heaven and demand happiness for yourselves. ...

'May the gods deign to accept our vows and our prayers! Oh! almighty Zeus, and thou, god with the golden lyre, who reignest on sacred Delos, and thou, oh, invincible virgin, Pallas, ... and may wisdom preside at the gathering of the noble matrons of Athens.

'Address your prayers to the gods and goddesses of Olympus, of Delphi, Delos and all other places; if there be a man who is plotting against the womenfolk or who, to injure them, is proposing peace to Euripides and the Medes ... pray the gods that they will overwhelm them with their wrath, both them and their families, and that they may reserve all their favours for you'.

[49]Dinarchus, *Against Aristogiton* 16, 'In the first place, at every sitting of the Assembly they publicly proclaimed curses against wrongdoers, calling down destruction on any who, after accepting bribes, made speeches or proposals upon state affairs'; Lycurgus, *Against Leocrates* 31, 'the man whose aims in going to law are honest, who brings proofs to bear against those who come under the herald's curse, does just the opposite, as I myself am doing'; Demosthenes, *Against Aristocrates* 97, 'The man who is amenable to the curse is the advocate who deceives and misleads the jury. That is why, at every meeting, the crier pronounces a commination, not upon those who have been misled, but upon whosoever makes a misleading speech to the Council, or to the Assembly, or to the Court'.

[50]*Cf.* Aristophanes, *Acharnenses* 44, where the herald describes the site of the assembly as in some sense sanctified; *cf.* also Aristophanes, *Ecclesiazusae* 129; Demosthenes, *Against Conon* 39.

discussion of matters pertaining to the national religion (περὶ ἱερῶν τῶν πατρίων), the reception of heralds and ambassadors, and the discussion of secular matters (καὶ ὁσίων).[51]

We can also see from this account that, although political and judicial questions may have occupied the majority of the business of the civic councils and popular assemblies, one other important area of their jurisdiction lay in the religious sphere, and it was such matters which were placed first on the agenda.[52] Business which could be classed in this bracket included 'the consultation of oracles, the sending of sacred delegations ... to the great festivals and the passing or revision of sacred laws'.[53] Additionally, civic government was responsible for introducing new gods to the civic pantheon.[54]

Thus, the citizen people of a Greek city-state had principal authority over the religious sphere of their civic life.[55] In many instances this authority was delegated to specific officials who could carry out tasks on behalf of the assembly.[56] Additionally, however, in a number of areas the assembly maintained their direct involvement.[57] First, it was only after having been agreed by the citizen body that the cult of a new deity could be officially recognized. Secondly, the people concerned themselves with the financial implications of state cults. Thirdly, it was the assembly which dealt with the majority of 'religious' crimes.[58] Associated with this high profile accorded to 'religious' matters, it is significant that

---

[51]Aeschines, *Against Timarchus* 22-23.

[52]L. Robert, *Bulletin de Correspondance Hellénique* 59 (1934) 513, argues also that epigraphic evidence from Mylasa in Caria confirms that religious matters held priority over other business; *cf.* also R. Parker, *Athenian Religion: a History* (Oxford: Clarendon Press, 1996) 123-24.

[53]*Cf.* L. Bruit Zaidman & P. Schmitt Pantel, *Religion in the Ancient Greek City*, 94; and, with regard to the Roman senate in Republican times, *cf.* M. Beard, 'Priesthood in the Roman Republic', in M. Beard & J. North (eds.), *Pagan Priests: Religion and Power in the Ancient World* (London: Duckworth, 1990) 31-33.

[54]*Cf.*, with regard to Athens in the first century, B.W. Winter, 'On Introducing Gods to Athens: an Alternative Reading of Acts 17:18-20', *Tyndale Bulletin* 47 (1996) 71-90.

[55]R. Parker, *Athenian Religion*, 124, argues 'The nerve-centre of the city's religion was now the democratic council'.

[56]L. Bruit Zaidman & P. Schmitt Pantel, *Religion in the Ancient Greek City*, 46-49.

[57]R. Garland, 'Priests and Power in Classical Athens', 85-86.

[58]The example is recorded by Demosthenes in *Apollodorus against Neaera* 116, of Archias who performed an inappropriate sacrifice, and whose crime was then considered by the assembly.

one of the subjects in which a public speaker needed to demonstrate proficiency was that of religious 'rites'.[59]

Following the decline of the great Hellenistic era and the subsequent rise of Roman domination in the East, it is unsurprising that many of the long established cities endeavoured to maintain links with their cherished past by fostering myths which celebrated the ancient foundation of their community.[60] It was, after all, those in the East (as opposed to the Roman West) who had an ancient imperial heritage to which they could turn, and which they could refashion to their advantage in the new political climate. Even some of the more recently founded cities followed suit and adopted myths of their own. Many such accounts had a strongly 'religious' or cultic flavour which honoured, for example, the patronage of a certain deity.[61] We have seen the famous example of this in the city of Ephesus in western Turkey. The cult of the goddess Artemis was clearly flourishing during the first century A.D. and her association with the city was an important part of the citizens' heritage.[62] Such local cults not only fuelled the intense rivalry which often existed between cities, but also provided a helpful focus for the allegiance and devotion of a community's self-awareness.

It is, thus, clear that the ancient ἐκκλησία of the Greek city continued to have a significant function within civic life of the first century A.D. The underlying principle of democracy may have faded somewhat by this time to be replaced by a more oligarchic structure;[63] but, while Rome wielded its considerable power over the individual Graeco-Roman cities, it is significant that these civic communities were permitted to preserve the technical terminology of their classical, democratic constitutions. The plenary meeting of council and citizens was permitted to continue to have a high profile

---

[59]R. Parker, *Athenian Religion*, 124.

[60]S. Mitchell, *Anatolia*, I.210.

[61]R. Wallace & W. Williams, *The Three Worlds of Paul of Tarsus*, 97-98.

[62]G.M. Rogers, *The Sacred Identity of Ephesos: Foundation Myths of a Roman City* (London: Routledge, 1991); and C.M. Thomas, 'At Home in the City of Artemis: Religion in Ephesos in the Literary Imagination of the Roman Period', in H. Koester (ed.), *Ephesos Metropolis of Asia: an Interdisciplinary Approach to its Archaeology, Religion and Culture* (Harvard Theological Studies, 41; Valley Forge: Trinity Press International, 1995).

[63]C.P. Jones, *The Roman World of Dio Chrysostom*, 4, describes Dio Chrysostom's town of Prusa as 'essentially an oligarchy of wealth, with the name and sometimes the substance, of democracy'.

in local affairs, although real power now rested with the council, which had become the preserve of the upper classes.[64]

It is also clear that integral to the ethos of local civic politics was a belief in the important patronage of the civic deities. This is evident not only in the ambiance in which official meetings of the political assembly were conducted and the priority which was given to religious matters, but also in the physical layout of the city centre itself where political and religious buildings were deliberately constructed side by side.

In this way, ἐκκλησία will have conjured in the mind of a Greek from the first century a popular civic assembly, albeit more oligarchic than democratic in conception. It was supremely concerned with political and judicial affairs, but also had an important religious dimension. Furthermore, its official business was conducted within a clearly religious context which reflected the underlying beliefs and superstitions of the majority of its citizens.[65]

IV. Leading Figures in the Graeco-Roman City

Having described the political structures which undergirded local administration and the religious context which embraced civic business in the Graeco-Roman cities of the eastern provinces, we turn now to consider the rôles of the leading figures within these communities, in particular the civic magistrates and priests.[66]

As we reflect on the rôle and influence of ancient priests and priestesses it is important that today's reader of first-century contexts

---

[64]F. Millar, *The Roman Empire and its Neighbours* (2nd ed.; London: Duckworth, 1981) 87.

[65]The phenomenon of civic religion did not die with the demise of the Greek city, *cf.* L. Bruit Zaidman & P. Schmitt Pantel, *Religion in the Ancient Greek City*, 233-34. J. Ferguson, *Greek and Roman Religion: a Source Book* (Noyes Classical Studies; Park Ridge: Noyes Press, 1980) 61-89, draws together a selection of sources ranging from Classical Greece through to the early Roman empire which confirm that a significant overlap between the religious and the secular continued.

[66]Here, we shall consider the civic or state religions, in distinction to the oriental mysteries. Although relevant also to the Graeco-Roman cities, attention will be given to the imperial cult in the next chapter. For the relationship between some of the mystery religions and the Graeco-Roman sacrificial system, *cf.* R. Gordon, 'Religion in the Roman Empire: the Civic Compromise and its Limits', in M. Beard and J. North (eds.), *Pagan Priests: Religion and Power in the Ancient World* (London: Duckworth, 1990) 248-52.

once again apply caution. In contrast to many expectations, the ancient pagan priest in the official religion 'never (or only in exceptional circumstances) stood apart from the political order. ... [P]riestly power was ... embedded within the social and political order'.[67] This reflection of reality is eloquently illustrated by Cicero in the opening of his speech to the college of pontiffs, dated 57 B.C.:

> Among the many divinely-inspired expedients of government established by our ancestors, there is none more striking than that whereby they expressed their intention that the worship of the gods and the vital interests of the state should be entrusted to the direction of the same individuals, to the end that citizens of the highest distinction and the brightest fame might achieve the welfare of religion by a wise administration of the state, and of the state by a sage interpretation of religion.[68]

Whilst it is widely held, although not provable at all historical points, that an overlap between the religious and the political was constantly present from the period of Archaic Greece until the Roman empire, the way in which this overlap was embodied necessarily altered as the dominant political models fluctuated from élitism to democracy, and back again to élitism.[69]

Under both the Republic and the empire, Graeco-Roman society experienced many considerable changes. In this period we see both the reinvestment of power in the hands of an élite few and possibly an even greater association between the religious and the political. The combination of these two developments became particularly evident as both religious and political authority was supremely focused in a single individual, rather than in the more democratic pattern prevalent in Classical Athens.[70] During the late

---

[67]M. Beard & J. North (eds.), *Pagan Priests: Religion and Power in the Ancient World* (London: Duckworth, 1990) 1-2. They also argue, *op. cit.*, 12-13, that the priests of the newer cults and mysteries may have more closely reflected what is understood in Western society today by the term 'priest'.

[68]Cicero, *De domo sua* 1.

[69]R. Garland, 'Priests and Power in Classical Athens', 91 (*cf.* also *op. cit.*, 73).

[70]M. Beard & J. North (eds.), *Pagan Priests*, 73, where, speaking of Classical Athens, they write, 'Priestly power is shown, once again, to have matched the distribution of political power. Whereas in Rome religious authority was diffused among the relatively small numbers of the élite, in Athens that authority was spread through the people (the *dêmos*) as a whole. The democratic system of government was mirrored in the patterns of religious office holding'.

Republic, the leading public figures claimed for themselves the titles of both priest and politician. Indeed, one of Julius Caesar's official titles in 63 B.C. was that of *pontifex maximus* (literally, 'chief priest', although not to be confused with the very different Jewish office of chief priest).[71] This title was later assumed by the emperor Augustus and, indeed, all Roman emperors through the first three centuries A.D. Augustus' reflections on this appointment were:

> I declined to be made *pontifex maximus* in place of a colleague still living, when the people offered me that priesthood which my father had held. But some years later I accepted the priesthood, on the death of that man who had used the opportunity offered by civil war to seize it for himself; this was in the consulship of Publius Sulpicius and Gaius Valgius and such crowds poured in from the whole of Italy for my election as are never recorded at Rome before.[72]

As visible confirmation of this development at the time of the Roman empire, the institutions of public sacrifice and priesthood were transferred symbolically to the domain of the emperor and his favoured élites.[73] It is remarkable that during the early Roman empire public depictions of the emperor portrayed him, not only as the principal benefactor, but also as the official celebrant in public sacrifices (although in reality there were many throughout the empire who were benefactors or actually carried out the ceremonies of sacrifice).[74] It is argued that this 'approved' picture proclaimed a

---

[71]*Cf.* R. Gordon, 'From Republic to Principate', in M. Beard & J. North (eds.), *Pagan Priests: Religion and Power in the Ancient World* (London: Duckworth, 1990) 182-83; *cf.* also *op. cit.*, 7; also *cf.* M. Beard, J. North & S. Price, *Religions of Rome: a History*, 189-92, for a consideration of how Augustus changed aspects of the post of *pontifex maximus*.

[72]Augustus, *Achievements* 10.2; cited in M. Beard, J. North & S. Price, *Religions of Rome: a Sourcebook* (Cambridge: Cambridge University Press, 1998) 206.

[73]R. Gordon, 'The Veil of Power: Emperors, Sacrificers and Benefactors', in M. Beard and J. North (eds.), *Pagan Priests: Religion and Power in the Ancient World* (London: Duckworth, 1990) 201, 'one of the bases of the Graeco-Roman system was to link official titles of priesthood with social status on the one hand, and with civic magistracy on the other'.

[74]R. Gordon, 'The Veil of Power: Emperors, Sacrificers and Benefactors', 201-202, 208-209, suggests that the emperor was thereby setting himself up as a model for the élites to emulate. See further, with relation to the imperial cult, S.R.F. Price, *Rituals and Power: the Roman Imperial Cult in Asia Minor* (Cambridge: Cambridge University Press, 1984).

significant message: 'as the emperor appropriated to himself the major political functions in the state, so necessarily he took over the major priestly function'.[75]

We often see in the Roman empire that practices which are instituted in Rome predictably filter down and are reflected in the provinces. Political pragmatism engendered widespread emulation and standardization across the empire. Unsurprisingly this merging of the principal religious and political offices in Rome was, therefore, mirrored also at the local level. There we see a similar 'elusive' or 'ambiguous' distinction between priest and magistrate.

> The priest or magistrate, in principle a member of a central or provincial élite group, obtains what is for the most part a symbolic good (the priesthood). In return he (or she) dispossesses him/herself of frequently enormous amounts of real goods, including the provision of games, feasts, monetary distributions and dispensations of oil or wine, help to the poor or orphaned, the construction of useful or prestigious civic buildings. What he or she finally accumulates, however, is symbolic capital, the most durable form of wealth, in the form of 'obligation, gratitude, prestige, personal loyalty'.[76]

Gordon goes on to describe this 'lack of clear distinction between magistracy and priesthood' as a 'civic compromise'.[77] It became clear to the magistrates in many of the provincial cities (as in Rome itself) that they could usefully enhance their influence by also incorporating in their profile the rôle of priest. In Athens, after all, elected officials regularly had to take oaths of religious allegiance and were questioned, before assuming office, regarding their loyalty and devotion to the gods.[78] Additionally, priests or priestesses also 'functioned like a civic magistrate, exercising a liturgical authority in

---

[75]M. Beard & J. North (eds.), *Pagan Priests*, 12, 48.

[76]R. Gordon, 'From Republic to Principate', 194; see also *idem*, 'Religion in the Roman Empire: the Civic Compromise and its Limits', 245.

[77]R. Gordon, 'From Republic to Principate', 197. This association between displays of wealth in the religious realm and power is seen also in ancient Greece; *cf*. T. Linders, 'Ritual Display and the Loss of Power', in P. Hellström & B. Alroth (eds.), *Religion and Power in the Ancient Greek World: Proceedings of the Uppsala Symposium 1993* (Acta Universitatis Upsaliensis. Boreas, 24; Uppsala: Ubsaliensis S. Academiae, 1996) 121-24.

[78]L. Bruit Zaidman & P. Schmitt Pantel, *Religion in the Ancient Greek City*, 94.

parallel to the legislative, judicial, financial or military authority of the city's officials'.[79]

These priestly and political offices could be granted to a member of the élites by the emperor as an act of generous benefaction, thereby at once eliciting from the recipient allegiance to him and reinforcing loyal dependence upon him as *pontifex maximus*.[80] Governor Pliny writes to the emperor Trajan specifically requesting that a priesthood be conferred upon him: 'the office either of *augur* or of *septemvir*, both of which are now vacant'.[81] Political influence, patronage and priesthood are, thus, closely entwined — supremely embodied in the emperor, but emulated, necessarily in an inferior way, by the élites.[82]

Thus, in contrast to the view propounded by William Fowler that religion by the time of the early empire had become stale and was in a state of decline, we see rather an energy, even a momentum, for change.[83] The best of posterity was maintained for the sake of continuity with antiquity, nonetheless modern channels of the religious were also introduced — channels which reinforced the political aims of the new régime and further underlined the revised *status quo*.[84] The emperor should, thus, be viewed as the innovator of all things new in the religious domain.[85] In a similar fashion, the Roman élites *used* their religious appointments to define the boundaries between themselves and the rest of the populace.[86]

---

[79]L. Bruit Zaidman & P. Schmitt Pantel, *Religion in the Ancient Greek City*, 49.

[80]R. Gordon, 'The Veil of Power: Emperors, Sacrificers and Benefactors', 221, 223-24.

[81]Pliny, *Letters* 10.13.

[82]R. Gordon, 'The Veil of Power: Emperors, Sacrificers and Benefactors', 226-28, offers a commentary on an illuminating inscription which honours Cleanax, son of Sarapion, of Cyme, dated between 2 B.C. and A.D. 2. Here civic and religious offices are clearly used in a not disinterested way as a means of reinforcing and enhancing personal honour.

[83]W.W. Fowler, *The Religious Experience of the Roman People, from the Earliest Times to the Age of Augustus* (Gifford lectures for 1909-10 delivered in Edinburgh University; London: Macmillan, 1911) 428-29. J.H.W.G. Liebeschuetz, *Continuity and Change in Roman Religion* (Oxford: Clarendon Press, 1979) 55-100, categorizes the early principate indeed as a period of religious revival and reform, albeit very necessary.

[84]As an effective innovation for reinforcing the political régime see also discussion of the imperial cult beginning on page 52 below.

[85]M. Beard, J. North & S. Price, *Religions of Rome: a History*, 252.

[86]M. Beard, J. North & S. Price, *Religions of Rome: a History*, 215.

The local élites in the eastern provinces soon discovered that operating this careful balance between cultivating those important aspects of their own local Greek tradition and yet still currying favour with the powers of central Roman administration enabled them to further their influence and reputation at both levels. Douglas Edwards writes:

> The antiquity of religious and mythic traditions heightened the power and prestige of leaders and secured or reaffirmed the relationship between rulers and ruled on a number of levels: between the emperor and the Greek cities, between local elites and their constituents, as well as between coequals, such as cities within a region.[87]

We can see, for example, the revival of veneration of Artemis in Ephesus as witnessed in Acts 19:24-37.[88] Reclaiming these ancient traditions had a stabilising effect on local communities which was significantly to the benefit of overall imperial control. Douglas Edwards writes, 'Persons who wished to participate in the imperial network of power as well as local and regional networks often had to acknowledge the power and presence of the cosmic realm associated with those arenas'.[89] This important link between ancient traditions and the demands of a new régime is reflected at the local level in a revival of the ancient cults. The leading civic figures could, of course, capitalize on this to their own ends. Edwards writes with reference to the Greek East:

> People drew on the antiquity of the worship of their deity (or deities), stressed the power and presence of the deity across the *oikoumene*, acknowledged individuals who mediated between the divine realm and human society, emphasized legitimate social customs and the current legal system promoted (but not always practiced) by powerful regional and international political figures, and made clear the deity's activity behind the scenes, influencing political and historical events. Members or associates of a local elite or aristocratic class often sought to use religious traditions to display for their audience (whether through literature or epigraphy or sculpture) the group's deity as the major arbiter of power within a newly defined all-pervasive web of power. They did so to make

---

[87]D.R. Edwards, *Religion and Power*, 28.
[88]For other examples see D.R. Edwards, *Religion and Power*, 29.
[89]D.R. Edwards, *Religion and Power*, 49-50.

their place within the larger society as a whole and as a means to consolidate their power base, in their locale, their region, and their cosmos.[90]

So, we see that the association between power and religion is represented in the accruing of both political and religious titles in a small élite. This was continually reinforced for the local population by the public expressions of this in sacrifice and benefaction. There were, however, further symbols of power, both political and religious, which could be harnessed to personal benefit. Edwards explains that 'Religious symbols continued as powerful instruments for negotiating the new contours of power brought on by the Flavian ascendancy'.[91] Coins were one particular medium which contributed beneficially to the public profile of a leading figure.[92]
Other prominent symbols of power included the massively expansionist building programme which was widely implemented throughout the empire during the first three centuries of the Principate and for the most part was funded at private expense.[93] The competition between cities in portraying grandiose civic centres was fierce. Buildings, monuments, statues, sculptures and inscriptions were all used as images to reflect both local power and the central power at Rome.[94] New building programmes were a means of identifying with the Augustan cultural renewal and reflecting the revised value system. This is expressed in an especially articulate way in the encomium to Rome which is commonly attributed to the second-century sophist Aelius Aristides:

> Now all the Greek cities rise up under your leadership, and the monuments which are dedicated in them and all their embellishments and comforts redound to your honour like beautiful suburbs. The coasts and interior have been filled with cities, some newly founded, others increased under and by you.[95]

---

[90]D.R. Edwards, *Religion and Power*, 14.

[91]D.R. Edwards, *Religion and Power*, 17.

[92]D.R. Edwards, *Religion and Power*, 11. *Cf.* also M. Beard, J. North & S. Price, *Religions of Rome: a Sourcebook*, 205, for examples of priestly symbols on coins minted by both Caesar and Nero.

[93]S. Mitchell, *Anatolia*, I.80.

[94]P. Zanker, *The Power of Images in the Age of Augustus* (Ann Arbor: University of Michigan Press, 1988) 312.

[95]Aelius Aristides, *Rome* 224.7.

Thus, we have during this period a growth in influence of a local élites, endorsed by central Rome, and with a limited power which was clearly visible at the local level. The line of command was fixed, from the Emperor, through his appointed senators and out into the provinces. Those who acknowledged and heeded this all-important chain stood to gain further influence, as Plutarch implies of the leading figure in the East. Such a figure no longer lives under the privileged freedom once enjoyed by the Athenians in the time of Pericles:

> You rule as a subject, over a city set under the jurisdiction of proconsuls, of the procurators of Caesar. ... This is not ancient Sardis or that old power of the Lydians. You must keep your robes in check, and cast your eye from the generals' office to the tribunal ... observing the Roman senators' shoes above your head.[96]

An important passage in Dio Chrysostom further underlines for us this important link between political power and religious observance:

> [He] who goes astray and dishonours him [Zeus] who entrusted him with his stewardship or gave him this gift, receives no other reward from his great authority and power than merely this: that he has shown himself to all men of his own time and to posterity to be a wicked and undisciplined man, illustrating the storied end of Phaethon, who mounted a mighty chariot of heaven in defiance of his lot but proved himself a feeble charioteer.[97]

V. Conclusion

Thus, we can see that not only in the constitutional structures, but also with regard to the leading figures of the cities of the Greek East, the overlap between the political and the religious was prominent. An important context in which the political life of the community was pursued was religious, and the leading figures of the community fulfilled both religious and political rôles. By the time of the Roman empire both priest and magistrate were selected from among the wealthier echelons of the community. Leadership had become the exclusive domain of the affluent, and any vestiges of democracy were

---

[96]Plutarch, *Moralia* 813D-E.
[97]Dio Chrysostom, *Orationes* 1.45-46, cited in D.R. Edwards, *Religion and Power*, 50.

in name only. These leaders were pragmatists whose actions were determined by an over-riding desire for political success and its concomitant personal honour. It is this picture, so dominant in the Greek cities of the Roman East, which will have crucially informed the understanding of its citizens.[98]

---

[98]S. Mitchell, *Anatolia*, I.204, 'In the face-to-face society of a small town there could have been no political secrets, and the knowledge of what its magistrates and councillors were doing gave the people its strongest political card'.

CHAPTER 3

LEADERSHIP IN THE ROMAN COLONY AND CITY

I. Introduction

Just as the Greeks had long heralded the concept of the city-state as the pinnacle of civilization,[1] so too the Romans came to view their conception of the city as the administrative structure best suited for establishing and developing civilized communities. In this chapter we shall consider not only the constitutions of the peculiarly Roman cities, in contrast to the older Greek cities which were subsumed under imperial control; but we shall also consider the leading political and religious figures in Roman civic administration. One significant difference which we shall find between the Greek and the Roman cities is that, for the most part, direct intervention and control from Rome was far more commonplace in the latter. As a consequence, we see a greater degree of uniformity in civic administration across the peculiarly Roman cities in both the western

---

[1]Cf. Cassiodorus, *Letters* 8.31, 'Let wild beasts live in fields and woods, men ought to draw together into cities'; and Aristotle, *Politica* 1252.20-1253.3, in his discussion of the preeminence of the city-state (πόλις), concludes that 'man is by nature a political (πολιτικός) animal'.

and eastern provinces of the empire than was potentially the case in the autonomous Greek city-states.[2]

This interventionism was an outworking of the Augustan policies of consolidation and expansion in the early empire. As part of the new régime, Rome needed urgently to develop means by which it could reinforce its own authority and jurisdiction over its subjects, raise the necessary taxation revenue to finance the imperial army, and maintain a credible semblance of law and order.[3] A convenient, and relatively simple, channel for implementing such policies was through both the long established and the newly founded cities within its provinces.[4] When Rome expanded its empire into the West, however, she found a notable lack of urbanization in comparison with the much longer established urban communities of the Greek East. In consequence, she set in train an extensive programme of development involving the establishment of numerous new cities.[5] This comparative newness of many of the communities in the West created the opportunity to impose from above a constitution which modelled closely the one which operated in the city of Rome itself and which could be implemented *ab initio*.

II. The Status and Constitution of Roman Cities

There existed a widely heeded hierarchy of status regarding the different types of Roman city and town in the early period of the

---

[2]*Cf.* F.F. Abbott & A.C. Johnson, *Municipal Administration in the Roman Empire* (New York: Russell & Russell, 1968) 56-57.

[3]C.R. Whittaker, 'Imperialism and Culture: the Roman Initiative', in D.J. Mattingly (ed.), *Dialogues in Roman Imperialism: Power, Discourse, and Discrepant Experience in the Roman Empire* (Journal of Roman Archaeology, Supplementary Series, 23; Portsmouth, R.I.: Journal of Roman Archaeology, 1997) 145, rightly views 'the city as both the major cultural construct and conveyancer of Roman imperialism abroad'.

[4]*Cf.* A.W. Lintott, *Imperium Romanum: Politics and Administration* (London: Routledge, 1993) 129; also A.T. Fear, *Rome and Baetica: Urbanization in Southern Spain c. 50 B.C. – A.D. 150* (Oxford Classical Monographs; Oxford: Oxford University Press, 1996) 79-83, who questions whether the prime purpose of establishing colonies was the romanization of the natives, although this may well have been a beneficial consequence.

[5]L.A. Curchin, *The Local Magistrates of Roman Spain* (Phoenix Supplementary volume, 28; Toronto: University of Toronto Press, 1990) 7.

empire.[6] The capital city of Rome was predictably regarded as supreme. Other towns within Italy enjoyed a privileged relationship with the capital which exempted them from direct taxation. Of lesser status were the Roman colonies, followed by the *municipia* (towns).

As already noted, during the expansionist periods of the second and first centuries B.C., Rome sought to establish a visible and strategic Roman presence in its newly acquired territories.[7] This was achieved by means of the founding of a number of colonies initially populated to a large extent by veteran soldiers or surplus inhabitants from an over-populated Rome. As compensation for being posted out of Italy, these colonists enjoyed a similar privilege of tax exemption as their counterparts in the Latin cities.[8] 'Such communities in the provinces had the prestigious status of Roman islands in a more or less foreign sea'.[9] Roman colonies were subdivided into those with Italian rights, and those without.

Five eastern cities visited by Paul were Roman colonies: Pisidian Antioch, Iconium, Lystra, Philippi and Corinth. Roman Corinth, re-founded by Julius Caesar as a colony in 44 B.C. after having been sacked by the Romans a century earlier in 146 B.C., exercised a strategic commercial interest with its prime location on the isthmus between mainland Greece and the southern Argolid, and from there she was able to control access to both east and west. Unlike many of the colonies instituted during the Roman Republican period, Corinth served largely to 'provide for freedmen and the urban poor of Rome';[10] and the evidence for any significant veteran

---

[6]*Cf.* J. Reynolds, 'Cities', in D.C. Braund (ed.), *The Administration of the Roman Empire (241 B.C. – A.D. 193)* (Exeter Studies in History, 18; Exeter: University of Exeter, 1988) 23; and F. Millar, *The Roman Empire and its Neighbours* (2nd ed.; London: Duckworth, 1981) 84-86.

[7]*Cf.* J.E. Stambaugh, *The Ancient Roman City* (Ancient Society and History; Baltimore: Johns Hopkins University Press, 1988) 244-47.

[8]*Cf.* R. Wallace & W. Williams, *The Three Worlds of Paul of Tarsus* (London: Routledge, 1998) 87.

[9]A.W. Lintott, *Imperium Romanum*, 130. *Cf.* also the widely cited statement by Aulus Gellius, *Noctes Atticae* 16.13, which describes the colonies as 'little copies and replicas (*effigies parvae simulacraque*) of the people of Rome'.

[10]*Cf.* Strabo, *Geography* 8.23; Appian, *Libyca* 136; M.E. Hoskins-Walbank, 'Evidence for the Imperial Cult in Julio-Claudian Corinth', in A. Small (ed.), *Subject and Ruler: the Cult of the Ruling Power in Classical Antiquity – Papers presented at a Conference held in the University of Alberta on April 13-15, 1994, to celebrate the 65th anniversary of Duncan Fishwick* (Journal of Roman Archaeology. Supplementary Series, 17; Ann Arbor: Journal of Roman Archaeology, 1996) 201.

population is lacking.[11] Antony Spawforth notes that 'a significant number — 19% — of wealthy and politically successful individuals classified as probably or certainly of freedman stock' were amongst the first inhabitants of the new Corinth.[12] Where the site of Corinth was favoured for its economic prospects, the colony of Philippi further to the north was founded by and in celebration of the military exploits of its namesake, Philip of Macedon.[13] In both cases, however, the association with the Roman capital was proudly acclaimed.

By the first century, the Roman *municipia* ('towns') had a lower status than the colonies,[14] and were also divided into two groups. Those with Roman status were treated in ways often similar to the treatment of the imperial colonies, with their citizens enjoying Roman citizenship; whereas those with merely Latin status were less highly regarded and only the leading figures, magistrates, of these cities possessed Roman citizenship.[15]

During the early imperial period, the emperor used his patronage to favour those cities which had significantly demonstrated their support for him. This support was often rewarded by the granting of full citizenship to the city. Equally, he withdrew privileges from those cities which had not demonstrated appropriate loyalty. Dio Chrysostom records instances of Caesar honouring the Spanish city of Gades, and Octavian honouring the cities of Utica and Tingi in this way;[16] and there are extensive details recording the occasion when Aphrodisias, in modern Turkey, was awarded its freedom in 39 B.C. after demonstrating brave resistance to a Parthian invasion.[17]

---

[11]*Contra* Plutarch, *Caesar* 57; *cf.* A.J.S. Spawforth, 'Roman Corinth: the Formation of a Colonial Elite', in A.D. Rizakis (ed.), *Roman Onomastics in the Greek East: Social and Political Aspects* (Meletemata, 21; Athens: Kentron Hellenikes kai Romaikes Archaiotetos, 1996) 170-71.

[12]A.J.S. Spawforth, 'Roman Corinth: the Formation of a Colonial Elite', 169.

[13]R. Wallace & W. Williams, *The Three Worlds of Paul of Tarsus*, 88. For further background, *cf.* also L. Bormann, *Philippi: Stadt und Christengemeinde zur Zeit des Paulus* (Supplements to Novum Testamentum, 78; Leiden: E.J. Brill, 1995).

[14]J.E. Stambaugh, *The Ancient Roman City*, 246.

[15]A.W. Lintott, *Imperium Romanum*, 130. Lintott categorizes also the smaller communities or villages, but these are less relevant for our present study since the early spread of Christianity should be regarded as a largely urban phenomenon.

[16]Dio Chrysostom, *Orationes* 41.24.1; 48.45.3; 49.16.1; *cf.* A.W. Lintott, *Imperium Romanum*, 165.

[17]*Cf.* J. Reynolds, 'Cities', 17.

Inevitably we find an atmosphere of intense competition existing between these cities of different social standing, each seeking to enhance their own status in the eyes of the emperor and Rome, and thereby extend the privileges available to them. Just as men and women, in Graeco-Roman society, compared themselves in terms of the honour in which they were held, Jon Lendon argues that precisely the same comparisons of honour were applied to cities.[18] A dramatic instance of this competitive spirit existed, for centuries, between the cities of Nicomedia and Nicaea and is witnessed for us by Dio Chrysostom.[19] Such competition was expressed in a city's very public attempts to honour the emperor, and give high profile to those activities which celebrated his prestige. In many instances this was demonstrated by massive and elaborate building programmes of impressive public monuments, funded by private patronage rather than from the public purse.[20] This is not to ignore the fact that there were also numerous examples of run-down city centres in the Roman empire.[21] Another ploy widely used by the local élites of a city was to foster relations with a particular senator from Rome — a respected individual who might have useful access to the emperor himself.[22] In each of these ways a city could seek to further its own standing and attract honours and privileges which were better than those enjoyed by its local competitors.

Thus, we see in the colonies and *municipia* of the Roman empire the products of a central policy of expansion being carried out from Rome. Part of this policy maintained an entrenched scale of comparison between cities of different status. Many cities entered

---

[18]J.E. Lendon, *Empire of Honour: the Art of Government in the Roman World* (Oxford: Clarendon Press, 1997) 74-77; also *op. cit.*, 80, 'The key to understanding relations between man and city in the ancient world is the realization that cities were fully anthropomorphized: they were thought to act just as humans did. Thus cities set out to control the acts of men, and men those of cities, just as men dealt with other men: employing — among other methods — honour-based forms of influence'.

[19]Dio Chrysostom, *Orationes* 38. For other examples, see J. Reynolds, 'Cities', 25.

[20]S. Mitchell, 'Imperial Building in the Eastern Roman Provinces', in S. Macready & F.H. Thompson (eds.), *Roman Architecture in the Greek World* (Occasional Paper, Society of Antiquaries of London, New Series, 10; London: Thames and Hudson, 1987) 18.

[21]J. Reynolds, 'Cities', 20, cites the instances of Euboea (*cf.* Dio Chrysostom, *Orationes* 7), and Panopeus (*cf.* Pausanias, *Geography* 10.4.1) both of which, during the second century A.D., were especially rundown.

[22]J. Reynolds, 'Cities', 31.

upon a costly and competitive round of pomp and circumstance, seeking to elicit greater standing in the eyes of Rome. This in turn served to advance further Rome's policy of expansion and development.

Both colonies and *municipia* were specifically Roman institutions and we have a wealth of information regarding their constitutions. Much of this data derives from cities in the West, notably imperial Spain, our knowledge of which has increased significantly in the last 25 years following important archaeological discoveries in the province. Much of the detail we now know derives from partial copies of specific local charters deriving from a number of western cities, and largely dating from the first centuries B.C. and A.D.[23] There is much standardization across these civic charters, with virtually identical wording in many parts. This has enabled scholars occasionally to allow one law to interpret lacunae in another, and thereby to construct a very detailed understanding of the structures which prevailed in local government. On this principle it is possible to look, for example, at data derived from the colony of Carthage in northern Africa or some of the Roman cities in Spain and note significant similarities reflected in the Roman colonies of Greece, such as Philippi and Corinth.[24]

We have seen that it was the case in the Greek cities that their constitutions broadly allowed the combined citizen assembly (ἐκκλησία) to ratify decisions of the council (βουλή). From the charters of Roman towns we infer that a more prescriptive constitution was firmly established either at the time of founding the community, or else subsequently adopted. In such towns the rôle of an assembly was more often restricted to that of election of civic officers.

---

[23]Important documents, deriving from both Italy and the provinces further west, include the *Tabula Heracleensis* or *Lex Julia Municipalis* (44 B.C., and apparently a charter for a number of towns in Roman Italy), the *Lex Municipii Tarentini* (between 88 and 61 B.C. in Italy), the *Lex Rubria de Gallia Cisalpina* (48-41 B.C., relating to towns in Cisalpine Gaul), the *Lex Coloniae Genetivae* (44 B.C., from the Spanish colony of Urso), the *Lex Municipalis Salpensana*, the *Lex Municipalis Malacitana*, the *Lex Irnitana* (from the Flavian period), and the *Fragmenta Villonensia* (fragments from charters deriving from Basilipo, Italica and Ostippo). For further details see L.A. Curchin, *The Local Magistrates of Roman Spain*, 12-16.

[24]See J.B. Rives, *Religion and Authority in Roman Carthage: from Augustus to Constantine* (Oxford: Clarendon Press, 1995) for his application of principles derivable from the Spanish colony of Urso to the situation in North African Carthage.

III. Leading Figures in the Roman Colony

1. Political Leadership in the Roman Civic Context

The Roman colonies and *municipia* adopted a fixed hierarchy of senior positions in civic leadership (*cursus honorum*). Progression up this ladder was highly esteemed although there was a significant distinction in status between a senior position of local leadership, for example a magistracy, and the superior status of those in the equestrian or senatorial classes. Most magistrates in Roman colonies and *municipia* would have enjoyed considerable standing within their own local community, and some even had comparable posts in neighbouring towns. Their wealth may have been significant, but none of this automatically gave them an entrée into the higher class of the knights (*equites*) and senators of imperial Rome.[25] Considerable progression and influence were needed to advance from the realms of the local élites to those of the higher class.

It is also important to note that a post on this *cursus honorum* should be viewed not as a job, but as a social status; thus, as Jon Lendon describes:

> offices were social distinctions, and ... the hierarchy that was marked to contemporaries was not any official hierarchy, in our sense, but a social hierarchy — a hierarchy of prestige and standing — in which official rank was a vital criterion of ranking.[26]

The civic charters which we possess, together with the extensive available numismatic and epigraphic evidence, enable us to have a particularly clear conception of the structure and responsibilities of the leading figures within Roman cities — the local élites.

The council of decurions (*ordo decurionum*) in a Roman colony or *municipium* was the court where most important civic decisions were ratified.[27] The number of decurions within a council varied between localities (probably in proportion to the size of the community), but is often detailed as one hundred. The *Lex Irnitana* prescribes regulations which come into force when the number drops

---

[25]L.A. Curchin, *The Local Magistrates of Roman Spain*, 125.
[26]J.E. Lendon, *Empire of Honour*, 21.
[27]J.B. Rives, *Religion and Authority in Roman Carthage*, 33.

below 63.[28] Members of this council were drawn from the local élites, and the civic charters laid down strict criteria which would qualify an individual to be eligible for election to this position. It was necessary to have been freeborn;[29] to be between the ages of 25 and 55 (in the early imperial period); to be a resident member of the community; to have moral integrity; and also to possess significant wealth (although it is not always clear what this should amount to).[30] The *ordo decurionum* had powers of approval and ratification, rather than executive responsibilities. For example, it was this council which approved proposals or agreed to decrees for public works which could then be carried out by the elected civic magistrates. It was also from this body of decurions that the magistrates were appointed each year: two duovirs, two aediles and two quaestors.

The two chief magistrates were annually elected from this council, and their principal rôle was to serve as chief justices. As such they were entitled *duoviri iure dicundo*. Additionally they presided over the meetings of the decurions.[31] In many towns, upon appointment to this post, the duovirs had to provide a substantial

---

[28]*Lex Irnitana* 31.

[29]Although there are exceptional examples from early Imperial Corinth where it is clear that freedmen had also been appointed to the civic magistracy. Gaius Babbius Philinus and Gaius Heius Pamphilus may be two such examples; *cf.* A.D. Clarke, *Secular and Christian Leadership in Corinth: a Socio-historical and Exegetical Study of 1 Corinthians 1-6* (Arbeiten zur Geschichte des antiken Judentums und des Urchristentums, 18; Leiden: E.J. Brill, 1993) 14; and A.J.S. Spawforth, 'Roman Corinth: the Formation of a Colonial Elite', 169 and 173-74, who also notes Philinus' probable freedman status, points out that, in time, the Babbii climbed into 'the provincial "aristocracy"', and argues that it was not until the reign of Claudius that there is 'unequivocal evidence for office-holding at Corinth by Greeks from other cities'. L.A. Curchin, *The Local Magistrates of Roman Spain*, 71, further argues that the appointment of freedmen to civic posts may have only been permissible in an early period. It appears to have been permitted in theory under Julius Caesar (*Lex Ursonensis* 105), although no explicit instance can be cited of this happening in Spain. The later *Lex Municipalis Malacitana*, however, explicitly precludes such an appointment. A.J.S. Spawforth, *op. cit.*, 170, however, suggests that 'colonial Corinth's reputation for being "freedmen-friendly" continued to attract freedmen in the years after the foundation'.

[30]L.A. Curchin, *Roman Spain: Conquest and Assimilation* (London: Routledge, 1991) 66.

[31]From the colony of Corinth I have identified in the extant epigraphic and numismatic evidence the names of fifty-eight individuals who fulfilled this post; *cf.* A.D. Clarke, *Secular and Christian Leadership in Corinth*, 14, together with Appendix A. *Cf.* also the more recent work of A.J.S. Spawforth, 'Roman Corinth: the Formation of a Colonial Elite', 167-82.

down-payment as a kind of institutionalized election promise. In addition to this down-payment, further financial outlays continued to mark the term of office of the magistrate. Indeed, the charter relating to the Spanish colony of Urso dictates that magistrates were obliged to arrange munificent public entertainments, largely at personal expense.

> All duoviri, except those first appointed after this law, shall during their magistracy at the discretion of the decuriones celebrate a gladiatorial show or dramatic spectacles to Jupiter, Juno, and Minerva, and to the gods and goddesses, or such part of the said shows as shall be possible, during four days, for the greater part of each day, and on the said spectacles and the said shows each of the said persons shall expend of his own money not less than 2,000 sesterces, and out of the public money it shall be lawful for each several duovir to expend a sum not exceeding 2,000 sesterces, and it shall be lawful for the said persons so to do with impunity.[32]

The duovirs were supported by two annually elected aediles and two quaestors. The former carried responsibility for 'managing the corn supply, the sacred buildings, the sacred and holy places, the town, the roads, the districts, the drains, the baths and the market and [for] checking weights and measures'.[33] As with the *duoviri*, there was an expectation that the aedile would demonstrate an ability to assume such an onerous task by some munificent gesture intended to benefit the city. There is the well-known example of an aedile from Corinth called Erastus who, in the mid-first century A.D., laid an extensive payment, strategically positioned outside the main theatre, specifically in return for being elected to the post.[34]

The more junior office of quaestor is found on very few Corinthian inscriptions, but is clearly outlined in some of the extant

---

[32]*Lex Ursonensis* 60. The following chapter of the charter stipulates lesser financial burdens on the aediles.

[33]*Lex Irnitana* 19.

[34]Cf. A.D. Clarke, *Secular and Christian Leadership in Corinth*, 15, 46-57. The possibility remains that this Erastus was a Christian in the Pauline congregation in Corinth; cf. the recent discussion in B.W. Winter, *Seek the Welfare of the City: Christians as Benefactors and Citizens* (First Century Christians in the Graeco-Roman World; Grand Rapids: Eerdmans, 1994) 179-97.

civic charters.[35] There has been the suggestion that the infrequent references to this post in many of the civic centres may reflect the perception that this was an insufficiently honourable post and thus did not warrant widespread attention. The chief responsibilities of the quaestors lay in the city treasury. The *Lex Irnitana* prescribes that 'they are to have the right and power of collecting, spending, keeping, administering and looking after the common funds'.[36]

In the city of Corinth, which had the additional privilege and responsibility of hosting three high profile games festivals — the biennial Isthmian games, the quadrennial Caesarean games, and the imperial contests — there was the additional civic post of agonothete. We know this to have been a position of particular honour by noting its prominent position on inscriptions which list the different posts held by a few Corinthian leaders.[37] As with the duovirs and aediles, this also was a position which had extensive accompanying costs. The agonothete, for example, had the responsibility of financing, to a large extent, the costly games.[38]

One further post of which we have particular evidence in Corinth was the periodically-filled position of curator of the grain supply (*curator annonae*). The requirement for this position was only during times of famine or excessive shortage of grain. Again this position was highly acclaimed by the people because it was the responsibility of this individual to ensure that there were sufficient grain resources to feed the hungry population in times of economic and potential social instability. This would often entail direct manipulation of market forces in order to increase the availability of grain for the hard-pressed local populace — the cost of which intervention was often borne personally by the *curator annonae*.[39]

---

[35]Cf. A.D. Clarke, *Secular and Christian Leadership in Corinth*, Appendix A, nos. 33, 48, 53, 143, 155, 157. Some 59 instances of quaestors are recorded in the *Conventus Tarraconensis; cf.* L.A. Curchin, *The Local Magistrates of Roman Spain*, 29.

[36]*Lex Irnitana* 20.

[37]D.J. Geagan, 'Notes on the Agonistic Institutions of Roman Corinth', *Greek, Roman and Byzantine Studies* 4 (1968) 69.

[38]Cf. further A.D. Clarke, *Secular and Christian Leadership in Corinth*, 17-18.

[39]Cf. further A.D. Clarke, *Secular and Christian Leadership in Corinth*, 16-17; and, for possible connections with Paul's reference to the 'present crisis' (τὴν ἐνεστῶσαν ἀνάγκην) in 1 Cor 7:26, see also B.W. Winter, 'Secular and Christian Responses to Corinthian Famines', *Tyndale Bulletin* 40 (1989) 86-106.

It is particularly significant that each of these leading posts was unsalaried, although other lesser officials were remunerated.[40] Furthermore, not only were the senior magistracies unsalaried, but we have seen that these posts also entailed not insignificant personal financial outlay. Jon Lendon describes the considerable burden which rested on the shoulders of the civic élites thus:

> There is no better illustration of the power, ubiquity, and complexity of the honour relations between man and city than the financial arrangements for the day-to-day running, adornment, and entertainment of the cities of the Roman empire. The capital aside, the great expenses of the cities — the provision of wood and oil for the baths, the elaborate religious festivals with public banquets and games, the building of temples, aqueducts, and great public structures — were met only in part by taxation. Instead, wealthy individuals, usually men but sometimes women as well, undertook these expenses themselves, spontaneously or as a function of the unsalaried magistracies of their towns — posts which were, moreover, time-consuming and which came to require a large upfront payment.[41]

It thus becomes apparent why positions of leadership within local civic administration came to be the preserve of the wealthy élites. After the time of Augustus we do not find examples of freedmen being appointed to the position of civic magistrate (even though some freedmen attracted considerably wealthy fortunes). Indeed, such an honour appears to have been expressly denied them in the later Spanish civic charters. It also becomes clear why a number of the civic charters which we possess explicitly prescribe a minimum property requirement on those who are to be appointed to high office, and even a charge on taking up the post. In later periods it is unsurprising that there is a growing reluctance on the part of the élites to assume high office precisely because of this concomitant high personal cost involved. Professor A.H.M. Jones writes:

> From the beginning of the second century, if not earlier, there are signs that the governing classes of the cities were beginning to regard civic office as an irksome task rather than a coveted honour.

---

[40]*Cf.* J. Reynolds, 'Cities', 35-36. A.T. Fear, *Rome and Baetica*, 85, suggests, for the Roman colony of Urso in Spain, the remarkably small figure of 16,200 sesterces *per annum* in salaries for paid officials.

[41]J.E. Lendon, *Empire of Honour*, 84-85.

The extravagant standard of living which the cities adopted and the emperors had failed effectively to curb threw a heavy burden on the civic officers, and the increasing demands of the central government … laid a yet heavier financial responsibility on them.[42]

In the light of the intense competition which existed between cities, it is not surprising that considerable pressure was often placed upon individuals in both Greek and Roman cities to offer their wealth in loyal service of their fellow citizens by accepting such onerous, but high profile, appointments. The inducement of the public acclaim and the promise in return of statues and inscriptions which would, albeit fleetingly, publicize the honourable gentleman were often too tempting to resist. Plutarch is well aware of the pressures which existed and goes as far as to advise the person without sufficient funds who nonetheless seeks high office to withdraw from what may well prove to be an embarrassingly onerous course. He warns:

> but if your property is moderate and in relation to your needs strictly circumscribed 'as by centre and radius', it is neither ignoble nor humiliating at all to confess your poverty and to withdraw from among those who have the means for public expenditures, instead of borrowing money and making yourself at once a pitiful and a ridiculous object in the matter of your public contributions; for men are plainly seen to lack resources when they keep annoying their friends or truckling to money-lenders so that it is not reputation or power, but rather shame and contempt, which they acquire by such expenditures.[43]

It is clear from the inducements that, for the most part, Graeco-Roman civic leaders should not, therefore, be regarded as philanthropists who selflessly sought to use their wealth simply for the benefit of their cities and the poorer members of their communities. On the contrary, it is clear from both the literary and the non-literary record that high office did attract a number of widely sought after and high profile privileges.[44] The local élites could be recognized by a distinct dress code, by having privileged seats on

---

[42]A.H.M. Jones, *The Greek City from Alexander to Justinian* (Oxford: Oxford University Press, 1966) 146.

[43]Plutarch, *Moralia* 822D; *cf.* also *Moralia* 822F; and Dio Chrysostom, *Orationes* 17.18.

[44]See A.D. Clarke, *Secular and Christian Leadership in Corinth*, 29-31.

public occasions,[45] and enjoying the benefit of immunity from some prosecution.[46] Such benefits were the exclusive prerogative of their high status. Indeed, in the Spanish charter from the colony of Urso fines are expressly detailed for those who are occupying seats in public places 'above their station'.[47]

A major characteristic and motivation of these leading figures was their love of esteem and honour (φιλοτιμία). Their desire for public office was prompted by the pledge of public acclaim and celebration in the form of monuments, statues and inscriptions set up by their city explicitly in recognition of their generosity. Dio Chrysostom wrote describing many who sought high office that they did so,

> not for the sake of what is truly best and in the interest of their country itself, but for the sake of reputation and honours and the possession of greater power than their neighbours, in the pursuit of crowns and precedence and purple robes, fixing their gaze upon these things and staking all upon their attainment.[48]

Thus, prominent civic leaders may not have been rewarded in monetary terms, but their status and generosity entitled them to significant social deference.[49] Pliny, in unrestrained flattery, seeks further patronage from the emperor Trajan by praising him for his generosity in the past: 'When I reflect upon your exalted station, and the greatness of your mind, it seems most fitting to point out to you some works worthy alike of your immortality and your fame, and no less useful than magnificent'.[50]

---

[45]Cf. J.E. Lendon, *Empire of Honour*, 22, for the scandal of a young man who refused to give up his seat to an ex-praetor.

[46]L.A. Curchin, *The Local Magistrates of Roman Spain*, 80.

[47]J.B. Rives, *Religion and Authority in Roman Carthage*, 31; *Lex Ursonensis* 125-27.

[48]Dio Chrysostom, *Orationes* 34.29. Plutarch, *Moralia* 788E, was no less flattering when he wrote, 'in public life one must escape, not from one tyrant, the love of boys or women, but from many loves which are more insane than that: love of contention, love of fame, the desire to be first and greatest, which is a disease most prolific of envy, jealousy and discord'; *cf.* also *idem, Moralia* 821.F.

[49]J.E. Lendon, *Empire of Honour*, 22.

[50]Pliny, *Letters* 10.41.

Thus, the pursuit of civic leadership in Greek and Roman civic contexts was often accompanied by a self-motivated love of honour.[51] Dio Chrysostom expresses the extent to which such honour was the very fabric of society and that for many, without the promise of reward, the task was not worth pursuing:

> You will find that there is nothing else, at least in the case of the great majority, that incites every man to despise danger, to endure toils, and to scorn the life of pleasure and ease ... However, this much is clear, that neither you nor any others, whether Greeks or barbarians, who are thought to have become great, advanced to glory and power for any other reason than because fortune gave to each in succession men who were jealous of honour and regarded their fame in after times as more precious than life. For the pillar, the inscription, and being set up in bronze are regarded as a high honour by noble men ... For all men set great store by the outward tokens of high achievement, and not one man in a thousand is willing to agree that what he regards as a noble deed shall have been done for himself alone and that no other man shall have knowledge of it.[52]

Those cities and citizens who benefited from the acts of generosity of their patrons were often extremely fickle, however. Their adulation and support were only as constant as the wealth of their benefactors. Dio Chrysostom records how the citizens of Rhodes, for example, were not above altering the inscription on a statue to honour the currently favoured benefactor and forget the benefits of its original honoree.[53]

It is apparent that although the Roman cities of the empire differed from their Greek counterparts in terms of civic constitution and the titles of their senior posts, by the time of the early empire much of the underlying, and unwritten, protocol of civic

---

[51]J.E. Lendon, *Empire of Honour*, 181, argues that, 'The honour of a man was inextricably bound up with the office he was holding and the offices he had held. To gain an office in the Roman world was to enjoy an accretion to one's honour'.

[52]Dio Chrysostom, *Orationes* 31.17, 20, 22.

[53]Dio Chrysostom, *Orationes* 31.8-9, 'I ask you to believe that the situation here among you is very bad and unworthy of your state, your treatment, I mean, of your benefactors and of the honours given to your good men. ... what occurs is quite absurd: your chief magistrate ... merely points his finger at the first statue that meets his eyes of those which have already been dedicated, and then, after the inscription which was previously on it has been removed and another name engraved, the business of honouring is finished'.

administration and engagement was consistent across both Roman and Greek urban communities. It is clear that those most active in the political affairs of city and province during the first century A.D. will, for the most part, have been representative of the established classes, characterized by both wealth and education, and motivated by an intense love of honour. We shall further see that in both Greek and Roman local politics, religion had an essential and high profile rôle to play.

2. Religious Leadership in the Graeco-Roman Civic Context

Having considered the political structures and dynamics of local administration in the Roman towns and cities, we turn now to consider the ways in which public religion was also fundamental to civic government.[54] Charles Whittaker argues that, 'The relationship of religion to society and politics ... is not so much that the former reflects the social order as that it shapes it'.[55] In this sphere also it appears that the colonies adopted a pattern prescribed by Rome herself. Andrew Fear describes the extensive religious rituals which marked the initial founding of an early Roman colony. Priests and augurs were involved in the reading of omens and the enactment of fertility rituals.[56] We noted above that the official civic games in the colony of Urso were explicitly dedicated to the Roman deities, Jupiter, Juno and Minerva.[57] The aediles were responsible for arranging similar entertainments, but additionally they were required to provide games in honour of Venus.[58]

Priesthoods within a city were especially honourable posts and such appointments were conferred on individuals as evidence of their loyalty. It is not uncommon, therefore, to see that magistrates and priests performed similar honorific functions and even were

---

[54]We have noted above, in discussion of the Greek cities, that there was no separation between the secular and the religious as might be more common in modern western society; this is borne out also with regard to the colonies; *cf.* for example, D. Engels, *Roman Corinth: an Alternative Model for the Classical City* (Chicago: University of Chicago Press, 1990) 92-107.

[55]C.R. Whittaker, 'Imperialism and Culture: the Roman Initiative', 148.

[56]A.T. Fear, *Rome and Baetica*, 70-73.

[57]*Lex Ursonensis* 70.

[58]*Lex Ursonensis* 71.

awarded both 'religious' and 'political' positions.[59] The office of
priest in public religion, therefore, should be regarded not so much as
a vocation, but rather as a reward for high status. While many
priesthoods were elected temporary posts, others were for life and
some instances are recorded of hereditary priesthoods.[60] Here also
there is a strict hierarchy of positions. The lowest rung was that of the
sevirs, and this position was normally awarded to freedmen. A more
senior position was that of the pontificate or flaminate; and the most
senior priesthood was provincial.[61] These religious officials also
enjoyed some of the privileges of the decurions, for example,
reserved seating at the games.[62] Indeed, analysis of the epigraphic
evidence from a number of cities makes it clear that many of the
priesthoods were widely regarded as higher positions than that of the
duovirs. The colonial charter of Urso specifically 'provides for the
setting-up of colleges of pontifices and augures, whose members are
to have the same privileges as those of the parallel priestly collegia
found at Rome. These provisions are explicitly said to be the same for
all coloniae'.[63]

It is apparent that whereas the inscriptions from both Greek
and Roman cities are able to tell us much about the status of these
high officials in society, and the literary sources portray something of
the honour in which they were held, we are reliant more upon the
Roman civic charters for information about their specific duties. From
these sources we are informed in some detail about the areas of
responsibility that the civic leaders had in the religious domain. The
charter from Spanish Urso, for example, refers to the responsibility of
the magistrates to ensure that the religious sites of the colony were
appropriately maintained.

> Every duovir or aedile or praefectus of the colonia Genetiva Julia
> shall severally during the year of his magistracy or imperium so far
> as shall be possible, without prejudice and without wrongful intent,

[59]See, for example, A.D. Clarke, *Secular and Christian Leadership in Corinth*,
Appendix A, 42 where Aulus Arrius Proclus is honoured for being an augur, an
aedile, an imperial priest of Neptune, a duovir and an agonothete in the early
part of the first century; *cf.* also nos. 75, 101, 146.
[60]S.R.F. Price, *Rituals and Power: the Roman Imperial Cult in Asia Minor*
(Cambridge: Cambridge University Press, 1984) 63.
[61]L.A. Curchin, *The Local Magistrates of Roman Spain*, 43.
[62]A.T. Fear, *Rome and Baetica*, 88.
[63]A.T. Fear, *Rome and Baetica*, 86-87.

take care that magistri be appointed for the chapels, temples, and shrines in such manner as the decuriones shall have determined; and that the said magistri shall, severally in each year, cause games in the circus, sacrifices, and services to be celebrated in such manner as the decuriones shall have decreed.[64]

The *Lex Ursonensis* also underlines the important rôle which the order of decurions had in religious affairs:

> All *duoviri* holding office after the establishment of the colony shall, within the ten days following the commencement of their magistracy, bring before the decurions, when not less than two-thirds are present, the question as to the dates and the persons to perform such sacrifices. Whatever a majority of the decurions present shall have decreed ... shall be lawful and valid, and such sacrifices and such festal days shall be observed in said colony.[65]

A similar involvement in religious affairs obtained also for the civic leaders in the Roman colony of Carthage, as James Rives records:

> In Carthage, then, the local ordo exercised an authority over public religion much the same as that of the Senate in republican Rome. It was responsible for selecting, organizing, and financing the sacra publica of the new colony, and in that process for defining its collective religious identity.[66]

It is also clear in the charter from the Roman colony of Urso that the city's leading figures had the additional responsibility of overseeing public sacrifices.[67]

The connection between high civic office and prominent religious positions (and the honours enjoyed by both) should not suggest that obeisance and celebration of the local gods was entirely a means of political manipulation and self-advancement. It is reasonable to assume that citizens in both the east and west of the empire had also a fundamental belief in the ability of the gods to affect the prosperity of their lives. These gods, furthermore, operated through the lives and influence of particular individuals. This is confirmed, for example, by a statement by Epictetus: 'That is why we

---

[64]*Lex Ursonensis* 128.

[65]*Lex Ursonensis* 44.

[66]J.B. Rives, *Religion and Authority in Roman Carthage*, 38-39. This perspective is reinforced more strongly at *op. cit.*, 51.

[67]J.B. Rives, *Religion and Authority in Roman Carthage*, 30; *Lex Ursonensis* 128.

even worship those persons as gods; for we consider that what has power to confer the greatest advantage is divine'.[68]

The imperial cult — an institution which accorded to a human being, the Roman emperor, honours similar to those of a god — was a highly significant element in the arena of civic life in both Greek and Roman cities.[69] In the light of what is already clear, it is unsurprising that the importance of the imperial cult to our study of leadership in the Graeco-Roman world also hinges upon the close association between politics and religion. Duncan Fishwick correctly observes:

> The real significance of the worship of the Roman emperor, particularly in its provincial application, lies not in the realm of religion at all but in a far different field: that of practical government, wherein lay the historic destiny of the Roman people.[70]

We have seen that honour was both root and branch of the system of Graeco-Roman leadership, whether at the imperial, the provincial, or the civic level. We shall find that the imperial cult also operated by means of the same system of honour and esteem.[71] Furthermore, Donald Engels points out that where, in earlier times, there had been a heavy reliance by independent city-states on the guidance of their civic gods, in the first-century climate where directive guidance often came from Rome, the imperial cult assumed an added importance.[72]

Although especially influential in the West, the imperial cult was well nigh ubiquitous throughout the Roman empire.[73] The eastern provinces were quicker to capitalize on adoption of what

---

[68]Epictetus 4.6.1, cited in D.R. Edwards, *Religion and Power: Pagans, Jews, and Christians in the Greek East* (Oxford: Oxford University Press, 1996) 91.

[69]D. Fishwick, *The Imperial Cult in the Latin West: Studies in the Ruler Cult of the Western Provinces of the Roman Empire* (Études préliminaires aux réligions orientales dans l'Empire romain, 108; vols. 1.i - 2.ii; Leiden: E.J. Brill, 1987) 1.i.33-34.

[70]D. Fishwick, 'The Development of Provincial Ruler Worship in the Western Roman Empire', in *Aufstieg und Niedergang der Römischen Welt* II.16.2 (1978) 1253. *Cf.* also S.R.F. Price, *Rituals and Power*, 16, 'The imperial cult is thus essentially a political phenomenon, either because it was exploited by the Roman state, or because the subjects made diplomatic capital out of it'.

[71]J.E. Lendon, *Empire of Honour*, 166.

[72]D. Engels, *Roman Corinth*, 92.

[73]For discussion of its influence in the East, see S.R.F. Price, *Rituals and Power*; for discussion of its influence in the West, see D. Fishwick, *The Imperial Cult in the Latin West*.

proved to be both a channel of imperial veneration and a means of personal and civic social advancement.[74] The Greek city-states, after all, had their own long history of honouring posthumously their greatest benefactors and rulers — a tradition which was especially cultivated in the post-Classical, individualistic and élitist period.[75]

The imperial cult provided an important platform for the local élites to enhance their own influence within their community. Peter Garnsey and Richard Saller write with regard to the imperial cult that it was 'a conveyor of imperial ideology, a focus of loyalty for the many, and a mechanism for the social advancement of the few'.[76] Expressions of honour to the emperor by way of decrees, libations or other acts of cult could be reciprocated by benefactions to the city, which in turn would elicit further honour from the client. This is the currency of reciprocity which was foundational to the institution of patronage. This fundamental relationship between patron and client was further reinforced by a recognition of the influence of a deity in that relationship.[77] It was perceived that the local élites were those best placed to broker power between divine, imperial and local authorities;[78] and it was these local élites who, charged with establishing the imperial cult in their localities, pursued this task with a clear eye to seeing the advancement of their own cause. James Rives argues that, '[t]hrough the imperial cult the local élite associated themselves with the emperor, the central power of the empire, and so promoted their own position with respect to the general populace of the city'.[79] This partnership between central and local government worked to mutual benefit. As always with patronage, both sides were working with self-interested agendas. Rives stresses that we need to redress any view which considers that the élites simply acted as agents of central government. They had their own political agendas

---

[74]Cf. D.W.G. Gill & B.W. Winter, 'Acts and Roman Religion', in D.W.J. Gill & C. Gempf (eds.), *The Book of Acts in its Graeco-Roman Setting* (The Book of Acts in its First Century Setting, 2; Grand Rapids: Eerdmans, 1994) 93-94; and S. Mitchell, *Anatolia: Land, Men, and Gods in Asia Minor* (2 vols.; Oxford: Clarendon Press, 1993) I.100.

[75]D. Fishwick, *The Imperial Cult in the Latin West*, 1.i.3, 5-7, 46.

[76]P. Garnsey & R.P. Saller, *The Roman Empire: Economy, Society, and Culture* (Berkeley: University of California Press, 1987) 166-67.

[77]D.R. Edwards, *Religion and Power*, 93.

[78]D.R. Edwards, *Religion and Power*, 94. He cites an example from Ephesus of a man who held political and religious office.

[79]J.B. Rives, *Religion and Authority in Roman Carthage*, 63.

to pursue, and followed the imperial line out of consensus. In some instances, this entailed the pursuance of local cults rather than Roman cults.[80] This nexus between the élites in local government, celebration of the imperial cult and patronage is seen in a Greek inscription from Sparta in c. A.D. 15.[81]

The importance of the emperor in Rome's expressions of its religion was reinforced by Augustus in his reorganization of the city in 7 B.C., when shrines (to the *Lares Augusti* and *Genius Augusti*) were built at the crossroads of each new ward of the city.[82] Furthermore, Augustus elevated his own standing by recording himself that he had repaired as many as 82 temples in 28 B.C.[83] Additionally, the emperor Augustus assumed for himself numerous priestly offices within Rome itself (although none outside the city).[84]

This single institution of the imperial cult provided a significant means of expressing imperial allegiance at the local civic level. This is dramatically seen in a competition devised in about 29 B.C. to reward 'the person who devised the greatest honour for the god [Augustus]'.[85] This personal interest is evident also in one notable event which took place in the Roman colony of Corinth at about the time Paul was writing to the Christian community in the city there. A significant provincial cult recognising the enthronement of Nero was instituted,[86] which was accompanied by imperial festivals attracting widespread publicity and redounding to the honour of the local élites.[87] (The debate is ongoing among ancient historians as to the degree to which initiative for the development of the imperial cult

---

[80]J.B. Rives, *Religion and Authority in Roman Carthage*, 169-70.

[81]*Supplementum Epigraphicum Graecum* 11.923.7-40, cited in M. Beard, J. North & S. Price, *Religions of Rome: a History* (Cambridge: Cambridge University Press, 1998) 254.

[82]M. Beard, J. North & S. Price, *Religions of Rome: a History*, 185.

[83]*Cf.* M. Beard, J. North & S. Price, *Religions of Rome: a History*, 196.

[84]M. Beard, J. North & S. Price, *Religions of Rome: a History*, 186-88.

[85]S.R.F. Price, *Rituals and Power*, 54.

[86]A.J.S. Spawforth, 'The Achaean Federal Cult Part I: Pseudo-Julian, Letters 198', *Tyndale Bulletin* 46 (1995) 151-68.

[87]For discussion as to how this may have affected the Christian believers at the time see B.W. Winter, 'The Achaean Federal Imperial Cult II: the Corinthian Church', *Tyndale Bulletin* 46 (1995) 169-78.

derived from the emperor himself or from the cities and leading personalities which sought to honour him.)[88]

Not only was the imperial cult ubiquitous, it also maintained its vitality over a long period, as witnessed by the continuing building of imperial temples into the beginning of the third century A.D.[89] It has even been argued that the cult's very vitality derives from 'its capacity to exploit the competitive values of the urban élite'.[90] Additionally, however, its vitality is owed in part to its innate flexibility and adaptability. It could not only be used in both the Greek and the Roman cities in different ways, but could also change with successive emperors.[91] In this respect, Paul Zanker writes:

> It was inevitable that the West would take over the ruler cult, since it gave local aristocracies a new vehicle for expressing and maintaining positions of power. The integration of the ruler cult into traditional religious ritual allowed each individual, and the community as a whole, to share the feeling of participation in the restoration of the state.[92]

The imperial cult was also a mechanism which fuelled the ongoing and intense rivalry between cities.[93] Fierce competition surrounded the fight to earn the right to build an imperial temple. A city with this right received the acclaimed title, *neokoros*. Once a city had achieved this honour, satisfaction was not complete until this honour had been repeated twice or more often.[94]

Thus we can see that it was a requirement of civic leaders in cities in the Roman West to pay due respect to the city's gods, as well

---

[88]S.R.F. Price, *Rituals and Power*, 53. *Cf.* also C.K. Williams, 'The Refounding of Corinth: Some Roman Religious Attitudes', in S. Macready & F.H. Thompson (eds.), *Roman Architecture in the Greek World* (Occasional Paper, Society of Antiquaries of London, New Series, 10; London: Thames and Hudson, 1987) 29-31.

[89]S.R.F. Price, *Rituals and Power*, 59.

[90]S.R.F. Price, *Rituals and Power*, 59.

[91]D. Fishwick, 'The Development of Provincial Ruler Worship in the Western Roman Empire', 1251.

[92]P. Zanker, *The Power of Images in the Age of Augustus* (Ann Arbor: University of Michigan Press, 1988) 331.

[93]S.R.F. Price, *Rituals and Power*, 126-32.

[94]This title became current in the late first century and was applied to the Greek city of Ephesus; with its two imperial temples, as detailed in S.J. Friesen, *Twice Neokoros: Ephesus, Asia and the Cult of the Flavian Imperial Family* (Religions in the Graeco-Roman World, 116; Leiden: E.J. Brill, 1993).

as the emperor and the Roman god Jupiter. This responsibility was accompanied by an extensive penalty for those failing to comply, as indicated by the *Lex Municipalis Salpensana*:

> The duovirs now charged with the highest jurisdiction in the said municipium, likewise the aediles and quaestors now holding office in the said municipium, each of them severally within the five days next following the issue of this law ... shall take oath in a public meeting, by Jupiter and by the divine Augustus and the divine Claudius and the divine Vespasianus Augustus and by the divine Titus Augustus and by the genius of the imperator Domitianus Augustus and by the dei Penates, that they will rightly perform whatsoever they believe to be in accordance with this law ... Any person failing to take such oath shall be condemned to pay to the citizens of the said municipium 10,000 sesterces, and in respect to the said money, the right to take legal action, to sue and to prosecute, shall belong at will to every citizen of the said municipium, and to any other person specified by this law.[95]

Tertullian, writing in the late second century, argues that these religious responsibilities associated with high office in a local city would prevent a Christian from accepting such positions.[96] Stephen Mitchell summarizes the obstacles:

> One cannot avoid the impression that the obstacle which stood in the way of the progress of Christianity, and the force which would have drawn new adherents back to conformity with the prevailing paganism, was the public worship of the emperors. ... In the urban setting of Pisidian Antioch where spectacular and enticing public festivals imposed conformity and a rhythm of observance on a compact population, where Christians could not (if they wanted to) conceal their beliefs and activities from their fellows, it was not a change of heart that might win a Christian convert back to paganism, but the overwhelming pressure to conform imposed by the institutions of his city and the activities of his neighbours.[97]

Bruce Winter, however, argues that the early Christian churches may well have enjoyed some of the exemptions which were

---

[95]*Lex Municipalis Salpensana* 41-45; *cf.* also A.D. Clarke, *Secular and Christian Leadership in Corinth*, 53; and A.G. Roos, '*De Titulo quodam latino Corinthi nuper reperto*', *Mnemosyne* 58 (1930) 160-65.

[96]Tertullian, *De idololatria* 17.3.

[97]S. Mitchell, *Anatolia*, II.10.

afforded to the Jewish communities, when Judaism was tolerated, as opposed to being a proscribed *religio illicita*. In particular, he argues that Gallio's edict may have offered immunity for Christians who did not comply with the imperial cult.[98]

It should not be concluded, however, that the imperial cult was *only* a disingenuous tool of the élites for personal advancement. Simon Price criticizes the view that the élites were sceptical about the ruler cult and did not take it seriously. He further argues that it was not exclusively the domain of the civic rulers, but rather that its influence was felt throughout the civic community.[99] The profile of the cult within the cities meant that it impinged also on the lives of people at a popular level.[100] 'All citizens had a share in the city, and in the imperial cult.'[101] It was at the high-profile festivals, games and processions where the imperial cult most touched the lives of the non-élites, and became a community-wide celebration.[102] Here the influence of the emperor was paraded alongside the munificence of the local benefactors. Furthermore, in the Roman cities, associations of ex-slaves, *Augustales*, could hold their own celebrations of the imperial cult.[103]

Thus, the imperial cult provided, amongst other formalities, a platform for the celebration of the principal ruler, the accrual of honour and profile to the local leaders, and the opportunity for all citizens to indulge in communal festivities; and as Jon Lendon summarizes,

---

[98]B.W. Winter, 'Gallio's Exemption of Achaean Christians from the Imperial Cult', (forthcoming).

[99]S.R.F. Price, *Rituals and Power*, 114-15.

[100]C.R. Whittaker, 'Imperialism and Culture: the Roman Initiative', 150, 'the public business of the cities, the politics, meetings, elections and courts, were integrated into what Gros calls "the liturgic circuits of the imperial cult", the whole ceremonial being an occasion for the display of social ranks and orders ... Although participation was probably not obligatory, official pressures and distribution of gifts or food and wine made an explicit attempt to ensure representation of different sectors of *ordo* and *populus* at the ceremonies'.

[101]S.R.F. Price, *Rituals and Power*, 114.

[102]S.R.F. Price, *Rituals and Power*, 101, 107-14.

[103]S.R.F. Price, *Rituals and Power*, 114. For examples from Roman Corinth see A.D. Clarke, *Secular and Christian Leadership in Corinth*, Appendix A, nos. 12, 22, 47, 108; *cf.* also R. Duthoy, 'Les *Augustales', *Aufstieg und Niedergang der Römischen Welt* II.16.2 (1978) 1254-1309.

The Roman imperial cult offers the most compelling insight into the complex relationship between honour as a practical way of getting things done in the Roman empire, honour as polite deception, and honour as self-deception.[104]

It is, thus, clear from both the Greek and Roman cities of the early Roman empire that local civic politics was inextricably linked with religious expression and cultic activity. Those who occupied leading positions in the administration of the city were called to perform also in the religious sphere, and were often rewarded with priesthoods. Cities competed also for recognition before the emperor and this was achieved not least by means of the ubiquitous imperial cult.

IV. Conclusion

Although the Roman colonies and towns differed in constitution from the older Greek cities, their civic leaders were in similar respects drawn from the élites, and likewise functioned in both a political and religious capacity. It has become apparent that significant personal wealth, demonstrated through patronage, was a necessary prerequisite for civic leadership. Such leadership had a strong component of self-interest where reputation, both in the present and in perpetuity, was a guiding principle.

Such leaders necessarily enjoyed a high profile within their local communities. The munificent round of public entertainments and sacrifices for the civic population, reinforced by statues, inscriptions and building works in strategic positions in the city, ensured that one's name and one's deeds were on the lips of almost all. This projection of the nature of leadership in Graeco-Roman society was consequently far-reaching in influence and will have been well understood by those in the mid-first century who were to be numbered amongst the early Christians.

---

[104]J.E. Lendon, *Empire of Honour*, 160.

CHAPTER 4

LEADERSHIP IN THE
VOLUNTARY ASSOCIATIONS

I. Introduction

Local civic government in the period of the early Roman empire was fundamentally oligarchic. It was the preserve of the socially advantaged, with wealth being one of the essential pre-requisites for effectively fulfilling such positions of leadership. The analysis of civic administration in the preceding chapters has necessarily, therefore, focused on structures which were largely the domain of the élites of local Graeco-Roman communities. Civic administration provided for such people a means by which they could both merit and repay the honour and esteem bestowed upon them by the citizen body.

Leadership within this civic domain may have been the exclusive preserve of the élites; however, it clearly impinged to a considerable extent on the lives of all citizens. The profile of these leading figures and the importance of their office were paraded before the whole civic community in acts of patronage and the continuing round of public activities in which leaders were involved.[1]

_____

[1]C.R. Whittaker, 'Imperialism and Culture: the Roman Initiative', in D.J. Mattingly (ed.), _Dialogues in Roman Imperialism: Power, Discourse, and Discrepant Experience in the Roman Empire_ (Journal of Roman Archaeology, Supplementary

This situation, nonetheless, begs the question whether leadership in the first-century world lay only within the grasp of the privileged and wealthy freeborn. Although the honorific posts in civic administration were almost exclusively available to the wise, well-born and powerful of society, there were other fora in which poorer individuals, including freedmen and even slaves, could exercise leadership. Indeed, patronal benefaction in the Graeco-Roman world is widely, but inaccurately, perceived as exclusively an institution of the wealthy. It should not be overlooked that patronage only functioned effectively in that society because it operated by means of the ubiquitous Mediterranean culture of honour and shame which was active at *all* levels of society, and not just at the more rarefied level of the élites.[2]

The present chapter will focus on the many and various voluntary associations, clubs, unions and guilds which existed throughout the Roman empire.[3] These groups were deeply integrated into the structures of the local community and crucially provided both a context in which the urban poor of Graeco-Roman society could exercise influence and a social unit which was small enough for each member of the group to have an identity.[4] It is significant that in these groups honour, privilege and prestige operated in a way which closely paralleled the system which lay at the heart of administration at the civic level. Furthermore, we see a similar nexus between political and religious elements of corporate life in both the

---

Series, 23; Portsmouth, R.I.: Journal of Roman Archaeology, 1997) 145, 'The Roman city was literally stuffed with political imagery which was, like advertising, ubiquitous, inescapable and subliminally absorbed'.

[2]H. Moxnes, '"He saw that the City was full of Idols" (Acts 17:16): Visualizing the World of the First Christians', in D. Hellholm, H. Moxnes & T.K. Seim (eds.), *Mighty Minorities?: Minorities in Early Christianity — Positions and Strategies: Essays in Honour of Jacob Jervell on his 70th Birthday, 21 May 1995* (Oslo: Scandinavian University Press, 1995) 115; *cf.* also J.E. Lendon, *Empire of Honour: the Art of Government in the Roman World* (Oxford: Clarendon Press, 1997) 105, 'Some of the ways in which individuals and institutions, from tiny clubs to cities to vast provinces, came to grips with the world around them were strangely similar; they all had honour, and all used honour's tools'.

[3]J.P. Waltzing, *Étude historique sur les corporations professionnelles chez les Romains depuis les origines jusqu'à la chute de l'Empire de l'Occident* (5 vols.; Hildesheim: Georg Olms, 1970) first published as long ago as 1895, lists some 2,500 Roman *collegia*.

[4]W. Cotter, 'Our *Politeuma* is in Heaven: the Meaning of Philippians 3:17-21', in B.H. McLean (ed.), *Origins and Method: Towards a New Understanding of Judaism and Christianity* (JSNT Supplement Series, 86; Sheffield: JSOT Press, 1993) 100-101.

associations and the higher echelons of civic life.[5] This correspondence between civic leadership and leadership in the associations further underlines the widespread impact which the local élites had upon the attitudes and practices of government at other levels of society.

It is significant, but not surprising, that the literary sources refer relatively rarely to the voluntary associations. This is partly because much of the available literary evidence derives predominantly from aristocratic circles, which in turn were more interested in reporting on public, than private activities. Where references are made to the clubs or associations, they are often in a derogatory or suppressive tone, and reflect the views which currently prevailed among the élites.[6] A more fertile source of evidence concerning such groups, however, surfaces in the legal documents of the Antonine period.[7] The voluntary associations were frequently the subject of imperial legislation and repeatedly revised limits of their liberties were encapsulated in law. The second major source of information regarding the associations can be found in the extant corpus of epigraphic material, most of which derives from the first three centuries of the Roman empire.[8] Inscriptions were not exclusively the domain of the wealthy, although they did predominantly reflect urban society; and there is a rich wealth of inscriptions produced by, although not always for, the less wealthy members of Graeco-Roman society who were fortunate enough to be part of an association (*collegium*).

Given that the voluntary associations were a widespread phenomenon in the Roman empire, it is remarkable that there has been so little secondary literature which has focused on these clubs. Following a brief period of considerable interest at the end of the nineteenth century,[9] during the early part of the twentieth century comparatively little was published which was concerned with these

---

[5]A.W. Lintott, 'Clubs, Roman', in *The Oxford Classical Dictionary* (Oxford: Oxford University Press, 1996) 352, 'The *collegia* illustrate the rule that all ancient societies from the family upwards had a religious basis'.

[6]E.A. Judge, *The Social Pattern of Christian Groups in the First Century: Some Prolegomena to the Study of New Testament Ideas of Social Obligation* (London: Tyndale Press, 1960) 41.

[7]*Cf.* J.P. Waltzing, *Étude historique sur les corporations professionnelles*, I.3.

[8]*Cf.* J.P. Waltzing, *Étude historique sur les corporations professionnelles*, I.4-5.

[9]*Cf.* the literature cited by J.P. Waltzing, *Étude historique sur les corporations professionnelles*, I.11-30.

associations.[10] In more recent years, however, there has been a renewed interest, most notably in relation to the field of New Testament studies. This interest is reflected in a number of short works focusing on the associations, together with one major volume of essays.[11]

II. Defining the Voluntary Associations

The description 'voluntary association' is often employed because it is sufficiently broad to encompass many of the different types of groups which existed in Graeco-Roman society — *collegium, secta, factio, thiasos, eranos, koinon, synodos, sodalitas*.[12] Sandra Walker-Ramisch offers the following definition:

> an organized association of persons who come together on a voluntary, contractual basis (rather than kinship, caste, national, or geographic association) in the pursuit of common interests, both manifest and latent. To the association each member contributes, by contractual agreement, a part of his/her time and resources.[13]

Inevitably such a broad classification is necessarily very generalized. At the time of the early Roman empire, the range of such groups was extensive, and associations could be classified according to a number of categories: some were public associations, others were

---

[10]*Cf.* the works cited by T. Seland, 'Philo and the Clubs and Associations of Alexandria', in J.S. Kloppenborg & S.G. Wilson (eds.), *Voluntary Associations in the Graeco-Roman World* (London: Routledge, 1996) 111.

[11]R.L. Wilken, 'Collegia, Philosophical Schools, and Theology', in S. Benko & J.J. O'Rourke (eds.), *Early Church History: the Roman Empire as the Setting of Primitive Christianity* (London: Oliphants, 1971) 268-91; J.S. Kloppenborg, 'Edwin Hatch, Churches and Collegia', in B.H. McLean (ed.), *Origins and Method: Towards a New Understanding of Judaism and Christianity* (JSNT Supplement Series, 86; Sheffield: JSOT Press, 1993) 212-38; B.H. McLean, 'The Agrippinilla Inscription: Religious Associations and Early Church Formation', *op. cit.*, 239-70; and J.S. Kloppenborg & S.G. Wilson (eds.), *Voluntary Associations in the Graeco-Roman World* (London: Routledge, 1996).

[12]S.G. Wilson, 'Voluntary Associations: an Overview', in J.S. Kloppenborg & S.G. Wilson (eds.), *Voluntary Associations in the Graeco-Roman World* (London: Routledge, 1996) 1.

[13]S. Walker-Ramisch, 'Associations and the Damascus Document: a Sociological Analysis', in J.S. Kloppenborg & S.G. Wilson (eds.), *Voluntary Associations in the Graeco-Roman World* (London: Routledge, 1996) 131.

only semi-official, and others still were purely private.[14] Furthermore, where many attracted a membership sharing a common profession (trade *collegia*), a good number shared a particular religious or cultic focus (priestly *collegia*), and others were centred on a particular family or household (domestic *collegia*).[15]

Common trades tended to cluster in the same locality in cities. This made it easier for professional *collegia* to be formed and to function from a common location as well as with a common trade.[16] Scholars are agreed that the prime aim of these professional *collegia* was not so much to operate as a trade union, concerned exclusively with professional issues such as standards, wages and conditions, but rather as a social group.[17] They met principally for recreational and religious purposes; indeed Philo denigrates the associations by recounting the reputation which many of the clubs (θίασοι) in Alexandria had:

> In the city there are clubs with a large membership, whose fellowship is founded on no sound principle but on strong liquor and drunkenness and sottish carousing and their offspring, wantonness.[18]

While the interests of the trade *collegia* were largely social, that is not to say that there was never a professional focus to such gatherings. Instances can be found where particular trade groups were able to exert influence on issues such as pay and conditions.[19] It may be that one such example is the combined action, albeit unsuccessful, of the silversmiths in Ephesus on experiencing a downturn in business

---

[14]J.P. Waltzing, *Étude historique sur les corporations professionnelles*, I.32.

[15]J.P. Waltzing, *Étude historique sur les corporations professionnelles*, I.33; *cf.* also A.D. Nock, C. Roberts & T.C. Skeat, 'The Guild of Zeus Hypsistos', *Harvard Theological Review* 29 (1936) 74.

[16]J.S. Kloppenborg, 'Collegia and *Thiasoi*: Issues in Function, Taxonomy and Membership', in J.S. Kloppenborg & S.G. Wilson (eds.), *Voluntary Associations in the Graeco-Roman World* (London: Routledge, 1996) 24.

[17]R.L. Wilken, 'Collegia, Philosophical Schools, and Theology', 280; *cf.* also J.S. Kloppenborg, 'Edwin Hatch, Churches and Collegia', 222, who says, 'The type of *collegia* functioned not like a modern labour union, to protect labour markets, but for social reasons, providing a quasi-civic structure in which members could receive and bestow honours on their fellows'.

[18]Philo, *In Flaccum* 136; *cf.* also *op. cit.*, 4; and Varro, *Res Rusticae* 3.2.16.

[19]J.S. Kloppenborg, 'Collegia and *Thiasoi*: Issues in Function, Taxonomy and Membership', 19.

following the spread of Christianity in the region.[20] The silversmith Demetrius called together the craftsmen and 'the workmen in related trades' to seek a solution to the threat that was being imposed to their business.

A distinction should be made between the official priestly *collegia* and the private associations. Many of the former were under the direct patronage of the emperor and also incorporated those from the élites. The *sodales Augustales* were included in this group and created a forum for freedmen, who did not normally have access to the civic magistracies, to exercise influence.[21] This is not to say that other private associations did not have a strongly religious dimension also.[22]

Many associations were based around the imperial or other private households (*collegia domestica*).[23] These groups, permitted by the masters and mistresses of the house, offered for the slaves and freedmen of the household a group identity. Such groups were able to appoint their own 'magistrates' and respond in an appropriate way to the benefactions given to them by the head of the household. The benefit to the head of the household was that those in his charge were occupied in pursuits of which he was aware, as opposed to some clandestine and possibly subversive association.[24] The Agrippinilla inscription of a Dionysiac religious guild (θίασος) dated from around A.D. 150, and originating in the Roman Campagna, gives evidence that there was the widest range of social status represented in a group, including both senator and slaves. The organization of this association was based on that of the Roman family of an ex-consul, and positions of pre-eminence were awarded

---

[20]Acts 19:23-40; *cf.* C.J. Hemer, *The Book of Acts in the Setting of Hellenistic History* (WUNT, 49; Tübingen: J.C.B. Mohr, 1989) 235-36; and E.A. Judge, *The Social Pattern of Christian Groups in the First Century*, 41.

[21]J.S. Kloppenborg, 'Collegia and *Thiasoi*: Issues in Function, Taxonomy and Membership', 17.

[22]Indeed, as J.P. Waltzing, *Étude historique sur les corporations professionnelles*, I.75, writes, 'À l'époque lointaine dont nous parlons, une corporation sans culte ne se conçoit pas'.

[23]*Cf.* for example the inscription *CIL* 6.9148 which refers to a 'collegium which is in the house of Sergia Paullina'.

[24]J.S. Kloppenborg, 'Collegia and *Thiasoi*: Issues in Function, Taxonomy and Membership', 23.

to those most closely related to the senatorial family of Marcus Gavius Squilla Gallicanus.[25]

The question has been raised as to whether Paul, as recorded in the book of Acts, interacted with some of the tentmaking professional guilds in his own capacity as a leatherworker or at least might have seemed to others as having formed a professional association;[26] and even whether some of the Pauline communities, as represented for example in Romans 16:5 and Colossians 4:15, might have begun as domestic *collegia*.[27]

III. The Social, Political and Religious Dimensions of Voluntary Associations

Those who are familiar with the social, political and religious dimensions of public civic life in the Graeco-Roman world will recognize a remarkable similarity to those expectations and practices of the voluntary associations. Although senior civic posts were the preserve of those in the local community who were regarded as wealthy, whereas the voluntary associations appealed in the majority to those with a lower social-standing, nonetheless these two sectors of society closely reflected each other in these specific categories.

1. The Social Dimension

The extensive by-laws of one particular burial society from the early second century in Lanuvium, Italy, are fortunately preserved, and shed much light on what was expected of members.[28] The official document records that the group was dedicated in the names of the gods Antinoüs and Diana, and met monthly in the temple of

---

[25]B.H. McLean, 'The Agrippinilla Inscription: Religious Associations and Early Church Formation', 247-48.

[26]*Cf.* J.S. Kloppenborg, 'Collegia and *Thiasoi*: Issues in Function, Taxonomy and Membership', 24; *cf.*, for example, Acts 18:3; and W.A. Meeks, *The First Urban Christians: the Social World of the Apostle Paul* (New Haven: Yale University Press, 1983) 32.

[27]J.S. Kloppenborg, 'Collegia and *Thiasoi*: Issues in Function, Taxonomy and Membership', 23.

[28]*CIL* 14.2.112, translated in N. Lewis & M. Reinhold (eds.), *Roman Civilization: Sourcebook, Vol. 2: The Empire* (New York: Harper & Row, 1966) 273-75.

Antinoüs in order to make contributions to a burial fund for its members. Thus:

> It was voted unanimously that whoever desires to enter this society shall pay an initiation fee of 100 sesterces and an amphora of good wine, and shall pay monthly dues of 4 asses. It was voted further that if anyone has not paid his dues for six consecutive months and the common lot of mankind befalls him, his claim to burial shall not be considered, even if he has provided for it in his will. It was voted further that upon the decease of a paid-up member of our body there will be due him from the treasury 300 sesterces, from which sum will be deducted a funeral fee of 50 sesterces to be distributed at the pyre [among those attending]; the obsequies, furthermore, will be performed on foot.

The association benefited from the patronage of Lucius Caesennius Rufus who donated the interest on 15,000 sesterces (amounting to some 400 sesterces) which accrued on both August 13th and November 27th. In addition to this specific patronage, the by-laws of this particular association reflect the expectation that membership would reflect a social mix. They expressly state that slaves were also members of the association and had rights of burial; indeed, those slaves who attained their freedom were expected to celebrate this by donating an amphora of good wine. Furthermore, slave masters were also among the members (and were expected to provide dinner for the association when their turn came around). It is thus clear that the honour system and a closely defined hierarchy applied in the Lanuvium burial society as reflected in the following:[29]

> It was voted further that any member who becomes *quinquennalis* in this society shall be exempt from such obligations [?] for the term when he is *quinquennalis*, and that he shall receive a double share in all distributions. It was voted further that the secretary and the messenger shall be exempt from such obligations [?] and shall receive a share and a half in every distribution.
> It was voted further that any member who has administered the office of *quinquennalis* honestly shall [thereafter] receive a share and

---

[29]This contrasts with the analysis given by R.H. Finger, *Paul and the Roman House Churches* (Scottdale: Herald, 1993) 52.

a half of everything as a mark of honor, so that other *quinquennales* will also hope for the same by properly discharging their duties.[30]

It is clear also that along with the honour of being the *quinquennalis* came the privilege of being both an officiant in the religious rites and a patron:

> It was voted further that on the festive days of his term of office each *quinquennalis* is to conduct worship with incense and wine and is to perform his other functions clothed in white, and that on the birthdays of Diana and Antinoüs he is to provide oil for the society in the public bath before they banquet.[31]

It thus emerges that standard social distinctions were observed in that those in positions of leadership in the *collegia* enjoyed particular privileges; specifically, officials enjoyed larger quantities of food at feasts than those of lower social status.[32] Although the membership of some associations reflected a level of social mix, this did not exclude the possibility of harsher punishment, for example flogging, being meted out in respect of the misconduct of members who were slaves in contrast to their free counterparts.[33]

Many of the associations were attractive to the lower social strata and, under the patronage of a chosen deity, and possibly also a wealthy individual, they gathered for the mutual benefit of their

---

[30]*CIL* 14.2.112, translated in N. Lewis & M. Reinhold (eds.), *Roman Civilization: Sourcebook, Vol. 2: The Empire,* 273-75.

[31]*CIL* 14.2.112, translated in N. Lewis & M. Reinhold (eds.), *Roman Civilization: Sourcebook, Vol. 2: The Empire,* 273-75.

[32]G. Theissen, *The Social Setting of Pauline Christianity: Essays on Corinth* (Philadelphia: Fortress Press, 1982) 154. He further suggests that this may well lie behind the inequalities in the celebration of the Lord's Supper recorded in 1 Cor 11; *cf.* also W.A. Meeks, *The First Urban Christians,* 159. J.E. Lendon, *Empire of Honour,* 97-98, writes, 'The existence of communities of honour far beneath the aristocracy can be illustrated in many contexts. Members of the lower classes naturally structured religious sodalities, trade guilds, and burial insurance clubs on the same basis as their social betters organized cities, relying on the better-off members to underwrite the expenses of the organization out of *philotimia,* in exchange for honour in the form of an ostentatiously higher-piled plate at club banquets, and statues, and honorific decrees passed by the members of the organization'; *cf.* also the 'privileges' cited in *op. cit.,* 98, fn. 328, 'For comic effect, Apuleius has bandits act like a *collegium* (*Met.* 7.7): when one is elected chief, he is clad in a splendid robe, kisses the members one by one, and takes his seat on the highest couch, *Met.* 7.9'.

[33]J.S. Kloppenborg, 'Edwin Hatch, Churches and Collegia', 234.

members. For the most part those of the significantly higher social strata, on the other hand, '[b]y virtue of their birth, means, and education ... had little need to resort to such organization to attain the ends — social and professional — that motivated persons beneath them in the social scale to form voluntary associations'.[34] Thus the associations provided the opportunity for many of those, without a public identity, to be part of a fictive kinship group in the otherwise pluralist, multi-cultural and highly-stratified society of the Roman empire.[35]

There was in the associations, as with the Graeco-Roman cities, also a fascination with the use of titles for official positions.[36] Such titles were favoured in that they further reinforced the social hierarchy. It is also significant that precisely those titles which were widely used in civic and priestly contexts were also adopted by leading officials in the context of the voluntary associations, for example: *magister, curator, quinquennalis, decurion, quaestor, mater collegii, pater collegii, sacerdos, hiereus, archiereus*.[37]

It was noted above that patronage was important to the functioning of the Lanuvium voluntary association.[38] Benefactions provided by the élites would readily be reciprocated by standard expressions of honour and respect in much the same way that the dynamic of benefactions operated in civic and provincial life.[39] Philo

---

[34]H. Remus, 'Voluntary Association and Networks: Aelius Aristides at the Asclepieion in Pergamum', in J.S. Kloppenborg & S.G. Wilson (eds.), *Voluntary Associations in the Graeco-Roman World* (London: Routledge, 1996) 148.

[35]B.H. McLean, 'The Place of Cult in Voluntary Associations and Christian Churches on Delos', in J.S. Kloppenborg & S.G. Wilson (eds.), *Voluntary Associations in the Graeco-Roman World* (London: Routledge, 1996) 189, writes, 'As cults, voluntary associations provided the opportunity to worship the gods of their homeland, and seek their protection and patronage by offering sacrifice'.

[36]W.A. Meeks, *The First Urban Christians*, 134, suggests that this is in notable contrast to the practice which seems to emerge in the early Pauline communities.

[37]Cf. A.W. Lintott, 'Clubs, Roman', 352; also W.A. Meeks, *The First Urban Christians*, 31; and J.S. Kloppenborg, 'Collegia and *Thiasoi*: Issues in Function, Taxonomy and Membership', 26.

[38]Cf. CIL 6.10234, where a Roman benefactress, Marcellina, provides a 50,000 sesterces endowment for a religious *collegium* to Asclepius and Hygia.

[39]J.S. Kloppenborg, 'Collegia and *Thiasoi*: Issues in Function, Taxonomy and Membership', 27. Cf. also B.H. McLean, 'The Agrippinilla Inscription: Religious Associations and Early Church Formation', 249, 'Private collegia and thiasoi were customarily dependent upon aristocratic individuals or families who established and financed them'.

gives the less than complimentary instance of Isodorus, a patron of many of the Alexandrian clubs, whose membership was galvanized into inciting opposition against Flaccus.[40] In this instance their actions were disruptive to the *status quo*. However, most 'patrons of collegia were often senators (in Rome) or civic officials or civic patrons (in other cities) which at least informally tied the collegia to the interests of the polis'.[41] The Agrippinilla inscription and statue may have been one association's attempt at honouring and securing the continued interest of their founding benefactress.

It is clear, therefore, that, notwithstanding the narrower cross-section of society which predominated in the membership of most associations, distinctions of social standing were still considered significant and specifically formed the basis of some of their regulations. It is, thus, noteworthy that precisely those social and organizational structures and power relations which were foundational to wider Graeco-Roman society and clearly represented in cities both in the East and the West were also reflected in the much smaller, and more localized representations of society which constituted the voluntary associations.[42]

2. *The Political Dimension*

As with local administration in the civic context, there was a certain amount of political activism by members of voluntary associations. It was this element which inevitably led to the periodic clampdown on the rights of such *collegia* when it seemed that they did not at heart support the Roman ideal.

During the politically unstable period of the Roman Republic, associations were repeatedly being suppressed, only to be followed shortly afterwards by the restitution of that freedom. In 64 B.C., the Roman senate construed associations as potentially seditious. They were accordingly banned 'by decree of the Senate' and deemed

---

[40]Philo, *In Flaccum* 137-39.

[41]J.S. Kloppenborg, 'Collegia and *Thiasoi*: Issues in Function, Taxonomy and Membership', 26.

[42]J.S. Kloppenborg, 'Collegia and *Thiasoi*: Issues in Function, Taxonomy and Membership', 26, writes, 'the organization of Roman voluntary associations was normally patterned on that of the city and the army. It is quite common to find collegia divided into *centuriae* or *decuriae* ... In many collegia, the group of decurions functioned as the administrative body'.

'against the public good'.[43] Their freedom to meet was soon restored in 58 B.C., only for those associations which were explicitly political in flavour to be almost immediately dissolved once again in 56 B.C. Later still, Julius Caesar withdrew the rights of all associations which were not considered to have had an ancient foundation. Jewish synagogues were expressly exempted from this restriction and continued to enjoy special privileges into the Augustan period.

With the political transformations introduced under the new imperial régime the fortunes of the *collegia* continued to fluctuate, sometimes favourably, other times facing selective restriction.[44] Augustus reinforced specific restrictions on *collegia* which were perceived as offering a potential threat to public security.[45] The Roman historian Suetonius records of this period:

> Many pernicious practices militating against public security had survived as a result of the lawless habits of the civil wars ... Numerous leagues, too, were formed for the commission of crimes of every kind, assuming the title of some new guild ... Therefore to put a stop to brigandage, he ... disbanded all guilds (*collegia*), except such as were of long standing and formed for legitimate purposes.[46]

In order to have legitimacy, *collegia* were required to seek Augustus' explicit permission, and they were to be seen to be working for the public good.[47] This nervous reaction to the latent power of the popular masses was reflected time and again by subsequent emperors, although often with very specific concern for a particular locality displaying social unrest.[48] But, notwithstanding these

---

[43]Asconius, *In senatu contra L. Pisonem* 8.

[44]J.P. Waltzing, *Étude historique sur les corporations professionnelles*, I.114. *Cf.* also P. Richardson, 'Augustan-Era Synagogues in Rome', in K.P. Donfried & P. Richardson (eds.), *Judaism and Christianity in First-Century Rome* (Grand Rapids: Eerdmans, 1998) 18.

[45]*Cf.* O.F. Robinson, *The Criminal Law of Rome* (London: Duckworth, 1995) 80.

[46]Suetonius, *Augustus* 32.

[47]W. Cotter, 'The Collegia and Roman Law: State Restrictions on Voluntary Associations 64 B.C.E.–200 C.E.', in J.S. Kloppenborg & S.G. Wilson (eds.), *Voluntary Associations in the Graeco-Roman World* (London: Routledge, 1996) 78.

[48]J.P. Waltzing, *Étude historique sur les corporations professionnelles*, I.116; *cf.* also Tertullian, *Apologeticum* 38-39, 'For, unless I mistake the matter, the prevention of such associations is based on a prudential regard to public order, that the state may not be divided into parties which would naturally lead to disturbance in the electoral assemblies, the councils, the curiae, the special conventions, even in the public shows by the hostile collisions of rival parties'; and the discussion of

restrictions, the *collegia* did continue to have a widespread presence throughout the early centuries of the empire.

Consistent with the restrictions stemming from this imperial sense of insecurity, for the most part the clubs did not have a large membership. Many would have numbered between thirty and forty, whilst some included up to two hundred.[49] This nervousness was implicit in Pliny's suggestion to the emperor Trajan that the membership of *collegia* should be limited in number. In his correspondence, the governor Pliny specifically argues that numbers should not exceed 150.[50] It was felt to be advantageous that the voluntary associations were largely localized in their membership, influence and networks. This is reflective of both the autonomy which prevailed in Greek civic administration, and the potential political threat imposed by an extensive trans-local group.[51]

Philo's attitude to the political manoeuvrings of the associations in the city of Alexandria was far from complimentary; indeed, such associations were banned in Alexandria by the emperor Tiberius. Philo describes them as 'constantly holding feasts under pretext of sacrifice in which drunkenness vented itself in political intrigue'.[52] Pliny, the governor of Bithynia in the early second century, corresponds with the emperor seeking advice about a group of firemen who have sought to form an association in the city. Trajan's reply highlights the political sensitivity which surrounds these groups:

> You are of the opinion that it would be proper to constitute a guild of firemen (*collegium fabrorum*) in Nicomedia, agreeably to what has

---

localized disturbance by H. Remus, 'Voluntary Association and Networks: Aelius Aristides at the Asclepieion in Pergamum', 147-48.

[49]W.A. Meeks, *The First Urban Christians*, 31. There is evidence, however, of a limited number of far larger groups which existed; *cf.* B.H. McLean, 'The Agrippinilla Inscription: Religious Associations and Early Church Formation', 239-70.

[50]Pliny, *Letters* 10.33.

[51]S. Walker-Ramisch, 'Associations and the Damascus Document: a Sociological Analysis', 135-36, highlights the perception that 'should a local association become a movement which transcended the jurisdictional boundaries of the *polis* to achieve an inter-city organization with a centralized authority, it would no longer be "familial" but "political," not the building blocks of empire but an independent public institution vying for political dominance'.

[52]Philo, *In Flaccum* 4. *Cf.* T. Seland, 'Philo and the Clubs and Associations of Alexandria', 110.

been practised in several other places. But it is to be remembered
that these sorts of societies have greatly disturbed the peace of your
province in general, and of those cities in particular. Whatever title
we give them, and whatever our object in giving it, men who are
banded together for a common end will all the same become a
political association (*hetairia*) before long. It will therefore be better
to provide suitable means for extinguishing fires, and enjoin owners
of house-property to employ these themselves, calling in the help of
the populace when necessary.[53]

Notwithstanding such imperial restrictions, '[e]pigraphy made
plain the fact that professional, athletic, literary, dining and cultic
associations flourished in every city of the Empire, despite the best
efforts of several emperors to eradicate them'.[54] Indeed, it is
significant that these associations could even be shrewdly harnessed
as a means of reinforcing the dominant social order, by offering
identity and purpose to an otherwise anonymous populace. Indeed,
Augustus himself instituted a number of clubs which were expressly
concerned with celebrating the imperial cult.[55] For the most part,
however, these groups survived where they did because they
reinforced the political *status quo*, rather than being subversive.[56]
There are, for example, numerous inscriptions from Pompeii which
highlight the political candidates (or patrons) whom a particular
collegium has opted to endorse.[57]

Thus, as in so many dimensions of life in the Graeco-Roman
world, those institutions which prospered were those which were
mutually beneficial across the social divides. Those in the *collegia*
sought the opportunity to have influence, albeit at a limited level; the
patrons valued the support that was afforded by the client *collegia*;
and the ruling élites could *use* the *collegia* as an effective means of
mediation between themselves and the non-aristocratic members of

---

[53]Pliny, *Letters* 10.34.

[54]J.S. Kloppenborg, 'Edwin Hatch, Churches and Collegia', 213.

[55]A.W. Lintott, 'Clubs, Roman', 352.

[56]*Cf.* S.G. Wilson, 'Voluntary Associations: an Overview', 3, who compares the early Christian communities and Jewish gatherings similarly. The majority of Jews and Christians were supportive rather than socially destabilizing, although instances of provocation and revolt are by no means absent.

[57]*CIL* 4.113; 206; 336; 497; 677; 710; 743; 826; 864; 960; 7164; 7273; 7473, cited in J.S. Kloppenborg, 'Collegia and *Thiasoi*: Issues in Function, Taxonomy and Membership', 30.

the community.[58] The generalization, nonetheless, holds good that 'although *collegia* might occasionally exert pressure on civic governance, their *raison d'être* was not principally economic but social';[59] and thus Seland argues, 'whether the ostensible purposes of the clubs were convivial, political, or economic, most often these features were intertwined'.[60] The religious *collegia*, however, might have more in the way of cultic activities.[61]

3. The Religious Dimension

It has become clear that public religion played a significant rôle in Greek and Roman civic life; indeed, 'the Greek city knows no separation between sacred and profane. Religion is present in all the different levels of social life, and all collective practices have a religious dimension'.[62] As such, no *collegium* would have been conceived as a purely religious group, only concerned with religious activities.[63] The religious element was fundamental and the word *collegium* 'had religious associations even when the object of the club was not primarily worship. Few, if any, *collegia* were completely secular'.[64] Accordingly, many of the names of associations were directly associated with a god; and some groups even convened in

---

[58]J.S. Kloppenborg, 'Collegia and *Thiasoi*: Issues in Function, Taxonomy and Membership', 27.

[59]J.S. Kloppenborg, 'Collegia and *Thiasoi*: Issues in Function, Taxonomy and Membership', 20.

[60]T. Seland, 'Philo and the Clubs and Associations of Alexandria', 112.

[61]J.S. Kloppenborg, 'Collegia and *Thiasoi*: Issues in Function, Taxonomy and Membership', 22.

[62]P. Schmitt-Pantel, 'Collective Activities and the Political in the Greek City', in O. Murray and S. Price (eds.), *The Greek City: from Homer to Alexander* (Oxford: Clarendon Press, 1990) 200.

[63]S. Walker-Ramisch, 'Associations and the Damascus Document: a Sociological Analysis', 135, 'To speak of a religious association in the ancient world is to speak anachronistically. "Religion" was embedded in institutions of the ancient world, and all associations, public and private, were "religious"'.

[64]A.W. Lintott, 'Clubs, Roman', 353; *cf.* also E. Hatch, *The Organization of the Early Christian Churches* (London: Longmans, Green, 1901) 27-28, who wrote, 'Almost all associations seem to have had a religious element. ... religion was ... the basis and bond of union'.

religious temples.[65] Edwin Hatch goes as far as to say that 'many men had two religions, that which they professed and that which they believed: for the former there were temples and State officials and public sacrifices; for the latter there were associations'.[66]

The insecurity of Rome towards the potential political influence of the *collegia* was not, therefore, dissimilar to the grounds of its nervousness towards those associations which were introducing new religious cults.[67] Cults were a powerful force of social cohesion, and, unless carefully regulated, new cults could potentially introduce localized social dislocation. More positively, voluntary associations were particularly active in the imperial cult, and were expressly supportive of the dominant Roman régime. Observation of the imperial cult at the level of the voluntary associations could also offer opportunities for freedmen to make a name for themselves. By demonstrating public spirit in this way, citizens could hope that in turn their own sons would have a greater chance to rise up the ladder and possibly gain for themselves some of the more coveted posts within local government.[68]

It should also be noted that there was an extensive practice of sacrifice within the associations. The minutes of two meetings of the Arval brothers in Rome, dated A.D. 60, record considerable sacrifices being made:

> Two entries, for the 1st and 3rd of January A.D. 60 ..., record that the master of the college sacrificed on the 1st a bullock to Jupiter, a

---

[65]A papyrus relating to a guild which honoured Zeus Hypsistos, dating from between 60 and 58 B.C., *P.Lond.* 2710, records that the association met in a temple; *cf.* A.D. Nock, C. Roberts & T.C. Skeat, 'The Guild of Zeus Hypsistos', 75; *cf.* also *CIL* 14.2112, cited above, referring to a burial society which met monthly in the temple of Antinoüs; also the many associations linked with religious cult on the island of Delos, noted by B.H. McLean, 'The Place of Cult in Voluntary Associations and Christian Churches on Delos', 186, 190.

[66]E. Hatch, *The Organization of the Early Christian Churches*, 28.

[67]W. Cotter, 'The Collegia and Roman Law: State Restrictions on Voluntary Associations 64 B.C.E.–200 C.E.', 78, argues, 'Since religion was integrated with social and political tradition, it is little wonder that the Roman administration was suspicious of ... new cults'. She also cites Dio Cassius 6.52.36: 'persons bringing in new divinities in place of the old, persuade many to adopt foreign practices, from which spring up conspiracies, factions and cabals, which are far from profitable to a monarch'.

[68]J. Reynolds, 'Cities', in D.C. Braund (ed.), *The Administration of the Roman Empire (241 B.C. – A.D. 193)* (Exeter Studies in History, 18; Exeter: University of Exeter, 1988) 49.

cow to Juno, a cow to Minerva and a bull to the *Genius*, or guardian spirit, of Nero on the occasion of his becoming consul, and that on the 3rd he renewed vows made a year before by sacrificing two bullocks to Jupiter and two cows to Juno, two cows to Minerva, two cows to Public Welfare, two bullocks to the deified Augustus, two cows to the deified Augusta, two bullocks to the deified Claudius.[69]

Thus, the social, political and religious interests of voluntary associations closely reflected those of local civic government. At both levels there were an intermingling of the political and religious dimensions and a reinforcement of distinctions in social class.

IV. Conclusion

Although much of the picture which we possess of the Graeco-Roman social world may derive from the sources of the literate aristocracy, we can nonetheless see that it need not be limited to this traditional perspective. It is colourfully supplemented by the caricature or satire; it is questioned by the philosopher who derides love of honour;[70] and there are also glimpses of the dynamics of honour among the non-élites in the associations. In this chapter it has been made clear that the careful gradations of honour were not the sole prerogative of the aristocracy. Comparison of honour took place even amongst slaves;[71] and the anomaly should be noted of those slaves and freedmen who were attached to the imperial household, that, although they could never climb to the ranks of the aristocracy, theirs was an honour which surpassed that of other slaves and freedmen.[72]

There were in these groups, therefore, individuals who yearned for high office but whose more limited circumstances precluded their ever achieving their dreams. In these associations, however, they

---

[69]E.M. Smallwood, *Documents Illustrating the Principates of Gaius, Claudius and Nero* (Cambridge: Cambridge University Press, 1967) 23. R. Wallace & W. Williams, *The Three Worlds of Paul of Tarsus* (London: Routledge, 1998) 102, note that such extensive sacrificing may not have seemed that dissimilar to the Jewish traditions practised in the Temple of Jerusalem.

[70]J.E. Lendon, *Empire of Honour*, 90-92.

[71]J.E. Lendon, *Empire of Honour*, 97.

[72]J.E. Lendon, *Empire of Honour*, 102.

were able to exercise their abilities in leadership.[73] It has also been clear that many of the associations were expressly organized in such a way as to reflect and reinforce the dominant social order, displayed first and foremost in the civic context.[74] In this way,

> the collegium provided a social setting in which persons who normally could never aspire to participation in the *cursus honorum* of the city and state could give and receive honors, enjoy the ascribed status that came with being a *quinquennalis* or *mater*, have a feeling of control over at least the destiny of the collegium, and enjoy regular banquets.[75]

Without these groups, it would have been hard for many of the non-aristocratic members of society to indulge in the public round of displaying honour which was so characteristic of the higher echelons of Graeco-Roman society. Jean-Pierre Waltzing describes at length how the 'artisan, the small merchant and the worker', normally at the bottom of the social and political ladder saw in the associations a means of escaping isolation, gaining influence and receiving honour.[76]

Notwithstanding this, we must appreciate that Graeco-Roman society, as stratified as it was, so driven by a love of honour, was not immune to social mobility. Jon Lendon helpfully observes that,

> the independent vitality of communities of honour outside the aristocracy was sapped by the co-option of their most successful individual members by the aristocracy, by the eagerness of such

---

[73]J. Reynolds, 'Cities', 49.

[74]S.G. Wilson, 'Voluntary Associations: an Overview', 2. *Cf.* also S. Walker-Ramisch, 'Associations and the Damascus Document: a Sociological Analysis', 136, who argues, 'The Graeco-Roman collegia ... not only mirror the organization of the *polis*, but are instrumental in the perpetuation of the dominant social order'.

[75]J.S. Kloppenborg, 'Collegia and *Thiasoi*: Issues in Function, Taxonomy and Membership', 26.

[76]J.P. Waltzing, *Étude historique sur les corporations professionnelles*, I.332, 'Grâce à elle, les artisans jouaient un rôle dans leur ville et ils se relevaient à leurs propres yeux; car ils figuraient parfois dans les fêtes publiques, et, presque exclus de la grande cité, ils avaient la conscience de former une cité plus restreinte, où ils étaient seuls maîtres, où ils ne rencontraient que des égaux, où ils pouvaient même commander; leur vanité y trouvait la même satisfaction que l'ambition du citoyen riche cherchait dans la gestion des fonctionnaires municipales, et que l'augustalité procurait aux affranchis'.

persons for honour at aristocratic hands. The Romans knew no inflexible castes; a man could rise from the lowest ranks of the free-born to the highest offices of a provincial town, to *claritas* in the eyes of the local quality.[77]

What happened, however, when within these lesser associations a man of honour was to be encountered? His aura and demonstrable honour would mean that his patronage would be sought, and his rank receive appropriate recognition.[78] Honour was so deeply integrated into Roman society that it operated at all levels.

---

[77]J.E. Lendon, *Empire of Honour*, 101.

[78]J.E. Lendon, *Empire of Honour*, 100-101, 'When an association could catch a man "loaded with dignity and replete with the honour of rods of office", its members naturally offered him the position of patron, "glorying and rejoicing". Their eyes were directed upwards, at what would please and attract their social superiors'.

CHAPTER 5

LEADERSHIP IN THE FAMILY AND HOUSEHOLD

I. Introduction

The institution of the Roman family provides a further widely influential context in which leadership was exercised in the first-century world.[1] The household was also both a model and a metaphor which the early Christians found useful in their attempts not only at self-definition and community organization, but also at describing their relationship with their God.[2] It is appropriate, therefore, to include it in our broader analysis of how people in the first century conceived of leadership, and consequently to discover

---

[1]W.K. Lacey, *'Patria Potestas'*, in B. Rawson (ed.), *The Family in Ancient Rome: New Perspectives* (London: Routledge, 1986) 123, argues indeed that it was the family (as characterized by the authority of the father figure) 'which was the fundamental institution underlying Roman institutions, and that, in consequence, public life followed the assumptions of private life, and not vice versa'.

[2]H. Moxnes, 'What is Family?: Problems Constructing Early Christian Families', in H. Moxnes (ed.), *Constructing Early Christian Families: Family as Social Reality and Metaphor* (London: Routledge, 1997) 26, writes, 'It was this urban context, with the institution of the household within a system of patronage and structures of personal authority, which provided the setting for the first Christians and which circumscribed their possibilities for social behaviour'.

how it may have influenced, whether consciously or not, some within the early Christian communities as they sought to adopt a model of leadership for their new context.[3]

In this chapter we shall seek to define what was meant in a Graeco-Roman context by 'family', and consider the rôle of the father within his household, the importance of honour between family members, the distinction between sons and slaves, and the place of religion in the context of the family. There are many other aspects of the dynamic of family life which are of interest to social historians and have been the subject of recent research, but the focus here is deliberately restricted to those areas which it is felt will prove most productive in our search for first-century models of group leadership in the Graeco-Roman urban context.

The English word 'family' carries a broad range of meanings which are dependent on context. It may refer to those people related by blood or marriage who both live at the same address and share the same surname (for example, husband and wife, with or without children); it may also be used to include those immediately related people even when they no longer have a common address or surname (as in the change of circumstance brought about through marriage or leaving home); it may sometimes include more distant relations, such as grandparents, grandchildren, uncles, aunts and cousins; it can even include those who have long since died, but are genealogically related; and in some contexts it can occasionally be used of two adults when accompanied by no more than two children under a defined age.[4] How 'family' is defined in a given context is further complicated when two families join or one family divides, as through marriage, divorce, separation, unmarried co-habitation, adoption or fostering. In some contexts, especially where property, inheritance or status is involved, then 'family' can once again have a very specific meaning, such as in reference to the family heirloom, the family business or the royal family.

It is commonly accepted that this English word 'family' has no exact counterpart in either Greek or Latin. For the Romans, *familia*

---

[3]J.S. Jeffers, 'Jewish and Christian Families in First-Century Rome', in K.P. Donfried & P. Richardson (eds.), *Judaism and Christianity in First-Century Rome* (Grand Rapids: Eerdmans, 1998) 149, argues that there were significant parallels between the rôles of and relationships within pagan, Jewish and Christian families of first-century Rome.

[4]This latter is sometimes applied when purchasing a so-called 'family ticket' in a recreational context.

was a term which carried a strictly defined range of legal meanings,[5] but which could also be used in a more flexible sense; *domus* had a slightly different semantic range. For the Greeks, where 'politics' described the management of the *polis* or city, 'economics' described the management of the *oikos* or household.[6]

Familia could include all those under the authority of one head (the father or *paterfamilias*), including a wife, natural and adopted children, grandchildren, and sometimes also slaves;[7] alternatively it might be restricted only to those related by blood; and in some archaic legal contexts it could even simply refer to an estate with its associated property.[8] *Domus*, on the other hand, was often used to describe the building which was the family home.[9] This was inevitably complicated in wealthier and aristocratic families where the head of the 'house' owned more than one residence.[10] In other contexts, the term defined the people attached to a house, including immediate family, slaves, freedmen and freedwomen and even clients. In this sense *domus* may be closer to the slightly archaic, even aristocratic, use of the English word 'household', which included the

---

[5]*Cf.* R.P. Saller, *Patriarchy, Property and Death in the Roman Family* (Cambridge Studies in Population, Economy and Society in Past Time, 25; Cambridge: Cambridge University Press, 1994) 75-76; K.R. Bradley, *Discovering the Roman Family: Studies in Roman Social History* (Oxford: Oxford University Press, 1991) 4; and J.F. Gardner, *Family and* Familia *in Roman Law and Life* (Oxford: Clarendon Press, 1998) 1.

[6]H. Moxnes, 'What is Family?: Problems Constructing Early Christian Families', 20.

[7]*Digest* 50.16.195.2-3, 'In the strict legal sense we call a *familia* a number of people who are by birth or by law subjected to the *potestas* (power) of one man, e.g., *paterfamilias* (father of a *familia*) ... We also habitually use *familia* of slaves'.

[8]R.P. Saller, *Patriarchy, Property and Death in the Roman Family*, 75; *cf.* also *Digest* 50.16.195.1-4, 'Let us see how the term *familia* is to be understood. It has various meanings, for it is applied both to property and to persons' (1); S. Dixon, *The Roman Family* (Baltimore: Johns Hopkins University Press, 1992) 2; and J.F. Gardner, 'Legal Stumbling-Blocks for Lower-Class Families in Rome', in B. Rawson & P. Weaver (eds.), *The Roman Family in Italy: Status, Sentiment, Space* (Oxford: Clarendon Press, 1997) 36.

[9]J.T. Bakker, *Living and Working with the Gods: Studies of Evidence for Private Religion and its Material Environment in the City of Ostia (100-500 AD)* (Dutch Monographs on Ancient History and Archaeology, 12; Amsterdam: J.C. Gieben, 1994) 21, 44, 52, distinguishes the *domus*, characteristic of dwellings belonging to those of 'more than average wealth', from other simpler habitations. These other dwellings, tenement houses or flats, will probably have been owned by the aristocracy, but rented out.

[10]R.P. Saller, *Patriarchy, Property and Death in the Roman Family*, 80-81.

household servants or domestic staff.[11] Wider still the circle of the *domus* could also include related kin. The *domus* was widely seen as a reflection of the status or honour of the head of the house, but it also stood for the good (or bad) name of that family.[12]

Clearly there is considerable overlap between *familia* and *domus*, and in many contexts, especially among poorer people, these two terms could be and were used synonymously. It should be recognized, therefore, that there are significant, potential pitfalls in trying to impose too restrictive a definition on a concept which was representative of social dynamics and behaviour. In the light of this, Richard Saller seeks rather to identify a range of 'context-specific' meanings, rather than a narrow definition.[13] An attempt to clarify what was meant by *familia* and *domus* in a first-century context is especially valuable, however, for our understanding of the relationship between the head of the house and those over whom he had authority.

The scholarly consensus emerging from research on the Roman family has gradually changed over the last century.[14] In the earlier part of the twentieth century the majority view, derived to a considerable extent from the extensive pool of ancient legal texts together with fruitful prosopographical analysis of the Roman élites, normally understood the Roman household structure to be that of the extended family, which could include a number of related nuclear families in the same building. The consensus has shifted, however, in recent decades.[15] Recognising that legal texts alone are unlikely to paint a true picture of social reality, since it is in their nature to circumscribe boundaries or outline ideals,[16] there has been a growing interest in specifically addressing the social historical aspects of the Roman family, and as part of this change of focus more attention has recently been given to the nature and function of the family among

---

[11]R.P. Saller, *Patriarchy, Property and Death in the Roman Family*, 81-82.

[12]R.P. Saller, *Patriarchy, Property and Death in the Roman Family*, 91-94.

[13]R.P. Saller, *Patriarchy, Property and Death in the Roman Family*, 74.

[14]S. Dixon, *The Roman Family*, 3-5.

[15]*Cf.* S.B. Pomeroy, *Families in Classical and Hellenistic Greece: Representations and Realities* (Oxford: Clarendon Press, 1997) 9.

[16]*Cf.* J. Crook, *'Patria Potestas'*, *Classical Quarterly* 17 (1967) 114, who writes, 'the Romans in law ... pushed things to the limits of logic, so that, given that *paterfamilias* had certain roles, their implications were rigorously drawn; they also kept law sharply apart from religion and morals, so that the legal character of *patria potestas* stands out in sociologically misleading clarity'.

the lower classes.[17] The resultant trend has been to regard the Roman family as principally nuclear in construct.[18] Richard Saller reflects this consensus thus:

> Neither *familia* nor *domus* has as a regular meaning the nuclear family, and yet much evidence suggests that this was the dominant family type. Funerary inscriptions and literary evidence, such as Cicero's statement[19] about the hierarchy of kinship bonds, seem to show that though the Romans had no word for it, they drew a conceptual circle around the mother-father-children triad and made it the center of primary obligations.[20]

To describe the Roman family as essentially nuclear does not mean, however, that it was identical to the modern urban conception of the nuclear family.[21] There was some fluidity in the range of inhabitants of a household which may, in addition to the primary 'mother-father-children triad', have included not only relatives, but also slaves, freedmen, lodgers and even trade apprentices.[22]

In 1994 and 1996, however, this revised perception of the family as being principally nuclear was challenged on methodological grounds in two independent studies. In a doctoral dissertation from Macquarie University, census returns from Roman Egypt were analysed and it was concluded that the family norm in that locality

---

[17]But note J.F. Gardner, *Family and* Familia *in Roman Law and Life*, who reconsiders the subject from the perspective of Roman law.

[18]K.R. Bradley, *Discovering the Roman Family*, 6, notes 'the emphasis historians have placed on the predominance in Roman society of the nuclear family — even though there is no Latin equivalent for the phrase — to the point that it is now almost unorthodox to think of the Roman family in any other way'. *Cf.* also J.A. Crook, *Law and Life of Rome* (Aspects of Greek and Roman Life; London: Thames and Hudson, 1967) 98.

[19]Cicero, *De officiis* 53-55.

[20]R.P. Saller, '*Familia, Domus* and the Roman Conception of the Family', *Phoenix* 38 (1984) 355.

[21]D.B. Martin, 'The Construction of the Ancient Family: Methodological Considerations', *Journal of Roman Studies* 86 (1996) 40, writes, 'The consensus is remarkable because practically all historians who support it admit that the portrait of the Roman family that emerges from many literary accounts and is enshrined in Roman law and language is nothing like the modern nuclear family'.

[22]S. Dixon, *The Roman Family*, 11.

should still predominantly be described as extended.[23] The author, Donald Barker, further argues that, with regard to Asia Minor and the western provinces of the Roman empire, the epigraphic evidence is currently insufficient to assert unequivocally that the predominant model was nuclear. Additionally, a critical article by a New Testament scholar[24] has brought into question the method adopted by the two historians Richard Saller and Brent Shaw in a seminal article they published in 1984.[25] Saller and Shaw together argued that:

> the emphasis in the funerary inscriptions on the nuclear family and the rarity of more distant kin offer a vital counterweight to linguistic and legal evidence which highlights the extended family, particularly the patriarchal family under *patria potestas*.[26]

In contrast to Saller and Shaw, Dale Martin, in his study of a number of funerary inscriptions from Asia Minor, adopted a different model of categorising the epigraphic evidence, and his analysis produced a notably different set of results. After reflection on these different results, Martin became critical of the Saller/Shaw approach and concluded that the debate as to whether the Roman family was principally nuclear or extended in format cannot be considered closed simply on the basis of their findings. His own conclusions are that:

> The Romans had no name for the 'nuclear family' as differentiated from the *familia* or *domus* not because the nuclear family did not exist in the sociological or biological sense (that is, in certain modernist discourses), nor because it was not important as a series of relationships, but because it was not important to them to

---

[23]D.C. Barker, *Household Patterns in the Roman Empire with Special Reference to Egypt* (2 vols.; PhD dissertation; Sydney: Macquarie University, 1994).

[24]D.B. Martin, 'The Construction of the Ancient Family: Methodological Considerations', 40-60.

[25]R.P. Saller & B.D. Shaw, 'Tombstones and Roman Family Relations in the Principate: Civilians, Soldiers and Slaves', *Journal of Roman Studies* 74 (1984) 124-56.

[26]R.P. Saller & B.D. Shaw, 'Tombstones and Roman Family Relations in the Principate: Civilians, Soldiers and Slaves', 145.

distinguish those relations firmly from other, less intimate, family relations.[27]

Even if the debate as to the predominant structure of the Roman family is presently unresolved, it is clear that upper and lower class families differed considerably; although it should not be overlooked that many lower class families were included within an upper class family, through patronage.[28] Inevitably, however, we know most about the families of the Roman élites, and this is almost entirely from the perspective of the adult, rather than the child or slave.[29] It is all the more important, therefore, to take into consideration the many funerary inscriptions from lower class families which modify the otherwise rather exclusive picture derived from the literary sources. Additionally there are New Testament prescriptive and descriptive references to the nature of urban Graeco-Roman households, and which, in particular, draw attention to some of the tensions which existed between the richer and poorer elements of society.[30] We are aware of houses large enough to accommodate meetings of Christian communities,[31] and, similarly, we are introduced to individuals in those communities who were masters of slaves, and were consequently considered comparatively more wealthy than some of their fellow-Christians.[32]

We need also to bear in mind that the early empire was a period of considerable social change with regard to the family. Motivated by a sense that honourable family values were

---

[27]D.B. Martin, 'The Construction of the Ancient Family: Methodological Considerations', 58.

[28]S. Dixon, *The Roman Family*, 14, 'There are always going to be great divergences in family structures, particularly between regions and classes and in response to various factors, geographic and economic'; *cf.* also *op. cit.*, 17.

[29]D.C. Verner, *The Household of God: the Social World of the Pastoral Epistles* (Society of Biblical Literature Dissertation Series, 71; Chico: Scholars Press, 1983) 47; and B. Rawson, 'Adult-Child Relationships in Roman Society', in B. Rawson (ed.), *Marriage, Divorce, and Children in Ancient Rome* (Oxford: Clarendon Press, 1991) 7.

[30]H. Moxnes, 'What is Family?: Problems Constructing Early Christian Families', 25; *cf.* for example, Acts 10-11; 16:13-15; 1 Cor 7:21-24; Eph 6:5-9; Col 2:2-4:1; Phlm; 1 Pet 2:18-25.

[31]Rom 16:3-5, 23; 1 Cor 16:19; Col 4:15; Phlm 2.

[32]Eph 6:9; Col 4:1; 1 Tim 6:2.

deteriorating, the emperor Augustus instituted a range of legislation which specifically dealt with family or household issues.[33]

II. The Father as the Leader of the Household

The leader of the household (*paterfamilias*) together with his associated authority and power (*patria potestas*) was unusually characteristic of the Roman people. In this regard the second-century Roman jurist, Gaius, is widely cited as saying: 'virtually no other men have over their sons a power such as we have'.[34] All relationships within the family were defined with reference to him, and unlike many modern societies this authority existed over both minors and adults.[35] Indeed, the family can be defined as precisely that which lies within the power of the *paterfamilias*, as Ulpian records in the *Digest*:

> In the strict legal sense we call a *familia* a number of people who are by birth or by law subjected to the *potestas* (power) of one man, e.g., *paterfamilias* (father of a *familia*), *mater* (mother of a *familia*), son or daughter of a *familia*, and so on in succession, e.g. grandsons, granddaughters, etc. *Paterfamilias* (head of a household) is the title given to the person who holds sway in the house, and he is correctly so called even if he has no children, for we are distinguishing not only him as a person, but his legal right: indeed, we call even a minor *paterfamilias*.[36]

---

[33]The *Lex Julia de maritandis ordinibus* (18 B.C.), the *Lex Julia de adulteriis coercendis* (18-16 B.C.) and the *Lex Papia Poppaea* (A.D. 9). These laws sought to offer financial and career incentives to increase the birth-rate. For further discussion, *cf.* A. Wallace-Hadrill, 'Family and Inheritance in the Augustan Marriage-Laws', *Proceedings of the Cambridge Philological Society* 207 (New Series, 27) (1981) 58; H. Last, 'The Social Policy of Augustus', in S.A. Cook, F.E. Adcock, & M.P. Charlesworth (eds.), *The Cambridge Ancient History* X (Cambridge: Cambridge University Press, 1966) 448; R.P. Saller, *Patriarchy, Property and Death in the Roman Family*, 1; and R.I. Frank, 'Augustus' Legislation on Marriage and Children', *California Studies in Classical Antiquity* 8 (1975) 41.

[34]Gaius, *Institutes* 1.55; *cf.* also Dionysius of Halicarnassus, *Roman Antiquities* 2.26.1ff. *Cf.* E. Eyben, 'Fathers and Sons', in B. Rawson (ed.), *Marriage, Divorce, and Children in Ancient Rome* (Oxford: Clarendon Press, 1991) 114-43.

[35]E.M. Lassen, 'The Roman Family: Ideal and Metaphor', in H. Moxnes (ed.), *Constructing Early Christian Families: Family as Social Reality and Metaphor* (London: Routledge, 1997) 105.

[36]*Digest* 50.16.195.2.

In principle of law, therefore, the Graeco-Roman family was predominantly patriarchal. Wife,[37] children and slaves were all under the authority of the *paterfamilias*, who had legal control over them, including, in theory, the power of life or death over them.[38] This is reflected in the statement by Dionysius of Halicarnassus in which he highlights the laws imposed by Romulus:

> the lawgiver of the Romans gave virtually full power to the father over his son, even during his whole life, whether he thought proper to imprison him, to scourge him, to put him in chains and keep him at work in the fields, or to put him to death, and this even though the son were already engaged in public affairs ... And not even at this point did the Roman lawgiver stop in giving the father power over the son, but he even allowed him to sell his son, without concerning himself whether this permission was compatible with natural affection.[39]

Thus, Eva Maria Lassen writes, 'A predominant — though not exclusive — function of Roman family metaphors was to evoke images of authority: authority of Gods over humans, senior officials over junior officials, state leaders over subjects'.[40]

With regard to this issue of paternal control in the family, however, scholarship has again seen a shift in emphasis in recent years. The earlier research dependent mostly on analysis and

---

[37]There were two types of marriage, that said to be with *manus* where the bride came under the power of her new husband and that *sine manu* where she would remain under the power of her father or guardian. The latter gradually came to be the more normal practice, but neither offers independence from a *paterfamilias*; *cf.* R.P. Saller, *Patriarchy, Property and Death in the Roman Family*, 76.

[38]J.F. Gardner, *Family and* Familia *in Roman Law and Life*, 2; *cf.* also for specific examples R.P. Saller, *Patriarchy, Property and Death in the Roman Family*, 115-17. S.J. Joubert, 'Managing the Household: Paul as *paterfamilias* of the Christian Household Group in Corinth', in P.F. Esler (ed.), *Modelling Early Christianity: Social-scientific Studies of the New Testament in its Context* (London: Routledge, 1995) 214-15, points out that 'Members of the Roman *familia* were subjected to the lifelong authority (*potestas*) of the *paterfamilias*, the oldest surviving male ascendant. His *potestas* over his ascendants and slaves was legally recognized and protected. Children had no power to own property in their own right and could not make valid wills, since the *paterfamilias* retained full power over all property in possession of the family'; *cf.* also E. Eyben, 'Fathers and Sons', 115, 'the *paterfamilias* had the right to expose his child, to scourge him, to sell him, to pawn him, to imprison him, and, *in extremis*, even to kill him'.

[39]Dionysius of Halicarnassus, *Roman Antiquities* 2.26.4-6.

[40]E.M. Lassen, 'The Roman Family: Ideal and Metaphor', 114.

interpretation of legal texts with their juridical bias inevitably focused on the authority, power and control vested in the head of the family[41] — thus, a fundamental aspect of the *paterfamilias* was his ownership of property, both objects and people.[42] More recent scholarship, concerned with a reflection of social history, culture and norms, has gone some way to weaken what is considered to be an overly austere portrait.[43] Jane Gardner says of those studies which focus on the legal perspective that they give to such matters,

> more prominence than they are likely to have held in the experience of most Romans; severe punishments, especially of adult children, let alone exercise of the 'ius vitae necisque' (power of life and death), were hardly likely to have been an everyday event in the lives of most Roman households; that is why rare (real or alleged) instances are the stuff of legends and moral treatises.[44]

It is argued, therefore, that in response to social pressures, the power of the father over his household gradually lessened by the time of the early Roman empire, and it would seem that the full extent of these powers was rarely if ever exercised, although his control over property continued.[45] Thus, the family of the early Roman empire may well have differed considerably from that of the earlier Republic, or even of Hellenistic or Classical Greece. This perception may be reflected in the consensual marriage relationship

---

[41]*Cf.* the view of P. Veyne summarized by R.P. Saller, 'Corporal Punishment, Authority, and Obedience in the Roman Household', in B. Rawson (ed.), *Marriage, Divorce, and Children in Ancient Rome* (Oxford: Clarendon Press, 1991) 144.

[42]R.P. Saller, *Patriarchy, Property and Death in the Roman Family*, 155.

[43]J.F. Gardner, *Family and* Familia *in Roman Law and Life*, 268-69.

[44]J.F. Gardner, *Family and* Familia *in Roman Law and Life*, 269.

[45]*Cf.* D.C. Verner, *The Household of God*, 80; *cf.* also R.P. Saller, *Patriarchy, Property and Death in the Roman Family*, 104, 'the early symmetry of paternal severity and filial duty gave way to mutual affection and devotion in the late Republic or early empire'; J.S. Jeffers, 'Jewish and Christian Families in First-Century Rome', 139; E.M. Lassen, 'The Use of the Father Image in Imperial Propaganda and 1 Corinthians 4:14-21', *Tyndale Bulletin* 42 (1991) 128, who suggests that *patria potestas* remained in law but was softened in practice, and could not have remained as significant in the context of a nuclear family; and S.J. Joubert, 'Managing the Household: Paul as *paterfamilias* of the Christian Household Group in Corinth', 215, who writes, 'However, in spite of the theoretically extreme powers vested in the role of the *patresfamiliarum*, their behaviour was moderated in practice by social pressures such as the values of their families, the morality of the day and the role of the gods in their lives'.

Plutarch seeks to describe: 'Every activity in a virtuous household is carried on by both parties in agreement, but discloses the husband's leadership and preferences'.[46] The third-century Roman lawyer may more accurately reflect the social reality which pertained in the early empire: 'paternal authority must be based on affection, not on cruelty'.[47]

By the time of the early empire, more marriages were contracted without the binding power of the husband. This is reflected in the non-literary sources where we see a number of married women who appeared to be wealthy independently of their husband's property.[48] Furthermore, affection was certainly a part of the Roman family ideal, and as a characteristic both of conjugal and parental relationships is reflected not only in numerous epitaphs,[49] but also in private correspondence.[50] One touching epitaph reads:

> Sacred to the Spirits of the Deceased. To Urbana, the sweetest, most chaste and exceptional wife. I am sure that nothing has been more wonderful than her. She deserves to be honoured by this inscription, since she spent her whole life with me utterly joyfully and without complication, with both married affection and with characteristic hard work. I have added these words so that those who read them may understand how deeply we loved one another. Paternus set this up to her who deserved it.[51]

---

[46]Plutarch, *Moralia* 139D.

[47]*Digest* 48.9.5, cited in E. Eyben, 'Fathers and Sons', 115.

[48]D.C. Verner, *The Household of God*, 39.

[49]*Cf.* B. Shaw, 'The Cultural Meaning of Death: Age and Gender in the Roman Family', in D.I. Kertzer & R.P. Saller (eds.), *The Family in Italy: from Antiquity to the Present* (New Haven: Yale University Press, 1991) 66-90; especially *op. cit.*, 67, 'The act of placing a tombstone, of having it inscribed, was integrally connected with the webs of duties and feelings concerning the dead and, by extension, a mirroring of their status while still among the living'.

[50]S. Dixon, 'The Sentimental Ideal of the Roman Family', in B. Rawson (ed.), *Marriage, Divorce, and Children in Ancient Rome* (Oxford: Clarendon Press, 1991) 99-100; and R.P. Saller, *Patriarchy, Property and Death in the Roman Family*, 2, 'The hundreds of letters of Cicero, our most intimate evidence for the day-to-day experiences of Roman families, give no hint of the exercise of the absolute legal powers of the father'. *Cf.* also, for example, the correspondence of Pliny, *Letters* 4.19.2-4, where he speaks most lovingly of his wife's affection.

[51]*CIL* 6.29580.

Cicero's correspondence, dating as it does from before the Augustan era, repeatedly presents something of the affection he holds for both his wife, Terentia, and his children, Tullia and Marcus.

> Ah, what a desperate pitiful case is mine! What now? Shall I ask you to come — a sick woman, physically and spiritually exhausted? Shall I *not* ask then? Am I to live without you? ... Be sure of one thing: if I have you, I shall not feel that I am utterly lost. But what is to become of my Tulliola? You at home must take care of that — I have nothing to suggest. But assuredly, however matters turn out, the poor little girl's marriage and good name must be a primary consideration. Then there is my son. What will he do? I hope that *he* will always be with me, my darling child. I cannot write any more now. Grief clogs my pen.[52]

This warmer perspective on the Roman father was, inevitably, not portrayed in the cold legal texts which formed the basis of much early scholarship on the family. The preoccupation with *patria potestas* has sometimes, therefore, misrepresented the nature of the father's rôle within the family.[53] The authority of the father, although in principle great, and in practice rarely exercised to its fullest extent, should nonetheless not minimise the fundamental expectation in the Roman family of filial obedience.

III. The Father and his Sons

We should not suppose that this authority or *patria potestas* was exercised by the father in the same way over both his offspring and his domestic staff. Indeed, one major distinction between the son and the slave was that the latter could be punished by means of a whip.[54]

Pietas, like *familia*, is a Latin word which proves difficult to translate into English.[55] It was that dutiful Roman quality of honour and respect which could be accorded to the gods, one's country or

---

[52]Cicero, *Letters to Friends* 6.3, cited in K.R. Bradley, *Discovering the Roman Family*, 177-78.

[53]R.P. Saller, *Patriarchy, Property and Death in the Roman Family*, 114.

[54]R.P. Saller, 'Corporal Punishment, Authority, and Obedience in the Roman Household', 155-64.

[55]To adopt its derivative 'piety', with its religious connotations, would be strongly misleading.

one's family.[56] It was a foundational quality of the empire and significantly embodied in the hero of Vergil's epic, Aeneas.[57] With regard to the family, *pietas* included the dutiful respect of children to their parents, and expressed principally obligation but also devotion and affection.[58] As such it was much more demanding than the unquestioning obedience which was expected of the slave.

It is this grasp of what is intrinsically honourable which prevented children from entering into litigation against their parents; thus the law could insist that: '[a]n action will not be given to certain persons, for example, to sons or freedmen proceeding against parents or patrons, since it carries *infamia'*.[59] The law also placed wider obligations of respect and honour on children towards their parents.[60]

This is not to deny that there was an element of reciprocity entailed within familial *pietas* — the parent had obligations also to the child; an aspect which further modifies the otherwise austere picture of the Roman father.[61] In this sense, the *patria potestas* is executed in a way that is consistent with *pietas*.[62] The father's relationship with his son is motivated by a genuine love, even though there may be a

---

[56]*Cf.* R.P. Saller, 'Corporal Punishment, Authority, and Obedience in the Roman Household', 146-51.

[57]Vergil, *Aeneid* 6.403.

[58]J.F. Gardner, 'Legal Stumbling-Blocks for Lower-Class Families in Rome', 35-36; *Digest* 37.15.1.2 describes a lack of respect for parents as *delictum ad publicam pietatem pertinens*.

[59]*Digest* 4.3.11.1.

[60]R.P. Saller, 'Corporal Punishment, Authority, and Obedience in the Roman Household', 148, draws attention to one aspect of the *Digest* entitled 'On the duties to parents and patrons'. This is not dissimilar to the Pauline reiterations of the Mosaic instructions to honour parents.

[61]*Cf.* R.P. Saller, 'Corporal Punishment, Authority, and Obedience in the Roman Household', 148-50; in his analysis of the *Digest*, R.P. Saller, *Patriarchy, Property and Death in the Roman Family*, 111-12, concludes that 'there are as many references to parental pietas as filial pietas: parents were obliged to look after the best interests of their children, just as children were obliged to respect and protect their parents'; also *op. cit.*, 110, 'the fundamental essence of pietas lay in a reciprocal devotion to family members that was broader than the notion of filial obedience'.

[62]E.M. Lassen, 'The Roman Family: Ideal and Metaphor', 107.

strictness in his dealings.[63] Additionally spouses had a mutual obligation of *pietas* towards each other.[64] Thus:

> the Romans did not construct a moral universe with sons and slaves as virtually indistinguishable members of a household obligated above all to obey its head. Regarded as having greater moral autonomy than slaves, children were caught up in a web of mutual obligations based on *pietas*, of which submission to the will of the *paterfamilias* was only one aspect. On the other side, the father was considered bound by *pietas* to his children and his wife, but not to his slaves.[65]

Pietas, therefore, distinguishes the father-child relationship from the master-slave relationship. The former is bound by mutual respect and obligations; the latter is marked by the slavish obedience and prompted by fear of punishment.[66] Consequently, the picture of the Roman family that focuses on *potestas* without taking due account of the impact of *pietas* in the overall equation is incomplete.[67]

IV. The Father and his Slaves

Both the traditional, but erroneous, caricature of the *paterfamilias* who had absolute dominion over his family, and the view that the Roman father was a more loving and affectionate figure, can thus blur a significant distinction which existed in family relationships. In reality, the head of the household exercised that dominion over the members of his household in varying ways depending on issues of status and honour. In the Roman household these Graeco-Roman norms of status and honour were as widely regarded as they were in public life. Honour was important between family members and, on a larger scale, the combined honour of the family in the eyes of

---

[63]J.S. Jeffers, 'Jewish and Christian Families in First-Century Rome', 143, who cites Seneca, *De providentia* 2.5, describing the difference between the way a father and a mother might deal with their children.

[64]R.P. Saller, *Patriarchy, Property and Death in the Roman Family*, 112.

[65]R.P. Saller, 'Corporal Punishment, Authority, and Obedience in the Roman Household', 150-51.

[66]R.P. Saller, 'Corporal Punishment, Authority, and Obedience in the Roman Household', 164.

[67]R.P. Saller, *Patriarchy, Property and Death in the Roman Family*, 226-27.

outsiders was also important.[68] The father, as we have seen, enjoyed a pre-eminent position of authority and respect. The son's relationship towards his father was characterized by *pietas* and obedience. It is important also, however, to consider the place of the slave within this dynamic.

It is clear that the slave was treated very differently from the son.[69] The slave could be punished most severely. Valerius Maximus cites a dream, in which:

> At the Plebeian Games, a certain *paterfamilias* had his slave brutally flogged and led him to execution, bearing the 'fork' (i.e., the cross-beam used for crucifixion), through the Circus Flaminius just before the sacred procession entered.[70]

This understanding of the social reality of family life is reflected also in Paul's use of an analogy based on the different status of the son and the slave in a Roman family.[71] A similar fundamental difference in the way the son and the slave are treated is reflected in Cicero's statement:

> we must distinguish between different kinds of domination and subjection. For the mind is said to rule over the body, and also over lust; but it rules over the body as a king governs his subjects, or a father his children, whereas it rules over lust as a master rules his slaves, restraining it and breaking its power.[72]

---

[68]P.F. Esler, 'Imagery and Identity in Gal 5:13-6:10', in H. Moxnes (ed.), *Constructing Early Christian Families: Family as Social Reality and Metaphor* (London: Routledge, 1997) 124.

[69]Exemption from corporal punishment also differentiated the free citizen from the slave, so that Paul, in Acts 22:22-29, is purported to have appealed on the grounds of his Roman citizenship that he should not have been so bound or subjected to beatings at the hands of the Roman tribune. Equally the military authorities are disconcerted that they have so offended the honour of a Roman citizen and publicly humiliated him in this way; *cf.* also B.M. Rapske, *The Book of Acts and Paul in Roman Custody* (The Book of Acts in its First Century Setting, 3; Grand Rapids: Eerdmans, 1994) 46-62; also R.P. Saller, *Patriarchy, Property and Death in the Roman Family*, 139-42.

[70]Valerius Maximus 1.7.4.

[71]*Cf.* especially Gal 4:1-2.

[72]Cicero, *Republic* 3.37.

It was widely regarded that slaves would remain loyal if they lived in fear of their masters.[73] Ulpian, the jurist, wrote, 'no household would be safe if slaves were not forced by the threat of danger to their own lives to protect their masters against enemies both from within and from outside the household'.[74] The loyalty and obedience of slaves could also be ensured by various incentives and rewards, including holidays and the possibility of eventual manumission (the granting of freedom from bondage as a slave).[75]

Honour was at the heart of the whole issue of punishment;[76] and the whip was used in punishment as a means of distinguishing between the honour which belonged to the son, and the lack of honour which was the lot of the slave.[77] This is not to deny the father's right to punish his own offspring by means of the whip, but the use of the whip on sons was considered inconsistent with the overriding desire to instil in them a sense of worthiness (*dignitas*).[78] Plutarch highlights the association between honour and punishment and also the distinction between the punishment of slaves by means of beatings and the training of one's own children by means of words:

> children ought to be led to honourable practices by means of encouragement and reasoning, and most certainly not by blows or ill-treatment, for it surely is agreed that these are fitting rather for slaves than for the free-born; for so they grow numb and shudder at their tasks, partly from the pain of the blows, partly from the degradation. Praise and reproof are more helpful for the free-born

---

[73]K.R. Bradley, *Slaves and Masters in the Roman Empire: a Study in Social Control* (Oxford: Oxford University Press, 1987) 45, 'Together the generosities and climate of fear which can be seen to surround servile life help to explain the survival over time of the Roman slavery system'.

[74]*Digest* 29.5.1.

[75]K.R. Bradley, *Slaves and Masters in the Roman Empire*, 45.

[76]R.P. Saller, *Patriarchy, Property and Death in the Roman Family*, 134.

[77]R.P. Saller, *Patriarchy, Property and Death in the Roman Family*, 133-53; especially, 137, 'One of the primary distinctions between the condition of a free man and a slave in the Roman mind was the vulnerability of the latter to corporal punishment, in particular lashings at another's private whim'.

[78]R.P. Saller, *Patriarchy, Property and Death in the Roman Family*, 142-43, 'The goal of proper appreciation of *dignitas* and use of power sets the discipline of children apart from the coercion of honorless slaves' (143).

than any sort of ill-usage, since the praise incites them toward what is honourable, and reproof keeps them from what is disgraceful.[79]

We are, of course, talking here in terms of generalization. It is clear that masters differed in their treatment of their slaves just as fathers differed in their treatment of their own children.[80] Anecdotal evidence of both severe and moderate masters, as well as harsh and affectionate fathers, would have been widespread in the period of the early Roman empire. Such variations, however, did not prevent the early Christians occasionally adopting the image of the father as applicable to leaders in the church, and, in continuity with the Old Testament, even to God himself. The underlying importance of comparative honour between fathers and sons or masters and slaves, however, was widely applicable in the Graeco-Roman world.[81]

V. The Father and Household Religion

Much as civic life was dominated by an overriding awareness of the influence the gods had over the local community, so also private family life carefully heeded and respected the powers which were believed to control its well-being.[82] The home was an important locus of cultic ritual; and domestic religion provided a valuable link with the past and the family's ancestry.[83] The household cult, however,

---

[79]Plutarch, in his 'The education of children', *Moralia* 8F.

[80]Pliny, *Letters* 8.16, records how he treated his slaves in large measure as if they had been sons.

[81]R.P. Saller, *Patriarchy, Property and Death in the Roman Family*, 152, does argue that the currency of honour affecting the treatment of children will have been more influential in the families of the élites for whom honour was of greatest importance.

[82]S.J. Joubert, 'Managing the Household: Paul as *paterfamilias* of the Christian Household Group in Corinth', 213, 'Kinship and its set of interlocking rules formed the central social institution ... Politics was the other major institution, with religion embedded in both of these. First-century people were thus socialized into a world where these values and institutions were part and parcel of their "taken-for-granted" reality'. With regard to the institution of the family in Classical Greece, D.C. Verner, *The Household of God*, 28, writes, 'Everyone who became a part of it passed into the service and under the protection of its gods'. *Cf.* also J.R. Clarke, *The Houses of Roman Italy, 100 B.C.-A.D. 250: Ritual, Space, and Decoration* (Berkeley: University of California Press, 1991) 1.

[83]J. Barclay, 'The Family as the Bearer of Religion in Judaism and Early Christianity', in H. Moxnes (ed.), *Constructing Early Christian Families: Family as*

was by no means as formalized as the public Roman religion with its officiating priests and civic magistrates. The private pursuit of religion within the confines of the family home had considerable flexibility to observe cultic rituals and recognize any divinity as each family saw fit.[84] It is precisely this privateness, flexibility (and even a degree of naïvety) which result in our knowing far less about domestic than state or civic religion.[85] As so often, again we find that it is the archaeological evidence which is most helpful for understanding household religion; it is very visible in many houses, as reflected in the number of shrines, niches and altars, as well as graffiti and artwork, which appear in some of the residences excavated in Ostia, Pompeii, Herculaneum and Delos.[86]

The hearth of the home was the focus of worship of the Roman goddess Vesta (the Greek goddess Hestia). She was the spirit of the home, and it was at this hearth that the household might gather daily to perform a sacrifice, propitiate her powerful will and thereby avert unforeseen crisis.[87] The hearth would be decorated with flowers, and sacrifices of cakes or wine would be made there.[88]

One particular group of gods, the family's *Lares*, was believed to fulfil a crucial protective or tutelary rôle over all the members of

---

Social Reality and Metaphor (London: Routledge, 1997) 67, writes, 'prayers, libations and the simple offerings of portions of food and incense appear to have been regular and ubiquitous features of domestic routine'.

[84]*Cf.* D.G. Orr, 'Roman Domestic Religion: the Evidence of the Household Shrines', *Aufstieg und Niedergang der Römischen Welt* 16.2 (1978) 1559; and J.T. Bakker, *Living and Working with the Gods*, 2.

[85]*Cf.* D.P. Harmon, 'The Family Festivals of Rome', *Aufstieg und Niedergang der Römischen Welt* 16.2 (1978) 1592; and J.R. Clarke, *The Houses of Roman Italy, 100 B.C.-A.D. 250: Ritual, Space, and Decoration* (Berkeley: University of California Press, 1991) 1.

[86]Although many such artefacts may well have been destroyed in the later Christian period; J.T. Bakker, *Living and Working with the Gods*, 13. This work is most valuable in this regard in that, instead of merely focusing on the household gods, the study is concerned also with the people involved in private religion. The evidence is mostly post-Trajan, however. *Cf.* also the French work which focuses on the household cult in Delos, M. Bulard, *Le religion domestique dans la colonie italienne de Délos, d'après les peintures murales et les autels historiés* (Bibliothèque des écoles françaises d'Athènes et de Rome, 131; Paris: Boccard, 1926).

[87]In later times purpose-built shrines replaced the importance of the hearth; J.R. Clarke, *The Houses of Roman Italy, 100 B.C.-A.D. 250*, 7.

[88]D.P. Harmon, 'The Family Festivals of Rome', 1593.

the household, including the slaves.[89] These were guardian spirits who oversaw the boundaries of the house or estate and were invoked for the safe return of its inhabitants.[90] Their protection was particularly invoked in regard to the major family events, including in particular births, marriages and deaths;[91] but also a boy's or girl's coming of age was an important moment when offerings of childhood objects were made to the *Lares*.[92]

The *Penates* (or spirits of the store-cupboard) were also considered protectors of the household.[93] They were originally sought for daily provision of the food supply, and were often depicted in the kitchen.[94] In this capacity they were proffered samples of food during mealtimes, but their brief was broadened over time such that they came to be regarded as 'the gods who have concern for all things in the *potestas* of the masters of the house'.[95] In many cases traditional gods were adopted as *Di Penates*, such as Jupiter or Minerva, although it is argued that originally the *Penates* may well have been an indistinct collection of deities.[96] There were also the ancestral spirits or *imagines*. David Orr suggests that there was much overlap between Vesta, the *Penates* and the *Lares* and

---

[89]*Cf.* D.G. Orr, 'Roman Domestic Religion: the Evidence of the Household Shrines', 1564-65; and J.T. Bakker, *Living and Working with the Gods*, 9; and J.R. Clarke, *The Houses of Roman Italy, 100 B.C.-A.D. 250*, 8, who argues that the Lares may have been the most important of the household deities.

[90]R.P. Saller, *Patriarchy, Property and Death in the Roman Family*, 89; *cf.* also *Digest* 25.3.1.2. *Cf.* also *CIL* 9.723, 'Gaius Salvius Eutychus, to the Lares who look after his hut, in fulfilment of a vow for the return of his mistress Rectina'. The Lares were also regarded for the protection beyond the home, and were worshipped at imperial boundaries or crossroads; see further, E. Simon, *Die Götter der Römer* (Munich: Hirmer, 1990) 119-25.

[91]J.T. Bakker, *Living and Working with the Gods*, 9.

[92]J.R. Clarke, *The Houses of Roman Italy, 100 B.C.-A.D. 250*, 9-10.

[93]A recent major historical work focusing on both the public and private Penates is A. Dubourdieu, *Les origines et le développement du culte des Pénates à Rome* (Collection de l'École française de Rome, 118; Rome: École française de Rome, 1989).

[94]*Cf.* D.G. Orr, 'Roman Domestic Religion: the Evidence of the Household Shrines', 1563; and A. Dubourdieu, *Les origines et le développement du culte des Pénates à Rome*, 66-67.

[95]D.P. Harmon, 'The Family Festivals of Rome', 1593.

[96]*Cf.* A. Dubourdieu, *Les origines et le développement du culte des Pénates à Rome*, 61; and J.T. Bakker, *Living and Working with the Gods*, 40-41, 192. Other major deities uncovered from Ostian archaeological evidence are Diana, Dionysus, the Dioscures, Fortuna, Hercules, Juno or Ceres, Mercurius, Silvanus and Venus.

'[c]learly there is a kind of collective mental set at work here. Perhaps the individual aspects of Lar, Vesta, and the Penates melded somewhat and by the early empire were grouped together as domestic deities'.[97]

The Genius or *numen* of a family was also the focus of domestic worship, and is referred to as 'its procreative force, and especially the living spirit of the *paterfamilias*'.[98] It was, as a fertility spirit, the Genius of the *paterfamilias* who 'guaranteed continuity of generation'.[99] Its association particularly with the head of the household is reflected in that it was worshipped especially on his birthday.[100]

It was the responsibility of the *paterfamilias* to ensure the co-operation of the household's gods or patron deities.[101] This would often take the form of a vow, and there are numerous inscriptions which record such moves or offer gratitude to the genius of a particular household or *paterfamilias* for protection offered, or relief from illness.[102]

> To Jupiter Best and Greatest who saves: and to the Genius of his household, Lucius Serenius Bassus, centurion of the Second Legion Adiutrix, for having been freed from a most serious illness; he willingly and properly fulfilled his vow.[103]

---

[97]D.G. Orr, 'Roman Domestic Religion: the Evidence of the Household Shrines', 1563. J.T. Bakker, *Living and Working with the Gods*, 10, suggests that the Lares and the Penates were sometimes even confused in antiquity; also, to add confusion, the Penates were occasionally used metonymously for the house or for the combined household gods and this may be symptomatic of the vitality of the cult and the depth of belief in the gods, cf. A. Dubourdieu, *Les origines et le développement du culte des Pénates à Rome*, 64, 70, 91, 94. He also points out that the Penates were still important in the fourth century A.D.

[98]D.G. Orr, 'Roman Domestic Religion: the Evidence of the Household Shrines', 1569-70.

[99]D.P. Harmon, 'The Family Festivals of Rome', 1595.

[100]Cf. also the ritual which marks a birth, M. Bulard, *Le religion domestique dans la colonie italienne de Délos, d'après les peintures murales et les autels historiés*, 7-56.

[101]J.T. Bakker, *Living and Working with the Gods*, 42. Cf. also J. Barclay, 'The Family as the Bearer of Religion in Judaism and Early Christianity', 67, who notes that 'domestic cult was intimately linked with the honour and prosperity of the head of the household'.

[102]R.M. Ogilvie, *The Romans and their Gods in the Age of Augustus* (London: Chatto & Windus, 1969) 100.

[103]CIL 3.6456.

> To Jupiter Best and Greatest, and to the gods and goddesses of
> hospitality, and to the Penates, for preserving his own well-being
> and that of his (family): Publius Aelius Marcianus, cohort prefect,
> dedicated this altar in fulfilment of a vow (?).[104]

Even the freedmen within a household recognized the security
offered by the household gods:

> The freedman Suavis and the overseer Faustus, the foremost among
> the dependants (*prim. in familia*), presented and gave the Lares and
> Genius together with the shrine out of their own money.[105]

Plutarch advises the new bride to maintain the family honour
by observing the same cult as her husband:

> A wife ought not to make friends of her own, but to enjoy her
> husband's friends in common with him. The gods are the first and
> most important friends. Wherefore it is becoming for a wife to
> worship and to know only the gods that her husband believes in,
> and to shut the front door tight upon all queer rituals and outlandish
> superstitions. For with no god do stealthy and secret rites performed
> by a woman find any favour.[106]

It is important to note that children were also not exempt from
involvement in household cult. They soon developed an instinct for
the honour in which the household gods were held, and were
encouraged to participate in and continue those familial traditions
and customs which had been handed down over the years. Such
observance on the part of the children demonstrated respect for the
paterfamilias.[107]

Thus, all members of the household were included within the
domestic cult.[108] Indeed, such a focus within a household, as in the
context of the city, was a tool of social reinforcement and
integration.[109] Thus, Cicero could write:

---

[104]*CIL* 7.237.

[105]*CIL* 2.1980.

[106]Plutarch, in his 'Advice on marriage', *Moralia* 140D.

[107]J. Barclay, 'The Family as the Bearer of Religion in Judaism and Early
Christianity', 68.

[108]A. Dubourdieu, *Les origines et le développement du culte des Pénates à Rome*, 68,
argues that the Penates were often situated, precisely for this reason, in areas of
the house which were accessible to all its members

[109]J.T. Bakker, *Living and Working with the Gods*, 194.

> What is more sacred, what more inviolably hedged about by every kind of sanctity, than the home (*domus*) of an individual citizen? Within its circle are his altars, his hearths, his household gods, his religion, his observances, his ritual; it is a sanctuary so holy in the eyes of all, that it were sacrilege to tear an owner therefrom.[110]

Cicero further describes both the ties of the nuclear family, the responsibilities towards the extended family, and the cohesion which derives from familial religion:

> But a still closer union exists between kindred. Starting with that infinite bond of union of the human race in general, the conception is now confined to a small and narrow circle. For since the reproductive instinct is by Nature's gift the common possession of all living creatures, the first bond of union is that between husband and wife; the next, that between parents and children; then we find one home with everything in common. And this is the foundation of civil government, the nursery, as it were, of the state. Then follow the bonds between brothers and sisters, and next those of first and then of second cousins; and when they can no longer be sheltered under one roof, they go out into other homes, as into colonies. Then follow between these, in turn, marriages and connections by marriage, and from these again a new stock of relations; and from this propagation and after-growth states have their beginnings. The bonds of common blood hold men fast through good-will and affection; for it means much to share in common the same family traditions, the same forms of domestic worship, and the same ancestral tombs.[111]

To this extent the exclusive conversion of a member of one's family to the monotheistic cult of Christianity will have had considerable implications for the honour of the family.[112]

---

[110]Cicero, *De domo sua* 109. This continues to be the case in many modern Asian cultures; thus, K.O. Sandnes, *A New Family: Conversion and Ecclesiology in the Early Church with Cross-cultural Comparisons* (Studien zur interkulturellen Geschichte des Christentums, 91; Bern: P. Lang, 1994) 3, writes, 'In societies where kinship ties are strong, solidarity with parents as well as with ancestors sets the standard of life within the family, maintains its honour and provides protection against evil powers. This gives family life a religious basis; contrariwise, it gives religion a household basis'.

[111]Cicero, *De officiis* 53-55.

[112]K.O. Sandnes, 'Equality within Patriarchal Structures: Some New Testament Perspectives on the Christian Fellowship as a Brother- or Sisterhood and a Family', in H. Moxnes (ed.), *Constructing Early Christian Families: Family as Social*

VI. Conclusion

Thus, we see that the Roman word *familia* could be either broadly or narrowly conceived. It sometimes was used in a restricted sense as a reference to a building or property; at other times it could include the nuclear blood-relatives, or even be extended to incorporate associated resident slaves and freedmen and freedwomen. It was enshrined in law that the *paterfamilias* had a significant rôle of authority over his entire household. Counterbalancing this theoretical authority, there was also a mutual bond of *pietas* between parents and children. Slaves, on the other hand, were treated, and where necessary punished, differently from free-born children in the household.

The house or family was also the focus of the household cult — an important dynamic of first-century culture. All members of the household were incorporated in these rituals, but it was the *paterfamilias* who was responsible for their correct observance.[113] The importance of this religious dimension to the cohesion of the family is demonstrated in the archaeological remains of a number of wealthier homes, where religious artefacts of shrines were very prominent.

Eva Maria Lassen points out that household metaphors were applied also to political and religious positions of honour in the public world.[114] In a very high profile way such language was also applied by Augustus and subsequent emperors to themselves in the self-description *pater patriae* ('father of the fatherland').[115] Thus, household terminology was not limited to the domestic sphere; and it should be of no surprise that we see it playing an important part also in early Christian texts as part of discussion of the church.[116]

Reality and Metaphor (London: Routledge, 1997) 154; *cf.* also G.E.M. de Ste Croix, 'Why were the Early Christians Persecuted?', in M. Finley (ed.), *Studies in Ancient Society* (London: Routledge and Kegan Paul, 1974) 238, 'The monotheistic exclusiveness of the Christians was believed to alienate the goodwill of the gods, to endanger what the Romans called the *pax deorum* (the right relationship between gods and men), and to be responsible for disasters which overtook the community'.

[113]J.T. Bakker, *Living and Working with the Gods*, 42.

[114]E.M. Lassen, 'The Roman Family: Ideal and Metaphor', 110-14.

[115]Eph 3:14-15, 'For this reason I bow my knees before the Father (τὸν πατέρα) from whom every family (πατριά) in heaven and on earth is named'.

[116]E.M. Lassen, 'The Roman Family: Ideal and Metaphor', 114, 'family metaphors constituted one of the means by which the Christian religion was communicated to the Romans'.

CHAPTER 6

LEADERSHIP IN THE
JEWISH SYNAGOGUES

I. Introduction

It is recognized that there are particular problems associated with historical investigation of Judaism during the first century A.D. These problems include the major difficulty of establishing in what ways Palestinian Judaism differed from diasporan Judaism (and, indeed, later rabbinic Judaism). Scholarship is hindered by the paucity of relevant literary sources which can clearly be dated prior to A.D. 70. The recent interest in what the epigraphic and other archaeological sources add to our picture has led to a significant increase in the quantity of apposite data we do possess, although the task of identifying, dating and interpreting these sources is incomplete. These non-literary sources initially seem far less eloquent than their literary counterparts, but access to what may be first-century Jewish buildings, inscriptions and art has enabled scholars to review our understanding of Judaism at the time of the early church — an understanding which was previously derived in large part from a descriptive, rather than prescriptive, reading of the rather later rabbinic sources.[1] This revised portrait reveals a spectrum of very

---

[1]A descriptive reading of the sources interprets the evidence as an accurate description of the nature of Judaism at the time, in contrast to a prescriptive

different types of Judaism, and to some extent it is as a result of these archaeological sources that the early scholarly perception of a 'normative' Judaism has been largely rejected.[2]

Within the broader study of ancient Judaism, research into the origins, function, organization and development of the ancient Jewish synagogue has in recent decades received significant scholarly attention.[3] Much archaeological evidence both from Palestine and the diaspora has caused many of the older theories regarding the origin and nature of this institution to be seriously questioned. The picture is now notably clearer for the situation as it pertained in the third and fourth centuries A.D. There continues to be, however, significant debate over the nature of the Jewish synagogue in the first century A.D.

Our main focus here is precisely with regard to this problematic period. The aim in this chapter is to review the present status of the debate in order that we might be in a better position to investigate the possible rôles played by synagogue officials within these Jewish communities, and the ways in which they may have been influenced by the surrounding Graeco-Roman culture. We shall then be able to consider in a later chapter how synagogue structures and officials may in turn have influenced the function, organization and leadership of the early Christian communities.[4]

---

reading which interprets the sources as an idealized prescription of what ought to have characterized Judaism. Cf. A.T. Kraabel, 'The Diaspora Synagogue: Archaeological and Epigraphic Evidence since Sukenik', *Aufstieg und Niedergang der Römischen Welt* II.19.1 (1979) 479; and S.J.D. Cohen, 'Women in the Synagogues of Antiquity', *Conservative Judaism* 33 (1980) 27.

[2]This old consensus is represented in the encyclopaedic works of E. Schürer, *The History of the Jewish People in the Age of Jesus Christ (175 B.C. – A.D. 135)* (rev. ed.; 3 vols.; Edinburgh: T. & T. Clark, 1979); and G.F. Moore, *Judaism in the First Centuries of the Christian Era: The Age of the Tannaim* (3 vols.; Cambridge: Harvard University Press, 1927-30).

[3]For a recent and helpful overview of the rising and falling tide of research over the past few decades into diasporan Judaism, cf. J.M.G. Barclay, *Jews in the Mediterranean Diaspora: from Alexander to Trajan (323 BCE-117 CE)* (Edinburgh: T. & T. Clark, 1996) 4-9; L.V. Rutgers, *The Hidden Heritage of Diaspora Judaism* (Contributions to Biblical Exegesis and Theology, 20; Leuven: Peeters, 1998) 15-44; and H.A. McKay, 'Ancient Synagogues: the Continuing Dialectic between two Major Views', *Currents in Research: Biblical Studies* 6 (1998) 103-42.

[4]Although, depending on dating of the synagogue evidence, it is not impossible that the Christian church may rather have influenced the Jewish synagogue in these matters.

It should be noted that whilst additional archaeological evidence has prompted a review of the debate, on many issues the jury is still considering their verdict and firm conclusions are unwisely drawn. There is presently little consensus either as to where the new pieces of the jigsaw should fit into the larger picture or how the gaps which still remain should be reconstructed.[5] The debate has polarized into two distinct camps. One camp favours a late date for the emergence of Jewish synagogue buildings, whilst the opposing camp adopts the view that the term synagogue, descriptive of both the institution and the building, was well-established in the first century A.D. The former are accused of adopting a correspondingly late composition or editorial date for otherwise relevant literary and archaeological sources; the latter are accused of conflating disparate evidence to suit their cause.[6] A study of the nature of Jewish synagogue leadership against the background of leadership in the wider Graeco-Roman culture may prove to be an instructive way forward.[7]

II. The Origins of the Synagogue

It is strange that the origins of what has for centuries been a major institution of the Jewish religion, namely the synagogue, continues to be a mystery. Much disagreement rests on whether the emergence of the synagogue as an institution significantly pre-dates the first buildings explicitly to be called synagogues. Early tradition, witnessed to by both Philo and Josephus[8] in the first century, as well as by the rabbis,[9] cites an origin, at the instigation of Moses himself,

---

[5]H.A. McKay, 'Ancient Synagogues: the Continuing Dialectic between two Major Views', 128-29.

[6]H.A. McKay, 'Ancient Synagogues: the Continuing Dialectic between two Major Views', 103-17, 129-32.

[7]Cf., for example, T. Rajak & D. Noy, 'Archisynagogoi: Office, Title, and Social Status in the Greco-Jewish Synagogue', Journal of Roman Studies 83 (1993) 75-93, discussed below on page 128.

[8]Philo, Life of Moses 2.211-16; De specialibus legibus 2.62; Josephus, Antiquities 16.43; Contra Apionem 2.175.

[9]Targum Pseudo-Jonathan, Ex 18:20; Mekhilta de-Rabbi Yishmael Tractate Amalek 3.174; Midrash Yalqut on Exodus 408; Mishnah Megillah 3.6; Babylonian Talmud Megillah 29a, 32a; Palestinian Talmud Megillah 4.75a. Cf. also H.L. Strack & P. Billerbeck (eds.), Kommentar zum Neuen Testament aus Talmud und Midrasch (7

of regular weekly meetings for the Jewish community.[10] More typically, scholars this century have variously defended dates from the seventh to the first centuries B.C. (in other words, a range spanning pre-exilic, exilic and post-exilic Judaism) for the foundation of this institution.[11] There has been a corresponding uncertainty as to where the synagogues first came into being, whether Babylon, Egypt, or Palestine.[12]

A long-standing traditional consensus, widely associated with the late nineteenth-century work of Alfred Edersheim,[13] has been that synagogues were first established by the Jews whilst in exile far from their temple during the Babylonian period.[14] Initially they met in

---

vols.; Munich: Beck, 1922-61) II.740 for the rabbinic suggestion that the establishment of the synagogue dates to the time of Abraham.

[10]Cf. also what may be implied in Acts 15:21, 'For from early generations Moses has had in every city those who preach him, for he is read every sabbath in the synagogues'; also the suggestion by some that Lev 23:4; Ps 26:8; 74:8; 90:1; Is 4:5; 19:19; Jer 39:8; and Ezk 11:16 may be references to the 'well-established institution' of synagogues, in L. Finkelstein, 'The Origin of the Synagogue', in J. Gutmann (ed.), *The Synagogue: Studies in Origins, Archaeology, and Architecture* (The Library of Biblical Studies; New York: Ktav, 1975) 13; and J.G. Griffiths, 'Egypt and the Rise of the Synagogue', in D. Urman & P.V.M. Flesher (eds.), *Ancient Synagogues: Historical Analysis and Archaeological Discovery* (Studia post-Biblica, 47; 2 vols.; Leiden: E.J. Brill, 1995) 3; and A. Kasher, 'Synagogues as "Houses of Prayer" and "Holy Places" in the Jewish Communities of Hellenistic and Roman Egypt', in D. Urman & P.V.M. Flesher (eds.), *Ancient Synagogues: Historical Analysis and Archaeological Discovery* (Studia post-Biblica, 47; 2 vols.; Leiden: E.J. Brill, 1995) 206.

[11]See the helpful summary of five key positions adopted by scholars in R. Hachlili, 'The Origin of the Synagogue: a Re-assessment', *Journal for the Study of Judaism in the Persian, Hellenistic and Roman Period* 28 (1997) 34-37. J. Gutmann, 'Synagogue Origins: Theories and Facts', in J. Gutmann (ed.), *Ancient Synagogues: the State of Research* (Brown Judaic Studies, 22; Chico: Scholars Press, 1981) 4, argues for a second century B.C. date ('a major historical event in second-century B.C.E. Judea ushered in the Pharisees and their new institution — the synagogue — whose existence is not historically demonstrable prior to the Hasmonean revolt'); also *idem, The Synagogue: Studies in Origins, Archaeology, and Architecture* (The Library of Biblical Studies; New York: Ktav, 1975) 72-76. For a summary, see also L.J. Hoppe, *The Synagogues and Churches of Ancient Palestine* (Collegeville: Liturgical Press, 1994) 7-14.

[12]J. Gutmann (ed.), *The Synagogue: Studies in Origins, Archaeology, and Architecture,* x.

[13]A. Edersheim, *The Life and Times of Jesus the Messiah* (2 vols.; London: Longmans, Green, and Co., 1900) I.18-20, 76-77, 430-39.

[14]Cf. J.G. Griffiths, 'Egypt and the Rise of the Synagogue', 3; and E.M. Meyers, 'Ancient Synagogues: an Archaeological Introduction', in S. Fine (ed.), *Sacred*

private homes, but, over time, formal meeting places were adopted.[15] In focus, these were principally places of prayer, and by the time of the New Testament, the synagogue, as both community and building, was well-established.[16] An opposing school, supported by a number of influential scholars, argues that this long dominant view rests on very little certain evidence.[17] It is argued that not until much later than the New Testament do we find clear archaeological data which corroborate the existence of synagogue buildings, thus making the traditional view of the origins and development of the synagogue somewhat improbable. Here we shall review some of the key literary and non-literary evidence for synagogues in both the diaspora and Palestine.

1. Literary Evidence

There are certainly a number of references in literary sources from the first century A.D. which speak of meetings of the Jewish community, often using the term synagogue.[18] In particular, the accounts of Jesus' ministry in the gospels and of Paul's journeys in Acts suggest the

---

Realm: the Emergence of the Synagogue in the Ancient World (Oxford: Oxford University Press, 1996) 10.

[15]The Hebrew *beth knesseth* ('house of assembly') may suggest that the origin of the synagogue was in 'secular assembly houses'; *cf.* R. Hachlili, 'The Origin of the Synagogue: a Re-assessment', 39.

[16]S. Zeitlin, 'The Origin of the Synagogue', *Proceedings of the American Academy for Jewish Research* 2 (1930-31) 69-81, reprinted in J. Gutmann (ed.), *The Synagogue: Studies in Origins, Archaeology, and Architecture* (The Library of Biblical Studies; New York: Ktav, 1975) 14-26, argued for a post-exilic origin which was linked with the rise of the Pharisees, where the focus on prayer and the reading of the Torah was secondary to other social and economic functions fulfilled by the community. The synagogue was initially a secular, rather than liturgical forum. Note that in the 1930s Zeitlin confidently wrote, *op. cit.*, 18, '*all* scholars are of the opinion that the synagogue as a fixed institution was in existence in Babylonia after the destruction of the first Temple. The rise of this institution was necessitated by the need of communal worship and instruction, felt after the destruction of the Temple' [italics added].

[17]*Cf.*, for example, P.V.M. Flesher, 'Palestinian Synagogues before 70 C.E.: a Review of the Evidence', in D. Urman & P.V.M. Flesher (eds.), *Ancient Synagogues: Historical Analysis and Archaeological Discovery* (Studia post-Biblica, 47; 2 vols.; Leiden: E.J. Brill, 1995) 27; and H.A. McKay, 'Ancient Synagogues: the Continuing Dialectic between two Major Views', 106.

[18]*Cf.* E.M. Meyers, 'Ancient Synagogues: an Archaeological Introduction', 9.

existence of synagogues both in Palestine and the diaspora during this period.[19] Knowledge of these synagogues by the first readers of the New Testament seems to be so much taken for granted, however, that little detail of them is provided within the text, and the modern reader is consequently left with a number of unanswered questions. What can be said is that these synagogues, whether descriptive of buildings or community gatherings, were the focus of reading, teaching and study of the Law. Jesus himself is recorded as using such occasions for public reading, teaching and healing, and these institutions were sufficiently organized such that expulsion from the community was conceivable.[20]

Some concern is raised, however, when it is noted that Paul does not explicitly refer to synagogues in his letters.[21] With a greater degree of scepticism, Richard Horsley argues that the New Testament references we do encounter are 'Lukan projections from his own later experience in diaspora "synagogues" back into the ministry of Jesus'.[22] It is argued, instead, that most of the references to synagogues in the pre-A.D. 70 New Testament sources speak of gatherings rather than buildings.[23] Others continue to argue,

---

[19]*Cf.* Mk 1:21, 23 (// Lk 4:33), 29 (// Lk 4:38), 39 (// Lk 4:44; Mt 4:23); 3:1 (// Mt 12:9; Lk 6:6); 5:22 (//Lk 8:41); 12:39 (// Mt 23:6; Lk 20:46); 13:9 (// Mt 24:17; Lk 21:12); Lk 4:15, 16 (// Mk 6:2; Mt 13:54), 20, 28; 7:5; 11:43; 12:11; 13:10; Mt 6:2, 5; 9:35; 10:17; 23:34; Jn 6:59; 18:20; Acts 6:9; 9:2, 20; 13:5, 14, 43; 14:1; 15:21; 17:1, 10, 17; 18:4, 7, 19, 26; 19:8; 22:19; 24:12; 26:11; Rev 2:9; 3:9.

[20]H.A. McKay, 'Ancient Synagogues: the Continuing Dialectic between two Major Views', 120.

[21]L.M. White, *The Social Origins of Christian Architecture: Building God's House in the Roman World: Architectural Adaptation among Pagans, Jews and Christians* (Harvard Theological Studies, 42; Valley Forge: Trinity Press International, 1996) 87.

[22]R.A. Horsley, *Archaeology, History, and Society in Galilee: the Social Context of Jesus and the Rabbis* (Valley Forge: Trinity Press International, 1996) 149. See also, *idem, Galilee: History, Politics, People* (Valley Forge: Trinity Press International, 1995) 224-26, where he writes 'It is thus clear from the synoptic Gospel tradition as our principal evidence that the *synagogai* in Galilee were not buildings, but assemblies or congregations of people'; and *op. cit.,* 227, 'We must thus conclude that a synagogue in ancient Galilee was not a building, but an assembly or congregation of people in a local community, and that the assembly gathered not simply for religious ceremonies but to deal with any and all community affairs such as fundraising, public projects, or common prayer'.

[23]*Cf.* H.A. McKay, 'Ancient Synagogues: the Continuing Dialectic between two Major Views', 121, who considers that the synagogues in the time of Jesus were more primitive than those descriptions later recorded by the evangelists.

however, that while it may be convenient to accuse Luke of anachronism (although commonly-accepted dating of Lukan material would allow little time for such anachronisms to be introduced), there is sufficient other literary and archaeological evidence to support the view that the New Testament text is accurate in its references to the existence of synagogues in the first century.[24]

The writings of Josephus provide some of the supportive first-century literary evidence referring to buildings as Jewish synagogues or meeting-places,[25] including, in particular, references to Caesarea Maritima, Dora and Tiberias.[26] Peter Richardson writes regarding Josephus' reports, however, that there may be a distinction between what can be assumed about the origin of the synagogues in the diaspora in contrast to those in Palestine. In particular he notes that Josephus does not refer to antecedents to the first-century Palestinian synagogues, whereas Josephus' evidence for synagogues in the diaspora is significantly earlier.[27]

Philo speaks of numerous synagogues,[28] notably in each of the five districts of the city of Alexandria as early as A.D. 38.[29] He also speaks of the Essene Jewish community which gathers in 'sacred spots (ἰερους ... τόπους) which they call synagogues'.[30] More

---

[24]R. Riesner, 'Synagogues in Jerusalem', in R. Bauckham (ed.), *The Book of Acts in its Palestinian Setting* (The Book of Acts in its First-Century Setting, 4; Grand Rapids: Eerdmans, 1995) 179-211.

[25]See the wider discussion in H.A. McKay, *Sabbath and Synagogue: the Question of Sabbath Worship in Ancient Judaism* (Religions in the Graeco-Roman World, 122; Leiden: E.J. Brill, 1994) 77-85.

[26]Josephus, *Jewish War* 2.285, where he refers to a synagogue in Caesarea which had been owned by a Greek, but which the Jews had repeatedly sought to purchase; *idem, Antiquities* 19.300-305, where a statue of Caesar was erected in the Jewish synagogue of Dora, and where Jews were being forbidden the right to assemble in their synagogue; and *idem, Life* 277-80, which concerns a meeting-house (προσευχή) of significant dimension in Tiberias.

[27]P. Richardson, 'Early Synagogues as Collegia in the Diaspora and Palestine', in J.S. Kloppenborg & S.G. Wilson (eds.), *Voluntary Associations in the Graeco-Roman World* (London: Routledge, 1996) 100.

[28]He most often uses the word προσευχή (in the sense of 'place of prayer'), as Luke does in Acts 16:13, 16.

[29]Philo, *In Flaccum* 41, 45-49, 53, where Flaccus is criticized for 'installing images in the meeting-houses (προσευχαῖς)' in Alexandria; Philo also reports of how widespread such places are, not only in Egypt, but also both further east and west, and that the Jewish meeting places in Alexandria were under threat of destruction.

[30]Philo, *Quod omnis probus liber sit* 81.

generally, he refers to numerous Jewish gatherings in 'many cities'.[31] These meetings were the focus of weekly opportunities for study and discussion.[32] Philo's preferred term for such Jewish communities is προσευχή, and inevitably scholars disagree as to whether προσευχή and συναγωγή were used synonymously; alternatively, one may have referred to religious and the other to civil gatherings, or indeed their application may reflect regional or chronological differences.[33] The lack of conclusive evidence suggests that Lester Grabbe is probably right to pursue what may be a more productive line by casting his net wide at this stage.[34]

If, therefore, we are limited to the literary evidence provided by Philo, Josephus and the New Testament gospels, with regard to Palestine we can only speak of synagogues in Galilee, northern Palestine, and amongst the Essenes of Palestine-Syria.[35] Of this, the material from Josephus in particular would support the notion of Palestinian synagogue buildings at this time. New Testament references to people entering, leaving or teaching in Palestinian

---

[31]Philo, *Life of Moses* 2.215-16; *De specialibus legibus* 2.62. *Cf.* also, *idem, De legatione ad Gaium* 20.132-37; and especially *op. cit.,* 20.156-58, 'Philo said Augustus "did not expel them from Rome or deprive them of their Roman citizenship because they remembered their Jewish nationality also. He introduced no changes into their synagogues, he did not prevent them from meeting for the exposition of the Law, and he raised no objection to the offering of first fruits, ... [and] if the distribution [of money or food in Rome] happened to be made on the Sabbath ... he instructed the distributors to reserve the Jews' share ... until the next day".' *Cf.* J.G. Griffiths, 'Egypt and the Rise of the Synagogue', 6.

[32]See the wider discussion in H.A. McKay, *Sabbath and Synagogue,* 65-77.

[33]For a review of the semantic range of προσευχή, συναγωγή and the Hebrew *beth knesseth* (בית כנסת), see R. Hachlili, 'The Origin of the Synagogue: a Re-assessment', 37-40.

[34]L.L. Grabbe, 'Synagogues in Pre-70 Palestine: a Reassessment', in D. Urman & P.V.M. Flesher (eds.), *Ancient Synagogues: Historical Analysis and Archaeological Discovery* (Studia post-Biblica, 47; 2 vols.; Leiden: E.J. Brill, 1995) 18. *Cf.* also A. Kasher, 'Synagogues as "Houses of Prayer" and "Holy Places" in the Jewish Communities of Hellenistic and Roman Egypt', 206, 'Until the first century, all the Jewish synagogues in Hellenistic and Roman Egypt were called "προσευχή"— a "place of prayer" or a "house of prayer" — at least according to inscriptions, papyrus documents, and literary sources'.

[35]P.V.M. Flesher, 'Palestinian Synagogues before 70 C.E.: a Review of the Evidence', 31-34; he does consider the references in Acts 22:19; 24:12; 26:11, and Jn 9:22; 12:42; 16:2 to synagogues in Jerusalem, but concurs with a number of scholars that these are post-70 A.D. retrojections. He also argues that Acts 6:9 reflects a meeting place for foreigners, and not, therefore, a synagogue in the strict sense.

synagogues are not conclusive as to whether specific buildings were in mind, although this would appear to be the more obvious interpretation.[36] The Lukan reference to a centurion who is honoured for having 'built' a synagogue for the Jewish community in Capernaum is, however, more compelling, if Luke's detail is not considered anachronistic.[37] The literary evidence from Philo, Josephus and Acts regarding the diaspora, however, suggests a much broader spread of synagogues in the first century.

2. Non-literary Evidence

We have noted above that archaeological research in recent decades is rapidly causing scholarly opinion about the origin of synagogues both in Palestine and the diaspora to be reconsidered. It used to be argued that there is no firm archaeological evidence for synagogues until the third century A.D., and then only from Palestine.[38] This view is no longer tenable; indeed, it is now argued by many that our earliest archaeological evidence for synagogue buildings derives from the diaspora.

Archaeological Evidence for Synagogues in the Diaspora

Archaeological evidence which presupposes the existence of synagogues in a number of Graeco-Roman cities has been uncovered. These sites, however, are relatively few and unfortunately far between.[39] In many cases, the earliest evidence comes to us in the form of datable inscriptions rather than unequivocal remains of

---

[36]Even the reference to 'the best seats in the synagogues (πρωτοκαθεδρίας ἐν ταῖς συναγωγαῖς) and the places of honour at feasts' (Mk 12:39) does not unequivocally suggest that a dedicated synagogue building was in mind, although, again, the implication of a permanent arrangement is preferable.

[37]Lk 7:5.

[38]J. Gutmann, 'The Origin of the Synagogue: the Current State of Research', in J. Gutmann (ed.), The Synagogue: Studies in Origins, Archaeology, and Architecture (The Library of Biblical Studies; New York: Ktav, 1975) 72-76.

[39]Unlike those in Palestine. Cf. G. Foerster, 'A Survey of Ancient Diaspora Synagogues', in L.I. Levine (ed.), Ancient Synagogues Revealed (Jerusalem: Israel Exploration Society, 1981) 164, 'If several synagogues were discovered within a more limited geographical area, it would probably be found that they possess common features in plan and ornament, as is the case with the ancient synagogues of Israel'.

Jewish buildings.[40] Where evidence of buildings which were clearly used as synagogues is largely dated later than the first century A.D., some epigraphic evidence is found for Jewish buildings dating from as early as the third century B.C. where they were called προσευχαί.[41]

It is in Egypt that we find the greatest wealth of archaeological and literary data referring to a diasporan Jewish community. Jewish refugees had inhabited Egypt as far back as the sixth century B.C.,[42] and Alexander himself encouraged Jews to settle into the new city 'on terms of equality with the Greeks'.[43] Even as early as the third century B.C. there is archaeological evidence for Jewish community meeting places in Egypt. An inscription, from 246-22 B.C. located in Schedia, some 20 miles from Alexandria, records:

> On behalf of King Ptolemy (III) and Queen Berenike, his sister and wife, and their children, the Jews (of Schedia near Alexandria have dedicated) the prayer-house (προσευχή).[44]

There are many more inscriptions in the second and first centuries B.C. which confirm that meeting places for the Jews were widespread in Egypt, and, indeed, that there was a vitality in such communities.[45] In Alexandria there were even districts of the city in

---

[40]Although P. Richardson, 'Augustan-Era Synagogues in Rome', in K.P. Donfried & P. Richardson (eds.), *Judaism and Christianity in First-Century Rome* (Grand Rapids: Eerdmans, 1998) 19-20, notes that 'the epigraphic conclusions only determine the period before which the synagogue must have been begun and do not bear on the origins of the various synagogues'.

[41]M. Hengel, 'Proseuche und Synagoge', in J. Gutmann (ed.), *The Synagogue: Studies in Origins, Archaeology, and Architecture* (The Library of Biblical Studies; New York: Ktav, 1975) 28, who argues that the foundation of synagogues lies neither in Palestine, nor Babylon, but in the diaspora of third-century B.C. Ptolemaic Egypt. Some scholars question this link between the prayer-house and the synagogue and assume these to have been two distinct buildings. The synagogue fulfilled a much broader rôle in the community than was the case with the prayer-house.

[42]J.M.G. Barclay, *Jews in the Mediterranean Diaspora*, 20.

[43]Josephus, *Jewish War* 2.487; *Contra Apionem* 2.35, 37.

[44]*CIJ* 1440; cf. also J.G. Griffiths, 'Egypt and the Rise of the Synagogue', 4-5; and *CIJ* 1441; 1442; 1443; 1449.

[45]Cf. J.G. Griffiths, 'Egypt and the Rise of the Synagogue', 6; and J.M.G. Barclay, *Jews in the Mediterranean Diaspora*, 26-27. For evidence of vitality throughout the diaspora in late antiquity, cf. L.V. Rutgers, *The Hidden Heritage of Diaspora Judaism*, 125-35.

which Jewish residence was concentrated.[46] There is thus little doubt that synagogues existed in Egypt during the Ptolemaic period, indeed Griffiths argues that it was here, rather than in Babylonia, that we find the origin of the Jewish synagogue.[47]

There is considerably less archaeological or literary evidence for the existence of synagogues in Cyrenaica. One important inscription, however, from the town of Berenice and dated to the mid-first century A.D. is not only instructive, but particularly significant in that it may be the earliest 'unequivocal' archaeological use of the term synagogue as a reference to both the community and the building.[48]

> In the 2nd year of the emperor Nero Claudius Caesar Drusus Germanicus, Choiak 16, the community (συναγωγή) of the Jews in Berenice has decided to inscribe on a stele of Parian marble (the names of) those who have contributed to the repair of the synagogue (συναγωγή).[49]

The most significant synagogue archaeological site from Syria is unquestionably that in Dura Europos, which seems clearly to have second and third century A.D. sections.[50] Again it appears originally to have been a private residence. This site is most interesting, however, for its extensive artwork depicting a number of biblical scenes.

Significant study has been made of the Jewish communities in Asia Minor.[51] Thomas Kraabel has focused considerable attention on

---

[46]Philo, *In Flaccum* 55; Josephus, *Jewish War* 2.495; *cf.* J.M.G. Barclay, *Jews in the Mediterranean Diaspora*, 29.

[47]J.G. Griffiths, 'Egypt and the Rise of the Synagogue', 3-16; *cf.* also A. Kasher, 'Synagogues as "Houses of Prayer" and "Holy Places" in the Jewish Communities of Hellenistic and Roman Egypt', 205-20.

[48]H.A. McKay, 'Ancient Synagogues: the Continuing Dialectic between two Major Views', 125, who argues that this should be recognized not only for its early date, but also for its possibly significant uniqueness.

[49]*Supplementum Epigraphicum Graecum* 17.823; but *cf.* also J.M.G. Barclay, *Jews in the Mediterranean Diaspora*, 236-37; and H.A. McKay, 'Ancient Synagogues: the Continuing Dialectic between two Major Views', 108.

[50]*Cf.* E.M. Meyers, 'Ancient Synagogues: an Archaeological Introduction', 12; and L.I. Levine, 'The Synagogue of Dura-Europos', in L.I. Levine (ed.), *Ancient Synagogues Revealed* (Jerusalem: Israel Exploration Society, 1982) 172-77.

[51]A very valuable and much cited study of Jewish communities in Asia Minor is P.R. Trebilco, *Jewish Communities in Asia Minor* (SNTS Monograph Series, 69; Cambridge: Cambridge University Press, 1991); which can be helpfully supplemented by the recent monograph, I. Levinskaya, *The Book of Acts in its*

the huge, originally third-century A.D. synagogue which was discovered in 1962 in Sardis, western Turkey (the largest example of an ancient synagogue as yet excavated). This building was not only large enough to accommodate a sizeable Jewish congregation numbering hundreds but it was centrally located in the city, and also richly decorated. This is clear evidence of a flourishing community,[52] and the significant number of inscriptions which highlight benefactions may well reflect the wealth, prominence and local success of this particular Jewish community.[53]

Although there is little in the way of archaeological remains of what can be assumed to be early Jewish synagogue buildings in Rome, it seems from the extremely rich epigraphic evidence that there may have been as many as sixteen synagogues in the city as early as the third and second centuries B.C.[54] Furthermore, the suggestion has been defended that five synagogues were founded in the city during the early first century A.D. The names of these synagogues ('of the Augustans', 'of the Agrippans', 'of the Herodians' and 'of the Volumnians') suggest that they were founded during or shortly after the lives of their respective namesakes and out of deference for the attitude towards and patronage of Jews by these leading figures in Rome.[55] Margaret Williams similarly argues that they may have been associations 'formed originally by Jewish members of the households of (respectively) the emperor Augustus, his right-hand man, Marcus Agrippa and Herod the Great's friend, Volumnius, a procurator in Syria in 8 B.C.E.'[56] Philo certainly refers to Augustus' not removing the Jews from Rome or denying them their rights.[57] Considerable research has been produced in defence of a first-century A.D. level in the archaeological remains of a synagogue

---

Diaspora Setting (The Book of Acts in its First Century Setting, 5; Grand Rapids: Eerdmans, 1996).

[52]L.V. Rutgers, *The Hidden Heritage of Diaspora Judaism*, 19-20.

[53]L.H. Feldman, 'Diaspora Synagogues: New Light from Inscriptions and Papyri', in S. Fine (ed.), *Sacred Realm: the Emergence of the Synagogue in the Ancient World* (Oxford: Oxford University Press, 1996) 53.

[54]L.H. Feldman, 'Diaspora Synagogues: New Light from Inscriptions and Papyri', 51.

[55]P. Richardson, 'Augustan-Era Synagogues in Rome', 20-23, 28.

[56]M.H. Williams (ed.), *The Jews among the Greeks and Romans*, 150.

[57]Philo, *De legatione ad Gaium* 20.157.

at the Roman port of Ostia.[58] On the basis of such a community, it is highly unlikely that Rome's seaport had a synagogue whilst at the same time the imperial capital did not also have one.[59]

Delos also provides us with very early evidence of the existence of synagogues. It seems that there was a synagogue here, which benefited from specific patronage, from as early as the second or first century B.C.[60] This synagogue was initially no more than the renovation of an existing building, but underwent two later phases of alteration.[61]

Archaeological Evidence for Synagogues in Palestine

The archaeological evidence for first-century synagogues in Palestine is less clear and more widely disputed. This may be because the earliest buildings were simply converted from other uses, and the extant archaeological remains are indistinguishable in architecture from other buildings. It may also be in part because the temple cult in the pre-A.D. 70 period obviated the need for synagogues in the region immediately surrounding Jerusalem.[62] It consequently became widely accepted among scholars that the earliest archaeological evidence for synagogues in Palestine is that of the second century

---

[58]L.M. White, *The Social Origins of Christian Architecture*; and *idem*, 'Synagogue and Society in Imperial Ostia: Archaeological and Epigraphic Evidence', *Harvard Theological Review* 90 (1997) 23-58 (also in K.P. Donfried & P. Richardson [eds.], *Judaism and Christianity in First-Century Rome* [Grand Rapids: Eerdmans, 1998] 30-63).

[59]P. Richardson, 'Augustan-Era Synagogues in Rome', 23.

[60]L.M. White, 'The Delos Synagogue Revisited: Recent Fieldwork in the Graeco-Roman Diaspora', *Harvard Theological Review* 80 (1987) 144, dates the following inscription to the second century B.C.: 'The Israelites (on Delos) who make offerings to hallowed, consecrated *Argarizein* honor Menippos, son of Artemidoros, of Herakleion, both himself and his descendants, for constructing and dedicating to the proseuche of God, out of his own funds, the ... (building?) and the walls and the ..., and crown him with a gold crown and ...'

[61]P. Richardson, 'Early Synagogues as Collegia in the Diaspora and Palestine', 97, 'The earliest Diaspora synagogue sites of which we have evidence were remodeled houses adapted to the needs of the worshipping community. The synagogue at Delos ... was renovated in the late second century B.C.E. and again in the mid-first century B.C.E., and continued on into the second century C.E.'

[62]P.V.M. Flesher, 'Palestinian Synagogues before 70 C.E.: a Review of the Evidence', 30-31; although see the article R. Riesner, 'Synagogues in Jerusalem', 179-211.

A.D.[63] Any earlier synagogues which may have existed were either indistinguishable from other buildings or were destroyed during the two Jewish revolts.[64]

During the past decades, however, archaeological evidence was found for what some scholars consider to have been six first-century synagogue buildings in Israel.[65] The need for applying caution when drawing firm conclusions from such data is heightened when it is noted that there was considerable diversity or variation between synagogues; and there are particular difficulties in 'the linking of a building's form to function'.[66]

Some scholars, however, continue to dispute the existence of such synagogue buildings prior to A.D. 70.[67] The principal hurdle in

---

[63]Y. Tsafrir, 'On the Source of the Architectural Design of the Ancient Synagogues in Galilee: a New Appraisal', in D. Urman & P.V.M. Flesher (eds.), *Ancient Synagogues: Historical Analysis and Archaeological Discovery* (Studia post-Biblica, 47; 2 vols.; Leiden: E.J. Brill, 1995) 70-86, argues that it is the third century before 'synagogues were built as a building of a specific form' in Galilee.

[64]M.J.S. Chiat, 'First-Century Synagogue Architecture: Methodological Problems', in J. Gutmann (ed.), *Ancient Synagogues: the State of Research* (Brown Judaic Studies, 22; Chico: Scholars Press, 1981) 49. It should be noted that some of the clear architectural evidence for synagogues points, nonetheless, to significant, presumably deliberate, similarities with other buildings in the Graeco-Roman world; *cf.* A. Ovadiah & T. Michaeli, 'Observations on the Origin of the Architectural Plan of Ancient Synagogues', *Journal of Jewish Studies* 38 (1987) 235.

[65]Masada, Herodium, Migdal, Chorazin, Capernaum, Gamala; of which Migdal and Chorazin (and possibly Herodium) have questionable evidence; *cf.* P.V.M. Flesher, 'Palestinian Synagogues before 70 C.E.: a Review of the Evidence', 34-35. M.J.S. Chiat, 'First-Century Synagogue Architecture: Methodological Problems', 55, however, has questioned the grounds for these conclusions and suggests instead that many Jewish communities would have met either in the city-square — an argument also made by S.B. Hoenig, 'The Ancient City-Square: The Forerunner of the Synagogue', *Aufstieg und Niedergang der Römischen Welt* II.19.1 (1979) 448-76 — or in any appropriately sized building in a town or village.

[66]M.J.S. Chiat, 'First-Century Synagogue Architecture: Methodological Problems', 56, where she states, 'Not enough is known about the function(s) of early synagogues to enable us to establish a link or relationship with their architectural form.' *Cf.* also A.T. Kraabel, 'Social Systems of Six Diaspora Synagogues', in J.A. Overman & R.S. MacLennan (eds.), *Diaspora Jews and Judaism: Essays in Honor of, and in Dialogue with, A. Thomas Kraabel* (South Florida Studies in the History of Judaism, 41; Atlanta: Scholars Press, 1992) 260, 'In all likelihood the faithful first met in homes, then raised the funds to convert one home to common use; such a process is known for other eastern religions in the Roman Empire, and is the rule for early Christianity'.

[67]*Cf.* H.C. Kee, 'The Transformation of the Synagogue after 70 C.E.: its Import for Early Christianity', *New Testament Studies* 36 (1990) 1-24; but see also the response

demonstrating their existence is the lack of archaeological remains of buildings which were *clearly and exclusively* used as synagogues in Roman Palestine of the first century.[68] The general consensus regarding this archaeological evidence, once the literary evidence is given due weight, however, is that synagogues were present in first-century Palestine;[69] although proof of their existence prior to the post-Maccabean period we do not presently have.[70]

3. Conclusion

We may never be able to solve the question as to the origin of the Jewish synagogue, because none of our extant literary sources discusses their recent foundation. It is noteworthy, however, that the earliest evidence from Palestine largely derives from the first century or later, as against that from the diaspora which begins to surface from a much earlier date.[71] One possible explanation of this disparity is that the presence of the temple of Jerusalem may well have dictated different circumstances for the Palestinian communities.

---

by R.E. Oster, 'Supposed Anachronism in Luke-Acts' Use of ΣΥΝΑΓΩΓΗ', *New Testament Studies* 39 (1993) 178-208; and the subsequent articles, H.C. Kee, 'The Changing Meaning of Synagogue: a Response to Richard Oster', *New Testament Studies* 40 (1994) 281-83; and *idem*, 'Defining the First-Century CE Synagogue: Problems and Progress', *New Testament Studies* 41 (1995) 481-500. J. Gutmann, 'Synagogue Origins: Theories and Facts', 1, argues, 'All hypotheses in support of an early origin for the synagogue are primarily arguments from silence — the pious wish conjured up for religious or pragmatic reasons to make the past yield results not necessarily warranted by factual evidence or historical possibility'.

[68]M.J.S. Chiat, 'First-Century Synagogue Architecture: Methodological Problems', 53, 'I would further suggest that at the time these five buildings were constructed, the first century C.E., there existed in Palestine various forms of assembly halls in which the Jewish people would gather to conduct a variety of communal affairs. If this is correct, the building in which these activities occurred would not have to conform to any particular set of specifications, particularly those of a sacred or "cultic" nature'.

[69]Cf. L.L. Grabbe, 'Synagogues in Pre-70 Palestine: a Reassessment', 23; and R. Riesner, 'Synagogues in Jerusalem', 184-87.

[70]Cf. L.L. Grabbe, 'Synagogues in Pre-70 Palestine: a Reassessment', 25, 'when we look at Palestine itself, evidence for the existence of synagogues is lacking before the first century B.C.E. and perhaps even until the first C.E.'

[71]P. Richardson, 'Early Synagogues as Collegia in the Diaspora and Palestine', 103-104.

The debate as to whether synagogue buildings existed in an identifiable form in the first century A.D., however, hinges on whether references to synagogues (or προσευχαί) during this period signify simply a 'gathering' of the Jewish community or the established 'meeting place' of that community,[72] and the comparative weight given to literary and archaeological evidence. If the archaeological evidence from both Palestine and the diaspora together with the unequivocal references in Philo and Josephus to buildings set aside for Jewish gatherings is given due weight, then the apparent paucity of explicit references to synagogue buildings in the New Testament material may be viewed with less suspicion. The conclusion carried forward here is that the terms συναγωγή and προσευχή were widely used to describe both the building and the institution,[73] and that, by the first century A.D., synagogue buildings were widespread in both Palestine and the diaspora.[74] Thus, as Lee Levine concludes:

> By the end of the Second Temple period the synagogue had become a central institution in Jewish life. It could be found everywhere, in Israel and in the Diaspora, east and west, in cities as well as in villages. The synagogue filled a wide variety of functions within the Jewish community and had become by the first century a recognised symbol of Jewish presence.[75]

It is also probable that the synagogue at this time was witnessing a period of development, especially following the destruction of the Jerusalem temple.[76] During this period, the Jewish synagogue varied considerably from locality to locality.[77] This variety

---

[72]H.C. Kee, 'The Changing Meaning of Synagogue: a Response to Richard Oster', 281-83; and R.A. Horsley, *Galilee*, 222, 'there is little or no solid evidence for the existence of synagogues as religious buildings in Galilee before the third century C.E.'; see also *idem*, *Archaeology, History, and Society in Galilee*, 131-53.

[73]*Cf.* T. Rajak & D. Noy, '*Archisynagogoi*: Office, Title, and Social Status in the Greco-Jewish Synagogue', 76; and P. Richardson, 'Augustan-Era Synagogues in Rome', 23.

[74]P. Richardson, 'Early Synagogues as Collegia in the Diaspora and Palestine', 95.

[75]L.I. Levine, 'The Second Temple Synagogue: the Formative Years', in L.I. Levine (ed.), *The Synagogue in Late Antiquity* (Philadelphia: American Schools of Oriental Research, 1987) 7.

[76]R. Hachlili, 'The Origin of the Synagogue: a Re-assessment', 45-47.

[77]M.H. Williams in 'The Structure of Roman Jewry Re-considered — Were the Synagogues of Ancient Rome entirely Homogeneous?', *Zeitschrift für Papyrologie und Epigraphik* 104 (1994) 129-41, argues for variety even within a specific locality.

is reflected in both the style and architecture of the buildings used for meeting and the names adopted to identify this meeting.[78] The range of names included 'place of gathering' (συναγωγή), 'place of prayer' (προσευχή, προσευκτήριον, εὐχεῖον), 'sanctuary' (τὸ ἱερόν), 'sabbath meeting place' (σαββατεῖον), 'place of instruction' (διδασκαλεῖον), 'the holy place' (ἅγιος τόπος), 'the house' (ὁ οἶκος), 'temple' (*templum*), and 'amphitheatre'. This range may reflect a corresponding variety of ways in which the synagogue was perceived in different locations. The most common term, 'synagogue' (συναγωγή), Lee Levine suggests, may have predominated precisely because it did not initially carry any special religious connotation.[79] There is, indeed, some limited evidence of pagan synagogues and *archisynagogoi*, although this also is disputed.[80]

III. The Function of the Synagogue

We turn now to look at the function of the synagogue in the early period of the common era. Our findings here will be important as we turn in due course to consider the rôle of the leading figures within the Jewish communities. The perspective of scholarship on the function of the synagogues has also changed significantly over recent decades, again largely in the light of new insights gleaned from the interpretation of non-literary sources, and a redressing of the method which was reliant upon reading back into the wide range of first-century situations conclusions derived almost exclusively from data deriving from later rabbinic sources.[81]

---

[78]E. Meyers, 'Synagogue', in D.N. Freedman (ed.), *Anchor Bible Dictionary* (vol. 6; New York: Doubleday, 1992) 253, 'The synagogues of the Greco-Roman Diaspora are diverse in style and varied in their architectural layout. Some are large, some are small. Some are basilical, some are broadhouses'.

[79]L.I. Levine, 'The Nature and Origin of the Palestinian Synagogue Reconsidered', *Journal of Biblical Literature* 115 (1996) 429-30.

[80]Cf. W. Schrage, 'ἀρχισυνάγωγος', *Theological Dictionary of the New Testament* 7 (1971) 844. For the contrary view see B.J. Brooten, *Women Leaders in the Ancient Synagogue: Inscriptional Evidence and Background Issues* (Brown Judaic Series, 36; Chico: Scholars Press, 1982) 5.

[81]Cf. R.A. Horsley, *Galilee*, 228, 'We have become critical of how earlier generations of scholars read ideas and opinions of later rabbinic texts back into first-century Pharisaism or "normative Judaism"'; and R. Riesner, 'Synagogues in Jerusalem', 186.

The traditional view assumed that the principal rôle of the synagogue was religious. It provided for its local community, in the absence of the temple, a centre for teaching and prayer.[82] As we have seen already, however, modern western society today draws a much sharper boundary between the religious, political and social spheres of life than would have been perceived by many ancient societies.[83] In the first century, both in rural and urban settings, the overlap between religious and social domains of life was considerable. The earlier consensus thus inaccurately conceived of the early synagogue as exclusively concerned with the sacred dimension.[84]

A broader picture, however, emerges from the first-century literary source of Josephus:

> from earliest times Jewish citizens had an assembly of their own in accordance with their native laws and their own place, in which they decide their affairs and controversies with one another ... Their laws and freedoms restored to them, they may, in accordance with their accepted customs, come together and have a community life and adjudicate suits among themselves, and at a place given them ... They may gather together with their wives and children and offer their ancestral prayers and sacrifices to God.[85]

---

[82]For this traditional view of the Jewish synagogue, see E. Schürer, *Die Gemeindeverfassung der Juden in Rom in der Kaiserzeit nach den Inschriften dargestellt, nebst 45 jüdischen Inschriften* (Leipzig: J.C. Hinrichs'sche Buchhandlung, 1879) 15-31; then, taken up by J.B. Frey in *Corpus Inscriptionum Iudaicarum: recueil des inscriptions juives qui vont du IIIe siècle avant Jésus-Christ au VIIe siècle de notre ère* (2 vols.; Sussidi allo studio delle antichità cristiane, 1, 3; Vatican City, Rome: Pontificio istituto di archeologia cristiana, 1936-52); and H.J. Leon, *The Jews of Ancient Rome* (Philadelphia: Jewish Publication Society, 1960) 167-94.

[83]See the discussion above on page 6. *Cf.* also R.A. Horsley, *Galilee*, 227-28, 'since religious affairs were not yet structurally differentiated from political-economic matters and village or town communities were not large or complex, much being structured by lineage and kinship relations, it is inherently unlikely that any distinctively religious social form(s) had evolved separate from the "civil" form(s)'; see also *op. cit.*, 230; and *idem, Archaeology, History, and Society in Galilee*, 146, 148.

[84]*Cf.*, for example, E. Schürer, *The History of the Jewish People in the Age of Jesus Christ*, II.425; G.F. Moore, *Judaism in the First Centuries of the Christian Era*, I.281-307. Also Josephus' reference (*Contra Apionem* 2.175) to the synagogue as a place where the reading of Scripture was important; and the New Testament evidence in Luke-Acts (Lk 4:16-22; Acts 13:13-16).

[85]*Cf.* Josephus, *Antiquities* 14.235; see also *idem, Antiquities* 19.300-305; and *Jewish War* 2.287-92; 7.44-47.

Accordingly, the view widely accepted by scholars today is that the ancient Jewish synagogue should be understood as more than merely a religious institution.[86] It also served a number of important social, civic, and educational functions.[87] (It may be precisely this range of functions which has contributed to our lack of specific detail regarding the ancient synagogue.)[88] The synagogue was, in a very broad sense, a 'community' building which was central to both the religious and social arenas of the Jewish community,[89] forming the focus of the local Jewish community's 'religious and religious-educational, religious-social activities ... as well as social-organizational occasions such as charity collections, announcements of lost property, sessions of the courts, etc.'[90] It is argued that this 'community' focus to the synagogue was reflected also in later synagogue architecture.[91] Even some of the Jewish buildings of

---

[86]J.T. Burtchaell, *From Synagogue to Church: Public Services and Offices in the Earliest Christian Communities* (Cambridge: Cambridge University Press, 1992) 206, 'What I refer to as a synagogal way of life was so integrated, so omnicompetent, so communitarian that our distinctions between public and private, or between sacred and secular, or between person and the community ... would be largely inapplicable. It was a society where various people were in charge — often many people — but ultimately they answered to the community for the entirety of its needs and interests'.

[87]*Cf.* E. Meyers, 'Synagogue', 253; Z. Safrai, 'The Communal Functions of the Synagogue in the Land of Israel in the Rabbinic Period', in D. Urman & P.V.M. Flesher (eds.), *Ancient Synagogues: Historical Analysis and Archaeological Discovery* (Studia post-Biblica, 47; 2 vols.; Leiden: E.J. Brill, 1995) 181-204; and L.H. Feldman, 'Diaspora Synagogues: New Light from Inscriptions and Papyri', 62-63.

[88]H.A. McKay, 'Ancient Synagogues: the Continuing Dialectic between two Major Views', 110.

[89]S. Zeitlin, 'The Origin of the Synagogue', in J. Gutmann (ed.), *The Synagogue: Studies in Origins, Archaeology, and Architecture*, 15-17, goes as far as to argue that the social rôle fulfilled by the synagogue developed prior to the religious dimension.

[90]D. Urman, 'The House of Assembly and the House of Study: Are they one and the same?', *Journal of Jewish Studies* 44 (1993) 241. Note also the research by Z. Safrai, 'The Communal Functions of the Synagogue in the Land of Israel in the Rabbinic Period', in D. Urman & P.V.M. Flesher (eds.), *Ancient Synagogues: Historical Analysis and Archaeological Discovery* (Studia post-Biblica, 47; 2 vols.; Leiden: E.J. Brill, 1995) where he concludes that the 'house of assembly' was the centre for the administration of the community.

[91]P. Richardson, 'Early Synagogues as Collegia in the Diaspora and Palestine', 102-103, 'Buildings have social meaning, expressing the goals, aspirations, and values of a community or society. These early synagogues were strikingly consistent. All express a high sense of community, especially in the arrangements

Galilean late antiquity have little to distinguish them in architectural form and style from contemporary public and civic structures.[92]

This is no less the case in the diaspora.[93] With regard to the impressive synagogue at Sardis,[94] this was probably the only sizeable building available to the Jewish community in the city, and it would be wrong to conclude that its only, or even primary, purpose was religious.[95] Here all the business, administrative, social and religious activities of the community would be conducted. Indeed a number of the synagogues from late antiquity were part of larger building complexes which reflect a wide range of uses.[96]

---

of the benches so that members — presumably male and female — were equally involved in the activities of the community ... The synagogues were plain, uncomplicated structures, with a primary emphasis on a "democratic" communal experience — the meeting space focused not on some function or office or liturgical feature but on the community itself. They were relatively unsophisticated'.

[92]R.A. Horsley, *Archaeology, History, and Society in Galilee*, 139.

[93]*Cf.* P. Richardson, 'Early Synagogues as Collegia in the Diaspora and Palestine', 104. For similar evidence from the rabbinic sources, *cf.* Z. Safrai, 'The Communal Functions of the Synagogue in the Land of Israel in the Rabbinic Period', in D. Urman & P.V.M. Flesher (eds.), *Ancient Synagogues: Historical Analysis and Archaeological Discovery* (Studia post-Biblica, 47; 2 vols.; Leiden: E.J. Brill, 1995) 181-204, esp. 203, 'the synagogue may be defined as the true community center, encompassing nearly the entire constellation of services that existed in the Jewish community. The officials of the synagogue were counted among the *parnasim* of the town and the line between synagogue and the communal leadership was blurred'.

[94]See page 113 above.

[95]A.T. Kraabel, 'The Synagogue at Sardis: Jews and Christians', in J.A. Overman & R.S. MacLennan (eds.), *Diaspora Jews and Judaism: Essays in Honor of, and in Dialogue with, A. Thomas Kraabel* (South Florida Studies in the History of Judaism, 41; Atlanta: Scholars Press, 1992) 228. He adds, *ad loc.*, 'A similar situation obtained even before this building existed: according to a Roman decree from the first century B.C.E., the Sardis Jews had been given their own "place" or "location" where decisions were made on community matters, religious and non-religious. This earlier meeting place could have been an entire building, an assembly hall, the forerunner of the mammoth synagogue described above; or it may have been nothing more than a designated space in some public building'. P. Richardson, 'Early Synagogues as Collegia in the Diaspora and Palestine', 103, writes, 'The range of functions that our earliest sources ascribed to these synagogues was fairly broad, and the physical remains matched the descriptions. No feature of early synagogues was modeled on the Jerusalem Temple, its character, divisions, or motifs'.

[96]L.V. Rutgers, *The Hidden Heritage of Diaspora Judaism*, 113-19.

Concerned, therefore, with the whole spectrum of community needs including 'political meetings, social gatherings, courts, schools, hostels, charity activities, slave manumissions,[97] meals (sacred or otherwise), and, of course, religious-liturgical functions',[98] the synagogue was collectively responsible for their widows and orphans and for maintaining the peace in multi-racial cities.[99] (This may have been important during a period of increasing hellenization when many Jews were less keen to emphasize their distinctiveness.)[100] Peter Richardson thus concludes:

> These early synagogues were community-oriented collegia, in which people gathered together (*synagein*) for multiple purposes as portrayed in the inscriptions and the documents of Josephus and Philo and reflected in the archaeological remains. These small communities ate meals together, observed Sabbaths and festivals, organized the collection of Temple tax dues, taught their children, arranged for the transmission of the first-fruits, heard civil law cases

---

[97]*Cf*. H.A. McKay, 'Ancient Synagogues: the Continuing Dialectic between two Major Views', 123; see *CIJ* 690 for a first-century A.D. example of manumission of a female slave in the prayer-house; and *Inscriptiones Graecae ad res Romanas pertinentes* I.881 for an A.D. 80 instance in the Crimea of a slave being manumitted in the prayer-house.

[98]L.I. Levine, 'The Nature and Origin of the Palestinian Synagogue Reconsidered', 430; also *idem*, 'The Synagogue in the Second Temple Period — Architectural and Social Interpretation' (in Hebrew), *Eretz Israel* 23 (1992) 331-44; E.M. Smallwood, *The Jews under Roman Rule from Pompey to Diocletian: a Study in Political Relations* (Studies in Judaism in Late Antiquity; Leiden: E.J. Brill, 1981) 133; the synagogues 'were responsible for the organization and administration of all aspects of the life of the community and not for a single aspect, religious worship, alone'; and J.T. Burtchaell, *From Synagogue to Church*, 204, 'The synagogue was an institution that, as it matured, took on lineaments which were political, liturgical, educational, financial, eleemosynary and ethnic'. *Cf*. also *y. Ber*. 2.5 [5d]; *y. Ta'an*. 4.5 [68b]; *y. Sanh*. 15.2 [26b]; *t. Sabb*. 16.22; *t. Ter*. 1.10; *y. Dem*. 3.1 [23b]; *Lev. Rab*. 6.2; *m. Mak*. 3.120.

[99]J.T. Burtchaell, *From Synagogue to Church*, 205.

[100]*Cf*. A.T. Kraabel, 'Unity and Diversity among Diaspora Synagogues', in J.A. Overman & R.S. MacLennan (eds.), *Diaspora Jews and Judaism: Essays in Honor of, and in Dialogue with, A. Thomas Kraabel* (South Florida Studies in the History of Judaism, 41; Atlanta: Scholars Press, 1992) 21, 'The Judaism of the synagogue communities of the Roman Diaspora is best understood, on the basis of the present evidence, as the grafting of a transformed biblical "exile" ideology onto a Greco-Roman form of social organization'.

and so on. When they had a building for these purposes — and not all did — the buildings were called *synagogai*.[101]

The highly significant Theodotus inscription, located near the Temple Mount in Jerusalem, cites a first-century synagogue as a hostel for Jewish travellers.[102] It may, indeed, have been the case that synagogues often offered shelter to travellers or the community's poor.[103] Although Paul Flesher argues that this inscription does not reflect a synagogue as a religious institution for *local* inhabitants of the city, it seems to me that his interpretation is unnecessarily limiting.[104] The inscription clearly cites reading the Torah and studying the commandments as the principal *raison d'être* of the synagogue, although it also served a number of other important community purposes.[105]

A closer look at synagogue life reveals a number of ways in which the Jewish community was adapting to the Graeco-Roman surrounding culture. Thomas Kraabel lists the following: dispensing with a priesthood and using a structure led by laymen; using a Greek translation of the Bible; developing a uniform model of community organization within the diaspora; adjusting to gentile life whilst maintaining essential cultic practices; and developing a new architecture for the meeting place.[106] We even see a distinction in authority and status between senior and more junior synagogues, with Jerusalem being the most senior.[107] This seems to reflect the Roman competition between cities and municipalities of differing status.[108] Further melding of the differences between synagogue and

---

[101]P. Richardson, 'Early Synagogues as Collegia in the Diaspora and Palestine', 103.

[102]This inscription has, inevitably, been the subject of considerable debate especially with regard to its date, which ranges from first to fourth century; *cf.* H.A. McKay, 'Ancient Synagogues: the Continuing Dialectic between two Major Views', 127-28; and R. Riesner, 'Synagogues in Jerusalem', 192-200.

[103]L.J. Hoppe, *The Synagogues and Churches of Ancient Palestine*, 17.

[104]P.V.M. Flesher, 'Palestinian Synagogues before 70 C.E.: a Review of the Evidence', 33-34.

[105]Z. Safrai, 'The Communal Functions of the Synagogue in the Land of Israel in the Rabbinic Period', in D. Urman & P.V.M. Flesher (eds.), *Ancient Synagogues: Historical Analysis and Archaeological Discovery* (Studia post-Biblica, 47; 2 vols.; Leiden: E.J. Brill, 1995) 182.

[106]A.T. Kraabel, 'Unity and Diversity among Diaspora Synagogues', 26.

[107]J.T. Burtchaell, *From Synagogue to Church*, 216-17.

[108]See the discussion above in chapter 3.

Graeco-Roman culture may be reflected in the evidence that the Jewish synagogues appeared to outsiders as *collegia*.[109]

Another way in which the Jewish synagogues may have reflected closely the mores of surrounding Graeco-Roman culture is witnessed to by the preponderance of epigraphic references to patronage. Luke records the account of a centurion having built a synagogue.[110] Patronage in the form of construction of buildings, we have seen, was widely the case in the Roman colonies, Graeco-Roman cities and voluntary associations of the Roman empire. It is not insignificant, therefore, that this practice pervaded also the Jewish synagogue communities. We shall consider this in more detail in the next section.

It may be argued that such adaptation was essential in the increasingly pluralist society of the Graeco-Roman world. Thomas Kraabel writes,

> the synagogue Judaism of the Roman Diaspora is best understood as the grafting of a biblical diaspora theology onto a Greco-Roman social organization. The shift to minority status in places outside the Homeland led to the abandonment of many elements of the ancestral religion, a new emphasis on others, and the adoption of the new environment's iconography, architecture, and organizational form.[111]

It has become clear that the Jewish communities of the ancient world were strongly influenced by the surrounding secular culture. Their synagogues fulfilled an important rôle in social, religious,

---

[109]P. Richardson, 'Early Synagogues as Collegia in the Diaspora and Palestine', 90-109.

[110]Lk 7:1-5.

[111]A.T. Kraabel, 'Unity and Diversity among Diaspora Synagogues', 30. *Cf.* also I. Levinskaya, *The Book of Acts in its Diaspora Setting*, 192, 'The elaborate structure and titulature of the synagogues echoed to a considerable extent the political organisation of Graeco-Roman cities'. J.T. Burtchaell, *From Synagogue to Church*, 208, writes, 'They cross-bred their ancestral polity with such international forms as seemed to be harmonious and, to boot, publicly appealing. There was no lack of models. The hellenistic and the Roman city = *polis*, the army = *stratia*, the sovereign's court and those of his subordinates and emissaries = *sunklêtos/philoi/-consilium*, ethnic enclaves = *politeumata*, civic associations = *thiasoi/eranoi/collegia*, settlements = *katoikiai*, villages = *kômai* all were familiar examples of social organizations to which Jewish communities everywhere could and did conform themselves, with rather parallel results in the homeland and in the dispersion'. But note the critique of Kraabel in L.V. Rutgers, *The Hidden Heritage of Diaspora Judaism*, 21.

educational and political spheres. There is limited literary and non-literary evidence that this applied as early as the first century in both Palestine and the diaspora, although this is not to deny that there was also diversity across different localities.[112] Some of the earliest Christian believers had been members of such synagogues, and this context may have contributed significantly to their conception of the nature of Christian communities.

IV. The Rôle and Function of Synagogue Leaders

We now turn to consider the rôle and function of leading officials within the ancient synagogue. Whereas there are a number of inscriptions which refer to synagogue officials, there is comparatively little primary source material which explains what their rôle was within the Jewish communities.[113] The evidence does, however, suggest a number of unexpected conclusions: it will become clear that '[t]he organization of the synagogue often paralleled that of non-Jewish communities and reminds one of Greco-Roman collegia or guilds';[114] and, again like much civic leadership, these positions were largely filled by laypeople, thus, 'as far as we can tell the leaders were not rabbis or priests'.[115] This view clearly is at odds with the older consensus which considered that 'the Pharisees before 70 CE and the rabbis after 70 CE [were] the leaders of the synagogue'.[116]

---

[112]L.M. White, *The Social Origins of Christian Architecture*, 78.

[113]P.W. van der Horst, *Ancient Jewish Epitaphs: an Introductory Survey of a Millennium of Jewish Funerary Epigraphy (300 BCE – 700 CE)* (Contributions to Biblical Exegesis and Theology, 2; Kampen: Kok, 1991) 89.

[114]L.H. Feldman, 'Diaspora Synagogues: New Light from Inscriptions and Papyri', 55.

[115]L.H. Feldman, 'Diaspora Synagogues: New Light from Inscriptions and Papyri', 55.

[116]S.J.D. Cohen, 'Were Pharisees and Rabbis the Leaders of Communal Prayer and Torah Study in Antiquity? The Evidence of the New Testament, Josephus, and the Church Fathers', in W.G. Dever and J.E. Wright (eds.), *The Echoes of Many Texts: Reflections on Jewish and Christian Traditions: Essays in Honor of Lou H. Silberman* (Brown Judaic Studies, 313; Atlanta: Scholars Press, 1997) 99, citing scholars such as George Foot Moore and Martin Hengel. S.J.D. Cohen, *op. cit.*, 102-14, discusses eight literary sources which might indicate 'Pharisaic or rabbinic leadership of communal prayer and/or Torah study'; none of which, he argues, provides conclusive proof; *cf.* also *op. cit.*, 112, 'The widely-held notion that Pharisees and rabbis led communal prayer and study seems to derive

A number of titles of leading synagogue officials emerge frequently in the epigraphic sources: *archisynagogos, archon, gerousiarch, prostates,* and father/mother of the synagogue. We shall look in turn at the evidence for these offices, and then draw together some common threads.

1. *The* archisynagogos

There are many literary references to the title *archisynagogos* or leader of the synagogue,[117] not least, for our period, in the New Testament itself.[118] The number of occurrences of the title, however, does not in itself assist us with elucidating the nature or function of this leader. It is further confused by the apparently interchangeable use of the titles *archon* and *archisynagogos* in the gospel sources.[119] Research into the titles and functions of officials from ancient Jewish synagogues has, until recently, focused almost exclusively on this available literary evidence.[120] The long-standing consensus is represented by Emil Schürer who suggested the *archisynagogos* was responsible for 'the arrangements of divine worship and the business of the synagogue as a whole'.[121]

---

ultimately from rabbinic literature, which conceives of the rabbis and their predecessors as *the* leaders of Judaism, indeed as synonymous with Judaism itself'.

[117]B.J. Brooten, *Women Leaders in the Ancient Synagogue,* 15-23.

[118]Mk 5:22, 35 (// Lk 8:49); 5:36, 38; Lk 13:14; Acts 13:15; 18:8, 17.

[119]*Cf.* Jairus as an *archisynagogos* (Mk 5:22, 35, 36, 38; Lk 8:49); and as an *archon* (Mt 9:18, 23; Lk 8:41); although T. Rajak & D. Noy, 'Archisynagogoi: Office, Title, and Social Status in the Greco-Jewish Synagogue', 85-86, argue that this inconsistency may simply have been because there was no formal *cursus honorum;* indeed '[o]ther notable features of honour-driven hierarchies are fluidity, inconsistency and elasticity in the number and formulation of titles: these are natural consequences of the valuing of honour over function'.

[120]L.I. Levine, 'Synagogue Officials: the Evidence from Caesarea and its Implications for Palestine and the Diaspora', in A. Raban and K.G. Holum (eds.), *Caesarea Maritima: a Retrospective after two Millennia* (Documenta et monumenta Orientis antiqui, 21; Leiden: E.J. Brill, 1996) 392-400, compares the different pictures emerging from the epigraphic and rabbinic sources, and from the Jewish communities in rural Palestine in contrast to the communities in urban Palestine or the diaspora.

[121]E. Schürer, *The History of the Jewish People in the Age of Jesus Christ,* II.434. *Cf.* also T. Rajak & D. Noy, 'Archisynagogoi: Office, Title, and Social Status in the Greco-Jewish Synagogue', 83, who are critical of the consensus which argues 'its

Recently available epigraphic evidence has considerably filled out our understanding of the status of the *archisynagogos*, however.[122] Tessa Rajak and David Noy argue that the title had a distinctly Jewish flavour, and yet it also 'evokes the Greco-Roman status distinctions in which standard civic inscriptions abound'.[123] In contrast to the perception that the *archisynagogos* was responsible for 'the sphere of the sacred', they gather evidence which suggests that the title was conferred as a recognition of the honour in which an individual was held.[124] Three applications of this title, in a number of inscriptions, support this conclusion. Examples are adduced where the title of *archisynagogos* is conferred as a permanent post. The phrase 'for life' (διὰ βίου or *perpetuus*) is occasionally added to the title.[125] Additionally, there are instances where the post of *archisynagogos* is kept within the same family in what may have been a hereditary honour.[126] Thirdly, there are examples of women and even child

---

highest and best-known leaders, by whom it was defined, were people who made prayer their business and who were assigned to the sphere of the sacred'.

[122]*Cf.* T. Rajak & D. Noy, '*Archisynagogoi*: Office, Title, and Social Status in the Greco-Jewish Synagogue', 75-93; L.I. Levine, 'Synagogue Officials: the Evidence from Caesarea and its Implications for Palestine and the Diaspora', 392-400; and L.H. Feldman, 'Diaspora Synagogues: New Light from Inscriptions and Papyri', 56-59. L.M. White, 'Synagogue and Society in Imperial Ostia: Archaeological and Epigraphic Evidence', 23-58, also notes a general oversight of epigraphic sources for our understanding of the ancient synagogue.

[123]T. Rajak & D. Noy, '*Archisynagogoi*: Office, Title, and Social Status in the Greco-Jewish Synagogue', 84.

[124]This is disputed by Williams who is unconvinced by the case made by Rajak and Noy; thus, M.H. Williams, 'The Structure of Roman Jewry Re-considered — Were the Synagogues of Ancient Rome entirely Homogeneous?', 135. Williams does not question, however, that the post of *archisynagogos* was accorded to those of very high status, albeit there were cultic duties attached to the rôle.

[125]*CIJ* 744, 'Most worthy Proutioses, *archisynagogos* for life (ὁ διὰ βίου), together with Bisinnia Demo, his wife, (constructed the building) from its foundation at his own expense'.

[126]*CIJ* 1404, which is dated by some to be earlier than A.D. 70 and located in Jerusalem, records an *archisynagogos* who is both the son and grandson of *archisynagogoi*, 'Theodotus, son of Vettenos, priest and archisynagogos, son of an archisynagogos and grandson of an archisynagogos, built this synagogue for purposes of reciting the Law and studying the commandments, and the hostel, chambers and water installations to provide for the needs of itinerants from abroad, and whose father, with the elders and Simonidus, founded the synagogue'. P.V.M. Flesher, 'Palestinian Synagogues before 70 C.E.: a Review of the Evidence', 33, is more circumspect about the date. *Cf.* also *CIJ* 584.

archisynagogoi.[127] Furthermore, there is no extant evidence that these posts were filled by annual election, or that there was a fixed number of such positions in a synagogue.[128]

We regularly see that the title of *archisynagogos* was conferred on those who were significant benefactors or who provided for the community out of their personal wealth,[129] and in support of this view there are a number of recorded instances where *archisynagogoi* are directly linked with the construction or renovation of the synagogue building, presumably funded at their personal expense.[130] This may indeed have been one of the principal responsibilities of such leaders, and could have limited such appointments to those who had the financial means to carry out these associated tasks.[131] If so, this closely parallels what we have seen to be the standard practice in

---

[127]*CIJ* 741 referring to a woman *archisynagogos* in the third century; and *CIJ* 587, which reports a three year old *archisynagogos* in the fifth century.

[128]L.H. Feldman, 'Diaspora Synagogues: New Light from Inscriptions and Papyri', 56.

[129]L.H. Feldman, 'Diaspora Synagogues: New Light from Inscriptions and Papyri', 58.

[130]*CIJ* 766 records an inscription from Acmonia, dated to the late first century, 'The building constructed by Julia Severa, Publius Tyrronios Klados, archisynagogos for life, and Lucius, son of Lucius, archisynagogos, and Popilios Zotikos, restored both out of their own funds and from the deposited sums, and they inscribed the walls and the ceilings, made secure the windows and made all the rest of the ornamentation, whom also the synagogue honoured with a gilded shield because of their virtuous disposition and both their good will and enthusiasm towards the synagogue', quoted from H.A. McKay, *Sabbath and Synagogue*, 222. This Julia Severa was a very significant person not just as regards the Jewish community. She was ἀρχιέρεια of the Imperial cult and also an agonothete.
Another inscription, dated A.D. 25 from Berenice, refers to a Marcus Tittius who was publicly honoured by the Jewish community. The public nature of this is noteworthy: 'On account of these things, it seemed good to the rulers and to the ethnic group of the Jews in Berenice both to honour him and crown him by name at every assembly and new moon with a crown of olive leaves and chaplet, and that the rulers should record the vote on a stele of Parian stone and place it in the most visible place in the amphitheatre. All votes white' (cited from H.A. McKay, *Sabbath and Synagogue*, 232). McKay, *op. cit.*, 240, suggests that this is proof that the Jewish community had civic power 'for they could place inscribed steles in the public amphitheatre'.

[131]L.H. Feldman, 'Diaspora Synagogues: New Light from Inscriptions and Papyri', 58, suggests 'Granted that the *archisynagogos* was wealthy, he served, in effect, as a patron of the Jewish community and, with his high-standing among both Jews and non-Jews, could act as a mediator for the Jewish community. He was consequently honored by the community'.

the secular world also.[132] Rajak and Noy conclude that the office of *archisynagogos* could only be achieved by those with financial means; '[b]eneficence played a major role in getting chosen and in the performance of the office itself',[133] and this 'echoing of the city's status system within the Jewish group represents at the very least an external acceptance within the group of civic political values'.[134]

Bernadette Brooten has written an influential monograph in which her main focus is to demonstrate the nature of the leadership exercised by women in the ancient synagogues.[135] In it she refers to three instances of epigraphic evidence where women are referred to as *archisynagogai*.[136] One of the most significant inscriptions in this regard is that of the wealthy female *archisynagogos*, Rufina. It is found on a marble plaque in Smyrna dating from the second or third century A.D., and refers to Rufina's construction of a tomb for the use of her slaves.

> Rufina, a Jewess, head of the synagogue, built this tomb for her freed slaves and the slaves raised in her house. No one else has the right to bury anyone (here). If someone should dare to do so, he or she will pay 1500 denars to the sacred treasury and 1000 denars to the Jewish people. A copy of this inscription has been placed in the (public) archives.[137]

It is apparent that we have here a wealthy woman who is holding the title of 'leader of the synagogue'. It is unclear, however, whether her official appointment in the synagogue was made in response to the honour in which she was held or the status which she had in the

---

[132]*CIJ* 738, possibly third century, refers to a woman benefactor, 'Tation, daughter of Straton, son of E(m)pedon, having built the house and the wall of the courtyard out of her own funds, gifted it to the Jews. The synagogue of the Jews honoured Tation, daughter of Straton, son of Empedon, by means of a golden crown and the privilege of sitting at the front'.

[133]*Cf.* also L.M. White, *The Social Origins of Christian Architecture*, 81.

[134]*Cf.* T. Rajak & D. Noy, '*Archisynagogoi*: Office, Title, and Social Status in the Greco-Jewish Synagogue', 84, 88-89; see also L.M. White, 'Synagogue and Society in Imperial Ostia', 26, 'One sees ... a diverse and socially active Jewish life in the Diaspora, where congregations hold the competing social and cultural pressures of self-definition and assimilation in creative tension'.

[135]B.J. Brooten, *Women Leaders in the Ancient Synagogue*.

[136]B.J. Brooten, *Women Leaders in the Ancient Synagogue*, 5-14.

[137]Translation from B.J. Brooten, *Women Leaders in the Ancient Synagogue*, 5.

community. What is clear is that she was in a position to offer patronage towards her dependants.

Although patronage is often associated with this senior post, it does not mean that the *archisynagogos* did not also have a leading rôle to play also in the public meeting. Indeed, the New Testament evidence would suggest that the leader of the synagogue 'performed an introductory function in the life and worship of their congregations'.[138] This is not inconsistent with the tasks of leading figures in the civic context, who were recognized on the basis of their wealth and status, were then appointed to these honoured posts, and fulfilled certain functions, including presiding at popular meetings.

2. *The* archon

Of all the synagogue titles, that of *archon* appears most commonly in the primary sources. It would appear that the position could be held by an individual on more than one occasion. It also appears, as with the *archisynagogos*, that some held the title as a permanent post. It is widely accepted now that this was first and foremost an honorary title.[139] As paralleled in non-Jewish communities in the Graeco-Roman world, however, honorary posts, even those held 'for life', were not devoid of public duties;[140] indeed there is some evidence that there were specific responsibilities, including involvement in some construction projects, associated with the position.[141] The difference between 'permanent' *archons* and others, consequently, could well have been one of status rather than function.

A small number of inscriptions which demonstrate that the title (or honour) was conferred upon children (of two, eight and twelve

---

[138]S. Applebaum, 'The Organization of the Jewish Communities in the Diaspora', in S. Safrai & M. Stern (eds.), *The Jewish People in the First Century: Historical Geography, Political History, Social, Cultural and Religious Life and Institutions* (Compendia Rerum Iudaicarum ad Novum Testamentum, 1; Assen: Van Gorcum, 1976) 493, who cites Acts 13:15 and 18:17 in support.

[139]P.W. van der Horst, *Ancient Jewish Epitaphs*, 89.

[140]M.H. Williams, 'The Structure of Roman Jewry Re-considered — Were the Synagogues of Ancient Rome entirely Homogeneous?', 133, citing A.H.M. Jones, *The Greek City from Alexander to Justinian* (Oxford: Oxford University Press, 1940) 175.

[141]S. Applebaum, 'The Organization of the Jewish Communities in the Diaspora', 495.

years old) and even upon those described as *archon* elect
(*mellarchontes*) — possibly also because their age precluded the full
title — support the notion that this was an honorary post.[142] In such
instances the title may well not have any associated function or
duties. Margaret Williams argues that such boys would have been
'given prominence and marked out for advancement by the
community because of the wealth and status of their fathers'.[143]

The title *archon* was occasionally further qualified, for example,
archon of all honour (πάσης τιμῆς) and *archon* extraordinaire (*alti
ordinis*). Both of these titles certainly give the suggestion that they
were closely related to the honour in which the holder of the office
was held. It has been noted above that many of the religious and
business associations of the early Roman empire adopted
organizational structures which were similar to those of the larger
civic institutions.[144] In this regard, Rajak and Noy suggest that 'the
archonship is an example of a civic title transferred to the Jewish
context'.[145]

It has become clear that there is 'a striking terminological
agreement between the political organization of cities in the
Hellenistic and Roman world and the organization of these
synagogues'.[146] Where there is little detail regarding the function of
these officials, the parallel with the language of the civic context may
well help us understand more clearly the type of esteem in which
they were held.

---

[142]H.J. Leon, *The Jews of Ancient Rome*, 179, concludes that 'the title of ἄρχων was
conferred on small children as a mark of honour, apparently in view of the
distinction of the family'. *Cf.* also P.W. van der Horst, *Ancient Jewish Epitaphs*, 89,
'The high status of some families ensured that their children would some day
become archons and by way of anticipation these (sometimes very young)
children were already designated as such'.

[143]M.H. Williams, 'The Structure of Roman Jewry Re-considered — Were the
Synagogues of Ancient Rome entirely Homogeneous?', 132.

[144]See the chapter above on 'Leadership in the Voluntary Associations'.

[145]T. Rajak & D. Noy, '*Archisynagogoi*: Office, Title, and Social Status in the Greco-
Jewish Synagogue', 84.

[146]*Cf.* P.W. van der Horst, *Ancient Jewish Epitaphs*, 96.

3. *The* gerousiarch

The office of *gerousiarch* is mentioned in twenty-four inscriptions, mostly from Rome.[147] It is assumed that the position of leader of the *gerousia*, or council of elders, was one of the senior administrative posts of the ancient synagogue. Philo refers to a *gerousia* in Alexandria and describes this group as 'the very rulers of the nation, the council of elders, who derived their very titles from the honour in which they were held and the offices which they filled'.[148] Predictably many of the inscriptions confirm that the office was given to older men.[149] This group of senior members of the local Jewish community was probably concerned with the financial aspects of communal life, together with maintenance of the community's buildings.[150] Once again, this closely parallels the pattern of highly honoured posts accorded to wealthy members of the local civic community.

4. *The Patron*

The title *prostates* carries, in some Greek contexts, the notion of patron and it has thus been assumed that such an individual would have been the patron of an ancient Jewish synagogue.[151] This title is also used as a description of 'the presiding officer of a religious association'. It has been noted that in one synagogue where we have a record of a *prostates* (Agrippesians), there is no comparable record of an *archisynagogos*. Although an argument drawn from silence, it may be that this reflects an example of variety in terminology across different synagogue communities. This particular community was

---

[147]*Cf.* L.H. Feldman, 'Diaspora Synagogues: New Light from Inscriptions and Papyri', 59; and P.W. van der Horst, *Ancient Jewish Epitaphs*, 91.

[148]Philo, *In Flaccum* 80.

[149]L.H. Feldman, 'Diaspora Synagogues: New Light from Inscriptions and Papyri', 59.

[150]M.H. Williams, 'The Structure of Roman Jewry Re-considered — Were the Synagogues of Ancient Rome entirely Homogeneous?', 134.

[151]The post may also have had associated legal responsibilities, where the patron would have been regarded as 'un défenseur et protecteur légal', J.B. Frey, *Corpus Inscriptionum Iudaicarum*, I.xcv.

one of the oldest in Rome, and it may be that the term *archisynagogos* did not become widely used until later.[152]

A number of inscriptions refer to a *pater* or *mater synagoges*.[153] Many scholars assume that this was an honorary post, equivalent to that of patron and granted to those with social prominence.[154] This again would closely follow widely adopted Graeco-Roman practice.[155] Those who fulfilled such positions were 'members of leading families', but such honorary posts did not necessarily exclude the holder from having associated administrative duties.[156]

5. Conclusions

It is significant that each of these terms occurs in the epigraphic sources. We have seen from the civic world that inscriptions were a widely-used means of publicly honouring leading figures or of drawing attention to benefactions. The Jewish communities seem to have adopted the same mechanism for rewarding their own leading figures and patrons.[157] Furthermore, in parallel with inscriptions from Graeco-Roman contexts, we see that women appear in their own right as generous patrons and leading figures of their (Jewish) communities. And, just as in the civic context honours can be given to those from other cities, so with the Jewish context there are those who are not themselves Jews who are honoured by the Jewish community for the contributions they make to that community.

Much debate has centred around whether these leading synagogue posts reflected the function of the office bearer, or were purely honorary; but these categories may be misleading and are

---

[152]M.H. Williams, 'The Structure of Roman Jewry Re-considered — Were the Synagogues of Ancient Rome entirely Homogeneous?', 138.

[153]*Cf.*, for example, *CIJ* 523.

[154]*Cf.*, for example, S. Applebaum, 'The Organization of the Jewish Communities in the Diaspora', 498.

[155]L.H. Feldman, 'Diaspora Synagogues: New Light from Inscriptions and Papyri', 61, argues that this post had 'no Jewish roots but apparently [was] taken over from pagan Hellenistic and especially Roman sources and particularly from mystery cults, where it denotes an initiate of an advanced degree'.

[156]B.J. Brooten, *Women Leaders in the Ancient Synagogue*, 72.

[157]*Cf.* the first-century A.D. instance of the Jewish community in Cyrene recognising the patronage of a benefactor, *Supplementum Epigraphicum Graecum* 16.931.

certainly used by scholars in different senses. It should be noted that in the civic context, posts were clearly offered on the basis of honour, and often in return for munificent benefactions. This meant that the qualifications for leading positions lay not in administrative or managerial skill, but in family background and financial liquidity. The posts may have been granted on the basis of honour, but that does not mean, in a different sense, that they were honorary, that is, sinecures with no related duties, responsibilities or useful function. The posts awarded to civic leaders or leaders of the *collegia*, although awarded on the basis of honour, did not exclude them from specific functions to fulfil, for example, the upkeep of roads and public buildings, the provision of entertainments or the presiding at sacrifices.

Louis Feldman notes from Jewish epigraphic evidence that 'of the fifty-three donor inscriptions from Asia Minor no fewer than nineteen, or 36 percent, identify the donors as women'.[158] Bernadette Brooten, in her monograph, investigates nineteen Greek and Latin inscriptions which appear to refer to women leaders ('head of synagogue', 'leader', 'elder', 'mother of synagogue', 'priestess').[159] She finds no evidence that supports the thesis that women had an office transferred to them by association with their husbands. She considers, rather, that such a view wrongly argues that theirs was purely an honorary office, in contrast to their male counterparts whose offices were functional. In support of this, it is rare that we see references to a wife bearing the same title as her husband.[160]

It would appear, however, that the issue is not simply whether titles given to leading synagogue officials were functional or honorific, but, whether functional or not, were they accorded on the basis of honour, respect, status and wealth, thus reflecting the current social norm in the wider Graeco-Roman society?[161] Clearly in those instances where young children were given a title, this implies no current function that they were capable of performing. This may, however, be similar to the situation in societies with inherited peerages: the honour is accorded to or inherited by the child who, in

---

[158]L.H. Feldman, 'Diaspora Synagogues: New Light from Inscriptions and Papyri', 51.
[159]B.J. Brooten, *Women Leaders in the Ancient Synagogue*, 1.
[160]P.R. Trebilco, *Jewish Communities in Asia Minor*, 104-26.
[161]For other questions which could be asked of Brooten, *cf.* L.V. Rutgers, *The Hidden Heritage of Diaspora Judaism*, 30-31.

due course, would be capable of carrying out the functions associated
with that title.

The nature of the evidence, reflecting the use of inscriptions so
common in the civic context, would argue that we have in the Jewish
synagogue setting a system where leading figures were recognized
and accorded positions of leadership on the basis of their status,
wealth and ability to act as patrons.[162] The position was clearly a
mark of the honour in which the person was held,[163] and was a
recognized means of rewarding their past generosity (and thereby
encouraging them to continue in their beneficence). Louis Feldman
points out, '[i]t is surely significant that of the forty *archisynagogoi*
mentioned in the thirty-two inscriptions, nine are presented as
donors, often of substantial gifts'.[164] There is notably little evidence
which describes the duties which they had to fulfil, but it is far from
necessary to conclude, given the broader Graeco-Roman context, that
these positions, whether for men or women, therefore had no related
functions or responsibilities.

The vagueness and variety of titles attributed to synagogue
leaders may best be explained by the vagueness of their rôle which
was first and foremost on the basis of honour. It is also noteworthy
that the number of individuals holding a given title in one synagogue
could vary.[165] This may be confirmed by Luke's imprecise description

---

[162]B.J. Brooten, *Women Leaders in the Ancient Synagogue*, 142, writes, 'In the
ancient world, philanthropy and power were also intimately connected with each
other, perhaps even more so than today, whereby it is not always clear whether
philanthropy was the prerequisite to holding office or vice versa'; also, *op. cit.*,
142, 'Without simplistically transferring the situation of the non-Jewish world
onto Judaism, it does seem reasonable to ask whether there might have been a
relationship between donations to and of synagogues and influence in the Jewish
community. This is not to ask whether synagogue functionaries attained their
titles through engaging in donative activity or whether maintaining the
synagogue building was one of their functions. Throughout the discussion of the
various titles, we have seen that while persons who bear titles often appear in
donative inscriptions, so too do those who bear none'.

[163]Philo speaks of members of the community sitting in order of rank or
seniority; Philo, *Life of Moses* 2.214-16; *De somniis* 2.127; *Hypothetica* 7.12-13.

[164]Cf. L.H. Feldman, 'Diaspora Synagogues: New Light from Inscriptions and
Papyri', 58.

[165]Williams' main contention is that one should not assume homogeneity
between the synagogues at Rome; M.H. Williams, 'The Structure of Roman Jewry
Re-considered — Were the Synagogues of Ancient Rome entirely
Homogeneous?', 136-37, 'Obviously the organisation of each will have been
similar, for the simple reason that there were certain basic functions, religious

of the leaders in the Jewish community in Rome as 'the leaders of the
Jews' (τοὺς ὄντας τῶν Ἰουδαίων πρώτους).[166]

It is clear, therefore, that, both in urban Palestine and the
diaspora, the Jews had adopted a number of practices characteristic
of Graeco-Roman culture, not least in the context of community
leadership. Lee Levine in a study on the archaeological evidence
regarding the synagogue at Caesarea notes that there was notable
Hellenistic influence on the Jewish community there. He also argues
that two very different perspectives on the ancient synagogue are
provided respectively by the rabbinic literature and the epigraphic
evidence. He writes,

> Inscriptions tell us much about the archisynagogue, *pater*, and *mater
> synagoges*, presbyter, *phrontistes* (treasurer or administrator), archon,
> and *grammateus*, all of which are connected in one way or another
> with the synagogue. Rabbinic literature, on the other hand, has
> preserved very little regarding most of these titles and, instead,
> offers a great deal of information about another set of synagogue
> officials: the *hazzan*, charity officers, teachers, and other religious
> functionaries, about whom the epigraphical corpus is to a large
> extent silent.[167]

Levine offers three possible grounds for this disparity which he
describes as internal-external, geographical and urban-rural.

One possibility is that the epigraphic sources are concerned
with the 'administrative and social running of the community',
whereas the rabbinic literature deals with the 'liturgical and
educational'. Thus they are each concerned with different spheres of
responsibility, internal and external.[168] Another pattern, although not
always consistent, is geographical. The picture as portrayed by the
rabbinic material complies more with the evidence in Jewish Palestine
whereas those terms found more commonly in the epigraphic sources

---

and social, which each community will have had to carry out. But we need not
assume that the officials to whom those tasks were entrusted, everywhere bore
the same titles'. Similarly, Burtchaell, although he does not rely on the epigraphic
evidence, prefers to speak of a typical synagogue, rather than a uniform or
universal one; J.T. Burtchaell, *From Synagogue to Church*, 202.

[166]Acts 28:17.

[167]L.I. Levine, 'Synagogue Officials', 394.

[168]L.I. Levine, 'Synagogue Officials', 395.

are diasporan in origin.[169] A further pattern which emerges is that those Palestinian inscriptions which are in Greek follow the trend in the diaspora, whereas the Hebrew and Aramaic inscriptions are closer to the picture which derives from rabbinic literature. The third possible explanation of the evidence is based on a distinction between the situation as found in rural communities and that which predominated in the cities.[170] The influence is clearly the process of assimilation of the Graeco-Roman culture. Levine concludes,

> Since each of the terms that appear in Greek synagogue inscriptions of the Diaspora and Palestine has its parallels in Greek and Roman institutions, it is certain that Jews exposed to the wider Hellenistic scene not only adopted its terminology, but undoubtedly something of its modes of organization and administration as well.[171]

V. The Status of Jews in Society

The comparison between the ways in which leading figures in the Graeco-Roman context and those in the Jewish communities were appointed, together with the suggestion that Jews were, deliberately or otherwise, pursuing assimilation with their surrounding culture, leads us also to consider the extent to which Jews succeeded in entering 'high' Graeco-Roman society, even if only at a local level.[172] On this issue there is no lack of literary and non-literary material

---

[169]L.I. Levine, 'Synagogue Officials', 395-96. One example of this is the more common practice in Palestine where synagogues were built by a communal effort, whereas in the diaspora, we expect more often to see this work carried out as a result of the benefaction of one individual.

[170]L.I. Levine, 'Synagogue Officials', 397, 'The assumption, then, might be that much of rabbinic literature (especially Tannaitic) together with the Palestinian epigraphical evidence (primarily the Hebrew and Aramaic inscriptions), derives primarily from the more rural segment of the population; Diaspora material, on the other hand, is basically reflective of an urban setting'.

[171]L.I. Levine, 'Synagogue Officials', 397.

[172]This issue is extensively handled in S. Applebaum, 'The Social and Economic Status of the Jews in the Diaspora', in S. Safrai & M. Stern (eds.), *The Jewish People in the First Century: Historical Geography, Political History, Social, Cultural and Religious Life and Institutions* (Compendia Rerum Iudaicarum ad Novum Testamentum, 2; Assen: Van Gorcum, 1976) 701-27; and more recently in J.M.G. Barclay, *Jews in the Mediterranean Diaspora;* and D.R. Edwards, *Religion and Power: Pagans, Jews, and Christians in the Greek East* (Oxford: Oxford University Press, 1996).

which supports the view that many Jews did indeed attain positions of influence in local civic contexts in the diaspora.

Egypt, with its long history of Jewish communities, had in the first century A.D. a significant number of Jews among its intellectual élite in the city of Alexandria. These had risen in prominence during the Ptolemaic period and had engineered for themselves a certain degree of political and legal autonomy within Alexandrian society.[173] Philo is the most well-known Alexandrian Jew who hailed from an aristocratic background. Philo's nephew, Tiberius Julius Alexander, also rose to prominence in Alexandrian society, however, and additionally gained influence elsewhere.[174] Beyond Egypt there are numerous instances of Jews rising to prominence in Graeco-Roman society, even to the extent of participation in non-Jewish cult.[175] With reference to an amphitheatre in Berenice, Cyrenaica,[176] John Barclay notes, 'It is certainly possible to imagine that the Jewish community in Berenice was sufficiently prominent and integrated into civic life to share in the use of major civic amenities'.[177] This may reflect a high Jewish profile in the civic arena together with a significant degree of assimilation in the political world of Cyrenaica.[178] The archaeological evidence in the Roman port of Ostia also reflects a thriving Jewish community during the second century.[179] It would seem evident that key Jewish figures were very highly placed socially and their influence within the city and to the benefit of the synagogue was significant.

In a recent monograph, Leonard Rutgers notes the extent to which Jewish communities had assimilated with the surrounding dominant culture:

> In view of the archaeological and epigraphical discoveries of the last century and a half, there can indeed no longer be any doubt that

---

[173]J.M.G. Barclay, *Jews in the Mediterranean Diaspora*, 19, 41-47.

[174]J.M.G. Barclay, *Jews in the Mediterranean Diaspora*, 105-106.

[175]J.M.G. Barclay, *Jews in the Mediterranean Diaspora*, 320-35.

[176]*Cf. Supplementum Epigraphicum Graecum* 16.931.

[177]J.M.G. Barclay, *Jews in the Mediterranean Diaspora*, 237, although he goes on to argue that there may even be the possibility that this 'amphitheatre' was an explicitly Jewish structure.

[178]J.M.G. Barclay, *Jews in the Mediterranean Diaspora*, 238.

[179]L.M. White, 'Synagogue and Society in Imperial Ostia: Archaeological and Epigraphic Evidence'; *cf.* also, with regard to social interaction with first-century society in Rome, P. Richardson, 'Augustan-Era Synagogues in Rome', 17-29.

Jews not only lived in the Diaspora, but that they also participated in the contemporary non-Jewish society intellectually, culturally, socially, and economically (and perhaps, to a very limited extent, even religiously).[180]

In contrast to some scholars, however, Rutgers questions whether this was because Jews felt at home in this surrounding culture. He suggests rather that such merging with Graeco-Roman society may have been in order to be better accepted by others in society.[181] This is reflected in their rising and falling fortunes at the hands of the Romans. At times they faced restrictions, expulsions and even persecution. At other times their traditions were explicitly accommodated under special legislation.[182]

VI. Conclusion

It has been noted through this chapter that the earlier scholarly consensus regarding the first-century synagogue was heavily reliant on the literary evidence of later rabbinic sources. More recently it has been found that the epigraphic evidence considerably enhances our understanding of the nature of the ancient synagogue. A picture then emerges which is not necessarily inconsistent with that of the first-century literary sources provided by Philo, Josephus and the New Testament writers.

When we turn to consider the nature of synagogue leadership, it is precisely in the epigraphic sources that we would expect to find a focus which highlights the honorific aspects of that structure.[183] At the same time, the succinct nature of inscriptions (many are brief epitaphs) means that they do not provide explanatory detail as to the function and rôle of these officials. It is necessary, therefore, to

---

[180]L.V. Rutgers, *The Hidden Heritage of Diaspora Judaism*, 20.

[181]L.V. Rutgers, *The Hidden Heritage of Diaspora Judaism*, 22.

[182]L.V. Rutgers, *The Hidden Heritage of Diaspora Judaism*, 189, 'The evidence ... warrants the conclusion that the constant factor in Roman policy towards the Jews was that there was no such constant factor'.

[183]M.H. Williams, 'The Structure of Roman Jewry Re-considered — Were the Synagogues of Ancient Rome entirely Homogeneous?', 130, 'Not only are there more inscriptions relating to the Jews of Rome than to any other Diasporan community but they are, thanks to Jewish copying of Roman epigraphic practices, unusually rich in the number of references they contain to public honours/offices (*honores*)'.

combine this epigraphic evidence with the record that we have known much longer from the literary sources, including, not least, the New Testament material itself. Our continuing caution must be neither to assume homogeneity throughout Palestine and the diaspora nor to use evidence from one site as proof of the prevailing situation in another area.

Notwithstanding this, there is sufficient evidence to show that Jews in the first century A.D. had filtered through to some of the highest echelons of local society in many parts of the diaspora. Many Jewish communities were adapting organizationally to patterns which closely mirrored those of Graeco-Roman civic institutions. In so doing they operated and benefited from the ubiquitous social values of honour and status, rather than reinforcing those values which may have been distinctive to their own culture.[184]

---

[184]M.H. Williams, 'The Structure of Roman Jewry Re-considered — Were the Synagogues of Ancient Rome entirely Homogeneous?', 132, suggests that the honorific titles adopted for the synagogue officials are 'directly borrowed from or modelled upon those found in the Graeco-Roman world', both civic and religious.

PART TWO

LEADERSHIP IN
THE CHRISTIAN COMMUNITY

CHAPTER 7

LEADERSHIP MODELS FOR THE CHRISTIAN COMMUNITY

I. Introduction

The earlier chapters of this book have sought to elucidate the nature of leadership within the cultural milieu in which the first converts to Christianity lived. In particular, a number of specific contexts which will have impinged at some level on the life of ordinary people in the first century were reviewed: the Graeco-Roman cities, the Roman colonies and cities, the voluntary associations, the family and household, and the Jewish synagogues. In all of these different contexts there were significant similarities in the way in which leadership was understood and exercised.

The *Graeco-Roman city* with its popular civic assembly (ἐκκλησία) practised a form of oligarchy in the first century in which the wealthy were elected to posts on the élitist executive council (βουλή). To all intents and purposes the traditional democracy of the classical city-state had been replaced by an authority vested in the hands of the local élites. These leaders sought to use their position to curry favour with the central power at Rome whilst at the same time enhancing their personal status and the honour in which they were held within the local civic community.

Similarly, in *Roman colonies and cities*, civic magistrates and other leading officials were elected on the basis of their status and wealth. The ability to participate fully in the round of expensive liturgies and the expectation of making generous benefactions were essential if one were to fulfil adequately a position of leadership in the civic sphere. These requirements were enshrined in the civic charters and constitutions.

At the less influential level of the Graeco-Roman *voluntary associations* some from the lower echelons of society found a context in which they also could exercise leadership. It is interesting that, by and large, these clubs adopted and operated a hierarchy of officials and a system of appointment that was remarkably similar to the patterns practised at the civic level. Here also, even among the less well-to-do, there were clear criteria for marking honour and showing due respect for recognized status.

The Roman *family*, revolving around the principle of near absolute authority (*patria potestas*) resting with the head of the household (*paterfamilias*) — an authority enshrined in law — had its own clear code of dutiful respect and honour (*pietas*) which each freeborn member of the family rightly accorded to the others. In the context of the family there were clear distinctions in social status between slave and free, and different expectations or forms of correction applied to each.[1]

There was also a significant similarity between the *Jewish synagogues* of the first century and other institutions in contemporary Graeco-Roman society, particularly in terms of the ways in which they honoured their leading and respected figures. Such people were recognized and honoured for their generosity towards and patronage of their local Jewish community. Time and again the key figures within the community were paraded in inscriptions as having made significant contributions from their own purse to the benefit of the synagogue. At this significant level, the degree of assimilation, in outward form at least, between the Jewish and the Graeco-Roman contexts is remarkable.

In each of these five contexts, therefore, it is clear that a similar economy of honour and status widely operated. Graeco-Roman society was highly stratified, and at all levels of community life people recognized and elevated the *status quo* whereby those of comparatively greater rank and social standing received due

---

[1]R.H. Finger, *Paul and the Roman House Churches* (Scottdale: Herald, 1993) 48.

deference and honour.[2] Since such principles of leadership permeated structures at so many different levels of community life, it is reasonable to assume that these dynamics will have impinged significantly on the lives of all in Graeco-Roman society of the first century, whether rich or poor, pagan or Christian.

It has also been clear in the preceding chapters, although in some ways less expected, that in each of these contexts the administrative, political and social aspects of leadership were inextricably linked with religious responsibilities and rituals. Where modern western societies traditionally draw a sharp distinction between the secular and the spiritual, between church and state, between the profane and the religious, in first-century Graeco-Roman society there was no such incongruity between these two spheres. Thus it has been demonstrated that in each of the areas which we have considered, leadership in the political, administrative or social realms also entailed leadership in a related religious dimension.

The ways in which local government in the traditional *Graeco-Roman city* was conducted reflected the underlying importance of the religious dimension. Official meetings of the civic council were marked by prayers, curses and sacrifices. The civic council was responsible for, indeed gave priority to, matters of civic religion. Additionally, it was the responsibility of the officials of the civic council to ensure that the guardian deities of the city were duly and appropriately honoured on all major civic occasions. Furthermore, both political and religious titles accrued to the same dominant élites.

In the *Roman colonies and cities*, significant emphasis was given in the civic founding charters to religious functions. The chief magistrates made appropriate oaths to the civic deities on assuming office, and were required to preside at public sacrifices. These leading figures were traditionally portrayed in the rich symbolism of the day thus emulating the emperor who was *pontifex maximus*. Time and again the epigraphic evidence demonstrates that amongst the most prestigious positions in local affairs were the priesthoods, whether of the high profile imperial cult or of other deities. Magistracies and civic priesthoods customarily were awarded to the same leading figures.

Many of the *voluntary associations* in the Graeco-Roman world also had a significant cultic focus. While some of the *collegia* were

---

[2]*Cf.* W.A. Meeks, *The Moral World of the First Christians* (Library of Early Christianity, 6; Philadelphia: Westminster Press, 1986) 32-38.

primarily religious associations and were named after a particular deity, other associations, based on a common trade or household, may have had a stronger social focus, but they would nonetheless carry out their formal, corporate activities within a pronounced religious context. On these occasions the expectation was similar to the practice at a civic level; that is, the leading figures would carry out a key presidential rôle.

In the context of the Roman *household*, domestic architecture confirms the view that there was a widespread preoccupation with the powerful influence which guardian deities had over the fortunes of a family. The head of the household had a primary rôle in ensuring that those gods associated with the family were appropriately honoured. Numerous inscriptions demonstrate the widespread concern to give due reverence to these powers, and it was at the least pragmatic that appropriate recognition and gratitude be accorded to these deities when the family's fortunes had been clearly favoured.

The epigraphic evidence significantly highlights that ancient Jewish *synagogues* had a corporate life which was considerably more embracing than simply the narrow confines of religious observance. This should not, however, occlude the importance of the religious dimension. Synagogues in Egypt were known as houses of prayer, and the reading and study of the Torah and the traditions of the fathers were a major focus of corporate activity.

It is thus clear that there were a number of key characteristics of leadership which permeated many levels of Graeco-Roman society. Pride of place was accorded on the basis of honour and wealth, rather than proven leadership skills, administrative ability or other qualifications. These respected leaders received public recognition. Additionally, as with many ancient societies, they did not separate into different spheres the religious and the political dimensions of their life. Those who were considered 'political' leaders were accorded also responsibility and a leading position in public religious observance.

II. The Influence of Graeco-Roman Society on Christian Communities

As we come to look in more detail at the early Christian communities, it is clear that these were not groups which were isolated from their surrounding culture. As with most Jews,

Christians continued to live, work and travel within the dominant culture of the Roman empire. We must, therefore, ask to what extent the new-found faith and practices of these first converts may have been influenced by or filtered through this ubiquitous Graeco-Roman culture in which these Christians continued to live and of which they continued to be a part. It is clear that on many levels there was assimilation of Graeco-Roman values and methods by Jews in the first century. The New Testament texts reveal that there were also elements of Graeco-Roman culture or principles of leadership which were assimilated by some Christians into the new Christian context.[3] In some cases, however, these practices were at odds with the expectations of the Christian gospel; and we are aware of them only through the corrective statements of New Testament writers.

The attitude of New Testament scholars to the degree of secular or pagan influence on early Christianity has long been the subject of disputation. In the wake of the Enlightenment and German rationalist philosophy, a dominant approach in Continental scholarship of the nineteenth century emerged arguing that early Christianity was at least subject to, and at most a product of, Greek influence. This perception was less widely adopted in Great Britain. The English scholar, Edwin Hatch, however, writing in the latter part of the nineteenth century, argued in a number of publications that there was widespread evidence that Greek ideas may have had a profound influence on the early church.[4] Although initially heavily criticized, it was this work of Edwin Hatch which set in motion a review in the English-speaking world of the extent to which early Christianity was also a Hellenistic phenomenon. The subsequent work of the History of Religion school focused further on the possible influence of hellenistic religions on the theology of early Christianity.[5] It is necessary, however, to draw a distinction between that work of the History of Religion school which argues that much Christian theology derived in a syncretistic way from other eastern religions, and, on the other hand, the seminal work of Edwin Hatch

---

[3]Many of these will be considered in chapter 8 below.

[4]*Cf.* E. Hatch, *The Organization of the Early Christian Churches* (London: Longmans, Green, 1901); and *idem, The Influence of Greek Ideas and Usages upon the Christian Church* (London: Williams and Norgate, 1890). See the analysis of S. Neill, *The Interpretation of the New Testament, 1861-1986* (2nd ed.; Oxford: Oxford University Press, 1988) 147-50.

[5]Associated in its early stages particularly with Richard Reitzenstein and Wilhelm Bousset.

which recognized that much of early Christianity came to expression within the context of a dominant Graeco-Roman culture. Many of those who first came to faith in Christ were previously immersed in such a social context. These people needed to assess the extent to which their Christian practices should differ from or be consistent with their background, much as first-century Jews in Palestine and the diaspora had variously struggled with these issues.[6] On some matters there were clear 'Christian' guidelines which had been taught, but which were not always observed. With regard to a number of these practices, Paul addresses, even seeks to redress, dominant cultural influences.[7] In a similar way the early Christians also faced a tension regarding the extent to which they should conform to Jewish cultural practices, such as circumcision, the refusal of food sacrificed to idols, and common table-fellowship. We gain an insight into these debates in, for example, Paul's letter to the Galatians, and the Lukan account of the Jerusalem Council.[8]

It is not necessary to assume, however, that all individuals within all early Christian communities were influenced by their surrounding culture in exactly the same way or to the same extent. There is no such consistency across Jewish synagogue communities throughout the diaspora. Neither is it necessary to assume that the early Christian communities were *directly dependent* for their models or structures of leadership on only one of the contexts outlined in the previous chapters.[9] It has been demonstrated that there were some elements of leadership and community organization common to many different contexts in first-century society. This ethos was so deeply engrained that explicit dependence by groups of Christians on exclusively one or another context would be difficult to demonstrate and unnecessary to maintain. In this chapter we shall consider the

---

[6]*Cf.* J.M.G. Barclay, *Jews in the Mediterranean Diaspora: from Alexander to Trajan (323 BCE-117 CE)* (Edinburgh: T. & T. Clark, 1996); and L.V. Rutgers, *The Hidden Heritage of Diaspora Judaism* (Contributions to Biblical Exegesis and Theology, 20; Leuven: Peeters, 1998).

[7]This will be the focus of chapter 8 below.

[8]*Cf.* Acts 15; Gal 2 in particular.

[9]W.L. Lane, 'Social Perspectives on Roman Christianity during the Formative Years from Nero to Nerva: Romans, Hebrews, *1 Clement*', in K.P. Donfried & P. Richardson (eds.), *Judaism and Christianity in First-Century Rome* (Grand Rapids: Eerdmans, 1998) 213, suggests that the household, synagogue and *collegia* may have each contributed to patterns of structure in the Christian house churches in Rome.

extent to which the early Christian communities may have been influenced by models of leadership derived from the range of contexts discussed in the preceding chapters.

III. The Christian Community and Cities

The civic context of local government will have been familiar to many of the earliest urban Christians. Local civic leadership had a high public profile in the city centres, witnessed to by the extensive and elaborate use of benefactions and inscriptions, and the frequent display of pomp and ceremony in public entertainments and religious functions.[10]

Robin Lane Fox,[11] who generally argues for the low social status of early Christians, nonetheless highlights instances in the book of Acts where Paul encounters high-ranking civic and provincial officials. One of the members of the Athenian civic council, the Areopagus, and presumably, therefore, a member of the local élites, is recorded as having become a convert following Paul's address to the Athenian civic body.[12] Luke also makes the suggestion that some of the asiarchs at Ephesus, 'men at the summit of provincial society', were considered to be friends of Paul.[13] Additionally Luke reports that, at Paphos, the seat of provincial administration on the island of Cyprus, Paul and Barnabas had an

---

[10]Contra R.H. Finger, Paul and the Roman House Churches, 46, who suggests that public life did not directly influence the 'day-to-day' living of first-century Christians in Rome.

[11]R. Lane Fox, Pagans and Christians (Harmondsworth: Viking, 1986) 293; cf. also, D.W.J. Gill, 'In Search of the Social Élite in the Corinthian Church', Tyndale Bulletin 44 (1993) 325-26; and D.R. Edwards, Religion and Power: Pagans, Jews, and Christians in the Greek East (Oxford: Oxford University Press, 1996) 42, 'The author of Acts portrays vividly the varied responses from local elites throughout the Greek East toward the new movement'.

[12]Acts 17:19-34.

[13]Acts 19:31. Cf. R.A. Kearsley, 'The Asiarchs', in D.W.J. Gill & C. Gempf (eds.), The Book of Acts in its Graeco-Roman Setting (The Book of Acts in its First Century Setting, 2; Grand Rapids: Eerdmans, 1994) 363-76, who refers to epigraphic evidence which challenges the view that Luke's reference to asiarchs was an anachronism. She writes, op. cit., 365, 'The wealth of honorific titles and high magistracies attributed to asiarchs in the inscriptions clearly demonstrates the asiarchs' importance in the cities and prosopographical studies reveal that their families intermarried extensively with other office-bearers, forming a close-knit social elite'.

audience with the Roman proconsul, Sergius Paulus, where there was the opportunity to preach the word of God.[14] This high-ranking official, we read, believed the message in response to the miracle he witnessed. Furthermore, in the Pauline correspondence we encounter a reference to what may have been a high-ranking civic official in the colony of Corinth, possibly an aedile, who was associated with the Christian community there.[15]

These Lukan and Pauline references reflect situations where at least a few early Christians are being portrayed as having had direct contact with leading civic and provincial officials.[16] This reinforces the view that the rarified world of the civic élites was not completely isolated from the general populace, but was rather dependent upon its continuing support. Public popularity was crucial to remaining in such high profile leadership positions, and many Christians, whether poor or more well-to-do, will have been abundantly aware of both imperial and local civic leadership. Accordingly, they would have seen in operation the dynamics which led to successful leadership.

It is apparent that, from earliest times, the widely adopted designation of the Christian communities was that of 'church' (ἐκκλησία), rather than 'synagogue'.[17] There were two significant contexts in which this word was used: it appears in the Septuagint as a designation of the assembly of the people of God, and, we have seen, it was also widely used in Graeco-Roman society, descriptive of the civic popular assembly. This choice of word may have raised problems for those Christians who, by virtue of their comparative wealth and social standing, were 'naturally' leaders in the local community and were expected to adopt similar positions of honour and respect within the Christian ἐκκλησία. Considerable influence was accorded to those within the secular ἐκκλησία who had the

---

[14]Acts 13:6-12.

[15]Rom 16:23; *cf.* the wider discussion of Erastus in chapter 8 below.

[16]*Cf.* also the contact between Christians in Thessalonica and the senior civic officials known as politarchs (Acts 17:6); G.H.R. Horsley, 'The Politarchs', in D.W.J. Gill & C. Gempf (eds.), *The Book of Acts in its Graeco-Roman Setting* (The Book of Acts in its First Century Setting, 2; Grand Rapids: Eerdmans, 1994) 419-31.

[17]*Cf.* the discussion in B.W. Winter, 'The Problem with "Church" for the Early Church', in D. Peterson & J. Pryor (eds.), *In the Fullness of Time: Biblical Studies in Honour of Archbishop Donald Robinson* (Lancer Books; Homebush West: Anzea, 1992) 203-17.

ability to persuade by means of oratory.[18] A similar emphasis on the importance of oratory underlies the approach of some from the Corinthian community, who were critical of Paul for his apparent lack of proficiency in this area.[19] It is clear that these early Christians were already operating with the expectation that the characteristics of leadership in the Christian ἐκκλησία should parallel those characteristics of leadership in the civic ἐκκλησία.[20]

IV. The Christian Community and Associations

A recent volume of conference papers has helpfully sought to assess the extent to which both the early Christian communities and the Jewish synagogues of the first century A.D. might also be classified among the associations of the Graeco-Roman world.[21] This is not presented as a new debate, but builds on arguments developed at the beginning of the twentieth century, although hotly contested, and which have been further developed in more recent decades.[22]

---

[18]C.P. Jones, *The Roman World of Dio Chrysostom* (Loeb Classical monographs; London: Harvard University Press, 1978) 9, writes, 'The spoken word was paramount: without oratory a Greek could not enter civic life, where he had to persuade his colleagues in the council or his inferiors in the assembly, to plead in courts of law, and to represent his city before governors and emperors'. This is reflected also by Plutarch, *Moralia* 792D, 'but the mental habit of public men — deliberation, wisdom, and justice, and, besides these, experience, which hits upon the proper moments and words and is the power that creates persuasion — is maintained by constantly speaking, acting, reasoning, and judging'; *cf.* also *op. cit.*, 801E; 802E; and Dio Chrysostom, *Orationes* 18.1-2; 24.3.

[19]*Cf.* the case presented, with regard to 1 Corinthians, by D. Litfin, *St. Paul's Theology of Proclamation: 1 Corinthians 1-4 and Greco-Roman Rhetoric* (SNTS Monograph Series, 79; Cambridge: Cambridge University Press, 1994); and, with regard to 2 Corinthians, by B.W. Winter, *Philo and Paul among the Sophists* (SNTS Monograph Series, 96; Cambridge: Cambridge University Press, 1997). This will be discussed in more detail in chapter 8 below.

[20]*Cf.* A.D. Clarke, *Secular and Christian Leadership in Corinth: a Socio-historical and Exegetical Study of 1 Corinthians 1-6* (Arbeiten zur Geschichte des antiken Judentums und des Urchristentums, 18; Leiden: E.J. Brill, 1993).

[21]J.S. Kloppenborg & S.G. Wilson (eds.), *Voluntary Associations in the Graeco-Roman World* (London: Routledge, 1996).

[22]*Cf.* the discussion in the following: W.A. Meeks, *The Moral World of the First Christians*, 113-14; J.S. Kloppenborg, 'Edwin Hatch, Churches and Collegia', in B.H. McLean (ed.), *Origins and Method: Towards a New Understanding of Judaism and Christianity* (JSNT Supplement Series, 86; Sheffield: JSOT Press, 1993) 212-38; and B.H. McLean, 'The Agrippinilla Inscription: Religious Associations and Early

In the Bampton Lectures of 1881, Edwin Hatch argued that some from Graeco-Roman society would have classified the Christian communities along with or at least analogous to the voluntary associations widely to be found in the Roman empire.[23] He wrote:

> to the eye of the outside observer they were in the same category as the associations which already existed. They had the same names for their meetings, and some of the same names for their officers. The basis of association, in the one case as the other, was the profession of a common religion.[24]

This perception of the early communities is reflected in some of the primary literary evidence. Certainly by the early second century

---

Church Formation', *op. cit.*, 239-70; W.O. McCready, 'Ecclesia and Voluntary Associations', in J.S. Kloppenborg & S.G. Wilson (eds.), *Voluntary Associations in the Graeco-Roman World* (London: Routledge, 1996) 59-73; P. Richardson, 'Early Synagogues as Collegia in the Diaspora and Palestine', *op. cit.*, 90-109; S. Walker-Ramisch, 'Associations and the Damascus Document: a Sociological Analysis', *op. cit.*, 128-45; P. Richardson & V. Heuchan, 'Jewish Voluntary Associations in Egypt and the Roles of Women', *op. cit.*, 226-51; and R.L. Wilken, 'Collegia, Philosophical Schools, and Theology', in S. Benko & J.J. O'Rourke (eds.), *Early Church History: the Roman Empire as the Setting of Primitive Christianity* (London: Oliphants, 1971) 268-91; R.H. Finger, *Paul and the Roman House Churches*, 51-53. W.O. McCready, *op. cit.*, 59-73, is careful to point out that there were also distinct differences between the early Christian communities and the contemporary associations, for example: the early churches were multi-dimensional in social status; the degree of intimacy in the churches was greater; the trans-local links were more developed; the familial structure of the groups was a major characteristic of the churches; additionally, members of the churches were expected to 'grow' and 'develop' in maturity.

[23]*Cf.* also W.O. McCready, 'Ecclesia and Voluntary Associations', 69, 'Early churches shared significant common features with voluntary associations, with the consequence that they were viewed as such, certainly by outsiders, and to a degree by insiders'.

[24]E. Hatch, *The Organization of the Early Christian Churches*, 30-31; *cf.* also *op. cit.*, 16-17, where he writes, 'with probably no single exception, the names of Christian institutions and Christian officers are shared by them in common with institutions and officers outside Christianity. It follows, from the mere conditions of the case, that those names were given by virtue of some resemblance in the Christian institutions and officers to institutions and officers which bore the same names already. ... If we find in the Roman Empire civil societies with organizations analogous to those of the Christian societies, civil officers with the same names and similar functions to those of ecclesiastical officers, the question arises and must be answered, whether the causes which are sufficient to account for them in the one case are not equally sufficient to account for them in the other'.

the Roman governor Pliny describes the Christian gatherings in the province of Bithynia as associations (*hetairiae*). In seeking advice from the emperor Trajan about how he should deal with the Christians in his province, Pliny describes their religious worship and common meal in ways which suggest strong affinities with the social and religious activities characteristic of life in the private voluntary associations. He describes,

> They had met regularly before dawn on a fixed day to chant verses alternately among themselves in honour of Christ as if to a god, and also to bind themselves by oath. ... After this ceremony it has been their custom to disperse and reassemble later to take food of an ordinary, harmless kind; but they had in fact given up this practice since my edict, issued on your instructions, which banned all political associations (*hetairiae*).[25]

It is also noteworthy in this excerpt from Pliny's correspondence that when Trajan advised a ban on the meeting of political clubs, it seems that the Christians were sufficiently regarded as such that they complied in some measure with this restriction.

The possibility of the Christian communities being perceived by outsiders as similar to the associations must have continued to be the case into the second and third centuries for Origen records and refutes Celsus' view that the Christian churches were really secretive associations;[26] and Tertullian writes at length trying to distance the Christian communities from the disruptive political clubs which were prevalent in his day. Closer similarities should be drawn, he insisted, with the non-activist, legalized societies of the time.[27]

A number of scholars in recent decades have continued to argue that, in some senses, these early Christian communities were analogous to the private associations widely seen in the early Roman empire.[28] The pre-A.D. 70 synagogues, both in Palestine and the

---

[25]Pliny, *Letters* 10.96.

[26]Origen, *Contra Celsum* 8.17, 'Celsus then proceeds to say that "we shrink from raising altars, statues, and temples; and this," he thinks, "has been agreed upon among us as the badge or distinctive mark of a secret and forbidden society"'.

[27]Tertullian, *Apologeticum* 38, 'Ought not Christians, therefore, to receive not merely a place among the law-tolerated societies, seeing they are not chargeable with any such crimes as are commonly dreaded from societies of the illicit class?'

[28]*Cf.* M. Sordi, *The Christians and the Roman Empire* (London: Routledge, 1994) 147; following E. Hatch, *The Organization of the Early Christian Churches*, 26-28, 38.

diaspora, are classified by some as *collegia*,[29] and it has even been suggested that the Philippian Christians explicitly modelled themselves on the organization and practices of the local associations in the colony.[30] At a number of points in the *Antiquities*, Josephus compares the gatherings of the Jewish synagogues with those of the clubs.[31] He notes, however, that Caesar's edict to forbid religious associations exempted the associations of the Jews. Also, Philo feels it necessary to highlight the ways in which the Jewish synagogues differed from the associations in Alexandria (which did not have a good reputation).[32] In particular, he frowns on the drunken excesses which were characteristic of many associations.[33] In comparing the Roman associations and the Pauline communities, Wayne Meeks writes:

> Both were small groups in which intensive face-to-face interactions were possible and encouraged. Membership was established by the free decision to associate rather than by birth, although factors of ethnic connections, rank, office, and profession were often important as the context for the associations. Both the Christian groups and the associations often incorporated persons who shared a common trade or craft. Both had a more or less important place for rituals and cultic activities. ... Both the private associations and the Christian

[29]P. Richardson, 'Early Synagogues as Collegia in the Diaspora and Palestine', 90-109; *cf.* also W.A. Meeks, *The First Urban Christians*, 32, '... the Jews in some cities were organized in the fashion of a *collegium*, with their single deity, officers and rules, private funds, and patrons'.

[30]W. Cotter, 'Our *Politeuma* is in Heaven: the Meaning of Philippians 3:17-21', in B.H. McLean (ed.), *Origins and Method: Towards a New Understanding of Judaism and Christianity* (JSNT Supplement Series, 86; Sheffield: JSOT Press, 1993) 92-104.

[31]T. Seland, 'Philo and the Clubs and Associations of Alexandria', in J.S. Kloppenborg & S.G. Wilson (eds.), *Voluntary Associations in the Graeco-Roman World* (London: Routledge, 1996) 115; Josephus, *Antiquities* 14.215-16, 259-60; *cf.* especially *op. cit.*, 14.235-36, 'Jewish citizens of ours have come to me and pointed out that from the earliest times they have had an association (σύνοδον) of their own in accordance with their native laws and a place of their own, in which they decide their affairs and controversies with one another; and upon their request that it be permitted them to do these things, I decided that they might be maintained, and permitted them so to do'.

[32]T. Seland, 'Philo and the Clubs and Associations of Alexandria', 115, 117.

[33]Philo, *De Ebrietate* 20-26.

> groups also depended to some extent on the beneficence of
> wealthier persons who acted as patrons ...[34]

Additionally, it has been argued, more specifically, that there was a
similarity between the early Christian communities and some of the
Graeco-Roman burial clubs (*collegium funeraticium* or *collegium
tenuiorum*).[35]

Whether or not it can be demonstrated that those in the early
Christian communities considered themselves tantamount to
members of a *collegium*, there is a strong likelihood that a significant
number of Christians may well have had professional experience of
such *collegia*.[36] Paul may have concentrated his mission amongst such
artisans. If this were so, then the system of honour and the structures
which prevailed in the associations would have been familiar to those
Christians who either had been or continued to be members of a
collegium. It is even suggested that the '(fictive) status elevation' so
fundamental to life in the *collegia* may have been at the root of some
of the social tensions exhibited by the Corinthian Christians and
tackled by Paul in 1 Corinthians.[37]

The Agrippinilla inscription of a family-based association may
provide one of the closer parallels to the Christian communities. This
group had a membership of over 400 people which suggests that it
included amongst its number some who were not strictly members of
the extended family. On the basis of this, Bradley McLean suggests
that 'the growth in the membership of family-based religious
associations was not limited by the size of private dwellings, nor by
consanguinity with the founding *familia*'.[38] This would be consistent
with Christian communities which were based around family units
and dwellings, and yet whose membership was not limited by either

---

[34]W.A. Meeks, *The First Urban Christians*, 78.

[35]R.L. Wilken, 'Collegia, Philosophical Schools, and Theology', 268-91. *Cf.* also,
with reference to the church in the early second century, R.L. Wilken, *The
Christians as the Romans Saw Them* (New Haven: Yale University Press, 1984) 31-
47.

[36]A.J. Malherbe, *Social Aspects of Early Christianity* (Baton Rouge: Louisiana State
University Press, 1977) 75.

[37]J.S. Kloppenborg, 'Edwin Hatch, Churches and Collegia', 222; and A.J.
Malherbe, *Social Aspects of Early Christianity*, 88-89.

[38]B.H. McLean, 'The Agrippinilla Inscription: Religious Associations and Early
Church Formation', 257.

of these factors.[39] A further similarity between the early Christian communities and the association of the Agrippinilla inscription is the socio-economic range within the group. In the Dionysiac cult this extended from the extremely powerful ex-proconsul Squilla Gallicanus, down to his many freedmen and slaves.[40] Turning to the Corinthian community, McLean suggests,

> the wealthier members of the Corinthian congregation probably offered to other members, especially social isolates such as new immigrants and newly manumitted slaves, various kinds of assistance. The structured social relationships in a church such as at Corinth, with its fictive kinship, probably facilitated opportunities for patronage, clientellism, employment and social and political mobility.[41]

Neither the Graeco-Roman associations nor the early Christian communities had a uniform organizational structure;[42] rather, there were local differences in leadership titles and administrative structures. Whether dedicated to Dionysos, Christ or some other god, these religious associations in the stratified world of Roman society provided the opportunity for at least limited improvement in one's status in the world.[43]

Elisabeth Schüssler Fiorenza argues with regard to the voluntary associations that '[o]n the whole, their social structures were socially less diversified and more homogeneous than those of the Christian groups'.[44] She further suggests that some religious clubs and associations 'were reserved specifically to persons of high status,

---

[39]B.H. McLean, 'The Agrippinilla Inscription: Religious Associations and Early Church Formation', 257.

[40]B.H. McLean, 'The Agrippinilla Inscription: Religious Associations and Early Church Formation', 257, concludes, 'The Agrippinilla association offers one such example of overlapping social networks in which social relations are structured, loyalties reinforced and social mobility, clientellism, patronage and political support fostered'.

[41]B.H. McLean, 'The Agrippinilla Inscription: Religious Associations and Early Church Formation', 269.

[42]J.S. Kloppenborg, 'Edwin Hatch, Churches and Collegia', 232.

[43]B.H. McLean, 'The Agrippinilla Inscription: Religious Associations and Early Church Formation', 256. He continues, *op. cit.*, 257, with regard to the slaves in the Agrippinilla association that 'their lowly status in the hierarchical Roman society was relativized by their membership in this religious society'.

[44]E.S. Fiorenza, *In Memory of Her: a Feminist Theological Reconstruction of Christian Origins* (2nd ed.; London: SCM Press, 1995) 180.

to certain ethnic groups, to lower-class people, or to women alone'.[45] In consequence, it is suggested that the early Christian communities were structurally closer to voluntary associations than to the patriarchal, familial model of the household. The erroneous conclusion is then carried forward that '[t]hose who joined the Christian house church joined it as an association of equals'.[46] In her reconstruction, the early Christian communities were essentially egalitarian where 'leadership' could, in theory, be exercised by any member regardless of social status. In principle this may have been the case, although in actuality there is more evidence to suggest that social and economic distinctives were all too apparent in the Christian communities. Fiorenza becomes aware of such disparity when she concedes that, within this so-called egalitarianism, it was also possible for wealthier members of a Christian community to exercise patronal influence within and on behalf of the community with which they were associated. It would seem that at the same time the place of women in the Christian communities benefited from the non-patriarchal egalitarianism, and yet the structure of patronage allowed women (and presumably men) to exercise an influence which was in direct proportion to their social status.[47]

There is continuing debate as to the degree to which either early Christian or Jewish communities should strictly be seen as associations. It is clear, however, that Christian communities later appeared to some outsiders as *collegia*; and it is not unreasonable that some of the earliest Christians were formerly, or continued to be, members of associations or at least familiar with such groups. Both of these allow the possibility of direct or indirect influence, although it must for now remain unproven whether Christian communities either viewed themselves as associations,[48] or were expressly

---

[45]E.S. Fiorenza, *In Memory of Her*, 180.

[46]E.S. Fiorenza, *In Memory of Her*, 181.

[47]E.S. Fiorenza, *In Memory of Her*, 181, wrongly asserts that there is 'no evidence that the Christian community bestowed particular honors and recognitions on its rich members'. This view is redressed by the situation which prevailed at the time of Paul's writing to the Corinthians; *cf.* A.D. Clarke, *Secular and Christian Leadership in Corinth*.

[48]They did not, for example, adopt for themselves any of the more common terms used by the associations, for example, θίασος or ἔρανος. Very few inscriptions refer to voluntary associations by the term ἐκκλησία, but J.S. Kloppenborg, 'Edwin Hatch, Churches and Collegia', 231, does, nonetheless, argue in categorical terms that 'In the environment of Greek cities, the term

modelled on such social and religious groups.[49] There are some significant differences, however, between Graeco-Roman associations and the early Christian communities. In particular, 'there is little evidence that [the Graeco-Roman associations] undertook to establish or reform moral rules or to instruct their adherents in ethical principles or rules for behavior'.[50]

V. The Christian Community and Families and Households

Many of the early Christians in Rome would have been:

> first-generation believers who were raised in pagan homes. Others were slaves in pagan households. Still others were Jewish converts who brought with them Jewish family concepts, influenced by Hellenistic and Roman beliefs.[51]

The Roman *familia* was so integral to Graeco-Roman society that members of the early church were bound to have been influenced by this powerful institution.[52] The family was a metaphor which was occasionally applied to the church.[53] It is certainly significant that the

---

would almost certainly be understood (by all involved) as one of the names for a voluntary association'.

[49]J.S. Kloppenborg, 'Edwin Hatch, Churches and Collegia', 231, 'there was a broad spectrum of forms of *collegia*, broad enough that most of the particularities seen in Pauline churches could fit comfortably within that spectrum'.

[50]W.A. Meeks, *The Moral World of the First Christians*, 114.

[51]J.S. Jeffers, 'Jewish and Christian Families in First-Century Rome', in K.P. Donfried & P. Richardson (eds.), *Judaism and Christianity in First-Century Rome* (Grand Rapids: Eerdmans, 1998) 150; see also *op. cit.*, 128-29, where he similarly points out that many first-century Christians in Rome will have had a pagan background, and those with a Jewish background will have anyway been strongly affected by surrounding Graeco-Roman culture; consequently, study of the dynamics of the pagan Roman family may shed some light on life in Christian families.

[52]*Cf.* W.L. Lane, 'Social Perspectives on Roman Christianity during the Formative Years from Nero to Nerva: Romans, Hebrews, 1 *Clement*', 208, 'The early church in Rome could not exist in such a milieu without something of that environment leaving its mark upon it'.

[53]Note especially the metaphor 'household of faith' in Gal 6:10 and 'household of God' in Eph 2:19; 1 Tim 3:15; and 1 Pet 4:17; *cf.* also the extensive discussion in D.C. Verner, *The Household of God: the Social World of the Pastoral Epistles* (Society of Biblical Literature Dissertation Series, 71; Chico: Scholars Press, 1983); and P.F.

context for the meetings of the early Christian communities was normally within a home.[54] The household unit was also one repeatedly referred to in New Testament texts. The conversion of the *paterfamilias* proved to be crucial in the spread of the early church.[55] Thus,

> the family-oriented society in which primitive Christianity took root provides the framework for what Acts tells us about the conversion of households. It is no surprise to find that the growth of the Christian faith ran on family lines in a family-oriented society.[56]

We have already seen that the Roman household provided a context for religious observance and the daily worship of familial deities.[57]

Esler, 'Imagery and Identity in Gal 5:13-6:10', in H. Moxnes (ed.), *Constructing Early Christian Families: Family as Social Reality and Metaphor* (London: Routledge, 1997) 121-49. A.J. Malherbe, 'God's New Family in Thessalonica', in L.M. White & O.L. Yarbrough (eds.), *The Social World of the First Christians: Essays in Honor of Wayne A. Meeks* (Minneapolis: Fortress Press, 1995) 116-25, argues that even though Paul does not explicitly describe the church as a family in 1 Thess, it is 'family' terminology which comes to the fore.

[54]*Cf.*, for example, Acts 2:46; 5:42; 16:15, 32, 34; 20:20; Rom 16:5; 1 Cor 16:19; Col 4:15; Phlm 2; also the wider discussion in V. Branick, *The House Church in the Writings of Paul* (Zaccheus Studies, New Testament; Wilmington: Michael Glazier, 1989); and W.A. Meeks, *The Moral World of the First Christians*, 110-13. This predominant practice of meeting in the home seems to have continued into the fourth century; *cf.* B.B. Blue, *In Public and in Private: the Role of the House Church in Early Christianity* (PhD dissertation; Aberdeen: Aberdeen University, 1989) 1; and the discovery of a Christian meeting place in a home in the third-century town of Dura-Europos.

[55]K.O. Sandnes, 'Equality within Patriarchal Structures: Some New Testament Perspectives on the Christian Fellowship as a Brother- or Sisterhood and a Family', in H. Moxnes (ed.), *Constructing Early Christian Families: Family as Social Reality and Metaphor* (London: Routledge, 1997) 152-53; *cf.* also L.M. White, 'Visualizing the "Real" World of Acts 16: Toward Construction of a Social Index', in L.M. White & O.L. Yarbrough (eds.), *The Social World of the First Christians: Essays in Honor of Wayne A. Meeks* (Minneapolis: Fortress Press, 1995) 258-59.

[56]K.O. Sandnes, 'Equality within Patriarchal Structures: Some New Testament Perspectives on the Christian Fellowship as a Brother- or Sisterhood and a Family', 153. *Cf.*, for example, the conversion of households in, for example, Acts 10:2; 11:14; 16:15, 31, 34; 18:8; 1 Cor 1:16; 16:15. *Cf.* also the following references to the unit of the household with relation to the Christian church: 1 Tim 5:14; 2 Tim 1:16; 3:6; 4:19.

[57]J.M.G. Barclay, 'The Family as the Bearer of Religion in Judaism and Early Christianity', in H. Moxnes (ed.), *Constructing Early Christian Families: Family as Social Reality and Metaphor* (London: Routledge, 1997) 73, points out, however, that the message of Christianity encouraged a significant break with strong

For these reasons the family may well have provided for some the most appropriate context for considering the nature and pattern for organising the local Christian community and defining its leadership.

The Christian homes which first hosted gatherings of the church provided both a location and a social context for these communities.[58] The family home could also be the context for preaching and teaching in the Graeco-Roman world, and Paul took advantage of this.[59] Philip Esler rightly points out,

> It is essential to note that these households were functioning families, containing family members and possibly slaves and visiting clients, not just the shells of houses taken over for meetings of the congregation. As a result, the congregations were actually swept up into the social realities, the roles, values and institutions, of particular families in the cities in which they were located.[60]

It might, therefore, be asked to what extent the context of the household influenced the dynamic of leadership within these early churches. For instance, was the authority which was customarily invested within the head of the household also dominant in the Christian congregation which met in his house?[61] Elisabeth Schüssler Fiorenza argues that, whereas in the public sphere men more generally had a dominant rôle, in the private sphere of the household the rôle of women was less-constrained. The unnecessary inference is

---

ancestral traditions. This may well lie behind the statement in 1 Pet 1:18 where his readers are reminded of the fact that Christ has redeemed them 'from the futile ways inherited from your ancestors'.

[58] A seminal article on this subject is that of F.V. Filson, 'The Significance of the Early House Churches', *Journal of Biblical Literature* 58 (1939) 105-12; more recent work on this subject includes, H.-J. Klauck, *Hausgemeinde und Hauskirche im frühen Christentum* (Stuttgarter Bibelstudien, 103; Stuttgart: Verlag Katholisches Bibelwerk, 1981); D.C. Verner, *The Household of God*; B.B. Blue, *In Public and in Private*; and L.M. White, *The Social Origins of Christian Architecture: Building God's House in the Roman World: Architectural Adaptation among Pagans, Jews and Christians* (Harvard Theological Studies, 42; Valley Forge: Trinity Press International, 1996).

[59] S.K. Stowers, 'Social Status, Public Speaking and Private Teaching: the Circumstances of Paul's Preaching Activity', *Novum Testamentum* 26 (1984) 64-73.

[60] P.F. Esler, 'Imagery and Identity in Gal 5:13-6:10', 135.

[61] *Cf.* H. Moxnes, 'What is Family?: Problems Constructing Early Christian Families', in H. Moxnes (ed.), *Constructing Early Christian Families: Family as Social Reality and Metaphor* (London: Routledge, 1997) 25, suggests that this is expressed in a number of places in the Pauline corpus.

then drawn, however, that therefore the woman or *'domina* of the house, where the ecclesia gathered, had primary responsibility for the community *and* its gathering'.[62] Evidence can certainly be adduced which suggests that in cases where women enjoyed prominent social status they also carried a prominent rôle within the Christian community which met in their house, but this is not to argue that men, for the most part, either in the Graeco-Roman or Christian contexts, were subordinate to women in matters of authority in the household.

The metaphor of the father was widely adopted. Paul viewed himself as an 'official emissary of the heavenly *paterfamilias'*,[63] and, in Ephesians, God himself is regarded as the supreme father (πατριά) over all.[64] Paul certainly refers to himself as the father of the Corinthian community,[65] but he also draws attention to other significant householders in that community who were leading figures, for example, Stephanas — a man wealthy enough, it would seem, to have slaves.[66] With regard to the Pastoral Epistles, leaders of the church are seen to be those who can manage their own households appropriately.[67] Indeed, the authority of the overseers 'was viewed as analogous to the householder's governing of his

---

[62]E.S. Fiorenza, *In Memory of Her*, 176.

[63]S.J. Joubert, 'Managing the Household: Paul as *paterfamilias* of the Christian Household Group in Corinth', in P.F. Esler (ed.), *Modelling Early Christianity: Social-scientific Studies of the New Testament in its Context* (London: Routledge, 1995) 217. *Cf.* also G. Theissen, *The Social Setting of Pauline Christianity: Essays on Corinth* (Philadelphia: Fortress Press, 1982) 107-109, who coined the term love-patriarchalism to describe Paul's ethic for Christian relationships; but note also the critique by D.G. Horrell, *The Social Ethos of the Corinthian Correspondence: Interests and Ideology from 1 Corinthians to 1 Clement* (Studies of the New Testament and its World; Edinburgh: T. & T. Clark, 1996) 126-31.

[64]Eph 3:14-15; *cf.* J.M.G. Barclay, 'The Family as the Bearer of Religion in Judaism and Early Christianity', 76.

[65]1 Cor 4:15. *Cf.* S.J. Joubert, 'Managing the Household: Paul as *paterfamilias* of the Christian Household Group in Corinth', 222; although he may have over-argued his case here in terms of the absolute obedience which Paul felt he could command of the Corinthian believers.

[66]1 Cor 1:16; 16:15-18. With regard to the social standing of Stephanas, see my article, A.D. Clarke, 'Refresh the Hearts of the Saints': a Unique Pauline Context?', *Tyndale Bulletin* 47 (1996) 287-89.

[67]1 Tim 3:4-5, 12. V. Branick, *The House Church in the Writings of Paul*, 21, argues that these references in the Pastoral Epistles suggest that the offices of overseer and elder were attributed to those who had demonstrated their ability as *paterfamilias*.

household'.[68] The issue of authority within the family — whether between husband and wife, between father and child, between master and slave, or even between patron and client — is one which receives repeated attention by Paul.[69] With regard to the house churches in Rome, William Lane concludes that,

> the host who possessed the resources and initiative to invite the church into his or her home assumed major leadership responsibilities deriving from the patronage offered. These included important administrative tasks, such as the provision of the common meals of the community, the extension of hospitality to traveling missionaries and other Christians, the representation of the community outside the domestic setting, in addition to pastoral oversight and governance. ... those who acted as patrons were in some sense also involved in governance of the community. A position of authority emerged out of the benefits that individuals of relatively higher wealth and social status could confer upon the community.[70]

It may also be significant that Paul found it necessary to focus in his correspondence on a number of 'family-related' issues.[71] For example, he urges those in the Thessalonian community to have marriages 'not like the Gentiles';[72] he also repeatedly refers, but more in a metaphorical sense, to the image of inheritance within the family;[73] and, furthermore, a number of New Testament writers deal at length with the situation facing slaves and they include specific instructions also for those Christians who were masters.[74] The socio-economic situation reflected in the Pauline correspondence makes it

---

[68]D.C. Verner, *The Household of God*, 160. Verner goes on to say, 'although the leaders of the church may not have been on the same social level as the members of their municipal aristocracy, they shared the same aristocratic social aspirations within a smaller sphere'.

[69]H. Moxnes, 'What is Family?: Problems Constructing Early Christian Families', 26.

[70]W.L. Lane, 'Social Perspectives on Roman Christianity during the Formative Years from Nero to Nerva: Romans, Hebrews, *1 Clement*', 211-12.

[71]F.V. Filson, 'The Significance of the Early House Churches', 105-12, argued that the household context for the early Christian churches may explain the significant interest in family issues expressed in early Christian writings.

[72]1 Thess 4:4-5.

[73]H. Moxnes, 'What is Family?: Problems Constructing Early Christian Families', 34.

[74]*Cf.* 1 Cor 7:21-23; Eph 6:5-9; Col 3:22; 4:1; 1 Tim 6:1-2; Tit 2:9; Phlm; 1 Pet 2:18.

reasonable to assume that a number of Christians in the early communities were wealthy enough to own slaves, whilst others in the same communities were themselves slaves. If the early Christian communities were based in houses where the *paterfamilias* would have been expected to hold sway, then there may also have been expectations upon slaves to adopt an appropriate place in comparison to the freeborn children of the household.

Given this social context, it is not unreasonable that there would have been considerable pressures and tensions on families where Christianity introduced a different set of values to those more commonly adopted in the surrounding culture.[75] Both Paul and Peter are aware, for example, of the possibility that some early Christian families were mixed, with only one believing partner, or where only a slave within a household was converted.[76] The situation which underlies Paul's correspondence with Philemon is one where the apostle seeks to impose a Christian perspective on what may have been a common first-century situation, that of a master seeking the return of his runaway slave.[77] Paul begins to interact with such tensions in his outlining of a revised set of household codes.[78]

The extent to which New Testament writers used the term 'brethren' may also be significant.[79] Karl Otto Sandnes argues that 'in

---

[75]J.M.G. Barclay, 'The Family as the Bearer of Religion in Judaism and Early Christianity', 73.

[76]1 Cor 7:12-17; 1 Pet 2:18-19; 3:1-6. *Cf.* K.O. Sandnes, 'Equality within Patriarchal Structures: Some New Testament Perspectives on the Christian Fellowship as a Brother- or Sisterhood and a Family', 154.

[77]The way in which the situation is to be reconstructed continues to be the subject of debate; *cf.* the helpful summary in K.P. Donfried & I.H. Marshall, *The Theology of the Shorter Pauline Letters* (Cambridge: Cambridge University Press, 1993) 177-79. For discussion of Paul's urging towards egalitarianism, with specific reference to the Onesimus/Philemon situation *cf.* K.O. Sandnes, 'Equality within Patriarchal Structures: Some New Testament Perspectives on the Christian Fellowship as a Brother- or Sisterhood and a Family', 150-65. He argues that Paul wished to modify the household model and maintain an element of equality; thus, *op. cit.*, 163, 'The autonomy of the paterfamilias in dealing with Onesimus is questioned. Thus the authority of Philemon is modified, although not denied or abandoned. A new relationship based on equality is in the making'.

[78]J.M.G. Barclay, 'The Family as the Bearer of Religion in Judaism and Early Christianity', 76.

[79]*Cf.* however the debate as to what 'brother' here means. K.O. Sandnes, 'Equality within Patriarchal Structures: Some New Testament Perspectives on the

the family terms of the New Testament, old and new structures come together. There is a convergence of household and brotherhood structures'.[80] This view is presented in contrast to that of Elisabeth Schüssler Fiorenza and Klaus Schäfer who argue rather that the earliest communities were more egalitarian in structure. The hierarchical pattern reflected by ancient households, they argue, was a later development.

VI. The Christian Community and the Synagogue

An encyclopaedic study by James Burtchaell of the organizational continuity between the ancient synagogues and early Christian churches concludes that there was 'a plausible continuity in community organization from the hellenistic Jewish synagogue to the early Christian church'.[81] He argues furthermore that functionally these two institutions were alike; that is, the range of community activities in which both synagogue and church engaged were similar.[82] The connection is predictably said to be,

> that the Jews who formed the archetypical churches followed the basic structural lineaments of community organization already familiar to them in the synagogue. This would not be unnatural, since it was synagogues they thought they were forming — at first.[83]

This is far from saying, however, that these two communities were identical in either organization or the titles adopted for official leaders; indeed, he points out that there were notable differences.[84] Burtchaell, however, overemphasizes the distinctions between Jewish synagogues and contemporary Graeco-Roman institutions,[85] and he,

---

Christian Fellowship as a Brother- or Sisterhood and a Family', 150-51, provides a brief summary of the key positions.
[80]K.O. Sandnes, 'Equality within Patriarchal Structures: Some New Testament Perspectives on the Christian Fellowship as a Brother- or Sisterhood and a Family', 151.
[81]J.T. Burtchaell, *From Synagogue to Church: Public Services and Offices in the Earliest Christian Communities* (Cambridge: Cambridge University Press, 1992) 339.
[82]J.T. Burtchaell, *From Synagogue to Church*, 340.
[83]J.T. Burtchaell, *From Synagogue to Church*, 340.
[84]J.T. Burtchaell, *From Synagogue to Church*, 340-48.
[85]J.T. Burtchaell, *From Synagogue to Church*, 265-67.

consequently, overargues his case that, 'the predominant model for social organization in the synagogue, during the period when it could have been influential upon the founding generation of Christians, was inveterately Jewish'.[86] I have argued, rather, that Jewish synagogue organization was significantly influenced by the surrounding Graeco-Roman culture, albeit maintaining some distinction.[87]

Our principal difficulty in assessing the influence of synagogues upon early Christian communities concerns defining the point at which Christian communities clearly saw themselves as distinct from Jewish groups.[88] Initially, Christianity is rightly viewed as a Jewish movement. We should note that a number of secular authorities viewed Christians, at first, indistinguishably from Jews.[89] The period that we are most concerned with here, however, is that covered by Paul's correspondence with a number of urban churches. These churches comprised both Jews and gentiles, but by this time they were already structurally and organizationally distinct from synagogues. The Claudian expulsion of Jews from Rome in the 40s (most argue A.D. 49) marks a point after which the two groups, in Rome at least, conceived of themselves as distinct.[90]

Nonetheless, for some of the first believers their long-standing continuity with Jewish tradition will certainly have suggested to them that elements of synagogue community life provided an appropriate model to adopt and modify. After all, early Christians

---

[86]J.T. Burtchaell, *From Synagogue to Church*, 209. *Cf.* the suggestion in G.F. Snyder, 'The Interaction of Jews with Non-Jews in Rome', in K.P. Donfried & P. Richardson (eds.), *Judaism and Christianity in First-Century Rome* (Grand Rapids: Eerdmans, 1998) 69-90, that Christianity was indebted more to Graeco-Roman than Jewish culture for much of the symbolism it adopted (and adapted).

[87]*Cf.* the discussion in chapter 6 above.

[88]*Cf.* J.D.G. Dunn, *The Partings of the Ways: Between Christianity and Judaism, and their Significance for the Character of Christianity* (London: SCM Press, 1991) 230-59.

[89]*Cf.* D.R. Edwards, *Religion and Power: Pagans, Jews, and Christians in the Greek East*, 24.

[90]R. Brändle & E.W. Stegemann, 'The Formation of the First "Christian Congregations" in Rome in the Context of the Jewish Congregations', in K.P. Donfried & P. Richardson (eds.), *Judaism and Christianity in First-Century Rome* (Grand Rapids: Eerdmans, 1998) 117-27; J.C. Walters, 'Romans, Jews and Christians: the Impact of the Romans on Jewish/Christian Relations in First-Century Rome', *op. cit.*, 175-95; and W.L. Lane, 'Social Perspectives on Roman Christianity during the Formative Years from Nero to Nerva: Romans, Hebrews, 1 Clement', *op. cit.*, 196-244.

were to meet for prayer and study of the Jewish scriptures, much as their contemporaries in the synagogues.[91] Furthermore, as was reflected in so many areas of Graeco-Roman culture, we have seen that the synagogues of the diaspora were not exclusively concerned with 'religious' aspects of life. So too the Pauline communities were not exclusively places for worship, prayer and study of the scriptures, but they also provided the context for sharing food and other possessions.

We might, in particular, expect those who worshipped in synagogues and later came to adopt the Christian faith to seek continuity with what they will have perceived to be their long-standing Jewish heritage. Amongst these might be numbered Crispus, the *archisynagogos* of Corinth who is recorded as having believed and been baptized in response to Paul's ministry, and is later mentioned in Pauline correspondence; Sosthenes, also an *archisynagogos* in Corinth; Titius Justus, a god-fearer in Corinth who was host to Paul; and Jason, arguably a wealthy Jew in Thessalonica who took a leading rôle in the Pauline congregation.[92]

In the early decades of the Christian church, the continuing influence of Jews within Christian congregations is evident in some of the tensions which existed in a number of Pauline communities. These derive from a clash over differences in lifestyle between Gentile and Jewish sections of the community. The difficulties reflected in Paul's correspondence with the Galatians is a case in point.[93]

It is not insignificant, however, that, although Jesus, Peter, James and Paul had all ministered within the context of the Jewish synagogue, the earliest Christian communities chose to be distinct from synagogues in the name they adopted to describe their

---

[91]Cf. L. Morris, 'The Saints and the Synagogue', in M.J. Wilkins & T. Paige (eds.), *Worship, Theology and Ministry in the Early Church: Essays in Honor of Ralph P. Martin* (JSNT Supplement Series, 87; Sheffield: JSOT, 1992) 39-52.

[92]Cf. references to Crispus in Acts 18:8 and 1 Cor 1:14; references to Sosthenes as co-writer in 1 Cor 1:1 and Sosthenes as ἀρχισυνάγωγος in Acts 18:17; reference to Titius Justus in Acts 18:7; and references to Jason in Acts 17:5-9 and Rom 16:21; cf. also F. Morgan-Gillman, 'Jason of Thessalonica (Acts 17,5-9)', in R.F. Collins (ed.), *The Thessalonian Correspondence* (Bibliotheca ephemeridum theologicarum lovaniensium, 87; Leuven: Leuven University Press, 1990) 39-49.

[93]Cf. E.P. Sanders, 'Jewish Association with Gentiles and Galatians 2:11-14', in R.T. Fortna & B.R. Gaventa (eds.), *The Conversation Continues: Studies in Paul and John in Honor of J. Louis Martyn* (Nashville: Abingdon Press, 1990) 170-88.

gatherings ('church', ἐκκλησία); the day on which they chose to meet; and, for the most part, the range of titles for community officers.

There is no conclusive evidence that the early Christian communities were exclusively dependent for their pattern of organization on any one of the institutions which we have considered — Graeco-Roman cities, Roman colonies and cities, voluntary associations, the family, or the Jewish synagogue.[94] Indeed, it has become clear that there was significant overlap in organization between a number of these institutions, such that Jewish synagogues were occasionally considered associations, and the difference between household cult and cultic association is not always clear.[95] Furthermore, the ancient ideal of the *polis* was seen to be the basis of organization of many other institutions, including the family.[96] Wayne Meeks has suggested that the early Christian ἐκκλησία 'was all the old things that observers in the first century might have seen in it: a Jewish sect, a club meeting in a household, an initiatory cult, a school. Yet it was more than the sum of those things, and different from the mere synthesis of their contradictory tendencies'.[97] It seems all the more plausible, therefore, that first-century Christians would have been familiar with and open to varying degrees of influence from all of these.[98] As we turn in more detail to the New Testament evidence it will become clear that the early Pauline communities were, to a large extent, organizationally independent of each other. They were able to adopt and adapt different dynamics of leadership, and were variously influenced dependent on the dominant personalities in each congregation. This is not to suggest, however,

---

[94]*Contra* J.T. Burtchaell, *From Synagogue to Church*. Note also the resistance to the view that the early church was structurally modelled on secular organization (as proposed by Hatch). This is clear in N.F. Josaitis, *Edwin Hatch and Early Church Order* (Recherches et synthèses, Section d'Histoire, 3; Gembloux: J. Duculot, 1971), cited in J.S. Kloppenborg, 'Edwin Hatch, Churches and Collegia', 224.

[95]*Cf.* S.K. Stowers, 'A Cult from Philadelphia: Oikos Religion or Cultic Association?', in A.J. Malherbe, F.W. Norris & J.W. Thompson (eds.), *The Early Church in its Context: Essays in Honor of Everett Ferguson* (Supplements to Novum Testamentum, 90; Leiden: Brill, 1998) 287-301.

[96]W.A. Meeks, *The Moral World of the First Christians*, 20, 'Most of the proper forms of human association, from that of husband and wife to that of government and citizens, fit neatly together within the polis's structure, like an elegant set of Chinese boxes'.

[97]W.A. Meeks, *The Moral World of the First Christians*, 120.

[98]W.A. Meeks, *The Moral World of the First Christians*, 110.

that all the measures adopted were equally acceptable to Paul.[99] In chapter 8 we shall consider the patterns of leadership adopted in a number of Pauline congregations, and in chapter 9 we shall review Paul's reaction to these, and his own preferred ideals of leadership. First, however, it will be necessary to address the nature of the evidence as it is presented in the New Testament.

VII. The Nature of the New Testament Evidence

A major difficulty which we face in assessing the local leadership in the urban context of the early Christian communities is the nature of the extant evidence. Unlike the pictures which can be derived of leadership in other Graeco-Roman contexts, where epigraphic and other archaeological data have considerably enhanced our understanding, sources for reconstructing the organization in the early Christian communities are largely limited to the literary evidence of the New Testament texts themselves. Most accessible are those letters written to specific congregations where the author has a clear knowledge of the context addressed. Amongst these, 1 Corinthians is perhaps paramount. It should be noted, however, that these letters, for the most part, offer one perspective on the historical situation, and therefore, in many cases, apprise us of only one side of the debate, conversation or dialogue which may have been taking place. Furthermore, much of the text of the epistles is didactic rather than descriptive; in other words, the writer is more often instructing his readers as to how they should conduct themselves and their affairs, as opposed to describing, in the nature of a historical account, what was actually happening. In our reading of the primary sources, we must avoid the so-called 'idealistic' fallacy which redraws history on the basis of Paul's corrective statements,[100]

---

[99]We could note, for example, the extent to which both Jews and Christians participated in pagan cult. This is implicit in Paul's discussion in 1 Cor 8-10. See also, P. Borgen, '"Yes," "No," "How Far?": The Participation of Jews and Christians in Pagan Cults', in T. Engberg-Pedersen (ed.), *Paul in his Hellenistic Context* (Studies of the New Testament and its World; Edinburgh: T. & T. Clark, 1994) 30-59.

[100]The 'fallacy of idealism' is described in B. Holmberg, *Paul and Power: the Structure of Authority in the Primitive Church as Reflected in the Pauline Epistles* (Coniectanea Biblica, New Testament Series, 11; Lund: CWK Gleerup, 1978) 205-207.

or, as James Burtchaell describes it, 'the consensus has taken [Paul's] reaction as the primary datum'.[101] We, however, must be careful to distinguish what may be determined about the social interactions which were actually taking place in these early communities, from the model of interaction which Paul, for example, wished to see and sought to impart.

The four gospels and the book of Acts, on the other hand, are presented more as historical descriptions, although in each case they also have a significant didactic purpose. Comparatively little is said in the book of Acts, however, about the way in which local communities were ordered. The task of determining the nature of those communities from which or to which the gospels were written is even more problematic.[102]

There has long been debate over whether there were any leaders as such in the earliest Pauline communities, and it is often suggested that leadership can only clearly be seen in the later sections of the New Testament.[103] Continental, protestant scholarship has repeatedly argued that we see within the pages of the New Testament evidence of a process of catholicization by which the church gradually fell away from its original ideal. This process continued throughout the rise of the Catholic church until checked in the sixteenth century by the Reformation. 1 Corinthians, a key text describing aspects of life in one of the early communities, was regarded by Ferdinand Christian Baur as showing some of the first signs of this process of catholicization.[104] The parties of Peter and Paul alluded to in 1 Corinthians 1 and 3 bear witness, he suggested, to a growing rift between Jewish and Gentile factions. It is in these early stages of the process, however, that we see the purer form of Pauline Christianity. There is no clear reference to overseers (bishops), elders or deacons in the epistle; these titles, rather, were characteristic of some of the later Pauline corpus. The consequent assumption was widely adopted that these first communities

---

[101]J.T. Burtchaell, *From Synagogue to Church*, 163.

[102]*Cf.* the debate recently invigorated by essays collected in R. Bauckham (ed.), *The Gospels for all Christians: Rethinking the Gospel Audiences* (Grand Rapids: Eerdmans, 1998).

[103]*Cf.* J.T. Burtchaell, *From Synagogue to Church*, for a helpful and wide-ranging historical overview of the debate.

[104]F.C. Baur, *The Church History of the First Three Centuries* (2 vols.; 3rd ed.; Theological Translation Fund Library, 16, 20; London: Williams and Norgate, 1878-79) I.60-65.

adopted a much freer form of organization, often labelled 'charismatic'.[105] James Burtchaell characterizes a measure of agreement on this view by Baur, Ritschl, Lightfoot, Hatch, von Harnack and Sohm: 'a drastic regression in the second century had replaced a casual and charismatic community with one that awarded definitive authority to bishops'.[106] This degree of consensus was reaffirmed in the twentieth century by Hans von Campenhausen and Eduard Schweizer.[107] In contrast to this consensus, now under strong attack from a number of quarters, I shall argue that it is not necessary to assume that absence of mention of offices meant that there were no leaders in these earliest communities.

In the following chapters, I shall endeavour to distinguish between the social processes which were active in a given Pauline community and the nature of godly leadership to which Paul appealed in his corrective statements. The former will not, of course, be transposable from congregation to congregation; but the latter may have a wider application. Accordingly, it will be necessary to focus, in turn, on specific congregations, and also to differentiate between what I have called the theory (those models or characteristics of leadership discernible both in Paul's corrective statements and in the lives of individuals who are held up as positive examples) and the practice (what can be discerned about the ways in which leaders within particular congregations were exercising their authority, influence or status).

---

[105]Cf. my discussion in A.D. Clarke, *Secular and Christian Leadership in Corinth*, 2-3.

[106]J.T. Burtchaell, *From Synagogue to Church*, 136.

[107]J.T. Burtchaell, *From Synagogue to Church*, 137.

CHAPTER 8

SECULAR LEADERSHIP IN THE CHRISTIAN COMMUNITY

I. Introduction

Reading the Pauline corpus in the light of our knowledge of the culture which prevailed in the Graeco-Roman world, this chapter will demonstrate some of the ways in which leadership was practised in the different local congregations of the Pauline churches. The evidence from Paul's letters shows that the dynamics of church organization and leadership were not the same across all Christian congregations; indeed, it is clear that Paul found it necessary to address a number of churches in very particular ways regarding issues of authority and leadership.[1] In this chapter, the situations which variously prevailed in some early Christian congregations will be considered and will be compared with those patterns of Graeco-Roman leadership which have emerged in the course of the preceding chapters. It is often the case that we only become aware of how leadership was exercised in particular Christian communities by

---

[1]J.M.G. Barclay, 'Thessalonica and Corinth: Social Contrasts in Pauline Christianity', *Journal for the Study of the New Testament* 47 (1992) 49-74, contrasts the very different social contexts in the church in Thessalonica and that in Corinth. These churches reacted very differently to the dominant Graeco-Roman culture, and elicited from Paul very different responses in his correspondence.

analysing Paul's corrective statements. The succeeding chapter will focus more specifically on the positive portrayal of Paul's contrasting understanding of the nature of leadership — leadership as he felt it should be practised in Christian communities in the first century.

II. 1 Corinthians — a Community Divided over its Leaders

It is widely noted by commentators that Corinth in the first century was a Roman colony, founded by Julius Caesar in its relatively recent past, 44 B.C. As such its pattern of civic government and administration followed largely that described above in chapter 3 concerning the Roman colony.[2] In consequence of being the provincial capital of Achaea, despite not having its own long-standing traditions, it was a city proud of its cultural prestige, economic strength and aura of Romanness. Where Corinth did differ from a number of colonies was in the extent to which, most especially in its early years, even freedmen could adopt significant positions of leadership within the city. Correspondingly, a competitive spirit of social upward mobility was more than usually prevalent in this colony.[3] A close reading of 1 Corinthians demonstrates that a similar preoccupation with social status was, at one time, characteristic also of the Christian church in the colony.

1. Social Status

In a series of significant articles published in 1974-75, Gerd Theissen argued persuasively that many of the problems arising in the early Corinthian community derived from social tensions between the rich and the poor.[4] Such a social mix is specifically noted by Paul in

---

[2]Cf. D.W.G. Gill, 'Corinth: a Roman Colony in Achaea', *Biblische Zeitschrift* 37 (1993) 259-64, for a recent demonstration of the Romanness of the colony.

[3]Strabo, *Geography* 8.6.22, 'Now after Corinth had remained deserted for a long time, it was restored again, because of its favourable position, by the deified Caesar, who colonized it with people who belonged for the most part to the freedmen class'; *cf.* also D. Engels, *Roman Corinth: an Alternative Model for the Classical City* (Chicago: University of Chicago Press, 1990) 18.

[4]These articles were subsequently gathered in a monograph, and translated into English; G. Theissen, *The Social Setting of Pauline Christianity: Essays on Corinth* (Philadelphia: Fortress Press, 1982).

1 Corinthians 1:26 where he records that 'not many of you were wise by human standards, not many were powerful, not many were of noble birth'.[5] Consequently, the church boasted at least some among its number who could describe themselves as among the relatively 'wise, powerful and well-born' of Corinthian society; in other words, within the ambit of their own social context, these people could consider themselves and were considered by some of their fellow Christians to be influential by virtue of their education, personal wealth or familial descent.[6] This assessment of the social diversity within the community is further supported by prosopographical analysis of some of the individuals specifically named in the correspondence; in particular, those who displayed evidence of higher social standing by virtue of official titles, property or ability to travel.[7] Especial interest has focused on the identification of the enigmatic figure Erastus — a member of the Corinthian Christian community who is mentioned by Paul in Romans 16:23 as being an *oikonomos* of the city.

Erastus is especially intriguing because of the possibility that he was, or became, one of Roman Corinth's civic leaders.[8] This view is principally dependent on the suggestion that the civic official (οἰκονόμος τῆς πόλεως) who is cited by Paul in his letter to the Romans may have been, for one year, an aedile in the colony of Corinth. As part of a generous benefaction, an Erastus in the mid-first century arranged for his name to be inscribed on a prominent pavement in front of the theatre in Corinth. The literary and archaeological evidence is tantalisingly insufficient as it stands either to prove or

---

[5]*Cf.* further D.W.G. Gill, 'In Search of the Social Élite in the Corinthian Church', *Tyndale Bulletin* 44 (1993) 323-37.

[6]See my discussion of the use of these terms by Dio Chrysostom, Plutarch, Aristotle, Philo and Josephus, together with prosopographical analyses of the community, in A.D. Clarke, *Secular and Christian Leadership in Corinth: a Socio-historical and Exegetical Study of 1 Corinthians 1-6* (Arbeiten zur Geschichte des antiken Judentums und des Urchristentums, 18; Leiden: E.J. Brill, 1993) 41-57.

[7]*Cf.* again, G. Theissen, *The Social Setting of Pauline Christianity*, 73-99.

[8]See the recently expanding secondary literature on this topic: D.W.G. Gill, 'Erastus the Aedile', *Tyndale Bulletin* 40 (1989) 293-301; A.D. Clarke, 'Another Corinthian Erastus Inscription', *Tyndale Bulletin* 42 (1991) 146-51; *idem, Secular and Christian Leadership in Corinth*, 46-56; B.W. Winter, *Seek the Welfare of the City: Christians as Benefactors and Citizens* (First Century Christians in the Graeco-Roman World; Grand Rapids: Eerdmans, 1994) 179-97; and J.J. Meggitt, *Paul, Poverty and Survival* (Studies of the New Testament and its World; Edinburgh: T. & T. Clark, 1998) 135-41.

dismiss an identification here. The possibility remains, however, that a prominent figure from Corinthian civic life was also closely associated with the Christian community in Corinth. Furthermore, there is the probability that the Erastus of Romans 16:23 was, whether or not an aedile, nonetheless a man of sufficient means and civic connections to be considered comparatively wealthy, at least by the standards of the Christian community. On the basis that wealthy Gentile benefactors were sometimes associated with Jewish synagogues, although not themselves members of the community, it must be accepted that the reference in Romans 16:23 does not require that Erastus was a Christian. If the Erastus referred to in Acts 19:22, and possibly also that in 2 Timothy 4:20, however, is the same as the Corinthian Erastus of Romans 16:23, then this would support the contention that the man mentioned in the Pauline correspondence was a Christian.[9]

Whether or not the identification of these Erasti is upheld, the general perception that there was a socio-economic imbalance within the Corinthian Christian community has been widely adopted by many scholars, even by those who have questioned Theissen's chosen method.[10] It also emerges through the course of 1 Corinthians that the more prominent individuals in the church were regarded within the community as its leading figures.[11] Some of them were exercising an authority over their fellow Christians on the basis of that greater status. In so doing, they were emulating patterns of leadership standardly adopted in wider Graeco-Roman society, and thereby were creating divisions within the Christian community. It is on closer inspection of a number of specific issues that we see such parallels between the ways in which some Christians were acting and the expectations and practices of many in the non-Christian surrounding culture.

2. Patronage

One of the first problems which Paul raises in 1 Corinthians is the matter of internal division and distinct parties, as reflected in the

---

[9]Cf. B.W. Winter, *Seek the Welfare of the City*, 196.

[10]But note the recent attack on this 'new consensus' by J.J. Meggitt, *Paul, Poverty and Survival*.

[11]This is notwithstanding the lack of reference to any titles or offices.

slogans, 'I am of Paul', 'I am of Apollos', 'I am of Cephas' and 'I am of Christ'.[12] Some in the Christian community were siding loyalties with leading Christian figures in much the same way that allegiance was offered by clients in secular society to their patrons or to other political figures.[13] Patronage, we have seen, was a key characteristic of leadership at various levels in the Graeco-Roman world, including the empire, the province, the city, the association and the household. For many of the inhabitants of first-century Corinth, patronage will have been witnessed either first-hand as patrons or clients, or at least second-hand as reflected in the hundreds of inscriptions, statues or other monuments which lined the public places in the city centre, or in the generosity expressed in the subsidising of grain prices or the provision of public games.[14] Roman citizens who were patrons to their own clientèles could at the same time be clients under the patronage of another, with the emperor himself as the supreme patron of the empire. It emerges that Christians, who themselves were leading figures within the Christian community, were similarly acting as clients to the apostolic figures highlighted in the partisan slogans, and seeking to further the reputation and status of their preferred figure.

There was the potential of significant benefits to be gained in siding loyalties with a particular patron, and it can be argued that the factions which characterized the Corinthian community were based on this sort of dynamic. Paul, indeed, points out that some in the community may have interpreted actions such as the baptizing of members of a household by a figure-head as an act of patronage or preferment; although Paul himself expressly states that he did not

---

[12]1 Cor 1:10-13; *cf.* also 1 Cor 3:5, 21-23.

[13]*Cf.* A.D. Clarke, *Secular and Christian Leadership in Corinth*, 92-95, and J.K. Chow, *Patronage and Power: a Study of Social Networks in Corinth* (JSNT Supplement Series, 75; Sheffield: JSOT Press, 1992).

[14]For the inscriptions, *cf.* the early archaeological reports published in B.D. Meritt, *Corinth — Greek Inscriptions 1896-1927. Corinth: Results, viii, Part I* (Cambridge MA, 1931); A.B. West, *Corinth — Latin Inscriptions 1896-1920. Corinth: Results, viii, Part II* (Cambridge MA, 1931); and J.H. Kent, *Corinth — Inscriptions 1926-1950. Corinth: Results, viii, Part III* (Princeton, 1966); for instances of leaders assisting in the grain supply, *cf.* B.W. Winter, 'Secular and Christian Responses to Corinthian Famines', *Tyndale Bulletin* 40 (1989) 86-106; and with regard to the patronage at the public games, *cf.* the instance of Lucius Castricius Regulus and the literary reference of Plutarch, *Moralia* 723, cited in A.D. Clarke, *Secular and Christian Leadership in Corinth*, 20.

wish to be regarded as a patron in this way.[15] According to the expectations of the day, such an act of patronage establishes a debt of gratitude and should properly be recognized by the client's reciprocating of honour. Although in this case the patrons are non-local figures in the Christian community (Paul, Apollos, Cephas and Christ), by deferring in this way to their patronage, the Christian clients were adopting the same currency of honour and prestige which operated in the surrounding secular society.

The way in which some of the Corinthian Christians were according honour and respect to their supposed leading figures, whether local or apostolic, was in their boasting.[16] 1 Corinthians is unusual within the New Testament because of the predominance of the motif of boasting. One major focus of this boasting was in certain people. At a number of points in the letter, Paul rebukes the Corinthians for their 'taking pride in people': he urges them to 'let no one boast about human leaders' (1 Cor 3:21); and he writes, 'I have applied all this to Apollos and myself for your benefit ... so that none of you will be puffed up in favour of one against another' (1 Cor 4:6).[17] Such boasting in people was commonplace in Graeco-Roman society, and although flattery of others was, on the surface, self-effacing, it elicited its own gratitude and possibly even reward. It was an acceptable mechanism in contemporary society of self-preferment and self-advancement.

An additional way in which clients could demonstrate their gratitude to a patron figure was by adopting the preferred deity of that patron figure as a cultic focus. This is most clearly evident with regard to the imperial cult throughout the empire, but not least in Corinth. The parallel with the situation in the Corinthian Christian community lies in the adoption by members of the community of favoured relations with individual apostolic figures and even with the figure of Christ himself.[18] The unfortunate effect of this action is to cause division within the Christian community.[19]

---

[15]In 1 Cor 1:13, he distances himself from any grounds for such adulation.

[16]Cf. A.D. Clarke, Secular and Christian Leadership in Corinth, 95-99.

[17]Cf. also the case made for the offender mentioned in 1 Cor 5 being a respected patron of the community in A.D. Clarke, Secular and Christian Leadership in Corinth, 73-88.

[18]1 Cor 1:12; 3:4.

[19]1 Cor 1:10.

3. Wisdom

Another area in which some of the Corinthian Christians displayed characteristics similar to those of pagan Graeco-Roman leaders and thereby introduced division was in their preoccupation with wisdom and proficiency in public speaking.[20] This is especially apparent in the number of contrasts which Paul draws in 1 Corinthians 1-3 between godly wisdom and the 'wisdom of the world' or 'human wisdom'.[21] It emerges that some of the Corinthian Christians had adopted expectations that Paul would function with the oratorical skill and training of an accomplished sophist.[22] In actuality he had adopted an anti-sophistic stance when he proclaimed the message to the Corinthians, thereby distancing himself and the delivery of his message from such characteristics of secular leaders.[23] Thus Paul states,

> When I came to you, brothers, I did not come with eloquence or superior wisdom as I proclaimed to you the testimony about God ... My message and my preaching were not in wise and persuasive words ... so that your faith might not rest on men's wisdom, but on God's power.[24]

Inevitably, Paul did not live up to the cultural expectations of these Christians and he therefore became the focus of severe criticism and unfavourable comparison with other apostolic figures. This criticism in turn created a means by which some of Paul's opponents in the church could draw attention to their own wisdom and thereby contrastingly display their own proficiency in this area and their consequent superior status. The Corinthians, in effect, could boast in their ability to critique Paul's skill in this way and in so doing they painted an enhanced picture of their own wisdom in direct relation to

---

[20]Cf. A.D. Clarke, *Secular and Christian Leadership in Corinth*, 101-105.

[21]Cf. 1 Cor 1:17, 20-21, 25, 27; 2:1-3, 5, 6-7, 13; 3:18, 19. A number of competing theories have been developed regarding the nature of this wisdom referred to by Paul. It is clear from the extensive contrasts Paul is making in this first major section of the epistle between the ways of God and the ways of the world, that this wisdom is not that of gnosticism or of the Hellenistic mysteries, but that of the sophists themselves.

[22]Cf. B.W. Winter, *Philo and Paul among the Sophists* (SNTS Monograph Series, 96; Cambridge: Cambridge University Press, 1997).

[23]This is most clear in Paul's defence of his proclamation in 1 Cor 2:1-5.

[24]1 Cor 2:1-5.

that of Paul.[25] These actions proved to be deeply divisive within the church.

4. Political Wrangling

Paul also makes explicit accusations that some of the Corinthian Christians had adopted secular attitudes in their actions and relationships. In 1 Corinthians 3:3-4, he accuses them of acting in a way which patterns that of wider Graeco-Roman, pagan society:

> as long as there is jealousy (ζῆλος) and quarreling (ἔρις) among you, are you not of the flesh, and behaving according to human inclinations? For when one says, 'I belong to Paul,' and another, 'I belong to Apollos,' are you not merely human?

Jealousy and quarreling, according to Paul, was symptomatic of 'worldly', or 'merely human' behaviour.[26] It should be noted that these attitudes and terms were characteristic of secular politics in the Roman world,[27] as is clearly seen in the statement of Dio Chrysostom:

> the high-minded, perfect man is above material wealth; but in the matter of reputation would he perhaps quarrel (ἐρίζοι) with and envy (φθονοῖ) those whom he sees more highly honoured by the crowd and winning greater plaudits?[28]

---

[25]Cf. D. Litfin, *St. Paul's Theology of Proclamation: 1 Corinthians 1-4 and Greco-Roman Rhetoric* (SNTS Monograph Series, 79; Cambridge: Cambridge University Press, 1994) 245, 'Though they were themselves on the outside — or perhaps even in some cases still more tantalizingly, on the fringe — of the circles of status, influence and sophistication in Corinth, they exalted those on the inside and themselves put on the airs of the aristocracy, affecting the stance of sophisticated critics as best they could'.

[26]Cf. A.D. Clarke, *Secular and Christian Leadership in Corinth*, 99-101; and, with regard to the sophistic characteristic of ζῆλος and ἔρις, see B.W. Winter, *Philo and Paul among the Sophists*, 170-76.

[27]L.L. Welborn, *Politics and Rhetoric in the Corinthian Epistles* (Macon: Mercer University Press, 1997) 1-42; but see also D.F. Epstein, *Personal Enmity in Roman Politics 218-43 B.C.* (London: Croom Helm, 1987) 28, 'The pursuit of *inimicitiae* and the destruction of one's enemies were firmly entrenched among those virtues Romans thought necessary for the acquisition of *dignitas, virtus*, status and nobility — qualities the Roman aristocracy pursued from birth'.

[28]Dio Chrysostom, *Orationes* 77/8.17.

The Corinthian Christian leaders, by their preoccupation with strife and wranglings more characteristic of secular politics, were causing deep-seated division within the Christian community.

5. Law Courts

Paul records in 1 Corinthians 6:1-11 that some in the congregation were taking their personal grievances before the civil judicial process which operated in the Roman colony. In doing so these Christians were using the secular lawcourts as a means of divisively enhancing their own status over that of their fellow Christians.[29] The implementation of vexatious litigation was a widely-used tool in the Graeco-Roman world by which influential figures in society could exercise legal privilege and use slander in order to further their own personal or political cause at the expense of the reputation of their opponent. The judicial process could be abused, becoming a mechanism to reinforce social standing and personal reputation, and could normally only be engaged in by those who were themselves of sufficient social standing to be confident about a successful outcome. Consequently, some from the Christian community were using the leverage of this judicial mechanism as a means of publicly bolstering their personal standing and status in front of their peers and social network, whilst also endeavouring to denigrate the status and diminish the popularity of their opponent. In so doing they were reinforcing division within the community.

6. Immorality

The church addressed in 1 Corinthians is popularly regarded as rife with immorality. One specific instance is highlighted in 1 Corinthians 5:1-5 where a man is known to be living with 'his father's wife'.[30] It is surprising to Paul that the church appears to have made no move to distance themselves from such behaviour. Although some scholars argue that their inaction may have been defended by the Corinthians

---

[29]Cf. A.D. Clarke, *Secular and Christian Leadership in Corinth*, 59-71; and B.W. Winter, 'Civil Litigation in Secular Corinth and the Church: the Forensic Background to 1 Corinthians 6.1-8', *New Testament Studies* 37 (1991) 559-72.
[30]Cf. A.D. Clarke, *Secular and Christian Leadership in Corinth*, 73-88.

on theological grounds, this is improbable given that Paul makes no attempt at this juncture to correct any faulty theology.[31] A stronger possibility, rather, is that the guilty man was in fact a high profile benefactor of the community whom the Christians felt unable, or possibly unwilling, to call to account for his actions. The community's reluctance to take action against this man would therefore have been out of deference to his superior status coupled with fear of loss of benefit from this patron figure.

This letter to the Corinthians also gives evidence, however, of other instances of immorality in lifestyle. 1 Corinthians 6:12-20 and 7:1-2 record further acts of immorality, greed or licentious behaviour within the church.[32] Again in these instances, it does not appear that a form of Christian doctrine peculiar to the Corinthians is being either defended by those in the community, or countered by Paul. Rather, we are again dealing with those who were using licentious behaviour as a means of drawing attention to their comparatively elevated social status. Philo projects what may be a similar attitude, namely that one's lifestyle reflected one's social standing.

> The mode of life of these two classes is a witness to the truth of what I say. For they who are called lovers of virtue are nearly all of them men inglorious, easily to be despised, lowly, in need of necessary things, more dishonourable than subjects, or even than slaves ... but those who take care of themselves are men of rank and wealth, holding leading positions, praised on all hands, recipients of honours, portly, healthy and robust, revelling in luxurious and riotous living, knowing nothing of labour, conversant with pleasures which carry the sweets of life to the all-welcoming soul by every channel of sense.[33]

Such licentious behaviour on the part of those Christians of higher status within the church would have served to exacerbate the division which existed in the community.

---

[31]Cf., for example, the theory of over-realized eschatology propounded by A.C. Thiselton, 'Realized Eschatology at Corinth', *New Testament Studies* 24 (1978) 510-26.

[32]Cf. A.D. Clarke, *Secular and Christian Leadership in Corinth*, 105-106. Cf. also, with regard to gluttony, B.W. Winter, 'Gluttony and Immorality at Élitist Banquets: the Background to 1 Corinthians 6:12-20', *Jian Dao* 7 (1997) 55-67.

[33]Philo, *Quod deterius potiori insidiari solet* 34; cf. also *op. cit.*, 33.

7. *Food Sacrificed to Idols*

Additionally, in 1 Corinthians 8-10, Paul addresses at length the issue of how the strong and weak were acting in regard to whether and where food sacrificed to idols was consumed. Here also there is an issue which is related to social status and the conflict which existed between those who were influential in both their household and the wider city and those who had a lower social status.[34] We have seen that the divisions between the secular and the religious dimensions of social life in Graeco-Roman society were indistinct. Religious pluralism was widespread in the Roman colony of Corinth and those who wished to maintain their social standing in this pagan culture would have felt it necessary to participate in the social customs of the time.[35] The principal problem which is being addressed in 1 Corinthians 8 and 10 was that some Christians were themselves participating in pagan feasts in the pagan temples and consequently eating in those surroundings meat that had been formerly sacrificed to idols.[36] To eat in the pagan temples was an activity which those of high status felt they could pursue by right; indeed it was access to such temples for feasting which differentiated them from their poorer fellow Christians. To withdraw from such functions, therefore, would have been to isolate oneself from established society and the possibility of social networking. On the other hand, for Christians to pursue this lifestyle was a means of drawing attention to their comparatively greater social status within the church, and thereby reinforcing social division.

---

[34]W.A. Meeks, *The Moral World of the First Christians* (Library of Early Christianity, 6; Philadelphia: Westminster Press, 1986) 112.

[35]B.W. Winter, 'Ethical and Theological Responses to Religious Pluralism in Corinth — 1 Corinthians 8–10', *Tyndale Bulletin* 41 (1990) 209-26, discusses the extent of religious pluralism in the colony, together with the ways in which both Jews and Christians responded to this situation. *Cf.* also *idem*, 'In Public and in Private: Early Christians and Religious Pluralism', in A.D. Clarke & B.W. Winter (eds.), *One God, One Lord: Christianity in a World of Religious Pluralism* (2nd ed.; Tyndale House Studies; Grand Rapids: Baker Book House, 1992) 125-48.

[36]1 Cor 8:10. *Cf.* B. Witherington, *Conflict and Community in Corinth: a Socio-rhetorical Commentary on 1 and 2 Corinthians* (Grand Rapids: Eerdmans, 1995) 186-202.

8. Head Covering

In 1 Corinthians 11:4 Paul urges that 'any man who prays or prophesies with something on his head disgraces his head'. We have seen above that in civic contexts it was the most senior figures who presided over religious ceremonies. Both statues and coins from Corinth and other Roman cities depict the emperor Augustus performing religious sacrifices with his head covered. What is noteworthy is that other, secondary, priestly figures at sacrifices do not have their heads covered. The use of head covering, thus, denoted status or seniority at a public function.[37] In Paul's view, with this cultural background, it is inappropriate for men to have their heads covered, because the chief official in their community and at their community functions is Christ.[38] If a man were to wear head covering it would be a statement that he viewed himself as the chief official. The suggestion is that there were those in the community whose positions of importance within broader Corinthian society were in this way being paraded also in the church. They were covering their heads in order to demonstrate their own importance — an action which was deeply divisive and of which Paul strongly disapproved.[39]

9. The Lord's Supper

It is clear also that celebration of the Lord's Supper in the Corinthian Christian community was marked by division.[40] Gerd Theissen has long argued that the division here arises from socio-economic differences within the community.[41] The distinction in the church between those who were wealthy and those who had no property is very visibly highlighted when they come together to share a meal.

---

[37]D.W.G. Gill, 'The Importance of Roman Portraiture for Head-Coverings in 1 Corinthians 11:2-16', *Tyndale Bulletin* 41 (1990) 248.

[38]1 Cor 11:3.

[39]D.W.G. Gill, 'The Importance of Roman Portraiture for Head-Coverings in 1 Corinthians 11:2-16', 260, argues, 'It seems to reflect the jostling for power and authority amongst the leading families within the church at Corinth ... It reflects the love of ambition usually met within an urban community of the Roman world such as a colony'.

[40]1 Cor 11:17-34.

[41]G. Theissen, *The Social Setting of Pauline Christianity*, 145-74.

Those who enjoyed higher status were able to display this by means of the quantity and type of food they could eat, while those who were poorer had to go without. In the context of Paul's discussion of this situation, he again repeats his concern about the divisions which are thereby caused within the community.[42]

10. Conclusions

1 Corinthians is a letter which, more transparently than any other in the Pauline corpus, sheds light on the social situation which prevailed in an early Christian community. What marks this congregation at this point in time is the range of social status represented amongst its members. Many of the root problems in the church derived from internal tensions between the relatively rich and the relatively poor. More particularly, Paul responded to those of high social status who were using that social status as a tool with which to alienate or crush the poor. It then becomes significant that this congregation, in contrast to many other Pauline churches, finds itself in little conflict with the surrounding Graeco-Roman culture.[43] Indeed, theirs is a comfortable life in direct contrast to that of the apostles.[44] The reason for this is that so many of the church's leaders continued to imbibe the culture of their surrounding society.

III. 2 Corinthians — a Community Boastful of its Leaders

2 Corinthians has been the subject of a number of dislocation theories. How many original letters comprise the present text and in what order were they sent?[45] These important questions are particularly significant for a diachronic study of the situation which prevailed in the Corinthian Christian community. In the present

---

[42]1 Cor 11:18.

[43]J.M.G. Barclay, 'Thessalonica and Corinth: Social Contrasts in Pauline Christianity', 57.

[44]Cf. the dramatic contrast painted between the Corinthians' lifestyle and that of Paul in 1 Cor 4:8-13.

[45]Cf. especially the recent suggestion that 2 Cor 10-13 was written between 1 Cor and 2 Cor 1-9, in D.G. Horrell, *The Social Ethos of the Corinthian Correspondence: Interests and Ideology from 1 Corinthians to 1 Clement* (Studies of the New Testament and its World; Edinburgh: T. & T. Clark, 1996) 296-312.

study the letter will be taken as a whole, and it will be assumed that all sections are addressing essentially similar circumstances. In the letter, Paul's opponents have a clear focus, and are repeatedly the subject of his attack.[46]

A number of recent studies have viewed the problems referred to in 2 Corinthians as a result of social disparity within the community: namely Peter Marshall's *Enmity in Corinth*, Timothy Savage's *Power through Weakness*, David Horrell's *The Social Ethos of the Corinthian Correspondence*, and Bruce Winter's *Philo and Paul among the Sophists*.[47] In particular a dominant group was exercising influence within the Christian ἐκκλησία according to standards widely adopted by wealthier people in Graeco-Roman society. We shall consider in particular how their actions were characterized by boasting and oratory.

1. Boasting

Paul suggests in 2 Corinthians 11:18 that some of his opponents at Corinth were boasting 'according to human standards'. This is described in more detail in 2 Corinthians 10:12-18 as self-commendation, and in 2 Corinthians 11:18 as boasting 'according to the flesh'.[48] It appears from 2 Corinthians 3:1 that Paul's opponents operated by means of letters of recommendation, and their expectation was either that they should be able to assess Paul's credentials and thereby make their own critique of him, or that Paul should provide statements which endorse his own credentials. The apostle, however, considered that their boasting was merely in 'external' matters, the things that are seen, rather than what is in the

---

[46]Cf. the references, both direct and indirect, in 2 Cor 2:17; 3:1; 10:2, 7, 11, 12; 11:4, 13, 15, 18.

[47]P. Marshall, *Enmity in Corinth: Social Conventions in Paul's Relations with the Corinthians* (WUNT, 2.23; Tübingen: J.C.B. Mohr, 1987); T.B. Savage, *Power through Weakness: Paul's Understanding of the Christian Ministry in 2 Corinthians* (SNTS Monograph Series, 86; Cambridge: Cambridge University Press, 1996); D.G. Horrell, *The Social Ethos of the Corinthian Correspondence*; B.W. Winter, *Philo and Paul among the Sophists*.

[48]Cf. T.B. Savage, *Power through Weakness*, 55-56. Cf. also G.B. Davis, *True and False Boasting in 2 Corinthians 10-13* (PhD dissertation; Cambridge: Cambridge University, 1998) for the view that Paul's response to the Corinthian criticisms derives from his use of Old Testament and Jewish attitudes to boasting.

heart.[49] The implication is that in adopting such comparisons and assessments Paul's opponents were living 'to please themselves'.[50]

Plutarch devotes an entire treatise to the subject of 'praising oneself inoffensively', in which he says 'in theory ... it is agreed that to speak to others of one's own importance or power is inoffensive, but in practice not many even of those who condemn such conduct avoid the odium of it',[51] and:

> For while praise from others ... is the most pleasant of recitals, praise of ourselves is for others most distressing. For first we regard self-praisers as shameless, since they should be embarrassed even by praise from others; second as unfair, as they arrogate to themselves what it is for others to bestow; and in the third place if we listen in silence we appear disgruntled and envious, while if we shy at this we are forced to join eulogies and confirm them against our better judgment, thus submitting to a thing more in keeping with unmanly flattery than with the showing of esteem — the praise of a man to his face.[52]

These statements by Plutarch highlight the widespread use of self-commendation or self-praise amongst those in the echelons of society with which he mixed, and compare significantly with the practices of some from the Christian community in Corinth.

2. Sophistic Appearance

In addition to self-adulation, Paul's opponents in 2 Corinthians were critical of the apostle himself.[53] In 2 Corinthians 10:10 Paul reports, 'For they say, "His letters are weighty (βαρεῖαι) and strong (ἰσχυραί), but his bodily presence (ἡ παρουσία τοῦ σώματος) is weak, and his speech contemptible"'; in 2 Corinthians 11:6, Paul has to defend, 'I may be untrained in speech (ἰδιώτης τῷ λόγῳ), but not in knowledge; certainly in every way and in all things we have made this evident to you'; and in 2 Corinthians 12:16, he says, 'Let it be assumed that I did

---

[49]2 Cor 5:12.
[50]2 Cor 5:15.
[51]Plutarch, *Moralia* 539A.
[52]Plutarch, *Moralia* 539D.
[53]*Cf.* B.W. Winter, *Philo and Paul among the Sophists*, 203-30.

not burden you. Nevertheless (you say) since I was crafty, I took you in by deceit'.

The adjectives 'weighty' and 'strong' (2 Cor 10:10) were used in sophistic circles to describe rhetorical techniques. Furthermore, the assessment of Paul's bodily presence amounts, in a first-century sophistic context, to a criticism of his skill in rhetorical delivery.[54] Thus Paul's presence among the Corinthians was being compared with the oratorical and debating skills of the accomplished sophists of the day and found wanting — Paul's speech was considered by his critics to be contemptible (ἐξουθενημένος).[55] Consequently, the canon of assessment which was being applied by his opponents was precisely that of the secular world.

This element of personal 'comparison' is seen clearly in 2 Corinthians 10:12, a practice which Paul refuses to adopt. He was being regarded as 'an unpresentable and inarticulate public speaker in a city highly conscious of rhetorical prowess'.[56] Paul's defence in 2 Corinthians 10:2-5 confirms that his opponents were adopting a strategy of argument that reflected patterns widely practised in Graeco-Roman society, and focused on such external matters.[57] Paul contrasts himself with such characterizations by saying, 'I beg you that when I come I may not have to be as bold as I expect to be towards some people who think that we live by the standards of this world. For though we live in the world, we do not wage war as the world does'. Paul goes on to demonstrate these weapons were precisely those of argument and oratory.[58]

In 2 Corinthians 11:5-6, Paul, acknowledging that it is a foolish exercise, is comparing himself with the so-called super-apostles. He concedes that he was an ἰδιώτης τῷ λόγῳ, which suggests either that he was untrained or was a novice in rhetoric.[59] Notwithstanding this, Paul certainly has some knowledge (γνῶσις) of rhetorical devices;

---

[54]Cf. Quintilian 11.3.12-13. This view is in contrast to those who argue that it is a reference to an illness of Paul.

[55]2 Cor 10:10. Cf. B.W. Winter, *Philo and Paul among the Sophists*, 207-13; also T.B. Savage, *Power through Weakness*, 65-67, who argues that there is a criticism here that Paul is duplicitous and lacks the strength to carry out his threats in person.

[56]B.W. Winter, *Philo and Paul among the Sophists*, 204.

[57]2 Cor 10:7.

[58]2 Cor 10:4-5.

[59]B.W. Winter, *Philo and Paul among the Sophists*, 213-15.

indeed these are displayed on occasions in his writings.[60] The problem, in the eyes of the Corinthians, is that Paul's manner of delivering his message does not match his conviction in the content of that message.[61] Paul, on the other hand, wants to avoid weakening the message of the cross merely for selfish reasons of self-aggrandizement.

In 2 Corinthians 12:16, Paul is accused of craftiness (πανοῦργος), deceit (δόλος), and financial exploitation. He points out to the Corinthians that just as Titus in no way exploited the Corinthians, Paul shares the same spirit and acted in like manner.[62] This is consistent with a perennial criticism levelled at first-century sophists.[63] If accused of 'peddling the word for profit' as the sophists did, Paul categorically denies the charge and affirms his own sincerity and transparency in these matters.[64]

We have here, therefore, influential figures from Corinth who were exercising their sway according to the canons of the secular world. For these people the model of leadership by which they were assessing Paul was that of the sophists. In like manner, it was this pattern which they had adopted as appropriate in the church.

IV. Romans — a Community with Leaders Preoccupied with Status

Debate continues as to whether it is possible to reconstruct the situation which existed in the Roman community or communities to which Paul wrote. The heart of the debate concerns the purpose of the letter: was it written as a 'summary of Christian doctrine' without specific circumstances in mind, or as an occasional letter? In recent times the former stance has been less widely adopted by scholars. If it was written as an occasional letter, however, does it reflect the

---

[60]Cf. Paul's forensic skill recorded in Acts 24, his use of a covert allusion in 1 Cor 6:4ff., his introduction of technical rhetorical terms in 1 Cor 2:1-5, and the possibility that his letter to the Galatians may conform to rhetorical structure; B.W. Winter, *Philo and Paul among the Sophists*, 215-18.

[61]T.B. Savage, *Power through Weakness*, 70-71.

[62]2 Cor 12:18.

[63]B.W. Winter, *Philo and Paul among the Sophists*, 218-19.

[64]2 Cor 2:17.

situation of its author or of its recipients?[65] A number of scholars find within Romans evidence which reflects some of the tensions which existed between Jewish and Christian congregations in the aftermath of the Claudian expulsion of 'Jews' from Rome.[66]

William Lane, in a recent article, helpfully charts the changing social perspective of Roman Christianity as variously presented in Romans, Hebrews and 1 Clement.[67] The situation which lies behind Paul's letter, especially Romans 16:3-15, was that of Christian groups meeting in various premises privately-owned by wealthier Christians who were acting in capacity as patrons. Specific patrons are mentioned by Paul who had shown him generosity when in the region of Corinth, namely Phoebe and Gaius.[68] Aquila and Priscilla were probably of a similar social group in Rome, and, automatically, therefore would have fulfilled a rôle as leaders.[69] These leaders

---

[65]Cf. W.L. Lane, 'Social Perspectives on Roman Christianity during the Formative Years from Nero to Nerva: Romans, Hebrews, 1 Clement', in K.P. Donfried & P. Richardson (eds.), Judaism and Christianity in First-Century Rome (Grand Rapids: Eerdmans, 1998) 196-202; and C.C. Caragounis, 'From Obscurity to Prominence: the Development of the Roman Church between Romans and 1 Clement', op. cit., 246-47, for a brief overview of the debate; especially, op. cit., 247, 'If he had any understanding of the Roman church at all — as he seems to have had — then not only the argumentative but also the hortatory passages of the letter must contain important information about the state of the Roman church'.

[66]Cf. R. Brändle & E.W. Stegemann, 'The Formation of the First "Christian Congregations" in Rome in the Context of the Jewish Congregations', in K.P. Donfried & P. Richardson (eds.), Judaism and Christianity in First-Century Rome (Grand Rapids: Eerdmans, 1998) 117-27; J.C. Walters, 'Romans, Jews and Christians: the Impact of the Romans on Jewish/Christian Relations in First-Century Rome', op. cit., 175-95; W.L. Lane, 'Social Perspectives on Roman Christianity during the Formative Years from Nero to Nerva: Romans, Hebrews, 1 Clement', 196-244; H. Moxnes, 'The Quest for Honor and the Unity of the Community in Romans 12 and in the Orations of Dio Chrysostom', in T. Engberg-Pedersen (ed.), Paul in his Hellenistic Context (Studies of the New Testament and its World; Edinburgh: T. & T. Clark, 1994) 203-30; and F. Watson, 'The Two Roman Congregations: Romans 14:1-15:13', in K.P. Donfried (ed.), The Romans Debate (Revised & expanded ed.; Edinburgh: T. & T. Clark, 1991) 203-15.

[67]W.L. Lane, 'Social Perspectives on Roman Christianity during the Formative Years from Nero to Nerva: Romans, Hebrews, 1 Clement', 196-244.

[68]Rom 16:2, 23; cf. W.L. Lane, 'Social Perspectives on Roman Christianity during the Formative Years from Nero to Nerva: Romans, Hebrews, 1 Clement', 211.

[69]Rom 16:3-5; cf. W.L. Lane, 'Social Perspectives on Roman Christianity during the Formative Years from Nero to Nerva: Romans, Hebrews, 1 Clement', 211, 'Wealth and patronage were almost certainly determining factors in the leadership they provided in Rome to those who looked to them as hosts and house church patrons'.

'emerged' within the community by virtue of their social standing, and the effect of Romans 16 is that of an apostolic legitimation of their service.[70]

Halvor Moxnes analyses, with illumination from Dio Chrysostom's orations, the extent to which personal honour and status were integral to life in Graeco-Roman cities.[71] He then argues that Paul was opposing, especially in Romans 12:3 and 16, disunity within the Christian community which stemmed from Christians who were pursuing a typically Graeco-Roman quest for honour.[72] The Graeco-Roman cultural context against which Paul responds is most clearly seen in Romans 13:1-7.[73] The congregation comprised a social mix and Paul's injunctions 'not to think too highly' 'is directed not to an individual character trait, but to a total system of relations between individuals of unequal status'.[74] Accordingly, Paul's exhortations concerning the weak and the strong in the community,[75] urge the latter firstly to imitate not the principles of Graeco-Roman society, but Christ who did not seek to please himself, and secondly to accept those, presumably of lower status, in the community.[76]

---

[70]W.L. Lane, 'Social Perspectives on Roman Christianity during the Formative Years from Nero to Nerva: Romans, Hebrews, 1 Clement', 212.

[71]C.P. Jones, *The Roman World of Dio Chrysostom* (Loeb Classical monographs; London: Harvard University Press, 1978) 25, points out how epigraphic evidence alone offers a positive view of benefaction where the literary evidence of, for example, Chrysostom's orations offers a more cynical view of how the system was abused.

[72]*Cf.* also, J.E. Lendon, *Empire of Honour: the Art of Government in the Roman World* (Oxford: Clarendon Press, 1997) 92-95, for instances in the post-apostolic church of ecclesiastical offices being sought merely for the honour that was attached to them, much as the secular authorities in the Graeco-Roman world had always done.

[73]H. Moxnes, 'The Quest for Honor and the Unity of the Community in Romans 12 and in the Orations of Dio Chrysostom', 214-16. *Cf.* also, with specific regard to benefaction terminology in Romans, B.W. Winter, 'The Public Honouring of Christian Benefactors: Romans 13.3 and 1 Peter 2.14-15', *Journal for the Study of the New Testament* 34 (1988) 87-103; and A.D. Clarke, 'The Good and the Just in Romans 5:7', *Tyndale Bulletin* 41 (1990) 128-42.

[74]Rom 12:3; and H. Moxnes, 'The Quest for Honor and the Unity of the Community in Romans 12 and in the Orations of Dio Chrysostom', 222.

[75]Rom 15:1-7.

[76]A.D. Clarke, '"Be Imitators of Me": Paul's Model of Leadership', *Tyndale Bulletin* 49 (1998) 353.

V. Philippians — a Community with Leaders Preoccupied with Politics

Many commentators on Paul's letter to the Philippians include standard reference to the cultural and political background of the Roman colony of Philippi.[77] An increasing number of scholars further find within this letter clear associations with that Roman background, both in vocabulary adopted and themes developed.[78] Indeed, conflict between the Christian and Roman social, cultural and religious contexts probably lies at the heart of some of the problems which Paul addresses in his letter.[79]

---

[77]Two recent monographs which handle this with exceptional detail are L. Bormann, *Philippi: Stadt und Christengemeinde zur Zeit des Paulus* (Supplements to Novum Testamentum, 78; Leiden: E.J. Brill, 1995); and P. Pilhofer, *Philippi vol. 1: die Erste Christliche Gemeinde Europas* (WUNT, 87; Tübingen: J.C.B. Mohr, 1995).

[78]*Cf.*, for example, M. Tellbe, 'The Sociological Factors behind Philippians 3:1-11 and the Conflict at Philippi', *Journal for the Study of the New Testament* 55 (1994) 98, who notes the *hapax legomena* πολιτεύεσθαι (Phil 1:27) and πολίτευμα (Phil 3:20), the references to the praetorian guard (Phil 1:13) and the house of Caesar (Phil 4:22), and the military and athletic images (Phil 1:27-30) and Stoic terminology. For further discussion of the possibility of Stoic terminology in the letter, *cf.* especially T. Engberg-Pedersen, 'Stoicism in Philippians', in T. Engberg-Pedersen (ed.), *Paul in his Hellenistic Context* (Studies of the New Testament and its World; Edinburgh: T. & T. Clark, 1994) 256-90. See also E.M. Krentz, 'Military Language and Metaphors in Philippians', in B.H. McLean (ed.), *Origins and Method: Towards a New Understanding of Judaism and Christianity* (JSNT Supplement Series, 86; Sheffield: JSOT Press, 1993) 105-27, who compares the vocabulary and themes in the letter with numerous Greek authors and notes what is an unusual preponderance of military language and metaphors within the epistle, especially Phil 1:27-30. Citing Epictetus 1.22.6; 3.22.83; 3.22.85, he argues, *op. cit.*, 115, that πολιτεύεσθαι can mean 'to engage in public life'; also T.C. Geoffrion, *The Rhetorical Purpose and the Political and Military Character of Philippians: a Call to Stand Firm* (Lampeter: Mellen Biblical Press, 1993) 91, who argues that even the word κοινωνία should here be understood as a political concept; *contra*, for example, J.P. Sampley, *Pauline Partnership in Christ: Christian Community and Commitment in Light of Roman Law* (Philadelphia: Fortress Press, 1980) 51-77, who reads κοινωνία in terms of *societas*, or 'consensual partnership'.

[79]*Cf.*, for example, M. Tellbe, 'The Sociological Factors behind Philippians 3:1-11 and the Conflict at Philippi', 111, who suggests, 'This distinctive Roman terminology was therefore most likely employed for the purpose of addressing the particular historical, political and sociological situation of the Philippian church'.

A key element of this interpretation revolves around the sense given to the verb πολιτεύεσθαι in Philippians 1:27[80] and the related noun πολίτευμα in Philippians 3:20.[81] Both of these words have strong political connotations, and suggest that Paul was aware of tensions amongst the Christians concerning the way in which the Christian community related to the wider social world of the Roman colony. The suggestion of conflict between the Philippian church and the surrounding society also surfaces in the language of Philippians 3:1-11.[82]

One convincing thesis is that these Christians were troubled by status inconsistency; in other words, their perceived status in the civic community was being adversely affected by their association with the Christian community.[83] On becoming Christians, they would have suffered social pressures following withdrawal from participation in the local civic and imperial cult. Such an action had significant political and social consequences. This was in noticeable

---

[80]*Cf.* R.R. Brewer, 'The meaning of πολιτεύεσθε in Philippians 1:27', *Journal of Biblical Literature* 73 (1954) 76-83, especially his suggested conveyance of the sense of Paul's statement, *op. cit.*, 83, 'Continue to discharge your obligations as citizens and residents of Philippi faithfully and as a Christian should'; also the helpful overview of the noun πολίτευμα by A.T. Lincoln, *Paradise Now and Not Yet: Studies in the Role of the Heavenly Dimension in Paul's Thought with Special Reference to his Eschatology* (SNTS Monograph Series, 43; Cambridge: Cambridge University Press, 1981) 97-101. This perspective is unconvincingly countered by E.C. Miller, 'Πολιτεύεσθε in Philippians 1:27: Some Philological and Thematic Observations', *Journal for the Study of the New Testament* 15 (1982) 86-96, who suggests that the sense of the verb should be located within the Judeo-Christian tradition, in connection with Torah usage; *cf.* also P. Perkins, 'Christology, Friendship and Status: the Rhetoric of Philippians', 516-17, who draws a link between *politeuma* and the Jewish independent political units in diasporan communities, for example, Alexandria; and G. Lüderitz, 'What is the Politeuma?' in J.W. van Henten & P.W. van der Horst, *Studies in Early Jewish Epigraphy* (Arbeiten zur Geschichte des antiken Judentums und des Urchristentums, 21; Leiden: E.J. Brill, 1994) 183-225, who discusses both the Graeco-Roman and Jewish contexts for the term, but not with respect to Philippians.

[81]P.C. Böttger, 'Die eschatologische Existenz der Christen. Erwägungen zu Philipper 3.20', *Zeitschrift für die neutestamentliche Wissenschaft* 60 (1969) 245, 247.

[82]M. Tellbe, 'The Sociological Factors behind Philippians 3:1-11 and the Conflict at Philippi', 98.

[83]P. Perkins, 'Christology, Friendship and Status: the Rhetoric of Philippians', *Society of Biblical Literature 1987 Seminar Papers* (Atlanta: Scholars Press, 1987) 510-12. Note also her suggestion that at the root of the Philippian community is the concept of the 'association', based on terms such as *societas* and *koinonia*; P. Perkins, *Ministering in the Pauline Churches* (New York: Paulist Press, 1982) 21-22.

contrast to the more advantageous situation faced by Jewish communities, which received a degree of Roman protection in many diasporan cities. Consequently, the possibility of closer association with the Jewish community may have presented an attractive compromise for the Philippian Christians. In particular, the option of 'seeking "status" as a *politeuma* of "Israelites" [a Jewish independent, political unit in a diasporan city] provided an alternative to the persistent danger of suspicion and persecution'.[84] The situation faced by these Christians was, therefore, something of a cleft stick.

Going back to the account in Acts 16:11-40, Mikael Tellbe understands that this conflict between the Christian gospel and Roman law and customs was first provoked when Paul and Silas were hauled before the civic magistrates (στρατηγοί) for 'advocating customs unlawful for us Romans to accept or practise',[85] thereby generating 'a clash between the apostolic preaching and the political ideology of the city of Philippi'.[86] Paul's κύριος language in the letter should then be seen in deliberate opposition to the alternative of pursuing the imperial cult.[87] What is distinctive about Christ is his path of humiliation towards exaltation portrayed in the Christ-hymn.[88] Peter Oakes similarly argues that this suffering was engendered by the refusal of some Christians to continue to observe the civic or imperial cult.[89] These actions would necessarily have

---

[84]P. Perkins, 'Christology, Friendship and Status: the Rhetoric of Philippians', 518. *Cf.* also *idem*, 'Philippians: Theology for the Heavenly Politeuma', in J.M. Bassler (ed.), *Pauline Theology: Volume I — Thessalonians, Philippians, Galatians, Philemon* (Minneapolis: Fortress Press, 1991) 92.

[85]Acts 16:20-21.

[86]M. Tellbe, 'The Sociological Factors behind Philippians 3:1-11 and the Conflict at Philippi', 108; he also refers to an expanded treatment in M. Tellbe, *Christ and Caesar: the Letter to the Philippians in the Setting of the Roman Imperial Cult* (ThM dissertation; Vancouver: Regent College, 1993) which the present author has not seen.

[87]M. Tellbe, 'The Sociological Factors behind Philippians 3:1-11 and the Conflict at Philippi', 111. It is pointed out that the noun is used some 15 times. Additionally, M. Tellbe, *op. cit.*, 112, points out the distinctive use of σωτήρ, a noun often applied to the emperor.

[88]M. Tellbe, 'The Sociological Factors behind Philippians 3:1-11 and the Conflict at Philippi', 113; *cf.* Phil 2:6-11 — a humiliation which entailed not grasping equality with God, taking the lowly place of a servant, and ultimately being crucified at the hands of the Romans.

[89]P. Oakes, 'Philippians: From People to Letter', *Tyndale Bulletin* 47 (1996) 371-74; *cf.* also, *idem, Philippians: From People to Letter* (DPhil dissertation; Oxford: Oxford University, 1995; Cambridge: Cambridge University Press, forthcoming); also D.

economic implications for Christians as they became marginalized from their fellow-citizens. The context of some of Paul's comments is clearly political and reflects his awareness that these Philippian Christians were exposed to a Roman imperial ideology.[90] In particular, a contrast is deliberately drawn between the nature of Christ as saviour and that of the emperor as saviour. Indeed Christ's authority is explicitly seen in Philippians 2:9-11 as greater than that of human rulers.

Judaizing Jewish-Christians in Philippi were aware of the social pressures on the Christians who had withdrawn from the imperial cult, and were appealing to them on the basis that identifying with the Jews would not only enhance their social status, but also afford them exemption from involvement in the civic cults since Judaism was a protected *religio licita*.[91] Without this the Christians would have been alienated both from the Jewish community and the Roman authorities.[92] Paul's response is to encourage the Philippians to identify rather with the example and sufferings of Christ.[93] If this reconstruction is plausible, the letter is, then, an encouragement that the Christians should not insist on their political rights in the earthly Roman or Jewish commonwealths; but rather they should focus on the fact that their citizenship was in heaven, from where would appear a non-imperial saviour figure.[94]

This dichotomy facing the Philippian Christians is resolved, Paul argues, neither by conforming to society's expectations, nor by total withdrawal from public life in the colony. Bruce Winter has

---

Peterlin, *Paul's Letter to the Philippians in the Light of Disunity in the Church* (Supplements to Novum Testamentum, 79; Leiden; New York: E.J. Brill, 1995) 135-70, who argues that the sizeable Philippian congregation comprised a social mix including peasants, town-dwelling day-labourers, slaves, as well as some more prominent people.

[90]For example, Phil 2:9-11; 3:20-21.

[91]M. Tellbe, 'The Sociological Factors behind Philippians 3:1-11 and the Conflict at Philippi', 117; *contra* D.J. Doughty, 'Citizens of Heaven: Philippians 3.2-21', *New Testament Studies* 41 (1995) 102-22, who argues for a post-Pauline authorship, with no clear reference to the presence of specific opponents.

[92]M. Tellbe, 'The Sociological Factors behind Philippians 3:1-11 and the Conflict at Philippi', 103; following J.M.G. Barclay, *Obeying the Truth: a Study of Paul's Ethics in Galatians* (Studies of the New Testament and its World; Edinburgh: T. & T. Clark, 1988) 56-59, with specific regard to Galatians.

[93]M. Tellbe, 'The Sociological Factors behind Philippians 3:1-11 and the Conflict at Philippi', 121.

[94]Phil 3:20.

made the case that one aspect of the situation which forms the background to Paul's letter to the Philippians is that of disunity and concord in the realm of *politeia*, defined as 'public life'.[95] The crux of this thesis is the interpretation given to the imperative πολιτεύεσθε in Philippians 1:27, namely 'live as citizens'. Such an interpretation contrasts with the apolitical renderings 'conduct yourselves', 'let your conduct', 'live', 'let your manner of life', or 'live your life' adopted by many English translations. Paul is thus urging his readers that they have a responsibility to act as citizens in the public sphere of the πόλις in a way which is also consistent with the message of the gospel. His injunction in Philippians 2:3 not to indulge in factionalism (ἐριθεία) and vain glory (κενοδοξία) similarly reflects the type of activity customarily adopted in the competitive world of public office;[96] equally, the murmurings (γογγυσμός) and disputations (διαλογισμός), which form the basis of Paul's criticism of the Philippians, reflect the language of political discord.[97] It is clear that some Christians had adopted this line of least resistance and were acting in a way which paralleled the expectations of Roman society.

There are clear similarities with Dio Chrysostom, when, for example, he speaks disparagingly to the citizens of Nicomedia of the vain-glory which nonetheless was part and parcel of so much political intrigue. Thus,

> vainglory has come to be regarded as a foolish thing even in private individuals, and we ourselves deride and loathe, and end by pitying, those persons above all who do not know wherein false glory differs from the genuine; besides no educated man has such a feeling about glory as to desire a foolish thing.[98]

In this speech, the orator is challenging the Nicomedians precisely because of their factionalism and vain-glory towards their bitter and local political rivals, the Nicaeans. There were fierce disputations over which city had primacy and who was entitled to the most prestigious rank. Such political wrangling was criticized by some as peculiar to Greek politics:

---

[95]B.W. Winter, *Seek the Welfare of the City*, 13-14, 57, 81-104.

[96]B.W. Winter, *Seek the Welfare of the City*, 98-100.

[97]Phil 2:14.

[98]Dio Chrysostom, *Orationes* 38.29; cited in B.W. Winter, *Seek the Welfare of the City*, 92.

In truth such marks of distinction, on which you plume yourselves, not only are objects of utter contempt in the eyes of all persons of discernment, but especially in Rome they excite laughter and, what is still more humiliating, are called 'Greek failings'![99]

Consequently, the situation reflected in Philippians is of a community which is facing social opposition, even persecution. For some there was the temptation to continue adopting the canons of political quarreling and intrigue. Wendy Cotter has intriguingly suggested that the disparaging language of Philippians 3:19, 'is in no significant way different than the repudiations launched against associations by Varro, Augustus, Flaccus and Claudius'.[100]   She writes, 'It must have been difficult for the Philippians to find a community model that would allow them to adopt certain offices of civic order without the attending ambitious and worldly behaviour typical of political and civic organizations'.[101]

VI. 1 & 2 Thessalonians — a Community influenced by Pagan Culture

The initial ministry of Paul, Silas and Timothy in the Greek city of Thessalonica was marked by suffering, as was the Thessalonians' response to that message.[102] This context of opposition would appear to be confirmed by the account in Acts 17:1-9. Both accounts, however, only give hints as to the basis of this conflict. John Barclay has argued that we should 'understand the Thessalonians' *thlipsis* as social harassment — an experience which became common for Christians in the Greco-Roman world'.[103] The roots of this harassment would then lie in gentile opposition to the Thessalonian

---

[99]Dio Chrysostom, *Orationes* 38.38.

[100]W. Cotter, 'Our *Politeuma* is in Heaven: the Meaning of Philippians 3:17-21', in B.H. McLean (ed.), *Origins and Method: Towards a New Understanding of Judaism and Christianity* (JSNT Supplement Series, 86; Sheffield: JSOT Press, 1993) 101.

[101]W. Cotter, 'Our *Politeuma* is in Heaven: the Meaning of Philippians 3:17-21', 104.

[102]1 Thess 1:6; 2:2, 14; 3:3-4, 7.

[103]J.M.G. Barclay, 'Conflict in Thessalonica', *Catholic Biblical Quarterly* 55 (1993) 514; and *idem*, 'Thessalonica and Corinth: Social Contrasts in Pauline Christianity', 52-53; also, *op. cit.*, 334, '1 Thessalonians shows us the precarious process by which a new Christian community carves out its place among the cults and associations of the Greco-Roman city'.

Christians' 'abandonment of Greco-Roman religion'.[104] Barclay goes as far as to suggest, from Acts 17, that there may be political overtones to the gentile reaction. In particular, there may have been a sense that this rejection of popular civic piety by the Christians was interpreted as a slight to the gods, on whose beneficence the Thessalonian citizens depended.[105] As the Thessalonians 'turned to God from idols, to serve the living and true God', this conversion was not simply a change of ideology, therefore, but also a change of cultic practice (which proved costly given the persecution which ensued).[106] We have already seen that Roman cult was central to the local community.[107] The Thessalonian Christian community may consequently have felt marginalized following its lack of conformity with pagan society. In particular Christians were no longer being

---

[104]J.M.G. Barclay, 'Conflict in Thessalonica', 514. Notwithstanding the emphasis in Acts that the opposition was at the *instigation* of the Jews, it was these Jews who effectively mobilized the opposition such that it assumed a gentile focus, notably the accusation in Acts 17:7 that the Christians were 'defying Caesar's decrees, saying that there is another king, one called Jesus'.

[105]J.M.G. Barclay, 'Conflict in Thessalonica', 514-15; *cf.* also K.P. Donfried, 'The Cults of Thessalonica and the Thessalonian Correspondence', *New Testament Studies* 31 (1985) 336-56, and *idem*, '2 Thessalonians and the Church of Thessalonica', in B.H. McLean (ed.), *Origins and Method: Towards a New Understanding of Judaism and Christianity* (JSNT Supplement Series, 86; Sheffield: JSOT Press, 1993) 128-44, who suggests that the hostility which the Christians experienced must have been related to the civic cults; and for a wider discussion of the Roman religious situation in Thessalonica, *cf.* H.L. Hendrix, *Thessalonicans Honor Romans* (ThD dissertation; Cambridge: Harvard University Press, 1984); and *idem*, 'Benefactor/Patron Networks in the Urban Environment: Evidence from Thessalonica', *Semeia* 56 (1992) 39-58; and, with reference to the Roman political overtones of Paul's statement 'peace and security' (1 Thess 5:3), *cf. idem*, 'Archaeology and Eschatology at Thessalonica', in B.A. Pearson (ed.), *The Future of Early Christianity: Essays in Honor of Helmut Koester* (Minneapolis: Fortress Press, 1991) 107-18.

[106]1 Thess 1:9; *cf.* also, P. Perkins, '1 Thessalonians and Hellenistic Religious Practices', in M.P. Horgan & P.J. Kobelski (eds.), *To Touch the Text: Biblical and Related Studies in Honor of Joseph A. Fitzmyer, S.J.* (New York: Crossroad, 1989) 327.

[107]D.A. deSilva, '"Worthy of his Kingdom": Honor Discourse and Social Engineering in 1 Thessalonians', *Journal for the Study of the New Testament* 64 (1996) 61, writes, 'Participation in the cults of Rome, the emperor, and the traditional pantheon showed one's *pietas* or εὐσέβεια, one's reliability, in effect, to fulfill one's obligations to family, patron, city, province, and empire. Participation showed one's support of the social body, one's desire for doing what was necessary to secure the welfare of the city, and one's commitment to the stability and ongoing life of the city'.

affirmed by the widespread Graeco-Roman values of honour.[108] As a result, the Thessalonian Christians, who are praised by Paul for having turned their backs on paganism, are then under popular suspicion precisely because of this action.[109]

Pagan society is, therefore, seen by Paul as a tempter, and it is such external pressures which are referred to in 1 Thessalonians 3:1-5, and which prompt Paul to send Timothy to 'strengthen and encourage' the Thessalonian Christians in the faith.[110] Paul's characterization of pagan society is negative and his message is that the church should not be guided by society's opinions or practices.[111] In the light of such provocation, he urges the Thessalonians not to retaliate, but instead to 'lead a quiet life ... mind your own business and ... work with your hands, so that your daily life may win the respect of outsiders'.[112]

This raises a second area which is forcefully addressed in the Thessalonian correspondence; namely the issue of idleness on the part of some of the believers. One of the problems Paul identifies in the Thessalonian church was the tendency for some of the poorer people to live off the patronage of wealthier Christians.[113] The Christian community in Thessalonica was predominantly made up of poorer people,[114] although its leaders were probably drawn from the

---

[108]D.A. deSilva, '"Worthy of his Kingdom": Honor Discourse and Social Engineering in 1 Thessalonians', 49-79.

[109]D.A. deSilva, '"Worthy of his Kingdom": Honor Discourse and Social Engineering in 1 Thessalonians', 65, 'attachment to Jesus and this new community has cost them the respect they formerly enjoyed from their neighbors, and to that extent has made them question their own self-worth'.

[110]D.A. deSilva, '"Worthy of his Kingdom": Honor Discourse and Social Engineering in 1 Thessalonians', 63.

[111]1 Thess 4:3-7, 11-12, 13-18; 5:3-8; cf. D.A. deSilva, '"Worthy of his Kingdom": Honor Discourse and Social Engineering in 1 Thessalonians', 65-66.

[112]1 Thess 4:11-12.

[113]B.W. Winter, '"If a Man Does not Wish to Work...": a Cultural and Historical Setting for 2 Thessalonians 3:6-16', Tyndale Bulletin 40 (1989) 305-15; cf. also R. Russell, 'The Idle in 2 Thess 3.6-12: an Eschatological or a Social Problem?', New Testament Studies 34 (1988) 112-13.

[114]Cf. N.O. Míguez, 'La composición social de la Iglesia en Tesalónica', Revista Bíblica 51.34 (1989) 65-89, who considers 2 Cor 8:2 and 1 Thess 2:9 as suggestive of the poorer background of most Thessalonian Christians. Cf. also A.J. Malherbe, Paul and the Thessalonians: the Philosophic Tradition of Pastoral Care (Philadelphia: Fortress Press, 1987) 98-101, who suggests that Paul's principal audience comprised Greek manual labourers.

wealthier in the community.[115] Jason, mentioned in Acts 17:5-9, seems to have taken a particularly prominent rôle.[116] It is widely assumed that he was a wealthy, Hellenistic Jew, converted under Paul's ministry, who played host to Paul and his fellow-workers, and whose house was consequently attacked by Jews. Jason's wealth not only afforded him a house in which he could offer hospitality, but it was also sufficient to post bond when the need arose.[117]

Notwithstanding the evidence that there were some in the church who were socially prominent, Paul's urge to the whole community is that the Thessalonian Christians become financially dependent on nobody.[118] In his subsequent letter, here assumed to be Pauline in authorship, he repeats an injunction which he had placed upon them in person: 'If a man does not wish to work, let him not eat'.[119] In this way Paul is concerned that Christians contribute to the welfare of the city, rather than be economically dependent on fellow citizens.[120]

So here we find a community which had formerly been heavily influenced by pagan culture. For the most part these were not wealthy individuals, but they are nonetheless strongly affected by the civic and cultic cultural background of Graeco-Roman Thessalonica. Paul's message is one of positive reinforcement to encourage them to remain strong in their faith and to resist society's pressures to conform. Additionally, in the congregation is a social mix. According

---

[115]Such leaders are those referred to in 1 Thess 5:12-13. *Cf.* J.L. Hill, *Establishing the Church in Thessalonica* (PhD dissertation; Durham: Duke University, 1990) 218-20. A broadly similar conclusion was drawn, although following a very different and not always convincing approach, by A.L. Chapple, *Local Leadership in the Pauline Churches: Theological and Social Factors in its Development: a Study Based on 1 Thessalonians, 1 Corinthians and Philippians* (PhD dissertation; Durham: Durham University, 1984) 206-60.

[116]Much of this reconstruction of Jason has to be in part speculative, but it could be that he is also referred to in Rom 16:21; *cf.* F. Morgan-Gillman, 'Jason of Thessalonica (Acts 17,5-9)', in R.F. Collins (ed.), *The Thessalonian Correspondence* (Bibliotheca ephemeridum theologicarum lovaniensium, 87; Leuven: Leuven University Press, 1990) 39-49. For the possibility of other leading figures in the Thessalonian church, *cf.* B.W. Winter, '"If a Man Does not Wish to Work...": a Cultural and Historical Setting for 2 Thessalonians 3:6-16', 306-307.

[117]F. Morgan-Gillman, 'Jason of Thessalonica (Acts 17,5-9)', 41.

[118]1 Thess 4:12.

[119]2 Thess 3:10.

[120]B.W. Winter, '"If a Man Does not Wish to Work...": a Cultural and Historical Setting for 2 Thessalonians 3:6-16', 314.

to the standard customs of patron/client relations, some of the poorer members of the community continued to be financially dependent on wealthier fellow Christians when there was no longer any need.

VII. Galatians — Communities with Proud Leaders

Paul's letter to the Galatian churches focuses especially on a refutation of the message of certain Judaizers. As he brings his letter to a close, however, he highlights for his readers particular areas in which they should avoid following practices which were also widely adopted in first-century society. His exhortation to them is rather to 'live by the Spirit', 'be led by the Spirit' and 'keep in step with the Spirit'.[121] In particular there is the insidious danger that pride may cause some to stumble. This danger is as real for 'those who are spiritual' as for those who are 'caught in a sin'.[122] It is noteworthy, indeed, that the focus of Paul's exhortation is on the dangers open to the 'spiritual' person, rather than the wrongdoing of the sinner.[123] In the necessary process of providing correction, this should be done in a gentle manner, specifically to avoid the temptation of becoming self-important in a moralistic way. Paul considers that those who were prominent among the Galatian churches were liable to think of themselves with self-importance, when instead they should recognize in reality that they have no grounds for such boasting.[124] There is a place for pride, however, but not that pride, so common in first-century society, which amounts to inflated superiority and derives from comparison with others.[125] What is called for, instead, is sober self-reflection before God.

The Galatian churches were under considerable pressure from Judaizers. Those Judaizers themselves, however, were characterized

---

[121]Cf. R.N. Longenecker, Galatians (Word Biblical Commentary, 41; Dallas: Word Books, 1990) 269, 'Such traditional material is not to be seen as unique to the Judaizers; rather, it probably was drawn by Paul from his own background (whether Jewish, Hellenistic, Christian, or some combination of these factors) and used by him in a manner he believed would be appreciated by his converts with their pagan and Christian backgrounds as well — traditions they would have known, at least to some extent, even before the intrusion of the Judaizers'.
[122]Gal 6:1.
[123]Cf. R.N. Longenecker, Galatians, 274.
[124]Gal 6:3.
[125]Gal 6:4.

by Paul as people determined 'to make a good impression outwardly'.[126] The irony of Paul's statement here lies in the way that the phrase 'make a good impression (εὐπροσωπῆσαι)', although a virtual *hapax legomenon*, might be expected to refer to physical beauty, but can here be inferred to be a reference to the circumcision to which the Galatians are being compelled to submit.[127] For these Jews, the circumcision of Christian gentiles becomes a grounds for personal boasting. Paul roundly opposes such a motivation. In contrast, he himself refuses to boast in anything except the cross of Christ.[128]

Pride was, thus, a problem for not only the Galatian Christians but also the Judaizers. Indeed, it was endemic to Greeks, Romans, Jews and Christians in the status-conscious world of the first century. Paul's response is unequivocally opposed.

VIII. Philemon — a Household Leader and Church Leader

The situation which lies behind the letter to Philemon is notoriously difficult to reconstruct given both the lack of explicit information provided by Paul and the ambiguous nature of some of his statements, possibly deliberate for the sake of diplomacy and politeness given the delicate nature of the situation.[129] Most scholarly interest is concerned with Onesimus, the nature of his relationship

---

[126]Gal 6:12.

[127]J.D.G. Dunn, *A Commentary on the Epistle to the Galatians* (Black's New Testament Commentaries; London: A. & C. Black, 1993) 335-36.

[128]Gal 6:13-14.

[129]*Cf.* the traditional view recently redefended by J.G. Nordling, 'Onesimus Fugitivus: a Defense of the Runaway Slave Hypothesis in Philemon', *Journal for the Study of the New Testament* 41 (1991) 97-119; a summary of views explaining how Onesimus came to meet Paul, by B.M. Rapske, 'The Prisoner Paul in the Eyes of Onesimus', *New Testament Studies* 37 (1991) 187-88; also the assessment of Onesimus' situation, by J.M.G. Barclay, 'Paul, Philemon and Christian Slave-Ownership', *New Testament Studies* 37 (1991) 161-86; the view that a solution to the reconstruction lies in a greater understanding of the importance of Jewish proselytism, by J.D.M. Derrett, 'The Functions of the Epistle to Philemon', *Zeitschrift für die Neutestamentliche Wissenschaft* 79 (1988) 63-91; and the radically different theories which argue that the fugitive slave hypothesis is untenable, proposed by P. Lampe, 'Keine Sklavenflucht des Onesimus', *Zeitschrift für die Neutestamentliche Wissenschaft* 76 (1985) 135-37; S.C. Winter, 'Paul's Letter to Philemon', *New Testament Studies* 33 (1987) 1-15; and A.D. Callahan, 'Paul's Epistle to Philemon: Toward an Alternative *Argumentum*', *Harvard Theological Review* 86 (1993) 357-76.

with Paul and Philemon, the circumstances which have led to his present situation, and Paul's attitude to slavery. In the present context, however, it is the rôle of Philemon which is of greater interest.[130]

Paul addresses the letter to Philemon, Apphia, Archippus and to the church which 'meets in *your* house'.[131] The singular pronoun 'your' has led the majority of commentators to assume that the house is that of Philemon, and the letter is primarily addressed to him.[132] It would appear that Philemon is a comparatively well-off householder within the Christian community of which he is a part. He is a man of sufficient means that he is able to offer hospitality to the church as they meet, and he can be prevailed upon to service Paul's request to provide a guest-room when he visits.[133] Philemon is a slaveowner, although we are not informed as to the extent of his household.[134] Furthermore, it can be inferred from Paul's use of commercial language in Philemon 17-18 that this householder was also a businessman.[135] It is generally accepted that the Onesimus of

[130]N.R. Petersen, *Rediscovering Paul: Philemon and the Sociology of Paul's Narrative World* (Philadelphia: Fortress Press, 1985) is one monograph which deals at length with the nature of the relationships between named individuals in the letter.

[131]Phlm 2.

[132]Although, *cf.* the unconvincing suggestion that Archippus is the chief recipient of the letter in S.C. Winter, 'Paul's Letter to Philemon', *New Testament Studies* 33 (1987) 1-2; the reconstruction in J. Knox, *Philemon among the Letters of Paul: a New View of its Place and Importance* (Chicago: University of Chicago Press, 1935) 26, that Onesimus was the slave of Archippus; and the intriguing suggestion by R.F. Hock, 'A Support for his Old Age: Paul's Plea on Behalf of Onesimus', in L.M. White & O.L. Yarbrough (eds.), *The Social World of the First Christians: Essays in Honor of Wayne A. Meeks* (Minneapolis: Fortress Press, 1995) 77, 81, that Paul's inclusion of the ἐκκλησία in the address follows Graeco-Roman cultural precedent that household matters were sometimes addressed more publicly; thus, 'The letter itself was read in the rhetorical situation of a quasi-public ἐκκλησία, or assembly, in which Philemon's action regarding Paul's plea on behalf of Onesimus was witnessed by those Christians who met in his house (vv. 1-2) and who were to judge this action against the honor that Philemon had gained by his love toward the saints (v. 5)'.

[133]Phlm 2, 22.

[134]Phlm 16.

[135]*Cf.* C.J. Martin, 'The Rhetorical Function of Commercial Language in Paul's Letter to Philemon (Verse 18)', in D.F. Watson (ed.), *Persuasive Artistry: Studies in New Testament Rhetoric in Honor of George A. Kennedy* (JSNT Supplement Series, 50; Sheffield: JSOT Press, 1991) 321-37; and J.D.G. Dunn, *The Epistles to the Colossians and to Philemon: a Commentary on the Greek Text* (The New International

Philemon 10 is also that of Colossians 4:9, and, consequently, that Philemon was a member of the church in Colossae.[136] His social standing within the Christian community, together with his position as host in his own house, presumably involved him in a leadership rôle.[137]

Paul's letter to Philemon concerns the nature of the relationship between Philemon and Onesimus, formerly master and slave, following Onesimus' conversion.[138] Paul argues that this conversion changes the nature of the slave's relationship with his master. 'In the Lord', their status has changed and they are now brothers.[139] Karl Sandnes argues that '[w]hat we see in the New Testament is not an egalitarian community which is being replaced by patriarchal structures; the brotherhood-like nature of the Christian fellowship is in the making, embedded in household structures'.[140] Thus, Paul recognizes Philemon's position as *paterfamilias*, benefactor and leader within his own house and, by extension, the church. His position or status is not countermanded, but the way in which Philemon undertakes to lead, however, is scrutinized by Paul. The nature of the relationship assumes a model of 'eschatological equality'.[141]

This house church, and the relationships represented by it, is at the same time influenced by secular values and by a Christian dynamic. Norman Petersen draws attention to Paul's highlighting of this two-fold dynamic: in Philemon 16, he describes Onesimus as

---

Greek Testament Commentary; Grand Rapids: Eerdmans, 1996) 336-39. Dunn further suggests, *op. cit.*, 301, that Philemon was a sufficiently successful businessman to afford time away from his affairs in order to pursue Christian ministry.

[136]*Cf.* J.D.G. Dunn, *The Epistles to the Colossians and to Philemon*, 300-301.

[137]K.O. Sandnes, 'Equality within Patriarchal Structures: Some New Testament Perspectives on the Christian Fellowship as a Brother- or Sisterhood and a Family', in H. Moxnes (ed.), *Constructing Early Christian Families: Family as Social Reality and Metaphor* (London: Routledge, 1997) 151-53.

[138]Phlm 10.

[139]Phlm 16; *cf.* K.O. Sandnes, 'Equality within Patriarchal Structures: Some New Testament Perspectives on the Christian Fellowship as a Brother- or Sisterhood and a Family', 156-57.

[140]K.O. Sandnes, 'Equality within Patriarchal Structures: Some New Testament Perspectives on the Christian Fellowship as a Brother- or Sisterhood and a Family', 151; *cf.* also *op. cit.*, 156.

[141]K.O. Sandnes, 'Equality within Patriarchal Structures: Some New Testament Perspectives on the Christian Fellowship as a Brother- or Sisterhood and a Family', 163.

both a slave and a brother, and distinguishes between that relationship which is in the flesh and that which is in the Lord (οὐκέτι ὡς δοῦλον ἀλλ' ὑπὲρ δοῦλον, ἀδελφὸν ἀγαπητόν, μάλιστα ἐμοί, πόσῳ δὲ μᾶλλον σοὶ καὶ ἐν σαρκὶ καὶ ἐν κυρίῳ).[142] The relationship between Philemon and Onesimus (that of master and slave or debtee and debtor) is one that was influenced by social, cultural and legal values.[143]

Paul highlights additional dimensions, however, to this scenario: first, the conversion of Onesimus alters the relationship between master and slave; secondly, Paul's relationship with Philemon, Paul argues, changes the dynamic of the situation;[144] and thirdly God is recognized as *paterfamilias*, and Jesus Christ as master over all the members of the household community.[145]

Paul wants the leadership which Philemon gives to members of the Christian community not to be characterized as that of a master over his slave. The generous patronage which Philemon has given and continues to give, patronage both to Paul and the church as a whole, is commended; but the associated hierarchical authority of the master is not to mark the relationships in the church. Petersen raises the question as to what implications the 'spiritual' relationship between Philemon and Onesimus has for their 'fleshly' relationship: 'can Philemon relate to his slave as a brother and still remain his structural master?'[146] In consequence, Paul asks Philemon not only to have Onesimus back, but to have him back as a brother, and furthermore to welcome him back as Philemon would welcome Paul himself (who is a brother, fellow-worker and partner in relation to Philemon).[147] This is significantly counter-cultural; but, notwithstanding this, in Philemon 21, Paul makes it clear that he expects Philemon to do even more than this![148]

---

[142]N.R. Petersen, *Rediscovering Paul*, 95.

[143]N.R. Petersen, *Rediscovering Paul*, 94, 'From a sociological perspective, Onesimus' flight is a relational breach that must be repaired because his action is not in conformity either with the sociological structure or with the social system (institution) that defines the ways in which slaves are to relate to masters'.

[144]Phlm 15-17; cf. N.R. Petersen, *Rediscovering Paul*, 95.

[145]N.R. Petersen, *Rediscovering Paul*, 91.

[146]N.R. Petersen, *Rediscovering Paul*, 96.

[147]N.R. Petersen, *Rediscovering Paul*, 92.

[148]N.R. Petersen, *Rediscovering Paul*, 97-98, 'The "even more" would therefore refer to Philemon's bringing the legal aspect of his worldly relationship with

What is also intriguing is the way in which Paul exercises authority in this situation. He notes that he could boldly instruct Philemon to comply with this injunction.[149] This, however, would be to use precisely those cultural categories of leadership which Paul is expressly asking Philemon to give up the right to. Paul's appeal is then on the basis of love, from one who is an old man, a fellow worker, a partner, a friend, and a brother.[150] Philemon's anticipated response is then to be considered as spontaneous, rather than under order force.[151]

Norman Petersen then draws the wrong conclusions:

> Our analysis of v. 17 and its context in Paul's letter indicates that despite the egalitarian implications of the notions of brother, fellow worker, and partner, Paul also claims a position of hierarchical superiority both over brothers and sisters and over his own fellow workers and partners. But the Letter to Philemon also seems to suggest that while all members of the church are brothers and sisters, those brothers and sisters who are fellow workers and partners also have a position of hierarchical superiority over those who are not.[152]

In the context of the letter, the significance lies in the fact that Paul is explicitly not claiming hierarchical superiority over Philemon; equally, he desires that no distinction is drawn between brothers and sisters in terms of status. Philemon's approach may have been to note these distinctions in status, according to standard cultural mores. Paul demonstrates that he is similarly aware of the normal stratification between Onesimus and Philemon and between Philemon and Paul, but he does not insist on his rights, and pleads with Philemon that, despite being a slave owner, he also deny himself these rights. Rather than concluding that Paul is making an

---

Onesimus into conformity with the social structural ground of their new churchly relationship, presumably by legally freeing Onesimus'.

[149]Phlm 8; cf. N.R. Petersen, *Rediscovering Paul*, 104.

[150]Phlm 1, 9, 17, 20.

[151]Phlm 14; cf. N.R. Petersen, *Rediscovering Paul*, 106. Cf. also, *op. cit.*, 107, with regard to Paul's returning Onesimus to Philemon (Phlm 12-14), '[Paul] has refrained from exercising his authority to compel Philemon to do as he wished, and he has also refrained from doing what he himself really wanted to do with Onesimus. He has not done either what he wanted to do or could have done, and now it is Philemon's turn to reciprocate'.

[152]N.R. Petersen, *Rediscovering Paul*, 107-108.

exception in this instance by not claiming his rightful authority here, it should be argued that this is Paul's standard view of ecclesial relationships and leadership.[153]

There are, nonetheless, responsibilities which go with Philemon's status. He rightfully acts as patron to the church by offering hospitality both to Paul and to the church which meets in his house; equally, he is commended for his actions in 'refreshing the hearts of the saints', and is urged to continue to do the same.[154] This action of 'refreshing the hearts of the saints' is commended of some of the leaders in the Corinthian community, but was also more widely exercised by the Christians in Corinth.[155]

IX. Conclusion

Many studies of Pauline ecclesiology have assessed what are prescriptive statements by Paul regarding church order but viewed them rather as descriptive of the situation which obtained. In this chapter it has been demonstrated that church life in each of the communities discussed varied considerably. As social groups, these churches did not fit neatly into a uniform, theological schema of Paul. It is also clear that each of these social groups was also part of the broader society in which the early Christians lived. They were, accordingly, influenced by the patterns of leadership which prevailed around them. We have seen the emergence within congregations of individuals who were preoccupied variously with issues of status, patronage and personality politics; those who sought to wield power by resorting to mechanisms provided by the legal system; those who resorted to political wranglings or favoured demonstrations of great human wisdom; as well as those who continued to sense the pull from their pagan religious past.

Not all leading figures, however, in these congregations were equally swayed by these 'worldly' influences. In the next chapter we shall consider the ways in which Paul's perception of Christian leadership differed, and how his own example, and that of others,

---

[153]This will be developed in chapter 9 below.

[154]Phlm 7, 20; cf. N.R. Petersen, *Rediscovering Paul*, 108.

[155]Cf. A.D. Clarke, '"Refresh the Hearts of the Saints": a Unique Pauline Context?', *Tyndale Bulletin* 47 (1996) 277-300.

was used to correct those wrong perceptions which otherwise dominated.

CHAPTER 9

PAULINE MINISTRY IN THE CHRISTIAN COMMUNITY

I. Introduction

The focus of the preceding chapters has been a consideration of models of leadership which prevailed in the Graeco-Roman world of the first century and the ways in which some of these principles may have influenced dynamics of local leadership within the Pauline Christian communities. The task in the present chapter is to assess the corrective statements, practices and examples which Paul presents in his correspondence as positive or negative paradigms of Christian leadership. These can be compared with those leadership practices which prevailed in different Pauline communities and were assessed in the preceding chapter.

Although the early Christians had a range of models of leadership or community organization available for them either to adopt or adapt, it becomes plain that Paul associates himself with none of these. Instead, his perception of the nature of leadership within the Christian church derives from his understanding of the unique nature of the Christian church, and the basis on which that community is founded.

In order to be able to construct from his letters a Pauline theology of Christian leadership, relevant material will be assessed as it emerges across the traditional Pauline corpus. This contrasts with the approach adopted in the preceding chapter where Paul's teaching to different communities was considered separately and contextually. The particular headings under which Paul's presentation of local church leadership will here be discussed are authority and ministry.

II. Authority

It has become apparent that the rise to power of individuals at many levels of Graeco-Roman society was predicated on the basis of wealth or family background, and the resultant status was publicly paraded, often by means of financial munificence and displays of wisdom or learning. The authority of individuals over a given community grew in proportion to the honour and esteem in which they were held by that community. Within the Pauline congregations also it has been suggested in the preceding chapter that some individuals were either accorded authority by a Christian community or exercised domination over a Christian community on the basis of similar criteria.[1] On what basis, however, did *Paul* consider that authority in the local church should be legitimated; in what ways should that authority be exercised; and on what grounds did he variously endorse or criticize the leadership of others within these communities?

A number of scholars have recently argued that Paul's style of leadership was both authoritarian and manipulative.[2] Graham Shaw has suggested that 1 Thessalonians 'is preoccupied with the assertion and exercise of the apostle's authority'.[3] He also argues that, in writing to the Galatians, Paul's authority was under considerable threat, and the letter consequently concerns those sanctions which the apostle could impose.[4] Furthermore, 1 Corinthians, he asserts, is 'an

---

[1]See the discussion in the preceding chapter, and, with specific reference to 1 Corinthians, see also, A.D. Clarke, *Secular and Christian Leadership in Corinth: a Socio-historical and Exegetical Study of 1 Corinthians 1-6* (Arbeiten zur Geschichte des antiken Judentums und des Urchristentums, 18; Leiden: E.J. Brill, 1993).

[2]The announced volume, S.H. Polaski, *Paul and the Discourse of Power* (Gender, Culture, Theory, 8; Sheffield: JSOT Press, 1999) had not been published at the time the present volume went to press.

[3]G. Shaw, *The Cost of Authority: Manipulation and Freedom in the New Testament* (London: SCM Press, 1983) 29.

[4]G. Shaw, *The Cost of Authority*, 41.

exercise in magisterial authority'.[5] Elizabeth Castelli has argued from a Foucauldian post-structuralist perspective that Paul used the motif of imitation as a rhetorical device of social control to reinforce his own power and thereby define his group's identity and insist on conformity.[6] Stephen Moore, also in the light of Foucauldian post-structuralism, similarly conceives of Paul as a manipulator.[7] More recently, Cynthia Kittredge has argued with reference to Philippians and Ephesians that 'the language of obedience operates in concert with the dynamics of opposition and identification with the author, and with the rhetoric of oneness'.[8] These assessments of the relationship between the apostle and those in his congregations reflect the cynical suspicion that Paul's dominant underlying agenda was one of control and manipulation.[9] (This is notwithstanding the

---

[5]G. Shaw, *The Cost of Authority*, 62.

[6]E.A. Castelli, *Imitating Paul: a Discourse of Power* (Literary Currents in Biblical Interpretation; Louisville: Westminster/John Knox, 1991) 24, writes that the Pauline letters should be regarded as 'a site at which power is negotiated, brokered, or inscribed — or even as a record of the conflict'. *Cf.* also *idem*, 'Interpretations of Power in 1 Corinthians', *Semeia* 54 (1992) 197-222. For a critical assessment of Castelli's use of Foucauldian theory see A.C. Thiselton, *Interpreting God and the Postmodern Self: On Meaning, Manipulation, and Promise* (Edinburgh: T. & T. Clark, 1995) 140-44.

[7]S.D. Moore, *Poststructuralism and the New Testament: Derrida and Foucault at the Foot of the Cross* (Minneapolis: Fortress, 1994) 109-110.

[8]C.B. Kittredge, *Community and Authority: the Rhetoric of Obedience in the Pauline Tradition* (Harvard Theological Studies, 45; Harrisburg: Trinity Press International, 1998) 175. *Op. cit.*, 109, with regard to Euodia and Syntyche in Philippians, she writes, 'Paul responds to the independent activity of the women partners in the gospel by constructing a model of voluntary renunciation of status, obedience to a superior, and imitation of himself as authoritative model'; and with regard to Ephesians, the attempt to bring about 'oneness' or unity is by resorting to 'obedience of subordinate to superordinate as the organizing principle'. C.B. Kittredge was a student of E.S. Fiorenza, who herself considers that a major emphasis of the Pauline communities is egalitarianism — E.S. Fiorenza, *In Memory of Her: a Feminist Theological Reconstruction of Christian Origins* (2nd ed.; London: SCM Press, 1995); contrast P. Ellingworth, 'Translating the Language of Leadership', *Bible Translator* 49 (1998) 137, 'The New Testament church, on the one hand, was a closely-knit community in which people physically unrelated could naturally call one another brothers or sisters. But on the other hand, it was not an egalitarian community in which all hierarchical structures were abolished or transcended. So much is clear from 1 Cor 12.28'.

[9]G. Shaw, *The Cost of Authority*, 1-25, regards much of the history of Christendom as reflecting an offensive and oppressive authoritarianism. *Cf.*, however, the comment of J.D.G. Dunn, *The Theology of Paul the Apostle* (Edinburgh: T. & T.

widespread perception that one of the criticisms levelled at the apostle by some of the Corinthians was rather that he lacked the 'obvious and objective power and authority associated with apostleship'.)[10]

Paul Avis, in his assessment of the place of authority in the Anglican church, affirms the widely-held view that 'authority has suffered a profound deconstruction at the hands of modernity'. He recognizes, however, that the roots of this current rejection of authority lie within the Enlightenment, and summarizes the standard argument thus:

> appeal to authority was the antithesis of reliance on one's own reason. From Descartes to Kant authority was held responsible for the binding and gagging of human reason ... If unquestioning submission to the prestige of authority excludes one's own judgement, then authority becomes tyrannical. ... The Enlightenment attempted to transfer the seat of authority from dogma to reason, from tradition to experience and from society to the individual.[11]

In today's climate of liberalism, pluralism and individualism the notions of authority and truth continue to be considered repressive.[12] In sympathy with these ideals, where post-modern commentators consider that the goal of Paul's actions and statements was to establish a conformity within the community which would reinforce the apostle's own power base, he is viewed negatively. It is to this end, it has been argued by some, that the metaphor of fatherhood, the authoritarian title of apostle and the controlling or suppressive injunctions to Pauline imitation were all intended to substantiate Paul's own position of authority and extend his power-base. The

---

Clark, 1998) 575, that Shaw demonstrates 'how far an unsympathetic reading or hermeneutic of suspicion can go'.

[10]S.J. Hafemann, '"Self-Commendation" and Apostolic Legitimacy in 2 Corinthians: a Pauline Dialectic?', *New Testament Studies* 36 (1990) 66.

[11]P.D.L. Avis, *Authority, Leadership and Conflict in the Church* (London: Mowbray, 1992) 26, 29. *Cf.* also *op. cit.*, 42, where he suggests that 'It is a disturbing paradox of modern history that, parallel to the advance of so-called Enlightenment and autonomy in the modern world, there has emerged wave after wave of irrational authoritarianism and repression'.

[12]*Cf.* the discussion of authority in L. Hirschhorn, *Reworking Authority: Leading and Following in the Post-modern Organization* (Organization Studies, 12; Cambridge, Mass.: MIT Press, 1997).

apostle then stands for that particular type of patriarchal authority which is viewed antagonistically by post-modern society.[13] It will here be questioned whether these perceptions of Paul's rôle are reflected in his epistles. It is clear that Paul adopted the metaphor of father, the title of apostle and the injunction to imitate. It is less certain that each of these necessarily presupposes a preoccupation with control.

Over recent years, the issue of Pauline authority has been a significant focus of Corinthian studies in particular. It has been widely argued that key to 1 Corinthians is an underlying dynamic by which Paul was forced to reassert his own authority in the face of a deeply critical internal opposition. Gordon Fee has championed this view in his extensive commentary.[14] We should not overlook, however, the fact that there were clearly some from the Corinthian church who did recognize his authority, and on that basis they prompted the writing of 1 Corinthians by themselves contacting him in order to elicit his advice.[15]

In 2 Corinthians, it is said that Paul was responding to 'the manipulative strategies of rival leaders'.[16] The dilemma which he faced in writing this 'second' epistle was whether he should 'exert his own leadership by following the same methods' as his detractors.[17] In contrast to those scholars who consider Paul's approach to be no less

---

[13]A.C. Thiselton, *Interpreting God and the Postmodern Self*, 135, considers the post-modern, suspicious agenda of those such as Shaw, Castelli and Moore as one which entails 'the universal doctrinal cynicism that all truth-claims are bids for power'. *Cf.* also *op. cit.*, 144, where he 'calls into question a postmodern tendency to doubt the integrity of all "order" as irredeemably linked with individual or corporate power-interests on behalf of some specific group'.

[14]G.D. Fee, *The First Epistle to the Corinthians* (The New International Commentary on the New Testament; Grand Rapids: Eerdmans, 1987); *cf.* also W. Schrage, *Der erste Brief an die Korinther* (Evangelisch-katholischer Kommentar zum Neuen Testament, 7; Neukirchen-Vluyn: Neukirchener Verlag, 1991-95); and J.C. Hurd, *The Origin of 1 Corinthians* (London: SPCK, 1965) 111-13. See, however, the contrary view made by B. Dodd, *Paul's Paradigmatic 'I': Personal Example as Literary Strategy* (JSNT Supplement Series; Sheffield: JSOT Press, 1999) 40-44.

[15]*Cf.*, for example, 1 Cor 1:11; 7:1; 11:18.

[16]A.C. Thiselton, *Interpreting God and the Postmodern Self*, 20. *Cf.* also *op. cit.*, 21, of Paul's opponents in 2 Cor, 'By contrast, the "false" apostles (11:13) use deceit and seduction (11:3, 13, 15), demand "submission" and exercise domination: they "make slaves of you, prey on you, put on airs" (11:20) and "you submit to it readily enough" (11:4)'.

[17]A.C. Thiselton, *Interpreting God and the Postmodern Self*, 20.

authoritarian or manipulative than his opponents, it will here be argued that Paul's response explicitly adopted a different approach.[18] Instead of defending himself against criticism by justifying his actions according to their criteria and thereby seeking to reestablish a following and enhance his personal power-base, Paul asserts that his opponents' principles and perceptions of the nature of Christian local leadership were often misconstrued. Thus, where Paul's opponents adopted a model of leadership widely acceptable to contemporary society, Paul, instead, considers that a quite different stance should be adopted by those in the Christian community. A number of passages from 1 Corinthians will serve to demonstrate this.

On the issue of eating, in pagan temples, meat which had previously been sacrificed to idols, Paul defends in 1 Corinthians 8-10 neither his own rights and authority nor those of other leading members of the Christian community. Indeed, he insists in these chapters that the dominant ethic should be that personal rights, not least his own, should be laid aside out of deference to the 'weaker' members of the community. As Bruce Winter has argued, 'Paul's overall concern is ... that determining ethical responses on this issue should be done not only within a credal but also a relational framework, in the first instance with respect to the weak Christian'.[19] The specific rights to which Paul was drawing attention were those of the established in society to conform to standard Graeco-Roman practice and to use pagan temples as the 'restaurants of antiquity'. These public occasions were especially enjoyed by those of high society, and yet they were conducted within a significantly 'religious' context.[20] Paul's injunction is that all actions should redound to the glory of God, should not cause any to stumble (whether Jews, Greeks or Christians), and should endeavour to benefit others.[21] In this way, *contra* Elizabeth Castelli, Paul's agenda was not to impose on the Corinthian community a conformity to his own values; rather, as Robert Jewett has contrastingly argued, it was to establish a tolerance

---

[18]A.C. Thiselton, *Interpreting God and the Postmodern Self*, 20, 'for the sake of Corinthian expectations, partly tongue-in-cheek Paul adopts a rhetorical form or style of "boasting" of credentials to establish and legitimate his "power", while in practice he deconstructs or undermines the game of power-play'.

[19]B.W. Winter, 'Ethical and Theological Responses to Religious Pluralism in Corinth — 1 Corinthians 8-10', *Tyndale Bulletin* 41 (1990) 223.

[20]B. Witherington, 'Not so Idle Thoughts about *Eidolothuton*', *Tyndale Bulletin* 44 (1993) 244-45.

[21]1 Cor 10:31-33.

by the strong towards the weak,[22] and to let the categories of love rather than knowledge dictate ethics;[23] his concern was not to see Pauline conformity but rather Christian liberty conditioned by love.[24]

This principle is significantly reinforced in 1 Corinthians 9 by a demonstration that the apostle himself laid down his own rights, including his right to financial support, for the sake of both the Corinthians and the gospel. In contradistinction to an action which might draw attention to Paul's high status over the Christian community, he urges the Corinthians, especially those who, like him, were strong in the faith, to forgo their rights together with those privileges which might have drawn attention to their status or power-base, all for the sake of those who were weaker in the faith. This interpretation of 1 Corinthians 9 means that the chapter need not be regarded as an anomalous digression within the broader context of Paul's argument in chapters 8 and 10.[25] Rather, it is an important demonstration that Paul himself, in contrast to defending his authority, set an example for the believers in laying aside his rights, and he implored his correspondents to do likewise.[26] In conclusion to this section of the epistle he urges the Corinthians to conform to his own pattern of weakness, not of power, and in so doing to follow Christ.[27]

Further in 1 Corinthians, the party-slogans of 1:12 and 3:4 have suggested to many commentators that there were tensions between the apostolic figures of Paul, Apollos and Cephas. In the light of such tensions or factions, it may have seemed that Paul's own power-base was being eroded, thus raising the need for him to restore confidence in his own position and authority over the community. It is,

---

[22]R. Jewett, *Christian Tolerance: Paul's Message to the Modern Church* (Philadelphia: Westminster Press, 1982) 126-33, who argues that in Rom 14-15 Paul proposes a strategy which counters notions of conformity, and, instead, encourages tolerance within the community.

[23]*Cf.* 1 Cor 8:1.

[24]J.D.G. Dunn, *The Theology of Paul the Apostle*, 659-60.

[25]*Cf.* S.J. Hafemann, *Suffering and Ministry in the Spirit: Paul's Defense of his Ministry in II Corinthians 2:14-3:3* (Grand Rapids: Eerdmans, 1990) 126-33.

[26]J.D.G. Dunn, *The Theology of Paul the Apostle*, 576, describes this as 'the principle of accommodation or adaptability'.

[27]1 Cor 10:33-11:1. *Cf.* M.M. Mitchell, *Paul and the Rhetoric of Reconciliation: an Exegetical Investigation of the Language and Composition of 1 Corinthians* (Hermeneutische Untersuchungen zur Theologie, 28; Tübingen: J.C.B. Mohr, 1991) 57, 'here again Paul presents himself as the opposite of a factionalist — he doesn't seek his own advantage, but the common advantage'.

therefore, significant that in 1 Corinthians 3 Paul is at pains rather to assert that he conceived of no competition between himself and Apollos, both being servants of the Lord who were influential in the coming to faith of some of the Corinthians.[28] This cooperation in the task to which they had been assigned by the Lord makes a mockery of those who would wish to see a partisanship and power struggle between these two apostolic figures.[29] The contrast which Paul draws in these verses does not reflect a tension between himself and Apollos, but rather one between the conduct of these two apostles and that of some of the other Corinthians.[30]

Having demonstrated that there was no rivalry between himself and Apollos, Paul then points out the more significant rôle which was played by God in the appointing of such servants, in assigning tasks to them, and, most importantly, in the work which he himself carried out. Where Paul had planted and Apollos had watered, it was God who had made things grow. Paul considered that his own strategic rôle had been in the laying of a foundation; Apollos had built upon that foundation; and others (presumably including some from amongst the Corinthian Christian community itself) could yet build further on this base.[31] From Paul's perspective, God's rôle had been preeminent, however. Rather than appealing to an exclusive relationship of authority over the Corinthians, therefore, he urges them to stop their focus on mere humans, for 'all things are yours, whether Paul or Apollos or Cephas or the world or life or death or the present or the future — all are yours, and you are of Christ, and Christ is of God'.[32]

It should also be noted that Paul does not cite as legitimation of his position of leadership his own secular status or credentials.[33] Indeed, as part of this discussion, he adopts a number of techniques which expressly invert the significance of social status. Paul's choice

---

[28]1 Cor 3:5. *Cf.* A.D. Clarke, *Secular and Christian Leadership in Corinth*, 119-21; *cf.* also B. Dodd, *Paul's Paradigmatic 'I'*, 55-56.

[29]1 Cor 3:4.

[30]B. Dodd, *Paul's Paradigmatic 'I'*, 33, 'Throughout this opening section Paul depreciates himself for christological emphasis, accents the unity of the missionary workers in their gospel work, and stresses the cruciform nature of life in Christ, laying a foundation for his solution to the church problems'.

[31]1 Cor 3:10, 12, 17; *cf.* B. Dodd, *Paul's Paradigmatic 'I'*, 56.

[32]1 Cor 3:21-23.

[33]Indeed in Phil 3:3-11 Paul eschews such outward credentials in favour rather of 'knowing Christ'.

of agricultural, artisan and household imagery in 1 Corinthians 3-4 (specifically the lowly task of gardener, builder and servant) may well have been regarded as offensive to those within the Christian community who sought to base their own authority on such widely-held criteria as secular honour and status.[34]

This stance is further reinforced by Paul's use of irony in 1 Corinthians 4:8-13 where he contrasts the élitist view of leadership, adopted by some Corinthians, with a far more menial perception of the rôle of the apostle. He caricatures the self-perception of the Corinthian leading figures as kings, both wealthy and wise, in contrast to the apostles whom God had 'put at the end of the procession' and who were regarded as 'the scum of the earth, the refuse of the world'.[35]

Much of Paul's response to the Corinthians, therefore, effectively yields ground to those Corinthians who considered that Paul did not cut a fine figure of leadership according to the much lauded, standard measures of Corinthian society. Where many in the church had sided loyalties with one or another apostolic figure, Paul's answer was not to canvas support for his own position, but rather to point out that both his and Apollos' rôles were menial in contrast to the more significant work of God. Thus, to follow either of these mere *servants* as if they were significant political leaders, would be a foolish course for the so-called 'wise' members of the Corinthian community to pursue.[36] In response to those who criticized Paul's lack of status, the apostle claims none of his usual rights, but argues that all those who were 'strong' should set aside such rights for the sake of the 'weak' and the gospel. In these responses there is no concerted attempt to reestablish a lost power-base.

It should also be noted however that authority was not the sole prerogative of the apostolic figures, even in the earliest communities. Paul in writing to the Corinthians urges them to submit to Stephanas, Fortunatus and Achaicus, as well as those like them.[37] The legitimation which Paul offers for their authority lies not with their status, and significantly no title is applied to them.[38] Rather their

---

[34]A.D. Clarke, *Secular and Christian Leadership in Corinth*, 120.
[35]1 Cor 4:13.
[36]1 Cor 3:18.
[37]1 Cor 16:16.
[38]K. Giles, *Patterns of Ministry among the First Christians* (Melbourne: Collins Dove, 1989) 17.

legitimation lies with the fact that they worked and laboured for the community (συνεργοῦντι καὶ κοπιῶντι). Similarly in 1 Thessalonians 5:12-13 Paul encourages the believers to respect those who exercised authority over them in the Lord and admonished them. Again the legitimation for that authority was that these people worked hard among them (τοὺς κοπιῶντας), and no official title was applied to them.[39]

It is clear that the issue of authority was extremely contentious. Paul's authority was being questioned by some and defended by others. Public popularity and effective authority were closely allied in the first-century world so familiar to these early Christians. Paul's view, however, was that the nature of the Christian ἐκκλησία was such that authority within that community should be differently conceived. This is especially demonstrated as we consider how Paul reflected on his rôle as father, model and apostle.

1. Paul as Father

Where Paul gave no evidence of tension between himself and Apollos and regarded both apostles as fulfilling for the Corinthians rôles which had been assigned by Christ, he appeals in 1 Corinthians 4:15, surprisingly, to the apparently exclusive relationship which he had with them as their 'father'. The conciliatory tone of the preceding chapters is considered by some commentators as anomalous in the light of the authority which Paul wields in this section. The collegiality of the relationship between Paul and Apollos in 1 Corinthians 3 contrasts starkly with the air of superiority adopted by him in 1 Corinthians 4:15-21, with its demand for a unique imitation of himself.

Brian Dodd has unconvincingly argued that 1 Corinthians 4:14 marks a shift in tone and that Paul's reference in the verse to 'these things (ταῦτα)' refers to the succeeding, rather than the preceding, section. Hereafter, Paul begins to assert his authority more conspicuously, both by reminding the Corinthians of his rôle as father and in the disciplining of the incestuous man in 1 Corinthians 5.[40] Eva Maria Lassen has adopted a different line of interpretation,

---

[39]C.K. Barrett, *Church, Ministry, and Sacraments in the New Testament* (The 1983 Didsbury Lectures; Exeter: Paternoster, 1985) 37.
[40]B. Dodd, *Paul's Paradigmatic "I"*, 65.

suggesting that the use of the father metaphor is contrasted ironically with the preceding picture depicted in 1 Corinthians 4:8-13. She suggests that Paul's invoking of the father image in verse 14, immediately following the outburst of 4:8-13, was in order to drive home 'the irony of the situation — the father experienced inferior status and degrading treatment while his children enjoyed the very best'.[41] The effect of this irony might well have been to shame and humiliate the Corinthians. Paul urges, however, that his professed aim was neither.

The Corinthians might conceivably have had any number of 'guardians' (ἐὰν γὰρ μυρίους παιδαγωγοὺς ἔχητε) in Christ;[42] but however many there might have been, they would all have had a limited basis for appeal to the Corinthians on the grounds of their relationship merely as guardians. Paul's appeal is that he had a particular relationship with them based on his bringing the gospel to them, thus making him their 'father'.

It is significant, however, that in 1 Corinthians 4:15 he neither excludes the possibility of other 'fathers' nor insists on being exclusively the one 'father' of the *whole* church.[43] There were many in the church, and Paul is not claiming sole responsibility for having 'fathered' all of them in the faith (although he did consider that he had been influential in the initial founding of the church).[44] Thus, instead of couching his argument in the somewhat more persuasive frame, 'you may have a myriad of guardians, *but only one father*', he suggests rather that the many who may have been guardians were different from the few who could call themselves fathers, among whom Paul certainly included himself. This is consistent with Paul's statement in 1 Corinthians 1:13-16 that he lays claim to having baptized only Crispus, Gaius, and the household of Stephanas. Thus, just as he made no attempt in previous chapters to further his own cause to the detriment of other apostolic figures to Corinth, so here also he does not exclude the possibility that some may have viewed Apollos (or Cephas) as also a 'father'. This further reinforces the case

---

[41]E.M. Lassen, 'The Use of the Father Image in Imperial Propaganda and 1 Corinthians 4:14-21', *Tyndale Bulletin* 42 (1991) 135-36.

[42]1 Cor 4:15.

[43]*Contra* G.D. Fee, *The First Epistle to the Corinthians*, 185, who stresses, with other commentators, the uniqueness of Paul's relationship with the Corinthians as their *only* father.

[44]1 Cor 3:6.

that his quarrel was not with the other apostles, and a wedge could not be driven between himself and them. Paul's appeal is that a father's relationship with his children provides a unique basis for appeal, a unique authority, but also a unique motivation. The possibility of there being more than one 'father', however, did not proportionately diminish Paul's grounds for appeal, authority or motivation. In any case, Paul's distinction here lies not between himself and other 'fathers', but between himself and those who were mere guardians.

As a 'father', with authority over them, there were a number of ways in which Paul might have acted. He could have adopted the domineering tone of an authoritarian and exercised harsh discipline. Alternatively, he could have appealed on the basis of moderation and love, and set for his children an example for them to follow. The option not reasonably available to one who is a father is inaction stemming from a lack of concern. Even in the context of the heated letter to the Galatians, Paul's approach was not authoritarian, as James Dunn points out:

> Paul is certainly threatening and fierce enough. But there is no ordering or commanding, not even his characteristic 'appeal' ... Some might see his language as bluster, some as cajoling, others simply as pleading and warning. Paul was certainly upset, anxious, and angry when he wrote the letter. But he was realistic enough to recognize that an authority overplayed was likely to be an authority repudiated. Even in this his fiercest letter he was aware that the success of his appeal depended first and foremost on the effect of the gospel on his readers.[45]

Equally in the antagonistic context of 2 Corinthians, Paul argues, 'Not that we lord it over your faith, but we work with you for your joy'.[46]

In 1 Corinthians 4:14-17 Paul lays down an appeal to those he loves (exemplified by his love for another of his 'sons', namely Timothy). His goal is that his 'children' should conform their lifestyle to that of the gospel, and with this he would be satisfied. Timothy *is* 'faithful in the Lord', and is, therefore, able to exemplify 'life in Christ Jesus' and offer in Paul's absence an appropriate model for the Corinthians.[47] Thus, Paul is not here enforcing his own authority as

---

[45]J.D.G. Dunn, *The Theology of Paul the Apostle*, 573-74.
[46]2 Cor 1:23.
[47]1 Cor 4:17.

superior to that of other appropriately qualified 'fathers', nor offering his own manner of life as the only one appropriate. Indeed, Timothy can be used as a means of reminding the Corinthians of what is appropriate behaviour. It is also noteworthy that in the context of other epistles Paul does not claim to be the only model for his congregations to emulate.[48]

Furthermore, there is a clear christological force to the appeal which further diminishes any element of unique importance being drawn by Paul to his own position. As Brian Dodd has argued, 'Paul depreciates himself to make a christological emphasis in chs. 1-4, and explicitly qualifies his example as one "in Christ" (11:1)'.[49] It is not, then, necessary to assume that Paul's goal was to develop a following for himself; indeed he has urged, with regard to Apollos, that the Corinthians do not 'take pride in one man over against another'.[50] Thus, in contradistinction to those models of leadership which were prevalent in Graeco-Roman society, Paul's legitimation comes not from his own qualities which might have commanded respect, but rather he defers to Christ alone.[51]

It may be argued that his continued adoption of the metaphor of fatherhood in 1 Corinthians 4:21, however, is different. Here there is a threat of judgment on those who were exercising leadership in an arrogant fashion.[52] As a 'father', he can either come to them 'with a whip, or in love and with a gentle spirit'. Thus, Paul's normally non-combative approach does not mean that those in the congregation should arrogantly assume that he carries no authority among them and will not come to them.[53] He is a 'father', and not a mere guardian, and thus he will not, indeed cannot, ignore his paternal instincts. While the implication is that Paul would prefer to come to them 'with love and a gentle spirit', the choice is theirs. He insists on his authority as a father, without wishing to be forced to carry it out in an authoritarian manner.

---

[48]A.D. Clarke, '"Be Imitators of Me": Paul's Model of Leadership', *Tyndale Bulletin* 49 (1998) 329-60.

[49]B. Dodd, *Paul's Paradigmatic "I"*, 131.

[50]1 Cor 4:6.

[51]E. Best, *Paul and his Converts: the Sprunt Lectures 1985* (Edinburgh: T. & T. Clark, 1988) 16.

[52]1 Cor 4:19, these 'leaders' are viewed, by some at least, as having 'power'.

[53]1 Cor 4:18.

Paul uses the term 'father' not only when speaking of the Corinthians,[54] but also of the Galatians,[55] of the Thessalonians,[56] of Timothy,[57] and of Onesimus.[58] It is widely noted that this metaphor of the relationship is only applied to those whom he has 'begotten in the faith'. Norman Petersen's conclusion that Paul's language of fatherhood in the letter to Philemon is related to the indebtedness of Onesimus (and Philemon) to him, rather than to the conversion of the slave under Paul's ministry is thus misfounded.[59]

It is significant that Paul here does apply to himself a title which was deeply integrated into Graeco-Roman society and culture. In his view, the metaphor of the family can, at least in some senses, be applied to the Christian community. Although the model of father/child was inherently, and especially at the time of the early Roman empire, a superior/inferior relation,[60] this does not necessarily entail an authoritarian relationship, however; and, in the case of Paul, this dynamic is clearly modified by love.[61] The metaphor is used carefully and variously by Paul: 'sometimes in order to describe his relationship to the congregation as a whole, sometimes to express a feeling of special concern for individuals, for instance Timothy'.[62] It is significantly juxtaposed however with much more menial titles. In 1 Corinthians Paul describes himself at once as a father and a manual labourer amongst them — indeed one whom God has placed last in line.[63]

Where Paul distances himself from the patterns of leadership in the voluntary associations and Graeco-Roman civic contexts, this image of 'father' is not avoided, and the notion of the Christian community as a family is in many ways acceptable to him. It is not, however, applied rigidly in a way which exclusively reinforces his own control. We have recognized that he makes occasional reference

[54]1 Cor 4:14; 2 Cor 6:13; 12:14-15.

[55]Gal 4:19.

[56]1 Thess 2:11.

[57]1 Cor 4:17; Phil 2:22.

[58]Phlm 10.

[59]Phlm 10, 19. N.R. Petersen, *Rediscovering Paul: Philemon and the Sociology of Paul's Narrative World* (Philadelphia: Fortress Press, 1985) 131.

[60]E. Best, *Paul and his Converts*, 29.

[61]E. Best, *Paul and his Converts*, 29.

[62]E.M. Lassen, 'The Use of the Father Image in Imperial Propaganda and 1 Corinthians 4:14-21', 127.

[63]1 Cor 3:6; 4:13, 15.

to himself as father, but generally not in order to reinforce a personal *patria potestas*. Instead, he concedes that a congregation may rightly include others among their fathers. God is, however, regarded as the supreme father who has sovereign authority and power over his family.[64]

Relationships between members of Christian communities are also identified by the term 'brother'.[65] Significant within this, however, is Paul's readiness equally to describe himself as a brother to fellow-believers in these churches.[66] His is not, therefore, an exclusive relationship with them, where he is only to be viewed as father; but, rather, it is an intimate one which should be characterized by mutual respect.

2. Paul as Model

Repeatedly Paul proposes himself as a model for those in his congregation to emulate and in this, he is unique among the New Testament writers.[67] In addition to these exhortations to imitation, Paul also, through the course of his correspondence, reveals elements of his own life and lifestyle through 'self-presentation, self-discussion and self-characterizations'.[68] It is significant, however, that Paul does not portray himself as the only appropriate object of imitation. Other fitting objects of imitation include Christ or God, his colleagues, other Christians and other churches. Whilst he commends imitation in others, he does not exempt himself also from modelling his own life on that of Christ.[69]

---

[64]Such a view is reflected most clearly in Eph 3:14-15; but see also some of the introductions to Pauline letters, for example, Rom 1:7; 1 Cor 1:3; 2 Cor 1:2; Gal 1:4; Phil 1:2; 1 Thess 1:3; Phlm 3; *cf.* also Gal 4:6.

[65]*Cf.*, for example, Rom 1:13; 7:1, 4; 8:12; 14:10, 13, 15, 21; 1 Cor 5:11; 6:1, 6; 7:12, 15; 8:11; 2 Cor 8:18.

[66]Rom 16:23; 1 Cor 1:1; 8:13; 16:12; 2 Cor 1:1; 2:13; 8:22; Phil 2:25; 1 Thess 3:2.

[67]For recent treatments of the mimesis motif in Paul, see A.D. Clarke, '"Be Imitators of Me": Paul's Model of Leadership', 329-60, and B. Dodd, *Paul's Paradigmatic 'I'*.

[68]B. Dodd, *Paul's Paradigmatic 'I'*, 14, who also notes that not all of Paul's references to himself are simply for hortatory reasons. *Cf.* also *op. cit.*, 61, with regard to 1 Cor 1:1-4:13, 'Paul's self-portrayal provides a contrastive example for the haughty, but from 4:14 Paul, on a literary level, sets a very concrete, ethical example for almost every issue he treats'.

[69]1 Cor 11:1.

Wilhelm Michaelis has influentially argued that the motif of Pauline imitation includes an implied call to obedience to apostolic authority.[70] More recently, Elizabeth Castelli has suggested that such calls to imitation are a rhetorical device by which Paul can reinforce his own power and his group's identity; thus, the invitation to emulate effectively defines Paul's superior authority over his readers, and the content of his model is less important, indeed 'conspicuously imprecise'.[71] A different conclusion, but widely adopted, has been to consider Paul's focus was to encourage emulation of the ethical example of the apostle, thereby downplaying the significance of a call to obedience or a statement of power.[72] Brian Dodd, most recently, adopts a *via media* arguing that 'the imitation of Paul can and should be understood both as a pedagogical technique and as an implied assertion of authority as a summons to conform to the pattern set by Paul as the regulative model'.[73]

In the course of 1 Thessalonians, Paul does not enjoin the Christians to emulation, but on a number of occasions he commends them for both imitating appropriate Christian examples and, in turn, becoming themselves a model for others — in other words, the mood is indicative as opposed to imperative.[74] It can be argued that the Thessalonians are being commended for their imitation, which consisted in 'responding to the gospel in a way which reflected and was consistent with both Paul's and the Lord's conduct in living and

---

[70]W. Michaelis, 'μιμέομαι κτλ.', *Theological Dictionary of the New Testament* 4 (1968) 659-74.

[71]E.A. Castelli, *Imitating Paul*, 32. *Contra* Castelli, B. Dodd, *Paul's Paradigmatic 'I'*, 31-32, rightly points out that Paul also recalls to the mind of his readers his personal example explicitly available to them during his previous visits.

[72]*Cf.*, for example, W.P. de Boer, *The Imitation of Paul: an Exegetical Study* (Kampen: J.H. Kok, 1962); and D.M. Stanley, 'Imitation in Paul's Letters: Its Significance for his Relationship to Jesus and to his own Christian Foundations', in P. Richardson and J.C. Hurd (eds.), *From Jesus to Paul: Studies in Honour of Francis Wright Beare* (Waterloo: Wilfrid Laurier University Press, 1984) 127-41.

[73]B. Dodd, *Paul's Paradigmatic 'I'*, 29. Cf. also *op. cit.*, 32, where he argues 'that Paul uses his personal example to ground and illustrate his argumentation in a rhetorically sophisticated manner, that he employs modelling as a technique of effective psychagogy, and that he often structures his argument on the basis of his personal example'.

[74]*Cf.* A.D. Clarke, '"Be Imitators of Me": Paul's Model of Leadership', 333-40; and J.H. Schütz, *Paul and the Anatomy of Apostolic Authority* (SNTS Monograph Series, 26; Cambridge: Cambridge University Press, 1975) 226, who writes of 1 Thess 2:14, 'This unusual verse suggests that imitation for Paul is not a matter of disciples following a master. It is not merely Paul who can be imitated'.

proclaiming that message'.[75] In contrast to building a power-base for himself, Paul's approval of the Thessalonians lies in their accepting the message of the gospel *not* as the message of Paul, but as the message of God.[76] His goal is that they 'live lives worthy of *God*, who calls you into *his* kingdom and glory'.[77] The appropriateness of the imitation is measured not in the conferring of status or dignity to Paul, but in the evidence that the Thessalonians' lifestyle has caused others, in turn, to respond to the gospel.[78]

It can also be seen that the content of Paul's lifestyle whilst he lived among the Thessalonians did not consist in a strategy of empire building, but in a quality of selflessness. In 1 Thessalonians 1:5 he reports that he and his fellow workers lived among the Thessalonians 'for their sake'. This is reinforced by the later account that the missionaries shared their very lives in toil and hardship so as not to be a burden.[79]

In 2 Thessalonians the community continues to be commended for their lifestyle.[80] In addition, the writer reports that he is holding up the Thessalonians as examples to others of perseverance and faith.[81] Although some commentators have argued that the tone in which the imitation motif is used in 2 Thessalonians is more imperatival than the indicative form of 1 Thessalonians, there remains no necessary assumption that the apostle is therefore being authoritarian. The goal of the imitation remains that the Thessalonians should live in a way that is worthy of God and glorifies Jesus.[82]

Paul's first letter to the Corinthians is a major locus of the imitation motif.[83] Again we should focus, not simply on the injunction itself, but also on the content of the imitation. It may seem ironic that in a letter in which the pursuance of personality-cults is criticized, he, nonetheless, presents himself as an object of imitation.

---

[75]A.D. Clarke, '"Be Imitators of Me": Paul's Model of Leadership', 337.

[76]1 Thess 2:13.

[77]1 Thess 2:12.

[78]1 Thess 1:8; 2:16.

[79]1 Thess 2:8-9.

[80]2 Thess 1:3, 4; 3:1, 4. *Cf.* A.D. Clarke, '"Be Imitators of Me": Paul's Model of Leadership', 340-42.

[81]2 Thess 1:4.

[82]2 Thess 1:5, 11, 12; 2:14.

[83]1 Cor 4:16; 11:1. *Cf.* A.D. Clarke, '"Be Imitators of Me": Paul's Model of Leadership', 342-47.

As has been argued above, however, the model which he is presenting is not one of power and influence. In 1 Corinthians 11:1, Paul issues the imperative that the Corinthians imitate him, as he imitates Christ. The substance of this imitation is presented in the preceding verse, namely that they are not to seek their own good, but the good of many.[84]

In writing to the Philippians, Paul presents a number of models for emulation: Christ, himself and certain other Christians.[85] Again, it should be noted that the context of Paul's injunction to imitate is one where he recognizes his own need to imitate Christ more closely, and a personal recognition that he still seeks to advance further towards this goal.[86] To this extent Paul's decision to offer himself as a model is consistent with Christian humility.[87] The primary model for imitation, not only for Paul but for all Christians, remains that of Christ himself.[88] Christ himself is presented as one who does not seek to hold on to power or glory, but forgoes such things, becomes a servant himself, and so leads others to recognize the glory of God.[89] Accordingly, the categories of power, control and authority by which Elizabeth Castelli interprets the letter are diametrically opposed to the case which Paul is actually making.

Where Paul is writing to a congregation which he has not formerly visited, namely that in Rome, we see no explicit call to apostolic imitation.[90] The Roman Christians are not in a position to recall Paul's conduct or lifestyle, and in these circumstances Paul refers them directly to the example of Christ.[91] The content of the model of Christ which is here presented is specifically that of not

---

[84]J.H. Schütz, *Paul and the Anatomy of Apostolic Authority*, 228, 'Thus while Paul urges himself on the community as an example to be followed, what he is urging is not obedience to his own commands, but obedience to the gospel itself as it actively sustains and should inform the life of the community'.

[85]Phil 2:5-11; 3:17; 4:9. Cf. A.D. Clarke, '"Be Imitators of Me": Paul's Model of Leadership', 348-50; also P.T. O'Brien, 'The Gospel and Godly Models in Philippians', in M.J. Wilkins & T. Paige (eds.), *Worship, Theology and Ministry in the Early Church: Essays in Honor of Ralph P. Martin* (JSNT Supplement Series, 87; Sheffield: JSOT, 1992) 273-84.

[86]Phil 3:8-14.

[87]P.T. O'Brien, *Gospel and Mission in the Writings of Paul: an Exegetical and Theological Analysis* (Grand Rapids: Baker Books, 1995) 84-85.

[88]Phil 2:5; 3:10.

[89]Phil 2:5-11.

[90]A.D. Clarke, '"Be Imitators of Me": Paul's Model of Leadership', 353.

[91]Rom 15:1-7.

pleasing oneself, and the goal is glorification of God, rather than of the apostle.

In addition to the specific references to imitation of Christ, himself or other churches, Paul also draws the attention of his readers to other examples of Christian individuals worthy of emulation. In 1 Corinthians 16:15-18 he mentions the leading figures of Stephanas, Fortunatus and Achaicus. These people are exemplary, not because they have furthered Paul's personal following, but because they have 'devoted themselves to the service of the saints' and have 'refreshed my spirit and yours also'. It is on this basis that they deserve recognition and their leadership within the community is legitimated.[92] What is further significant is that this legitimation is not on the basis of social status, for Fortunatus and Achaicus may well have been slaves or former slaves. This legitimation is solely on the basis of their labouring amongst the saints. Ironically, as servants (εἰς διακονίαν τοῖς ἁγίοις) they should receive the submission (ὑποτάσσησθε) of others within the community.

Paul also draws the attention of the Corinthians to the example of Timothy. Timothy is one who faithfully models the life of Paul and who labours for the cause of the gospel in a way that is similar to that of Paul.[93] The effect of drawing attention to Timothy in this way is to focus, not on Paul, but on the work of the Lord which both Paul and Timothy are effectively carrying out. The Philippian Christians are also referred to the example of Timothy. Paul states that 'I have no-one else like him, who takes a genuine interest in your welfare'.[94] In pointing out the father/son relationship between Paul and Timothy, particular attention is drawn again to Timothy's focus in the work of the gospel.[95] No less, Epaphroditus is heralded before the Philippians as one who should be the object of their honour, for he again was one who 'almost died for the work of Christ'.[96] It could well be that both Timothy and Epaphroditus are being referred to in Philippians 3:17 as 'those who live according to the pattern we gave you'.[97]

---

[92]Cf. A.D. Clarke, '"Refresh the Hearts of the Saints": a Unique Pauline Context?', *Tyndale Bulletin* 47 (1996) 287-89; and *idem, Secular and Christian Leadership in Corinth*, 126.

[93]1 Cor 4:17; 16:10-11. Cf. also, A.D. Clarke, *Secular and Christian Leadership in Corinth*, 126.

[94]Phil 2:19.

[95]Phil 2:20.

[96]Phil 2:29-30.

[97]A.D. Clarke, '"Be Imitators of Me": Paul's Model of Leadership', 349.

Throughout these repeated references to imitation it is clear
that the object of imitation is not exclusively Paul, but is always
ultimately Christ.[98] The injunction to imitate should not, therefore, be
seen as an authoritarian tool by which Paul enforces conformity to his
own ideal, thus elevating his own status and power-base. Similarly,
this context in which Paul uses the motif of emulation is significantly
at odds with the nature of much leadership in wider Graeco-Roman
society. We have seen that the culture of such leadership was
dependent on self-promotion and the elaborate pursuit of public
popularity.

3. Paul as Apostle

If Paul's adoption of the title 'father' and his recourse to the
injunction to imitate do not serve as tools of authoritarianism in his
hands, then his proud use of the title 'apostle' may yet provide the
strongest evidence for a domineering and suppressive leader.

For Paul the title 'apostle' is closely allied with his calling both
from God and to the gospel of Christ.[99] This is clearly demonstrated
in his introductions to the Romans ('Paul, a slave of Christ Jesus,
called an apostle, set apart for the gospel of God') and to the
Galatians ('When [God] who set me apart from my mother's womb
and called me through his grace was pleased to reveal his Son in me,
in order that I might preach his gospel among the nations ...').[100] His
commitment to preaching the gospel is thoroughgoing;[101] and were
he to preach a message contrary to the grace of Christ, he would be
accursed.[102] John Schütz has argued that this gospel is thus
considered by Paul to be normative, both for him as the preacher
who can preach no other, and for the hearers who should respond to
no other;[103] it reflects 'the proper realm of human existence'.[104] As far
as the Galatians should be concerned, a rejection of the gospel which

---

[98]E. Best, *Paul and his Converts*, 69.

[99]*Cf.* J.H. Schütz, *Paul and the Anatomy of Apostolic Authority*, 35; and J.D.G. Dunn,
The Theology of Paul the Apostle, 572.

[100]Rom 1:1; Gal 1:15-16.

[101]Rom 1:16-17; 1 Cor 1:17; 9:23; Gal 2:7-8.

[102]Gal 1:8.

[103]J.H. Schütz, *Paul and the Anatomy of Apostolic Authority*, 116-23.

[104]J.H. Schütz, *Paul and the Anatomy of Apostolic Authority*, 117.

Paul preached is a rejection of the calling of God.[105] It is in this way that the authority which Paul has over those congregations to whom he is an apostle is inextricably bound up with and circumscribed by the gospel and God's commissioning.

On the basis of this apostleship and for the sake of this gospel, Paul exercises an authority over those congregations which he has founded. In writing to the Corinthians, he remarks that their response to the gospel makes them the authenticating sign or seal of his apostleship.[106] To the Galatians he can plead that they become like him, because it was he who first preached the gospel to them.[107] Since the legitimation of Paul's authority lies in the calling which he has received from God[108] and the gospel of grace which he preaches, he has no conflict with those who endorse this same message and build on this same foundation. This is seen with regard to Paul's relationship with Apollos in the Corinthian church,[109] with regard to Paul's relationship with Peter in the Galatian churches,[110] and with regard to those to whom Paul refers in his letter to the Philippians who preach the gospel albeit out of impure motives, wanting to challenge Paul's position.[111] Such people may not be contributing to Paul's own power-base, but Paul is nonetheless content in that they offer no threat to the gospel, and, indeed, are even advancing the cause of the gospel. Nor does Paul seek to claim credit for work done by others or encroach on their 'territory'. This is most clearly presented in 2 Corinthians 10:13-16.[112]

Similarly, those who preach or live contrary to this gospel offer no personal threat to Paul, therefore he does not need to defend himself against them. They do, however, threaten the state of grace enjoyed by his followers and thus may cause them to return to a state

---

[105]Gal 1:6.

[106]1 Cor 9:2.

[107]Gal 4:12-13.

[108]2 Cor 2:17.

[109]1 Cor 3:1-15.

[110]Gal 2:7-8.

[111]Phil 1:12-18. J.H. Schütz, *Paul and the Anatomy of Apostolic Authority*, 161, writes, 'The motives of the proclamation of the gospel are subordinated to the fact of its proclamation and then regarded as secondary. ... Here again we have an example of the over-riding supremacy of the message, a supremacy which serves as the norm for judging the action of apparently disparate groups of preachers'.

[112]*Cf.* J.D.G. Dunn, *The Theology of Paul the Apostle*, 578.

of slavery. To this extent Paul opposes the Galatian agitators who were causing the Galatian Christians to reject the grace of God.[113] He also opposes Peter for living contrary to the gospel in a hypocritical fashion, which caused Barnabas to be led astray and was forcing the Galatians to judaize.[114] It is at this point that Paul presents a defence, but not of his own position.

In 2 Corinthians Paul is aware of those who are denying his own apostolic status.[115] Here Paul certainly senses the need to defend or recommend himself and to a degree that is not otherwise demonstrated in his letters. John Schütz considers that here Paul attempts to 'beat them at their own game'.[116] Again, however, there is a christological focus to Paul's defence just as in Galatians 1:10 there is a christological focus to his calling and ministry which would be at odds with an attempt to please people. His concern continues to be that the Corinthians are becoming separate from Christ.[117] Equally, his focus is professedly on the gospel rather than on himself.[118] Schütz argues further that whereas Paul's legitimacy comes from the gospel, his opponents' 'claims are entirely self-authenticating because they are entirely self-referential'.[119]

A major tension which Paul faces is whether he should seek to defend his own apostolicity in the same terms as those of the so-called 'super' or 'false' apostles.[120] Furthermore, should Paul be inveigled into resorting to self-commendation?[121] Paul's self-commendation in 2 Corinthians 10:17-18 is distinct from the self-

---

[113]Gal 5:1-6.

[114]Gal 2:11-14.

[115]2 Cor 10:2, 12; 11:5, 13; 12:11.

[116]J.H. Schütz, *Paul and the Anatomy of Apostolic Authority*, 168.

[117]2 Cor 11:2-3.

[118]2 Cor 11:7.

[119]J.H. Schütz, *Paul and the Anatomy of Apostolic Authority*, 185; cf. 2 Cor 10:12.

[120]J.H. Schütz, *Paul and the Anatomy of Apostolic Authority*, 185, 'Paul has only two choices when confronted with this kind of problem. He may let it go unopposed, which would mean sanctioning what is implicitly "another gospel". Or he may wrestle with the question of the apostolic self, which is in effect to play their game. This he does even while disowning the effort, for obvious reasons'.

[121]S.J. Hafemann, '"Self-Commendation" and Apostolic Legitimacy in 2 Corinthians: a Pauline Dialectic?', 69, considers that self-commendation is 'the key to understanding the focus of Paul's apologetic in 2 Cor'. Cf. also *op. cit.*, 71, 'Thus, in addition to the explicit *positive* uses of συνιστάνειν ἑαυτόν throughout 2 Corinthians, 2 Corinthians itself becomes such a self-commendation despite Paul's equally explicit rejection of allegations that he engages in such a practice'.

commendation of his opponents in that it is really the 'Lord's commendation' or 'boasting in the Lord'.[122] Thus the grounds for Paul's authority over the Corinthians lies not in his abilities (or lack of them) but in his commissioning by the Lord.[123] Indeed, the proof of Paul's apostleship, his letter of recommendation, is none other than the Corinthians themselves.[124]

What Paul seeks to build up is not his own power-base, so much as the community of Christians. To this end Paul speaks at length, most notably in 1 Corinthians 8-14, of the principle of seeking the benefit of the community (using the noun οἰκοδομή and the verb οἰκοδομέω).[125] This is one of the measures by which the actions of all the believers, not least himself, are to be measured; indeed the authority which Paul has over the Corinthians is precisely an authority for building up, rather than destroying.[126]

A further and highly significant factor of his own apostleship is that 'Paul's sense of power is cast in terms of one dominant and very unusual image, the cross. This gives the whole understanding of power a thoroughly dialectical texture. Power appears as weakness and weakness as power'.[127] Timothy Savage has convincingly demonstrated this element with particular reference to 2 Corinthians.[128] Where Paul's opponents construct an appearance of strength in contrast to the weakness of the apostle, Paul's unexpected response is to assent to his own weaknesses and sufferings.[129] The message of the cross, the gospel with which Paul is commissioned,

---

[122]S.J. Hafemann, '"Self-Commendation" and Apostolic Legitimacy in 2 Corinthians: a Pauline Dialectic?', 76.

[123]2 Cor 3:4-5, 'Such confidence as this is ours through Christ before God. Not that we are competent to claim anything for ourselves, but our competence comes from God. He has made us competent as ministers of a new covenant ...'

[124]2 Cor 3:1-2.

[125]J.D.G. Dunn, The Theology of Paul the Apostle, 597.

[126]2 Cor 10:8.

[127]J.H. Schütz, Paul and the Anatomy of Apostolic Authority, 187.

[128]T.B. Savage, Power through Weakness: Paul's Understanding of the Christian Ministry in 2 Corinthians (SNTS Monograph Series, 86; Cambridge: Cambridge University Press, 1996); cf. also S.J. Hafemann, Suffering and Ministry in the Spirit: Paul's Defense of his Ministry in II Corinthians 2:14-3:3; together with the more technical, idem, Suffering and the Spirit: an Exegetical Study of II Cor. 2:14-3:3 within the Context of the Corinthian Correspondence (WUNT, 2.19; Tübingen: J.C.B. Mohr, 1986). Cf. 2 Cor 4:7; 6:4-10; 12:7-10.

[129]2 Cor 12:15.

appears as foolishness to many who hear it.[130] Correspondingly, God chooses the weak, foolish and lowly rather than the strong, wise and significant.[131] Furthermore, Paul's own lifestyle is repeatedly presented as one of weakness. Savage argues that 'The things which the Corinthians find so objectionable about their apostle — his failure to boast, his timid personal presence, his amateurish speech, his refusal of support — all represent deliberate attempts by Paul to remain humble before an exalted God'.[132] For Paul to defend his own leadership in terms of power, wisdom and social standing — precisely those characteristics which Paul recognized in some of the Corinthians[133] — would then be to undermine the christological basis to his apostolicity.

4. Summary

Thus, where there has been an Enlightenment or post-modern trend by some commentators to view Paul's relationship with his churches as suppressive and authoritarian, it may rather be argued that it was Paul's opponents who could often be accused of such arrogance. In contrast, Paul repeatedly adopts a line which is diametrically opposed to 'worldly' ways of exercising authority. He views his own authority as deriving from Christ and being circumscribed both by the gospel and his specific commission. The nature of that ministry is characterized by weakness rather than power, and seeks to build up rather than suppress. Paul certainly has an authority over the congregations which he has founded. That authority is exercised as both an apostle and father, but is distinct from the false apostles and the mere guardians of the Corinthian church. As both father and apostle, Paul is concerned to see that the believers are living in accordance with the gospel with which he was commissioned. To this end he offers to them a number of models which they should emulate. Chief amongst these is that of Christ, whom he also seeks to imitate. In addition he presents other examples, including himself; and commends those churches which successfully offer to their fellow churches appropriate models.

---

[130] 1 Cor 1:18.
[131] 1 Cor 1:27-29.
[132] T.B. Savage, *Power through Weakness*, 185.
[133] 1 Cor 1:26; *cf.* A.D. Clarke, *Secular and Christian Leadership in Corinth*, 41-45.

III. Ministry or Service

Paul Ellingworth observes from recent English translations of the Bible 'a general tendency ... to use "leader" and related terms to translate a whole range of Hebrew and Greek expressions which in fact have rather varied connotations'.[134] The term 'leader' is more commonly used in the context of modern democratic societies where authority is circumscribed 'to a greater or lesser extent by the power of major shareholders, labour and company legislation, and trade union activity'. Such a term may well conjure something quite different within a Graeco-Roman, hierarchical and status-conscious society where 'ruler' and 'the language of rule and obedience' may be more apt.[135] It then appears all the more striking that the New Testament did not apply to positions of ecclesiastical office the terms 'office' or 'rule' (ἀρχή), 'honour' (τιμή), or 'power' (τέλος).[136] Paul, together with other New Testament writers, preferred, rather, to speak of service or ministry, using the διακονία word-group.[137] Indeed, Eduard Schweizer writes,

> As a general term for what we call 'office', namely the service of individuals within the Church, there is, with a few exceptions, only one word: διακονία. Thus the New Testament throughout and uniformly chooses a word that is entirely unbiblical and non-religious and never includes association with a particular dignity or position.[138]

---

[134]P. Ellingworth, 'Translating the Language of Leadership', 129. This is most marked, he suggests, with regard to the Good News Bible translation, and a number of instances are cited from both the Old and New Testaments. Ellingworth suggests, op. cit., 131-32, three possible reasons for the popular introduction of 'leader' and its cognates where they are not explicit in the original biblical text: firstly, to avoid uncommon technical terms, for example tetrarch; second, to make explicit something which is only implicit, for example when οἱ Ἰουδαῖοι refers to Jewish leaders; and thirdly, it may 'mask a subtle ... form of transculturation, in which presuppositions from modern (especially western democratic) society are projected onto an ancient, in principle hierarchical, form of social organisation'.

[135]P. Ellingworth, 'Translating the Language of Leadership', 137-38.

[136]E. Schweizer, Church Order in the New Testament (London: SCM Press, 1961) 171.

[137]Cf. Rom 12:7; 15:31; 1 Cor 16:15.

[138]E. Schweizer, Church Order in the New Testament, 173-74.

The word 'ministry', a common translation of the Greek word διακονία, continues to be widely used in both the modern church and current discussions of New Testament ecclesiology. Although widely used, its meaning is rarely defined, and often remains somewhat amorphous.[139] Phrases such as 'entering the ministry', 'ministry of the word', 'healing ministry', and 'women's ministry' serve to demonstrate something of the breadth of application of the word. This English word has roots in the Greek word διακονία and the Latin word *ministerium*, both frequently associated in scholarship with the idea of service. In ecclesiastical contexts, however, the term has often been used more specifically of the religious work of the ordained clergy, and it is this sense which predominates in many English dictionaries.[140]

The seeds of modern conceptions of *diakonia* can be seen in the 1931 doctoral dissertation of the German theologian, Wilhelm Brandt, who 'found this word denoting in Christian writings a caring kind of service exemplified in its most sublime form in the actions of Jesus at the supper, where he described himself "as one who serves", and in the self-giving which led to his death'.[141] This conclusion was taken up by Hermann Beyer in an article in Gerhard Kittel's *Theological Dictionary of the New Testament*, and thereafter influenced much later

---

[139]*Cf.* J.N. Collins, *Diakonia: Re-interpreting the Ancient Sources* (Oxford: Oxford University Press, 1990) 4.

[140]In recent decades *diakonia* is more commonly not seen as the sole prerogative of the ordained minister. J.N. Collins, 'Once more on Ministry: Forcing a Turnover in the Linguistic Field', *One in Christ* 27 (1991) 241, has suggested that this change of perception is reflected in successive editions of the Revised Standard Version translation of Eph 4:12. Where the 1946 edition reads that the threefold task of leading figures in the church is 'for the equipment of the saints, for the work of ministry, for building up the body of Christ', the 1971 edition, by altering punctuation, significantly changes the brief of these leaders, who are now responsible 'to equip the saints for the work of ministry, for building up the body of Christ'. In contrast to received tradition, the task of ministry should now be understood as belonging to the saints, rather than solely the prerogative of the apostles, prophets, evangelists, pastors and teachers. Along with this theological change, J.N. Collins, *Diakonia*, 3-4, notes an associated change in more recent English translations of the Bible of adopting 'service' in place of 'ministry' as a translation of the Greek word διακονία.

[141]J.N. Collins, 'Once more on Ministry: Forcing a Turnover in the Linguistic Field', 239; also W. Brandt, *Dienst und Dienen im Neuen Testament* (Gütersloh, 1931).

discussion of the term.[142] *Diakonia*, the resulting consensus argues, has roots in Greek menial and undignified contexts, commonly associated with serving at tables.[143] The term, however, was imbued with considerably deeper and more elevated connotations by association with the life of Jesus. It came to describe service marked by a peculiarly Christian value of love and self-giving. New Testament occurrences of this abstract noun together with its cognates — the verb, διακονέω, and the noun, διάκονος — are then most often applied in ecclesiastical contexts, associated with ministry, service or the diaconate.[144] Even with this 'ecclesiastical flavour', scholars have disagreed, however, as to whether the primary meaning is ethical or 'constitutive of institutionalised ministry or church office'.[145]

John Collins is critical of this consensus derived from what he considers to be the very blinkered lexicographical studies of Brandt and Beyer; and he consequently seeks to establish to what extent such modern interpretations of *diakonia* are rightly derived from their earlier use in the New Testament text. He summarizes,

> the recurrent theme of 'diakonia' in early writings has seemed to ... many modern theologians to provide at least one constant; apostle, presbyter, and believer, we are to take it, found common cause with him who came to serve. They had thereby been placed in such a novel religious condition that neither the linguistic storehouse of the Jewish Septuagint nor the legal, administrative or religious language of the contemporary pagan Greek world, creative and even fanciful as that was in the religious sector, could furnish them with a basic

---

[142]H.W. Beyer, 'διακονέω, διακονία, διάκονος', *Theological Dictionary of the New Testament* 2 (1964) 81-93.

[143]This view has been recently maintained by L.R. Hennessey, '*Diakonia* and *Diakonoi* in the Pre-Nicene Church', in T. Halton & J.P. Williman (eds.), *Diakonia: Studies in Honor of Robert T. Meyer* (Washington: Catholic University of America Press, 1986) 60-86; E.S. Fiorenza, '"Waiting at Table": a Critical Feminist Theological Reflection', in N. Greinacher & N. Mette (eds.), *Diakonia: Church for Others* (Concilium, 198; Edinburgh: T. & T. Clark, 1988) 84-94; and J. Pinnock, 'The History of the Diaconate', in C. Hall (ed.), *The Deacon's Ministry* (Leominster: Gracewing, 1991) 9-24.

[144]J.N. Collins, *Diakonia*, 3, notes an earlier distinction in European ecclesiastical circles between 'ministry' and 'diaconate'.

[145]J.N. Collins, *Diakonia*, 37.

terminology — prepacked, ready for use. Instead they had to process their own.[146]

It is this commonly-held view which Collins seeks to bring into question.[147] He questions firstly whether the servile 'waiting at table' association was a dominant idea in extra-Biblical Greek usage, and secondly whether the early Christians did 'Christianize' its application. He demonstrates this firstly by considering those gospel traditions which associate διακονία and its cognates with the ministry of Jesus.[148] Key in this regard is the programmatic statement of Mark 10:45. Collins notes that scholars differ widely on their understanding of the nature of the Son of Man's service as described in this verse; with such lack of agreement, he then concludes that there is little confident grounds for assuming that the modern ecclesiological and technical uses of *diakonia* find precedent in the much more general use of the concept as recorded in Mark.[149] From this stance he then considers the use of the term in other early Christian literature, noting that it was much more widely adopted than might have been anticipated by its relatively infrequent use in Septuagintal sources; furthermore, its use in these New Testament and patristic sources equally shows little evidence of carrying the modern notion of *diakonia*.[150]

Having found little evidence in the New Testament and early Christian literature for today's commonly accepted meaning of *diakonia*, Collins then turns to the non-Christian Greek sources in

---

[146]J.N. Collins, *Diakonia*, 39-40.

[147]J.N. Collins, *Diakonia*, 71; *cf.* also *op. cit.*, 94, 'an approximation to a service of love is the notion now usually taken from those passages about διακονία in the New Testament that have a bearing on functions in the church; on the modern view the mere presence of a word of this group in any statement tends to give the statement an ecclesiological significance'. With regard to the ministry of the word 'διακονία τοῦ λόγου', he writes, *op. cit.*, 96, 'Would the term have come naturally to a Greek writing about a preaching ministry or would a Greek have needed to be a Christian to use it?'

[148]J.N. Collins, *Diakonia*, 46-62, particularly with regard to Mk 10:42-45 and Lk 22:25-27. *Cf.* P. Ellingworth, 'Translating the Language of Leadership', 130, who points out that in Lk 22:26 Jesus is recorded as advocating precisely that quality of servanthood which is contrasted with that of civil, military and religious leaders, thus, ὁ ἡγούμενος [γινέσθω] ὡς ὁ διακονῶν; whereas in Mt 2:6 Jesus is described, in civil leadership terms, as an ἡγούμενος, albeit one who will 'shepherd (ποιμανεῖ; RSV, "govern") the people of Israel'.

[149]J.N. Collins, *Diakonia*, 61-62.

[150]J.N. Collins, *Diakonia*, 63.

order to uncover whether there was indeed a peculiarly 'Christian' interpretation given to the concept by the early church. It emerges that the διακονία group of words is used comparatively sparingly, the context is not always servile, and yet there is a 'remarkable consistency over nearly a thousand years'.[151] If frequency of use is significant, the most common context is that of 'waiting at table'.[152] Collins argues, however, that a dominant underlying notion, also applying in, but not restricted to, those contexts where 'waiting at table' is implied, is 'activity of an in-between kind'.[153] More fully, the notions of 'work', 'motion', 'mediation',[154] and 'agency' were widely associated with διακονία and its cognates; and the idea of menial service was correspondingly not dominant.[155] He then proposes that the idea of 'waiting at tables' was not at the root of *diakonia*, but could be present as an element of the go-between's task. The *task* of the go-between was dominant; any associated idea of a servile *manner* was not essential. Indeed,

> the function of waiting at tables is so integral to the religious dimension of the meal that slaves are not permitted to engage in it. The *diakonia* of tables is a privileged, religious ritual with a dignity accruing to it from the age of Homer.[156]

It is this element, that the terms carry no *necessary* sense of lowliness, servitude or inferior status, which, Collins considers, undermines the dominant consensus.[157] The notion of 'waiting at table' *may* be present but 'cannot be called "the basic meaning"'. The implication of

---

[151]J.N. Collins, *Diakonia*, 74.

[152]J.N. Collins, *Diakonia*, 75; 'service at table' accounting for 'about a quarter of all instances' and a further quarter might broadly be considered menial contexts.

[153]J.N. Collins, *Diakonia*, 335.

[154]J.N. Collins, 'Once more on Ministry: Forcing a Turnover in the Linguistic Field', 244.

[155]J.N. Collins, *Diakonia*, 93-95; *cf.* also *op. cit.*, 194, 'the words show no signs of having developed in meaning over the course of changing literary eras, the sense "to serve at table" cannot be called "the basic meaning" — in fact that sense has to be perceived as a particular application of a word capable of signifying doing messages and being another person's agent — and "the more comprehensive idea of 'serving'" is vague and inadequate. If the words denote actions or positions of "inferior value," there is at the same time often the connotation of something special, even dignified, about the circumstance'.

[156]J.N. Collins, 'Once more on Ministry: Forcing a Turnover in the Linguistic Field', 243.

[157]J.N. Collins, *Diakonia*, 335.

'inferior value' *may* be present, but there is often 'the connotation of something special, even dignified'.[158]

Having established these elements in the long tradition of extra-Biblical Greek usage, Collins then turns to usage of the διακονία word group in Paul and Acts. He suggests that '[i]n the long history of the usage there is no evidence of any change in meanings except in the case of the Christian designation "deacon"'.[159] Indeed, he argues that the ideas of spokesman, emissary and mediator continue to be closely associated particularly in occurrences of the phrase 'ministry of the word'.[160] They carry the implication of 'mandated authority' which is 'a prerogative of the apostle and those whom the apostle commissions'.[161] The διάκονος is, then, not the one who serves the congregation, but the one who serves the overseer 'whose "agent" the "deacon" is'.[162] Furthermore, Collins distances himself from those 'who present this language as designating something "dishonourable", "counting for nothing", and "despised by all"'.[163]

Collins has produced a thoroughly researched and judiciously argued criticism of a long-standing consensus. As he suggests, proponents of this consensus have rarely challenged the early dogmatism of Beyer, Brandt and Schweizer. Collins may thus have demonstrated the following: although the early church used the διακονία word group much more frequently than contemporary and earlier Greek society, they nonetheless did not imbue it with additional meaning.

It does not necessarily follow from Collins' conclusions, however, that the New Testament writers did not speak of *diakonia* in servile contexts (just as extra-Biblical Greek writers often applied the term to servile contexts), nor does it mean that they did not conceive of 'ministry' (whether described as διακονία or not) as nonetheless 'serving others'. We shall, therefore, consider first whether διακονία words in the New Testament were used in servile contexts, and

---

158J.N. Collins, *Diakonia*, 194.

159J.N. Collins, *Diakonia*, 335.

160J.N. Collins, *Diakonia*, 195; a view followed by D.L. Bartlett, *Ministry in the New Testament* (Overtures to Biblical Theology; Minneapolis: Fortress Press, 1993) 43-44; *cf.* especially 1 Cor 3:5; 2 Cor 3:6; 6:4; 11:23.

161J.N. Collins, *Diakonia*, 336.

162J.N. Collins, *Diakonia*, 337.

163J.N. Collins, 'Once more on Ministry: Forcing a Turnover in the Linguistic Field', 244; and *idem, Diakonia*, 336, 'the notion of "service to fellow human beings" as a benevolent activity does not enter'.

secondly whether Paul conceived of the broader work of the Christian leader as one of service.

Collins does concede that διακονία words 'In the gospels ... mainly designate menial attendance of one kind or another'.[164] We see, for example, that the clearly menial word 'slave' (δοῦλος) is sometimes linked with the verb 'to serve' (διακονέω) in the sense of serving at tables. Collins points out that it is the Hellenistic evangelist who brings out this connection. In Luke 17:7-10, for example, a parable is recorded which cites a slave (δοῦλος) who waits at table (διακονέω) for his master, and who expects no more than to fulfil this duty as an 'unworthy slave'. The distinction in status and expectations between the master and the slave is emphasized. Similarly in Luke 12:37 a parable is recorded where the slaves of a master (δοῦλοι) are commended for being ready for their master's return. They are rewarded by being themselves sat at table and waited on (διακονέω) by the master. The notion of spokesman is not intended. Rather the reversal of status is here significant. One further significant passage, Luke 22:24-27, again contrasts those who serve at table with those who are the masters:

> A dispute also arose among them as to which one of them was to be regarded as the greatest. But he said to them, 'The kings of the Gentiles lord it (κυριεύουσιν) over them; and those in authority over them are called benefactors. But not so with you; rather the greatest among you must become like the youngest, and the leader like one who serves (ὁ διακονῶν). For who is greater, the one who is at the table or the one who serves (ὁ διακονῶν)? Is it not the one at the table? But I am among you as one who serves (ὁ διακονῶν).'

Here Jesus distinguishes himself and his disciples from the Gentile rulers who are authoritarian. The image is expressly that the greater person is not the one sitting at table, but rather the greater person is the one who serves as Jesus has done. Consequently, those disciples who seek to be great, should rather achieve greatness by serving. Again the idea is not that of the spokesman, rather 'His astonishing act in the estimation of service was precisely to reverse, in ethical estimation, the relation between serving and being served'.[165] Collins seeks to downplay the significance of this by pointing out that in both Luke 22:16 and 17 a figure of speech is used — a simile. Jesus is

---

[164]J.N. Collins, *Diakonia*, 245.
[165]L.R. Hennessey, '*Diakonia* and *Diakonoi* in the Pre-Nicene Church', 65.

among them *as* one who serves, the greatest amongst them should be
as the youngest, and the one who rules *as* the one who serves.[166]
Collins further stretches the point by arguing that 'the simile refers
only to events there at table; the image of waiter would be an
unnatural figure by which to allude beyond the supper to situations
like Jesus' care for the disciples or for the sick'.[167] The rôle of Jesus in
this specific instance was that of one who broke bread and passed a
cup, and Collins wrongly concludes that the general notion of serving
beyond this context is unnecessary.

In the pericope Mark 9:33-35 which includes the phrase 'If any
one would be first, he must be last of all *and servant of all*', Collins
again weakens the significance of the verse by comparing the varying
contexts of the synoptic accounts and concluding that 'the teaching
has an uncertain home in the tradition'.[168] He later concludes, 'No
special significance, consequently, attaches to the occurrences of the
term διάκονος in these sayings, and there is no call to explain its
presence by way of a connection with its currency in the language of
church order or in any other part of a presumed Christian lexicon'.[169]

One passage to which Collins does not refer (because it does
not contain one of the διακονία words) is the account recorded in
John 13. Here Jesus portrays himself in the form of a servant by
washing his disciples' feet. He then contrasts the rôle of a servant
(δοῦλος) with that of the lord and teacher, and urges his disciples to
follow his example of being servant.[170] The notion of service is, thus,
evident irrespective of Collins' technical interpretation of διακονία.
Equally Jesus does not adopt 'titles of domination', nor does he
exhort in an authoritarian way.[171]

It may be considered that Collins has found ways to diminish
from the synoptic accounts the notion of service as a dominical
imperative. Not all commentators will be convinced, however, by
these attempts, and many will still consider that an important
message of the evangelists remains that the one who 'came not to be

---

[166]J.N. Collins, *Diakonia*, 246, 'we are thereby alerted to the fact that the point of
the teaching is not going to be found in its literal reading'.

[167]J.N. Collins, *Diakonia*, 247.

[168]J.N. Collins, *Diakonia*, 247. Cf. *op. cit.*, 330-31, where he notes that the parallel
Mk 9:35 includes 'slave *of all*', but does not suggest that this allows for any more
widespread an application.

[169]J.N. Collins, *Diakonia*, 248.

[170]Jn 13:13-17.

[171]P. Ellingworth, 'Translating the Language of Leadership', 137.

served, but to serve' also sought to enjoin his followers to adopt a similarly 'serving' attitude. It will now be considered whether a similar notion is maintained also within the Pauline corpus. In general, Collins argues that the notions of spokesman and emissary predominate, and, in particular in 1 Corinthians 3:5 and 2 Corinthians 3:6, 6:4, and 11:23 he is not speaking 'in an imprecise way about servants'.[172]

In his discussion of 1 Corinthians 3:5, however, it would seem that Collins wrongly interprets Paul's statements and he overlooks the theme of status which underlines so much of Paul's exhortation in the opening chapters of the letter.[173] It is argued that the main force of Paul's paraenesis is that Paul (and Apollos) come with the authorization of God.[174] It is clear that, as apostles, their appointment derives from the Lord; equally their task is assigned by the Lord.[175] Paul appears here, however, to be contrasting his own task with that of God, as opposed to emphasizing any element of mediation or agency.[176] Indeed, his own rôle as planter and Apollos' rôle as the one who waters are expressly belittled in comparison with the far more significant rôle of the one who makes things increase. It is important for Paul to demonstrate how his stance is at odds with the position adopted by the Corinthians who rather elevated personal standing and took pride in human leaders. The language of servanthood is reinforced by the agricultural and artisan metaphors which are self-applied in this section.[177] It may be argued that Paul's use of the neuter interrogative pronoun τί, as opposed to the masculine form τίς, implies a stress on the task which is performed, rather than on the importance of the relationship between the διάκονος and the Lord. Thus, he writes that the one who plants and the one who waters are comparatively 'nothing'.[178] This is in stark contrast to the position adopted by the Corinthians who were

---

[172]J.N. Collins, *Diakonia*, 195.

[173]J.N. Collins, *Diakonia*, 196. *Cf.* also the discussion in P. Ellingworth, 'Servant, Slave or what?', *Bible Translator* 49 (1998) 123-26, with regard to what these terms imply about social status.

[174]J.N. Collins, *Diakonia*, 196-97.

[175]1 Cor 3:5.

[176]1 Cor 3:5-6.

[177]A.D. Clarke, *Secular and Christian Leadership in Corinth*, 119-21.

[178]1 Cor 3:7.

variously saying 'I am of Paul' and 'I am of Apollos'.[179] Rather than saying we are significant emissaries, the emphasis appears to be that these apostles should be viewed, as they viewed themselves, as no more than servants who consequently should not be the focus of attention. As such, Paul inverts the contemporary social values which were being adopted by some in the Christian community, and adopts metaphors which were associated with menial and vulgar work, thereby eschewing self-exaltation.[180]

In 2 Corinthians 6:4 Paul again describes himself as one of God's ministers (θεοῦ διάκονοι). Again it is considered by Collins that this title 'indicates Paul's role as the authoritative mouthpiece of God, and for his readers has precise connotations of a person entrusted with God's full message, charged with the duty to deliver it, and endowed with the right to be heard and believed'.[181] Also in 2 Corinthians 11:23 Paul applies the metaphor of 'servant of Christ' to himself. In both of these cases, however, Paul juxtaposes the self-designation with a catalogue of sufferings and deprivations which amount to his credentials. As such the term διάκονος does not emphasize a position of status with respect to association with God as his mouthpiece, rather it is one of suffering and hardship with respect to the Corinthians and in contrast to the apostle's opponents. Paul's point is precisely that he is boasting about things which show his weakness, rather than his status.[182]

---

[179]1 Cor 3:4.

[180]Cf. the statements by Plutarch, Pericles 1.4-2.1, 'while we delight in the work, we despise the workman, as, for instance, in the case of perfumes and dyes; we take a delight in them, but dyers and perfumers we regard as illiberal and vulgar folk. ... Labour with one's own hands on lowly tasks gives witness, in the toil thus expended on useless things, to one's own indifference to higher things. ... For it does not of necessity follow that if the work delights you with its grace, the one who wrought it is worthy of your esteem'; and Philo, Quod deterius potiori insidiari solet 33-34, who contrasted the established of society with those who worked with their hands and were consequently without status: 'Those who take care of themselves are men of mark and wealth, holding leading positions, praised on all hands, recipients of honours, portly, healthy and robust, revelling in luxurious and riotous living, knowing nothing of labour (πόνον οὐκ εἰδότες), conversant with pleasures which carry the sweets of life to the all-welcoming soul by every channel of sense'. Cf. also B.W. Winter, '"If a Man Does not Wish to Work...": a Cultural and Historical Setting for 2 Thessalonians 3:6-16', Tyndale Bulletin 40 (1989) 303-15.

[181]J.N. Collins, Diakonia, 198.

[182]2 Cor 11:30.

Notwithstanding the interpretation given by Collins to Paul's use of διάκονος in the above passages, in 1 Corinthians 9:19 and 2 Corinthians 4:5 Paul expressly declared himself to be a slave (here δοῦλος) of the Corinthian Christians and to be prepared to make himself a slave for the sake of winning people to the gospel. In these instances there can be no reference to Paul's rôle as either divine spokesman or mediator. Rather he is establishing himself in relation to the Corinthians as one who serves. (He also applies the word 'slave' to his relationship to God.)[183]

In the hymn of Christ in Philippians it can further be seen that Jesus is portrayed as the one who disdained equality with God, and assumed the form of a servant, and further humbled himself, becoming obedient to death.[184] It is this same attitude or mind which Paul commends all Christians to have, just as he himself endeavours also to know Christ.[185] Thus, he urges the Galatians, Christians are to 'serve' (δουλεύω) one another in love.[186]

1. Status

At a number of points in our assessment of Paul's perception of Christian leadership it has been clear that he adopts a line which rejects many of the measures of human status which were widely-held by Graeco-Roman society. Additionally, Paul's response to the Corinthian preoccupation with personality-cult, boasting and wisdom also reflects a rejection of such worldly categories of status. Paul views Christian leaders not as those of the highest status within their community, but as those who serve.

Characteristic of the Corinthian church was the exclusive loyalty or allegiance which some members displayed towards patron-like figures, such as Paul, Apollos and Cephas. This is most clearly seen in the party-spirit of factionalism which Paul criticizes in 1 Corinthians 1:10-13.[187] Paul was keen to distance himself from being the object of such treatment, and points out that he had not

---

[183]Rom 1:1; Gal 1:10; Phil 1:1. It is confusing that many English translations can use the same word 'servant' to interpret both δοῦλος and διάκονος.
[184]Phil 2:6-8.
[185]Phil 2:5; 3:10.
[186]Gal 5:13. Cf. P.T. O'Brien, *Gospel and Mission in the Writings of Paul*, 100.
[187]Cf. A.D. Clarke, *Secular and Christian Leadership in Corinth*, 112-13.

acted towards individuals within the community in a way which could be interpreted as suggestive of a patron to his clients.[188] He highlights later in the epistle that this factionalism was responsible for producing a climate of factionalism, jealousy and envy, more characteristic of the world, than of a Christian community.[189]

There is also the possibility that the Corinthian community was protecting one of their patron figures from public censure and possible expulsion, namely, the immoral brother mentioned by Paul in 1 Corinthians 5.[190] The community is challenged by Paul for not reacting to this instance of sexual immorality with a disciplinary hearing, but rather for showing pride despite the event. At first glance it seems puzzling that Paul's own response is not to offer a lesson in what is acceptable practice. One explanation is that the offender is a much respected figure of the community; and, if he were a patron, it would be difficult, not to say unpragmatic, to expel him. Paul urges the community instead to act in precisely the way that he would were he to have been present. This person is to be 'handed over to Satan'.[191] In Paul's eyes, the secular status of a believer does not pave the way for positive discrimination.

For leaders in Graeco-Roman society the display of wisdom enhanced one's respect in the community. In 1 Corinthians Paul repeatedly draws a distinction between the wisdom of the world and that which is available to the spiritual person and derives from God.[192] It is pointed out that God, in his wisdom, did not call Christians on the basis of their human wisdom.[193] Indeed, few in the Corinthian church at least could lay claim to being 'wise' according to human standards.[194] Human wisdom reviles the saving message of the cross;[195] human wisdom is that wisdom which is shamed by even the foolishness of God;[196] and human wisdom, the kind of wisdom

---

[188]Specifically, the few baptisms which he undertook should not be interpreted as representative of a patron/client relationship; 1 Cor 1:14-16.

[189]1 Cor 3:1-23.

[190]Cf. A.D. Clarke, *Secular and Christian Leadership in Corinth*, 73-88.

[191]1 Cor 5:4-5.

[192]Cf. for example, 1 Cor 1:21, 25; 2:5; 3:19. Cf. also P. Lampe, 'Theological Wisdom and the "Word about the Cross": The Rhetorical Scheme in 1 Corinthians 1-4', *Interpretation* 44 (1990) 118.

[193]1 Cor 1:27-28.

[194]1 Cor 1:26.

[195]1 Cor 1:17-18, 21-24.

[196]1 Cor 1:25.

adopted by 'the rulers of this age' precipitated the crucifixion of the Lord of glory.[197] Such wisdom is thus both inappropriate and insufficient to characterize godly leadership; indeed, the truly spiritual among the Corinthians should have appreciated that godly wisdom derives from God and is inaccessible to those who have not the Spirit of God, whereas human wisdom is taught merely by humans.[198] Those who elevate human wisdom, therefore, are denying the superiority of godly wisdom.

Paul repeatedly draws the Corinthians' attention to his own rejection of human wisdom. In 1 Corinthians 1:12-17 he stresses that Paul should not be the focus of adulation or personal following in that he was neither crucified for the Corinthians, nor were many of the Corinthians baptized in his name. On the contrary, Paul was seeking to fulfil his own calling to preach the gospel in a way which was not dependent on human wisdom. This latter point is further emphasized in 1 Corinthians 2:1-5.[199]

2. Summary

It can be concluded, then, that Collins' insistence that διάκονος has a technical connotation of intermediary or spokesman is not convincing with regard to the New Testament evidence. In addition, it has been seen from both the synoptic and the Pauline texts that there remains a significant emphasis on the servile nature, not only of Jesus' and Paul's ministries, but this is also commended by both Jesus and Paul as something which should more widely be characteristic of all Christians. This is further reinforced by Paul's general rejection of 'worldly' ways of recognizing status.

---

[197]1 Cor 2:6-8; cf. A.D. Clarke, Secular and Christian Leadership in Corinth, 114-17.
[198]1 Cor 2:12-13.
[199]Described by D. Litfin, St. Paul's Theology of Proclamation: 1 Corinthians 1-4 and Greco-Roman Rhetoric (SNTS Monograph Series, 79; Cambridge: Cambridge University Press, 1994) 204-209, as the locus classicus of Paul's theology of proclamation.

IV. Conclusion

We may be able to see in conclusion that the way in which Paul exercised authority over those in his communities is significant. In certain circumstances he maintains neither his own rights nor authority, but rather modifies his lifestyle out of deference to those who are 'weak' in the community. This practice of letting love, rather than knowledge, dictate personal ethics he urges on others. With regard to the party divisions which may have been in the community, instead of pursuing the option of reinforcing his own following, Paul expresses no animosity towards Apollos, but urges the Corinthians to see both himself and Apollos as mere servants. There are others also in the Christian communities to whom respect should be accorded. These positions of leadership are legitimated on the basis not of social status, but function.

Paul, on a number of occasions, applies to himself the title of 'father' to the community. It is significant, however, that this usage is contrary to the honorific application of the titles Father/Mother of the synagogue found on a number of Jewish inscriptions. This is not a title redolent with status, conveyed upon the community's chief benefactor. Paul's fatherhood is, rather, exercised out of love. His relationship with them as father gives him, not simply a unique authority, but a unique motivation of loving concern.

On numerous occasions Paul enjoins believers to imitate a given model, variously God, Christ, himself, other believers or other churches. This non-exclusive use of the imitation motif should not be conceived as a call to obedience, or as a means by which Paul can reinforce group boundaries to his own advantage. Paul's own life is modelled on that of Christ, and this is the ultimate goal of the motif.

One of Paul's preferred titles is that of 'apostle', a commission which derives from God and is founded in the gospel. Paul's ministry is challenged not when his apostleship is challenged, but when believers are being drawn away from Christ and his grace. Apostleship is regarded as a ministry of weakness, rather than status and grace.

There has been considerable debate over what is conveyed by the διακονία word group, specifically whether this is a Greek technical term for an intermediary or go-between, or whether the early Christians had made it a Christian technical term for loving service. This particular debate may be inconclusive at present. Nevertheless, in both the gospel records and the Pauline epistles the notion of service and humility is powerfully conveyed irrespective of the notion of *diakonia*.

In each of these areas Paul demonstrates a conviction that true Christian leadership in God's ἐκκλησία is quite distinct from the patterns of leadership which were immediately accessible throughout Graeco-Roman urban culture of the first century. Much leadership in that society was dependent on an integrated power-base. Paul's own example and directive were opposed to such models. The nature of the Christian church and the message of the Christian gospel required a quite different style of leadership.

CHAPTER 10

CONCLUSIONS

I. Christian 'Leaders' Serving as 'Ministers'

We have seen that Graeco-Roman society in the first century had an exceptionally developed pattern of social hierarchy where high status was clearly recognized and publicly honoured. There was a corresponding preoccupation, at many different levels of society, with honorific titles associated with positions of leadership. Some of these elements of community organization were evident also in local congregations of the early church. It is all the more significant when we come to Paul's view of leadership in the context of the church, therefore, to note that he avoids the terms 'leader' or 'leadership' with reference to Christian communities, preferring to speak rather of service or ministry (διακονία) and co-workers.

For Paul, the nature of the Christian ἐκκλησία demands a significantly different model of organization from that which prevailed in the civic ἐκκλησία. It is then all the more anomalous that considerable focus is given in many modern contexts to church 'leaders' and church 'leadership'. Those descriptions which Paul did use include that of deacon and bishop (overseer). These terms have since been embellished in some ecclesiastical quarters by adding as a prefix one particular term, familiar in first-century contexts, which Paul seems to have avoided, namely 'arch-' (derived from one of the

Greek words for 'leader', ἄρχων).[1] In this way the importance of official titles in church contexts is reinforced and the appearance of a hierarchy is created which would have been as familiar in the cultural context of the first-century world, both Graeco-Roman and Jewish, as it is today. On this issue Paul is clearly countercultural. Not only is the word 'leader' avoided by him, but he also eschews the associated concepts of leadership.

To the extent that Paul distances himself from any who would call themselves his followers or disciples,[2] he does not regard himself as a leader. Similarly, he is no master and has no servants, just fellow-workers, fellow-partners and fellow-soldiers. This is an important contrast to the ministry of Jesus who attracted disciples and expressly called people to follow him. Thus it is important to note that, although Paul looks to Jesus as a model, there are aspects of Jesus' ministry which cannot be emulated by the apostle.

Avoiding the notion of leader, Paul did, however, regard himself as a servant. In this regard he does adopt the pattern modeled by Jesus, who came to serve.[3] He is a servant both of Christ and to the church, and as such he labours and applies to himself metaphors of manual work, such as builder and planter (quite at odds with the sophists of the day who could proudly say 'our hands never knew labour'). Similarly he considers that where there is a hierarchy in the church, God deems that it is these serving apostles who are on the lowest rung.[4]

Given Paul's countercultural stance, preferring the notion of service (or 'ministry') to that of leadership, it may seem strange that he also established himself as one who should be imitated.[5] It is significant, however, that he did not regard himself either as the exclusive model to believers, nor even as one of particular importance. Indeed, he expressly commended others who were equally worthy of imitation. A particular model was considered appropriate not because of who that person was but because of the

---

[1]A different, but equivalent, prefix preferred in some churches is the less archaic designation 'senior'.

[2]*Cf.* 1 Cor 1:10-17. It was commonplace in the first century for religious, philosophical and political leaders of the day to attract and foster the support of disciples.

[3]Mk 10:45; Jn 13:1-17; Phil 2:6-9.

[4]1 Cor 3:21-23; 4:9.

[5]It is on this point that a number of scholars have misread Paul's approach, and interpreted the motif of imitation rather as authoritarian.

extent to which that life was conformed to the gospel. Consequently, all such models were secondary in importance. Their supreme goal was imitation of Christ.

Of all the patterns of community organization which were available to the early church (the civic contexts, the voluntary associations, the family and the Jewish synagogues), the one which could be most easily modified so as to be appropriate to the context of the Christian community was that of the family. The metaphor of the family was directly applied to the church, and many of its relationships were described in terms of brother/sister and father/child. Paul does occasionally refer to himself as a father, but also as a brother.

The metaphor of a father is useful to Paul in that it highlights the nature of his concern and love for a congregation. Significantly he does not apply it to himself, however, in an exclusive way. He is also aware that there are connotations of authority which are associated with fatherhood, but his earnest endeavour is that these need never be applied.[6] More commonly Paul describes himself as a brother to his fellow believers, thus drawing attention away from any sense of seniority. For somebody from a different natural family to be associated with another as a brother was not lightly done in Graeco-Roman contexts.

In each of these aspects of church organization it emerges that Paul was calling those in Christian communities to make the necessary and deep-seated adjustments from their cultural background. The nature of the church required a pattern of organization which could not immediately be transferred from the culture of the day. Paul's unflinching criticism of some of the churches to which he was writing was that they were being inappropriately drawn to such models.

II. Institutionalization

There has been a long-standing consensus among scholars that the New Testament reflects a process of institutionalization where formerly 'charismatic' churches (viz. the church at the stage of development when Paul wrote 1 Corinthians) gradually became institutionalized and adopted a hierarchical structure (viz. the church

---

[6] 1 Cor 4:14-21.

represented in the later Pastoral Epistles). We see from the ancient literary and archaeological sources, however, that a distinction between charismatic and hierarchical leadership was not especially evident in first-century Graeco-Roman society. This was a society that was deeply stratified, and elements of a similar stratification are evident even in the early expressions of the church which lie behind Paul's early correspondence.

This scholarly 'consensus' was put off the scent of leadership in the earliest Pauline communities precisely because of the lack of specific references to leadership in some of Paul's epistles, not realising that his deliberate avoidance of this term was an eschewing of what it stood for, rather than a signal that leadership did not exist at this stage. Our analysis of a range of community contexts in the first century has demonstrated rather that leadership was operative in the early Christian communities. Indeed, it was often determined by social status rather than other 'charismatic' qualities.

BIBLIOGRAPHY

Abbott, F.F. & Johnson, A.C. *Municipal Administration in the Roman Empire* (New York: Russell & Russell, 1968).

Alcock, S.E.   *The Early Roman Empire in the East* (Oxbow Monograph, 97; Oxford: Oxbow, 1997).

Alcock, S.E.   'Minding the Gap in Hellenistic and Roman Greece', in S.E. Alcock & R. Osborne (eds.), *Placing the Gods: Sanctuaries and Sacred Space in Ancient Greece* (Oxford: Clarendon Press, 1994) 247-61.

Alcock, S.E.   *Graecia Capta: the Landscapes of Roman Greece* (Cambridge: Cambridge University Press, 1993).

Applebaum, S.   'The Organization of the Jewish Communities in the Diaspora', in S. Safrai & M. Stern (eds.), *The Jewish People in the First Century: Historical Geography, Political History, Social, Cultural and Religious Life and Institutions* (Compendia Rerum Iudaicarum ad Novum Testamentum, 1; Assen: Van Gorcum, 1976) 464-503.

Applebaum, S.   'The Social and Economic Status of the Jews in the Diaspora', in S. Safrai & M. Stern (eds.), *The Jewish People in the First Century: Historical Geography, Political History, Social, Cultural and Religious Life and Institutions* (Compendia Rerum Iudaicarum ad Novum Testamentum, 2; Assen: Van Gorcum, 1976) 701-27.

Avis, P.D.L.   *Authority, Leadership and Conflict in the Church* (London: Mowbray, 1992).

Bakker, J.T.   *Living and Working with the Gods: Studies of Evidence for Private Religion and its Material Environment in the City of Ostia (100-500 AD)* (Dutch Monographs on Ancient History and Archaeology, 12; Amsterdam: J.C. Gieben, 1994).

Barclay, J.M.G.   'The Family as the Bearer of Religion in Judaism and Early Christianity', in H. Moxnes (ed.), *Constructing Early Christian Families: Family as Social Reality and Metaphor* (London: Routledge, 1997) 66-80.

Barclay, J.M.G.   *Jews in the Mediterranean Diaspora: from Alexander to Trajan (323 BCE-117 CE)* (Edinburgh: T. & T. Clark, 1996).

Barclay, J.M.G.   'Conflict in Thessalonica', *Catholic Biblical Quarterly* 55 (1993) 512-30.

Barclay, J.M.G.   'Thessalonica and Corinth: Social Contrasts in Pauline Christianity', *Journal for the Study of the New Testament* 47 (1992) 49-74.

Barclay, J.M.G.   'Paul, Philemon and Christian Slave-Ownership', *New Testament Studies* 37 (1991) 161-86.

Barclay, J.M.G.   *Obeying the Truth: a Study of Paul's Ethics in Galatians* (Studies of the New Testament and its World; Edinburgh: T. & T. Clark, 1988).

Barclay, J.M.G. & Sweet, J.   *Early Christian Thought in its Jewish Context* (Cambridge: Cambridge University Press, 1996).

Barker, D.C.   *Household Patterns in the Roman Empire with Special Reference to Egypt* (2 vols.; PhD dissertation; Sydney: Macquarie University, 1994).

Barrett, C.K.   *Church, Ministry, and Sacraments in the New Testament* (The 1983 Didsbury Lectures; Exeter: Paternoster, 1985).

Bartlett, D.L.   *Ministry in the New Testament* (Overtures to Biblical Theology; Minneapolis: Fortress Press, 1993).

Bauckham, R. (ed.)   *The Gospels for all Christians: Rethinking the Gospel Audiences* (Grand Rapids: Eerdmans, 1998).

Baur, F.C.   *The Church History of the First Three Centuries* (2 vols.; 3rd ed.; Theological Translation Fund

Library, 16, 20; London: Williams and Norgate, 1878-79).

Beard, M.   'Priesthood in the Roman Republic', in M. Beard & J. North (eds.), *Pagan Priests: Religion and Power in the Ancient World* (London: Duckworth, 1990) 19-48.

Beard, M., North, J. & Price, S.   *Religions of Rome: a History* (Cambridge: Cambridge University Press, 1998).

Beard, M., North, J. & Price, S.   *Religions of Rome: a Sourcebook* (Cambridge: Cambridge University Press, 1998).

Beard, M. & North, J. (eds.) *Pagan Priests: Religion and Power in the Ancient World* (London: Duckworth, 1990).

Best, E.   *Paul and his Converts: the Sprunt Lectures 1985* (Edinburgh: T. & T. Clark, 1988).

Beyer, H.W.   'διακονέω, διακονία, διάκονος', *Theological Dictionary of the New Testament* 2 (1964) 81-93.

Blue, B.B.   *In Public and in Private: the Role of the House Church in Early Christianity* (PhD dissertation; Aberdeen: Aberdeen University, 1989).

Borgen, P.   '"Yes," "No," "How Far?": the Participation of Jews and Christians in Pagan Cults', in T. Engberg-Pedersen (ed.), *Paul in his Hellenistic Context* (Studies of the New Testament and its World; Edinburgh: T. & T. Clark, 1994) 30-59.

Bormann, L.   *Philippi: Stadt und Christengemeinde zur Zeit des Paulus* (Supplements to Novum Testamentum, 78; Leiden: E.J. Brill, 1995).

Böttger, P.C.   'Die eschatologische Existenz der Christen: Erwägungen zu Philipper 3.20', *Zeitschrift für die neutestamentliche Wissenschaft* 60 (1969) 244-63.

Bradley, K.R.   *Discovering the Roman Family: Studies in Roman Social History* (Oxford: Oxford University Press, 1991).

Bradley, K.R.   *Slaves and Masters in the Roman Empire: a Study in Social Control* (Oxford: Oxford University Press, 1987).

Brändle, R. & Stegemann, E.W.   'The Formation of the First "Christian Congregations" in Rome in the Context of the Jewish Congregations', in K.P. Donfried & P.

Richardson (eds.), *Judaism and Christianity in First-Century Rome* (Grand Rapids: Eerdmans, 1998) 117-27.

Brandt, W.   *Dienst und Dienen im Neuen Testament* (Gütersloh, 1931).

Branick, V.   *The House Church in the Writings of Paul* (Zaccheus Studies, New Testament; Wilmington: Michael Glazier, 1989).

Brewer, R.R.   'The meaning of πολιτεύεσθε in Philippians 1:27', *Journal of Biblical Literature* 73 (1954) 76-83.

Brooten, B.J.   *Women Leaders in the Ancient Synagogue: Inscriptional Evidence and Background Issues* (Brown Judaic Series, 36; Chico: Scholars Press, 1982).

Bruit Zaidman, L. & Schmitt Pantel, P.   *Religion in the Ancient Greek City* (Cambridge: Cambridge University Press, 1995).

Bulard, M.   *Le religion domestique dans la colonie italienne de Délos, d'après les peintures murales et les autels historiés* (Bibliothèque des écoles françaises d'Athènes et de Rome, 131; Paris: Boccard, 1926).

Burtchaell, J.T.   *From Synagogue to Church: Public Services and Offices in the Earliest Christian Communities* (Cambridge: Cambridge University Press, 1992).

Callahan, A.D.   'Paul's Epistle to Philemon: Toward an Alternative *Argumentum*', *Harvard Theological Review* 86 (1993) 357-76.

Campbell, J.Y.   'The Origin and Meaning of the Christian Use of the Word Ἐκκλησία', in J.Y. Campbell, *Three New Testament Studies* (Leiden: E.J. Brill, 1965) 41-54.

Caragounis, C.C.   'From Obscurity to Prominence: the Development of the Roman Church between Romans and *1 Clement*', in K.P. Donfried & P. Richardson (eds.), *Judaism and Christianity in First-Century Rome* (Grand Rapids: Eerdmans, 1998) 245-79.

Castelli, E.A.   'Interpretations of Power in 1 Corinthians', *Semeia* 54 (1992) 197-222.

Castelli, E.A.   *Imitating Paul: a Discourse of Power* (Literary Currents in Biblical Interpretation; Louisville: Westminster/John Knox, 1991).

Chapple, A.L.   *Local Leadership in the Pauline Churches: Theological and Social Factors in its Development: a Study Based on 1 Thessalonians, 1 Corinthians and Philippians* (PhD dissertation; Durham: Durham University, 1984).

Chiat, M.J.S.   *Handbook of Synagogue Architecture* (Brown Judaic Studies, 29; Chico: Scholars Press, 1982).

Chiat, M.J.S.   'First-Century Synagogue Architecture: Methodological Problems', in J. Gutmann (ed.), *Ancient Synagogues: the State of Research* (Brown Judaic Studies, 22; Chico: Scholars Press, 1981) 49-60.

Chow, J.K.   *Patronage and Power: a Study of Social Networks in Corinth* (JSNT Supplement Series, 75; Sheffield: JSOT Press, 1992).

Clarke, A.D.   '"Be Imitators of Me": Paul's Model of Leadership', *Tyndale Bulletin* 49 (1998) 329-60.

Clarke, A.D.   '"Refresh the Hearts of the Saints": a Unique Pauline Context?', *Tyndale Bulletin* 47 (1996) 277-300.

Clarke, A.D.   *Secular and Christian Leadership in Corinth: a Socio-historical and Exegetical Study of 1 Corinthians 1-6* (Arbeiten zur Geschichte des antiken Judentums und des Urchristentums, 18; Leiden: E.J. Brill, 1993).

Clarke, A.D.   'Another Corinthian Erastus Inscription', *Tyndale Bulletin* 42 (1991) 146-51.

Clarke, A.D.   'The Good and the Just in Romans 5:7', *Tyndale Bulletin* 41 (1990) 128-42.

Clarke, J.R.   *The Houses of Roman Italy, 100 B.C.-A.D. 250: Ritual, Space, and Decoration* (Berkeley: University of California Press, 1991).

Cohen, S.J.D.   'Were Pharisees and Rabbis the Leaders of Communal Prayer and Torah Study in Antiquity? The Evidence of the New Testament, Josephus, and the Church Fathers', in W.G. Dever and J.E. Wright (eds.), *The Echoes of Many Texts: Reflections on Jewish and Christian Traditions: Essays in Honor of Lou H. Silberman* (Brown Judaic Studies, 313; Atlanta: Scholars Press, 1997) 99-114.

Cohen, S.J.D.   'Women in the Synagogues of Antiquity', *Conservative Judaism* 33 (1980) 23-9.

Collins, J.N.   'Once more on Ministry: Forcing a Turnover in the Linguistic Field', *One in Christ* 27 (1991) 234-45.

Collins, J.N.   *Diakonia: Re-interpreting the Ancient Sources* (Oxford: Oxford University Press, 1990).

Cotter, W.   'The Collegia and Roman Law: State Restrictions on Voluntary Associations 64 B.C.E.–200 C.E.', in J.S. Kloppenborg & S.G. Wilson (eds.), *Voluntary Associations in the Graeco-Roman World* (London: Routledge, 1996) 74-89.

Cotter, W.   'Our *Politeuma* is in Heaven: the Meaning of Philippians 3:17-21', in B.H. McLean (ed.), *Origins and Method: Towards a New Understanding of Judaism and Christianity* (JSNT Supplement Series, 86; Sheffield: JSOT Press, 1993) 92-104.

Croix, G.E.M. de Ste   'Why were the Early Christians Persecuted?', in M. Finley (ed.), *Studies in Ancient Society* (London: Routledge and Kegan Paul, 1974) 210-49.

Crook, J.A.   *'Patria Potestas'*, *Classical Quarterly* 17 (1967) 113-22.

Crook, J.A.   *Law and Life of Rome* (Aspects of Greek and Roman Life; London: Thames and Hudson, 1967).

Curchin, L.A.   *Roman Spain: Conquest and Assimilation* (London: Routledge, 1991).

Curchin, L.A.   *The Local Magistrates of Roman Spain* (Phoenix Supplementary vol., 28; Toronto: University of Toronto Press, 1990).

Davis, G.B.   *True and False Boasting in 2 Corinthians 10-13* (PhD dissertation; Cambridge: Cambridge University, 1998).

De Boer, W.P.   *The Imitation of Paul: an Exegetical Study* (Kampen: J.H. Kok, 1962).

Derrett, J.D.M.   'The Functions of the Epistle to Philemon', *Zeitschrift für die Neutestamentliche Wissenschaft* 79 (1988) 63-91.

DeSilva, D.A.   '"Worthy of his Kingdom": Honor Discourse and Social Engineering in 1 Thessalonians', *Journal for the Study of the New Testament* 64 (1996) 49-79.

Dixon, S.   *The Roman Family* (Baltimore: Johns Hopkins University Press, 1992).

Dixon, S.   'The Sentimental Ideal of the Roman Family', in B. Rawson (ed.), *Marriage, Divorce, and Children in Ancient Rome* (Oxford: Clarendon Press, 1991) 99-113.

Dodd, B.   *Paul's Paradigmatic 'I': Personal Example as Literary Strategy* (JSNT Supplement Series: Sheffield: JSOT Press, 1999).

Donfried, K.P.   '2 Thessalonians and the Church of Thessalonica', in B.H. McLean (ed.), *Origins and Method: Towards a New Understanding of Judaism and Christianity* (JSNT Supplement Series, 86; Sheffield: JSOT Press, 1993) 128-44.

Donfried, K.P.   'The Cults of Thessalonica and the Thessalonian Correspondence', *New Testament Studies* 31 (1985) 336-56.

Donfried, K.P. & Marshall, I.H.   *The Theology of the Shorter Pauline Letters* (Cambridge: Cambridge University Press, 1993).

Doughty, D.J.   'Citizens of Heaven: Philippians 3.2-21', *New Testament Studies* 41 (1995) 102-22.

Dubourdieu, A.   *Les origines et le développement du culte des Pénates à Rome* (Collection de l'École française de Rome, 118; Rome: École française de Rome, 1989).

Dunn, J.D.G.   *The Theology of Paul the Apostle* (Edinburgh: T. & T. Clark, 1998).

Dunn, J.D.G.   *The Epistles to the Colossians and to Philemon: a Commentary on the Greek Text* (The New International Greek Testament Commentary; Grand Rapids: Eerdmans, 1996).

Dunn, J.D.G.   *A Commentary on the Epistle to the Galatians* (Black's New Testament Commentaries; London: A. & C. Black, 1993).

Dunn, J.D.G.   *The Partings of the Ways: Between Christianity and Judaism, and their Significance for the Character of Christianity* (London: SCM Press, 1991).

Duthoy, R.   'Les *Augustales', *Aufstieg und Niedergang der Römischen Welt* II.16.2 (1978) 1254-1309.

Edersheim, A.   *The Life and Times of Jesus the Messiah* (2 vols.; London: Longmans, Green, and Co., 1900).

Edwards, D.R.   *Religion and Power: Pagans, Jews, and Christians in the Greek East* (Oxford: Oxford University Press, 1996).

Ellingworth, P.   'Servant, Slave or what?', *Bible Translator* 49 (1998) 123-26.

Ellingworth, P.   'Translating the Language of Leadership', *Bible Translator* 49 (1998) 126-38.

Engberg-Pedersen, T. 'Stoicism in Philippians', in T. Engberg-Pedersen (ed.), *Paul in his Hellenistic Context* (Studies of the New Testament and its World; Edinburgh: T. & T. Clark, 1994) 256-90.

Engels, D.   *Roman Corinth: an Alternative Model for the Classical City* (Chicago: University of Chicago Press, 1990).

Epstein, D.F.   *Personal Enmity in Roman Politics 218-43 B.C.* (London: Croom Helm, 1987).

Esler, P.F.   'Imagery and Identity in Gal 5:13-6:10', in H. Moxnes (ed.), *Constructing Early Christian Families: Family as Social Reality and Metaphor* (London: Routledge, 1997) 121-49.

Eyben, E.   'Fathers and Sons', in B. Rawson (ed.), *Marriage, Divorce, and Children in Ancient Rome* (Oxford: Clarendon Press, 1991) 114-43.

Fear, A.T.   *Rome and Baetica: Urbanization in Southern Spain c. 50 B.C. – A.D. 150* (Oxford Classical monographs; Oxford: Oxford University Press, 1996).

Fee, G.D.   *The First Epistle to the Corinthians* (The New International Commentary on the New Testament; Grand Rapids: Eerdmans, 1987).

Feldman, L.H.   'Diaspora Synagogues: New Light from Inscriptions and Papyri', in S. Fine (ed.), *Sacred Realm: the Emergence of the Synagogue in the Ancient World* (Oxford: Oxford University Press, 1996) 48-66.

Feldman, L.H.   *Jew and Gentile in the Ancient World: Attitudes and Interactions from Alexander to Justinian* (Princeton: Princeton University Press, 1993).

Feldman, L.H. & Reinhold, M. (eds.)   *Jewish Life and Thought among Greeks and Romans: Primary Readings* (Edinburgh: T. & T. Clark, 1996).

Ferguson, J.   *Greek and Roman Religion: a Source Book* (Noyes Classical Studies; Park Ridge: Noyes Press, 1980).

Filson, F.V.   'The Significance of the Early House Churches', *Journal of Biblical Literature* 58 (1939) 105-12.

Fine, S. (ed.)   *Jews, Christians and Polytheists in the Ancient Synagogue* (London: Routledge, 1999).

Finger, R.H.   *Paul and the Roman House Churches* (Scottdale: Herald, 1993).

Finkelstein, L.   'The Origin of the Synagogue', in J. Gutmann (ed.), *The Synagogue: Studies in Origins, Archaeology, and Architecture* (The Library of Biblical Studies; New York: Ktav, 1975) 3-13.

Finley, M.I.   *Politics in the Ancient World* (Cambridge: Cambridge University Press, 1987).

Finley, M.I.   *Authority and Legitimacy in the Classical City-State* (Offprint from Kongelige Danske Videnskabernes Selskab Historisk- filosofiske Meddelelser 50:3, 1982; Copenhagen: Munksgaard, 1982) 3-23.

Fiorenza, E.S.   *In Memory of Her: a Feminist Theological Reconstruction of Christian Origins* (2nd ed.; London: SCM Press, 1995).

Fiorenza, E.S.   '"Waiting at Table": a Critical Feminist Theological Reflection', in N. Greinacher & N. Mette (eds.), *Diakonia: Church for Others* (Concilium, 198; Edinburgh: T. & T. Clark, 1988) 84-94.

Fishwick, D.   *The Imperial Cult in the Latin West: Studies in the Ruler Cult of the Western Provinces of the Roman Empire* (Études préliminaires aux réligions orientales dans l'Empire romain, 108; vols. 1.i - 2.ii; Leiden: E.J. Brill, 1987).

Fishwick, D.   'The Development of Provincial Ruler Worship in the Western Roman Empire', *Aufstieg und Niedergang der Römischen Welt* II.16.2 (1978) 1201-53.

Flesher, P.V.M.   'Palestinian Synagogues before 70 C.E.: a Review of the Evidence', in D. Urman & P.V.M. Flesher (eds.), *Ancient Synagogues: Historical Analysis and*

Archaeological Discovery (Studia post-Biblica, 47; 2 vols.; Leiden: E.J. Brill, 1995) 27-39.

Foerster, G.   'Architectural Models of the Greco-Roman Period and the Origin of the "Galilean" Synagogue', in L.I. Levine (ed.), *Ancient Synagogues Revealed* (Jerusalem: Israel Exploration Society, 1981) 45-48.

Foerster, G.   'A Survey of Ancient Diaspora Synagogues', in L.I. Levine (ed.), *Ancient Synagogues Revealed* (Jerusalem: Israel Exploration Society, 1981) 164-71.

Fowler, W.W.   *The Religious Experience of the Roman People, from the Earliest Times to the Age of Augustus* (Gifford lectures for 1909-10 delivered in Edinburgh University; London: Macmillan, 1911).

Frank, R.I.   'Augustus' Legislation on Marriage and Children', *California Studies in Classical Antiquity* 8 (1975) 41-52.

Frey, J.-B.   *Corpus Inscriptionum Iudaicarum: recueil des inscriptions juives qui vont du IIIe siècle avant Jésus-Christ au VIIe siècle de notre ère* (2 vols.; Sussidi allo studio delle antichità cristiane, 1, 3; Vatican City, Rome: Pontificio istituto di archeologia cristiana, 1936-1952).

Friesen, S.J.   *Twice Neokoros: Ephesus, Asia and the Cult of the Flavian Imperial Family* (Religions in the Graeco-Roman World, 116; Leiden: E.J. Brill, 1993).

Gardner, J.F.   *Family and* Familia *in Roman Law and Life* (Oxford: Clarendon Press, 1998).

Gardner, J.F.   'Legal Stumbling-Blocks for Lower-Class Families in Rome', in B. Rawson & P. Weaver (eds.), *The Roman Family in Italy: Status, Sentiment, Space* (Oxford: Clarendon Press, 1997) 35-53.

Gardner, J.F. & Wiedemann, T. (eds.)   *The Roman Household: a Sourcebook* (London: Routledge, 1991).

Garland, R.   'Priests and Power in Classical Athens', in M. Beard and J. North (eds.), *Pagan Priests: Religion and Power in the Ancient World* (London: Duckworth, 1990) 73-91.

Garnsey, P. & Saller, R.P. *The Roman Empire: Economy, Society, and Culture* (Berkeley: University of California Press, 1987).

Geagan, D.J. 'Notes on the Agonistic Institutions of Roman Corinth', *Greek, Roman and Byzantine Studies* 4 (1968) 69-80.

Geoffrion, T.C. *The Rhetorical Purpose and the Political and Military Character of Philippians: a Call to Stand Firm* (Lampeter: Mellen Biblical Press, 1993).

Giles, K. *Patterns of Ministry among the First Christians* (Melbourne: Collins Dove, 1989).

Gill, D.W.G. 'In Search of the Social Élite in the Corinthian Church', *Tyndale Bulletin* 44 (1993) 323-37.

Gill, D.W.G. 'Corinth: a Roman Colony in Achaea', *Biblische Zeitschrift* 37 (1993) 259-64.

Gill, D.W.G. 'The Importance of Roman Portraiture for Head-Coverings in 1 Corinthians 11:2-16', *Tyndale Bulletin* 41 (1990) 245-60.

Gill, D.W.G. 'Erastus the Aedile', *Tyndale Bulletin* 40 (1989) 293-301.

Gill, D.W.G. & Winter, B.W. 'Acts and Roman Religion', in D.W.J. Gill & C. Gempf (eds.), *The Book of Acts in its Graeco-Roman Setting* (The Book of Acts in its First Century Setting, 2; Grand Rapids: Eerdmans, 1994) 79-103.

Gordon, R. 'From Republic to Principate: Priesthood, Religion and Ideology', in M. Beard and J. North (eds.), *Pagan Priests: Religion and Power in the Ancient World* (London: Duckworth, 1990) 179-98.

Gordon, R. 'The Veil of Power: Emperors, Sacrificers and Benefactors', in M. Beard and J. North (eds.), *Pagan Priests: Religion and Power in the Ancient World* (London: Duckworth, 1990) 201-31.

Gordon, R. 'Religion in the Roman Empire: the Civic Compromise and its Limits', in M. Beard and J. North (eds.), *Pagan Priests: Religion and Power in the Ancient World* (London: Duckworth, 1990) 235-55.

Grabbe, L.L. 'Synagogues in Pre-70 Palestine: a Reassessment', in D. Urman & P.V.M. Flesher (eds.), *Ancient Synagogues: Historical Analysis and Archaeological*

Discovery (Studia post-Biblica, 47; 2 vols.; Leiden: E.J. Brill, 1995) 17-26.

Griffiths, J.G.   'Egypt and the Rise of the Synagogue', in D. Urman & P.V.M. Flesher (eds.), *Ancient Synagogues: Historical Analysis and Archaeological Discovery* (Studia post-Biblica, 47; 2 vols.; Leiden: E.J. Brill, 1995) 3-16.

Gutmann, J.   *Ancient Synagogues: the State of Research* (Brown Judaic Studies, 22; Chico: Scholars Press, 1981).

Gutmann, J.   'Synagogue Origins: Theories and Facts', in J. Gutmann (ed.), *Ancient Synagogues: the State of Research* (Brown Judaic Studies, 22; Chico: Scholars Press, 1981) 1-6.

Gutmann, J.   *The Synagogue: Studies in Origins, Archaeology, and Architecture* (The Library of Biblical Studies; New York: Ktav, 1975).

Gutmann, J.   'The Origin of the Synagogue: the Current State of Research', in J. Gutmann (ed.), *The Synagogue: Studies in Origins, Archaeology, and Architecture* (The Library of Biblical Studies; New York: Ktav, 1975) 72-76.

Hachlili, R.   'The Origin of the Synagogue: a Re-assessment', *Journal for the Study of Judaism in the Persian, Hellenistic and Roman Period* 28 (1997) 34-47.

Hafemann, S.J.   '"Self-Commendation" and Apostolic Legitimacy in 2 Corinthians: a Pauline Dialectic?', *New Testament Studies* 36 (1990) 66-88.

Hafemann, S.J.   *Suffering and Ministry in the Spirit: Paul's Defense of his Ministry in II Corinthians 2:14-3:3* (Grand Rapids: Eerdmans, 1990).

Hafemann, S.J.   *Suffering and the Spirit: an Exegetical Study of II Cor. 2:14-3:3 within the Context of the Corinthian Correspondence* (WUNT, 2.19; Tübingen: J.C.B. Mohr, 1986).

Hansen, M.H.   *The Athenian Democracy in the Age of Demosthenes: Structure, Principles, and Ideology* (The Ancient World; Oxford: Blackwell, 1991).

Hansen, M.H.   *The Athenian Assembly: in the Age of Demosthenes* (Oxford: Blackwell, 1987).

Harmon, D.P.   'The Family Festivals of Rome', *Aufstieg und Niedergang der Römischen Welt* 16.2 (1978) 1592-1603.

Hatch, E.   *The Organization of the Early Christian Churches* (London: Longmans, Green, 1901).

Hatch, E.   *The Influence of Greek Ideas and Usages upon the Christian Church* (London: Williams and Norgate, 1890).

Hemer, C.J.   *The Book of Acts in the Setting of Hellenistic History* (WUNT, 49; Tübingen: J.C.B. Mohr, 1989).

Hendrix, H.L.   'Benefactor/Patron Networks in the Urban Environment: Evidence from Thessalonica', *Semeia* 56 (1992) 39-58.

Hendrix, H.L.   'Archaeology and Eschatology at Thessalonica', in B.A. Pearson (ed.), *The Future of Early Christianity: Essays in Honor of Helmut Koester* (Minneapolis: Fortress Press, 1991) 107-18.

Hendrix, H.L.   *Thessalonicans Honor Romans* (ThD dissertation; Cambridge: Harvard University Press, 1984).

Hengel, M.   'Proseuche und Synagoge', in J. Gutmann (ed.), *The Synagogue: Studies in Origins, Archaeology, and Architecture* (The Library of Biblical Studies; New York: Ktav, 1975) 27-54.

Hengel, M.   'Die Synagogeninschrift von Stobi', in J. Gutmann (ed.), *The Synagogue: Studies in Origins, Archaeology, and Architecture* (The Library of Biblical Studies; New York: Ktav, 1975) 110-48.

Hennessey, L.R.   '*Diakonia* and *Diakonoi* in the Pre-Nicene Church', in T. Halton & J.P. Williman (eds.), *Diakonia: Studies in Honor of Robert T. Meyer* (Washington: Catholic University of America Press, 1986) 60-86.

Hill, J.L.   *Establishing the Church in Thessalonica* (PhD dissertation; Durham: Duke University, 1990).

Hirschhorn, L.   *Reworking Authority: Leading and Following in the Post-modern Organization* (Organization Studies, 12; Cambridge, Mass.: MIT Press, 1997).

Hock, R.F.   'A Support for his Old Age: Paul's Plea on Behalf of Onesimus', in L.M. White & O.L. Yarbrough (eds.), *The Social World of the First Christians: Essays in*

Honor of Wayne A. Meeks (Minneapolis: Fortress Press, 1995) 67-81.

Hoenig, S.B.   'The Ancient City-Square: The Forerunner of the Synagogue', Aufstieg und Niedergang der Römischen Welt II.19.1 (1979) 448-76.

Hoff, M.C. & Rotroff, S.I. (eds.)   The Romanization of Athens: Proceedings of an International Conference held at Lincoln, Nebraska (April 1996) (Oxbow Monograph, 94; Oxford: Oxbow Books, 1997).

Holmberg, B.   Paul and Power: the Structure of Authority in the Primitive Church as Reflected in the Pauline Epistles (Coniectanea Biblica, New Testament Series, 11; Lund: CWK Gleerup, 1978).

Hoppe, L.J.   The Synagogues and Churches of Ancient Palestine (Collegeville: Liturgical Press, 1994).

Horbury, W.   'Septuagintal and New Testament Conceptions of the Church', in M. Bockmuehl & M.B. Thompson (eds.), A Vision for the Church: Studies in Early Christian Ecclesiology in Honour of J.P.M. Sweet (Edinburgh: T. & T. Clark, 1997) 1-17.

Horbury, W. & Noy, D.   Jewish Inscriptions of Graeco-Roman Egypt: with an Index of the Jewish Inscriptions of Egypt and Cyrenaica (Cambridge: Cambridge University Press, 1992).

Horrell, D.G.   The Social Ethos of the Corinthian Correspondence: Interests and Ideology from 1 Corinthians to 1 Clement (Studies of the New Testament and its World; Edinburgh: T. & T. Clark, 1996).

Horsley, G.H.R.   'The Politarchs', in D.W.J. Gill & C. Gempf (eds.), The Book of Acts in its Graeco-Roman Setting (The Book of Acts in its First Century Setting, 2; Grand Rapids: Eerdmans, 1994) 419-31.

Horsley, G.H.R.   'An archisynagogos of Corinth?', New Documents illustrating Early Christianity 4 (1987) 213-220.

Horsley, R.A.   Paul and Empire: Religion and Power in Roman Imperial Society (Harrisburg: Trinity Press International, 1997).

Horsley, R.A.   *Archaeology, History, and Society in Galilee: the Social Context of Jesus and the Rabbis* (Valley Forge: Trinity Press International, 1996).

Horsley, R.A.   *Galilee: History, Politics, People* (Valley Forge: Trinity Press International, 1995).

Hoskins-Walbank, M.E.   'Evidence for the Imperial Cult in Julio-Claudian Corinth', in A. Small (ed.), *Subject and Ruler: the Cult of the Ruling Power in Classical Antiquity – Papers presented at a Conference held in the University of Alberta on April 13-15, 1994, to celebrate the 65th anniversary of Duncan Fishwick* (Journal of Roman Archaeology. Supplementary Series, 17; Ann Arbor: Journal of Roman Archaeology, 1996) 201-13.

Hurd, J.C.   *The Origin of 1 Corinthians* (London: SPCK, 1965).

Jeffers, J.S.   'Jewish and Christian Families in First-Century Rome', in K.P. Donfried & P. Richardson (eds.), *Judaism and Christianity in First-Century Rome* (Grand Rapids: Eerdmans, 1998) 128-50.

Jewett, R.   *Christian Tolerance: Paul's Message to the Modern Church* (Philadelphia: Westminster Press, 1982).

Jones, A.H.M.   *The Greek City from Alexander to Justinian* (Oxford: Oxford University Press, 1966).

Jones, C.P.   *The Roman World of Dio Chrysostom* (Loeb Classical monographs; London: Harvard University Press, 1978).

Josaitis, N.F.   *Edwin Hatch and Early Church Order* (Recherches et synthèses, Section d'Histoire, 3; Gembloux: J. Duculot, 1971).

Joubert, S.J.   'Managing the Household: Paul as *paterfamilias* of the Christian Household Group in Corinth', in P.F. Esler (ed.), *Modelling Early Christianity: Social-scientific Studies of the New Testament in its Context* (London: Routledge, 1995) 213-223.

Judge, E.A.   *The Social Pattern of Christian Groups in the First Century: Some Prolegomena to the Study of New Testament Ideas of Social Obligation* (London: Tyndale Press, 1960).

Kasher, A.   'Synagogues as "Houses of Prayer" and "Holy Places" in the Jewish Communities of Hellenistic and Roman Egypt', in D. Urman & P.V.M. Flesher (eds.), *Ancient Synagogues: Historical Analysis and Archaeological Discovery* (Studia post-Biblica, 47; 2 vols.; Leiden: E.J. Brill, 1995) 205-220.

Kearsley, R.A.   'The Asiarchs', in D.W.J. Gill & C. Gempf (eds.), *The Book of Acts in its Graeco-Roman Setting* (The Book of Acts in its First Century Setting, 2; Grand Rapids: Eerdmans, 1994) 363-76.

Kee, H.C.   'Defining the First-Century CE Synagogue: Problems and Progress', *New Testament Studies* 41 (1995) 481-500.

Kee, H.C.   'The Changing Meaning of Synagogue: a Response to Richard Oster', *New Testament Studies* 40 (1994) 281-3.

Kee, H.C.   'The Transformation of the Synagogue after 70 C.E.: its Import for Early Christianity', *New Testament Studies* 36 (1990) 1-24.

Kent, J.H.   *Corinth — Inscriptions 1926-1950. Corinth: Results, viii, Part III* (Princeton, 1966).

Kittredge, C.B.   *Community and Authority: the Rhetoric of Obedience in the Pauline Tradition* (Harvard Theological Studies, 45; Harrisburg: Trinity Press International, 1998).

Klauck, H.-J.   *Hausgemeinde und Hauskirche im frühen Christentum* (Stuttgarter Bibelstudien, 103; Stuttgart: Verlag Katholisches Bibelwerk, 1981).

Kloppenborg, J.S. 'Collegia and *Thiasoi*: Issues in Function, Taxonomy and Membership', in J.S. Kloppenborg & S.G. Wilson (eds.), *Voluntary Associations in the Graeco-Roman World* (London: Routledge, 1996) 16-30.

Kloppenborg, J.S. 'Edwin Hatch, Churches and Collegia', in B.H. McLean (ed.), *Origins and Method: Towards a New Understanding of Judaism and Christianity* (JSNT Supplement Series, 86; Sheffield: JSOT Press, 1993) 212-38.

Kloppenborg, J.S. & Wilson, S.G. (eds.) *Voluntary Associations in the Graeco-Roman World* (London: Routledge, 1996).

Knox, J.   *Philemon among the Letters of Paul: a New View of its Place and Importance* (Chicago: University of Chicago Press, 1935).

Kraabel, A.T.   'Unity and Diversity among Diaspora Synagogues', in J.A. Overman & R.S. MacLennan (eds.), *Diaspora Jews and Judaism: Essays in Honor of, and in Dialogue with, A. Thomas Kraabel* (South Florida Studies in the History of Judaism, 41; Atlanta: Scholars Press, 1992) 21-33.

Kraabel, A.T.   'The Synagogue at Sardis: Jews and Christians', in J.A. Overman & R.S. MacLennan (eds.), *Diaspora Jews and Judaism: Essays in Honor of, and in Dialogue with, A. Thomas Kraabel* (South Florida Studies in the History of Judaism, 41; Atlanta: Scholars Press, 1992) 225-36.

Kraabel, A.T.   'Social Systems of Six Diaspora Synagogues', in J.A. Overman & R.S. MacLennan (eds.), *Diaspora Jews and Judaism: Essays in Honor of, and in Dialogue with, A. Thomas Kraabel* (South Florida Studies in the History of Judaism, 41; Atlanta: Scholars Press, 1992) 257-67.

Kraabel, A.T.   'The Diaspora Synagogue: Archaeological and Epigraphic Evidence since Sukenik', *Aufstieg und Niedergang der Römischen Welt* II.19.1 (1979) 477-510.

Krentz, E.M.   'Military Language and Metaphors in Philippians', in B.H. McLean (ed.), *Origins and Method: Towards a New Understanding of Judaism and Christianity* (JSNT Supplement Series, 86; Sheffield: JSOT Press, 1993) 105-27.

Lacey, W.K.   '*Patria Potestas*', in B. Rawson (ed.), *The Family in Ancient Rome: New Perspectives* (London: Routledge, 1986) 121-44.

Lampe, P.   'Theological Wisdom and the "Word about the Cross": The Rhetorical Scheme in 1 Corinthians 1-4', *Interpretation* 44 (1990) 117-31.

Lampe, P.   'Keine Sklavenflucht des Onesimus', *Zeitschrift für die Neutestamentliche Wissenschaft* 76 (1985) 135-7.

Lane, W.L.   'Social Perspectives on Roman Christianity during the Formative Years from Nero to Nerva: Romans, Hebrews, *1 Clement*', in K.P. Donfried & P.

Richardson (eds.), *Judaism and Christianity in First-Century Rome* (Grand Rapids: Eerdmans, 1998) 196-244.

Lane Fox, R.   *Pagans and Christians* (Harmondsworth: Viking, 1986).

Lassen, E.M.   'The Roman Family: Ideal and Metaphor', in H. Moxnes (ed.), *Constructing Early Christian Families: Family as Social Reality and Metaphor* (London: Routledge, 1997) 103-20.

Lassen, E.M.   'The Use of the Father Image in Imperial Propaganda and 1 Corinthians 4:14-21', *Tyndale Bulletin* 42 (1991) 127-36.

Last, H.   'The Social Policy of Augustus', in S.A. Cook, F.E. Adcock, & M.P. Charlesworth (eds.), *The Cambridge Ancient History* X (Cambridge: Cambridge University Press, 1966) 425-64.

Lendon, J.E.   *Empire of Honour: the Art of Government in the Roman World* (Oxford: Clarendon Press, 1997).

Leon, H.J.   *The Jews of Ancient Rome* (Philadelphia: Jewish Publication Society, 1960).

Levine, L.I.   'The Nature and Origin of the Palestinian Synagogue Reconsidered', *Journal of Biblical Literature* 115 (1996) 425-448.

Levine, L.I.   'Synagogue Officials: the Evidence from Caesarea and its Implications for Palestine and the Diaspora', in A. Raban and K.G. Holum (eds.), *Caesarea Maritima: a Retrospective after two Millennia* (Documenta et monumenta Orientis antiqui, 21; Leiden: E.J. Brill, 1996) 392-400.

Levine, L.I.   'The Synagogue in the Second Temple Period — Architectural and Social Interpretation' (in Hebrew), *Eretz Israel* 23 (1992) 331-44.

Levine, L.I.   'The Second Temple Synagogue: the Formative Years', in L.I. Levine (ed.), *The Synagogue in Late Antiquity* (Philadelphia: American Schools of Oriental Research, 1987) 7-31.

Levine, L.I.   'The Synagogue of Dura-Europos', in L.I. Levine (ed.), *Ancient Synagogues Revealed* (Jerusalem: Israel Exploration Society, 1982) 172-7.

Levine, L.I. (ed.)   *The Synagogue in Late Antiquity* (Philadelphia: American Schools of Oriental Research, 1987).

Levinskaya, I.   *The Book of Acts in its Diaspora Setting* (The Book of Acts in its First Century Setting, 5; Grand Rapids: Eerdmans, 1996).

Lewis, N. & Reinhold, M. (eds.)   *Roman Civilization: Sourcebook, Vol. 2: The Empire* (New York: Harper & Row, 1966).

Liebeschuetz, J.H.W.G. *Continuity and Change in Roman Religion* (Oxford: Clarendon Press, 1979).

Lincoln, A.T.   *Paradise Now and Not Yet: Studies in the Role of the Heavenly Dimension in Paul's Thought with Special Reference to his Eschatology* (SNTS Monograph Series, 43; Cambridge: Cambridge University Press, 1981).

Linders, T.   'Ritual Display and the Loss of Power', in P. Hellström & B. Alroth (eds.), *Religion and Power in the Ancient Greek World: Proceedings of the Uppsala Symposium 1993* (Acta Universitatis Upsaliensis. Boreas, 24; Uppsala: Ubsaliensis S. Academiae, 1996) 121-4.

Lintott, A.W.   'Clubs, Roman', in *The Oxford Classical Dictionary* (Oxford: Oxford University Press, 1996) 352-3.

Lintott, A.W.   *Imperium Romanum: Politics and Administration* (London: Routledge, 1993).

Litfin, D.   *St. Paul's Theology of Proclamation: 1 Corinthians 1-4 and Greco-Roman Rhetoric* (SNTS Monograph Series, 79; Cambridge: Cambridge University Press, 1994).

Longenecker, R.N.   *Galatians* (Word Biblical Commentary, 41; Dallas: Word Books, 1990).

Lüderitz, G.   'What is the Politeuma?' in J.W. van Henten & P.W. van der Horst, *Studies in Early Jewish Epigraphy* (Arbeiten zur Geschichte des antiken Judentums und des Urchristentums, 21; Leiden: E.J. Brill, 1994) 183-225.

McCready, W.O.   '*Ecclesia* and Voluntary Associations', in J.S. Kloppenborg & S.G. Wilson (eds.), *Voluntary Associations in the Graeco-Roman World* (London: Routledge, 1996) 59-73.

McKay, H.A.   'Ancient Synagogues: the Continuing Dialectic between two Major Views', *Currents in Research: Biblical Studies* 6 (1998) 103-42.

McKay, H.A.   *Sabbath and Synagogue: the Question of Sabbath Worship in Ancient Judaism* (Religions in the Graeco-Roman World, 122; Leiden: E.J. Brill, 1994).

McLean, B.H.   'The Place of Cult in Voluntary Associations and Christian Churches on Delos', in J.S. Kloppenborg & S.G. Wilson (eds.), *Voluntary Associations in the Graeco-Roman World* (London: Routledge, 1996) 186-225.

McLean, B.H.   'The Agrippinilla Inscription: Religious Associations and Early Church Formation', in B.H. McLean (ed.), *Origins and Method: Towards a New Understanding of Judaism and Christianity* (JSNT Supplement Series, 86; Sheffield: JSOT Press, 1993) 239-70.

Malherbe, A.J.   'God's New Family in Thessalonica', in L.M. White & O.L. Yarbrough (eds.), *The Social World of the First Christians: Essays in Honor of Wayne A. Meeks* (Minneapolis: Fortress Press, 1995) 116-25.

Malherbe, A.J.   *Paul and the Thessalonians: the Philosophic Tradition of Pastoral Care* (Philadelphia: Fortress Press, 1987).

Malherbe, A.J.   *Social Aspects of Early Christianity* (Baton Rouge: Louisiana State University Press, 1977).

Marshall, P.   *Enmity in Corinth: Social Conventions in Paul's Relations with the Corinthians* (WUNT, 2.23; Tübingen: J.C.B. Mohr, 1987).

Martin, C.J.   'The Rhetorical Function of Commercial Language in Paul's Letter to Philemon (Verse 18)', in D.F. Watson (ed.), *Persuasive Artistry: Studies in New Testament Rhetoric in Honor of George A. Kennedy* (JSNT Supplement Series, 50; Sheffield: JSOT Press, 1991) 321-37.

Martin, D.B.   'The Construction of the Ancient Family: Methodological Considerations', *Journal of Roman Studies* 86 (1996) 40-60.

Meeks, W.A.   *The Moral World of the First Christians* (Library of
                   Early Christianity, 6; Philadelphia: Westminster
                   Press, 1986).

Meeks, W.A.   *The First Urban Christians: the Social World of the
                   Apostle Paul* (New Haven: Yale University Press,
                   1983).

Meeks, W.A. & Wilken, R.L. *Jews and Christians in Antioch in the First
                   Four Centuries of the Common Era* (Society of Biblical
                   Literature: Sources for Biblical Study 13; Missoula:
                   Scholars Press, 1978).

Meggitt, J.J.   *Paul, Poverty and Survival* (Studies of the New
                   Testament and its World; Edinburgh: T. & T. Clark,
                   1998).

Meritt, B.D.   *Corinth — Greek Inscriptions 1896-1927. Corinth:
                   Results, viii, Part I* (Cambridge MA, 1931).

Meyers, E.M.   'Ancient Synagogues: an Archaeological
                   Introduction', in S. Fine (ed.), *Sacred Realm: the
                   Emergence of the Synagogue in the Ancient World*
                   (Oxford: Oxford University Press, 1996) 3-20.

Meyers, E.M.   'Synagogue', in D.N. Freedman (ed.), *Anchor Bible
                   Dictionary* (vol. 6; New York: Doubleday, 1992) 251-
                   263.

Michaelis, W.   'μιμέομαι κτλ.', *Theological Dictionary of the New
                   Testament* 4 (1968) 659-74.

Míguez, N.O.   'La composición social de la Iglesia en Tesalónica',
                   Revista Bíblica 51.34 (1989) 65-89.

Millar, F.   *The Roman Empire and its Neighbours* (2nd ed.;
                   London: Duckworth, 1981).

Miller, E.C.   'Πολιτεύεσθε in Philippians 1:27: Some Philological
                   and Thematic Observations', *Journal for the Study of
                   the New Testament* 15 (1982) 86-96.

Mitchell, M.M.   *Paul and the Rhetoric of Reconciliation: an Exegetical
                   Investigation of the Language and Composition of
                   1 Corinthians* (Hermeneutische Untersuchungen zur
                   Theologie, 28; Tübingen: J.C.B. Mohr, 1991).

Mitchell, S.   *Anatolia: Land, Men, and Gods in Asia Minor* (2 vols.;
                   Oxford: Clarendon Press, 1993).

Mitchell, S.   'Imperial Building in the Eastern Roman Provinces', in S. Macready & F.H. Thompson (eds.), *Roman Architecture in the Greek World* (Occasional Paper, Society of Antiquaries of London, New Series, 10; London: Thames and Hudson, 1987) 18-25.

Moore, G.F.   *Judaism in the First Centuries of the Christian Era: The Age of the Tannaim* (3 vols.; Cambridge: Harvard University Press, 1927-30).

Moore, S.D.   *Poststructuralism and the New Testament: Derrida and Foucault at the Foot of the Cross* (Minneapolis: Fortress, 1994).

Morgan-Gillman, F.   'Jason of Thessalonica (Acts 17,5-9)', in R.F. Collins (ed.), *The Thessalonian Correspondence* (Bibliotheca ephemeridum theologicarum lovaniensium, 87; Leuven: Leuven University Press, 1990) 39-49.

Morris, L.   'The Saints and the Synagogue', in M.J. Wilkins & T. Paige (eds.), *Worship, Theology and Ministry in the Early Church: Essays in Honor of Ralph P. Martin* (JSNT Supplement Series, 87; Sheffield: JSOT, 1992) 39-52.

Moule, C.F.D.   *The Birth of the New Testament* (3rd ed.; Harper's New Testament Commentaries; San Francisco: Harper & Row, 1982).

Moxnes, H.   'What is Family?: Problems Constructing Early Christian Families', in H. Moxnes (ed.), *Constructing Early Christian Families: Family as Social Reality and Metaphor* (London: Routledge, 1997) 13-41.

Moxnes, H.   '"He saw that the City was full of Idols" (Acts 17:16): Visualizing the World of the First Christians', in D. Hellholm, H. Moxnes & T.K. Seim (eds.), *Mighty Minorities?: Minorities in Early Christianity — Positions and Strategies: Essays in Honour of Jacob Jervell on his 70th Birthday, 21 May 1995* (Oslo: Scandinavian University Press, 1995) 107-31.

Moxnes, H.   'The Quest for Honor and the Unity of the Community in Romans 12 and in the Orations of

Dio Chrysostom', in T. Engberg-Pedersen (ed.), *Paul in his Hellenistic Context* (Studies of the New Testament and its World; Edinburgh: T. & T. Clark, 1994) 203-30.

Murphy O'Connor, J. 'Galatians 4:13-14 and the Recipients of "Galatians"', *Revue Biblique* 105 (1998) 202-207.

Neill, S. *The Interpretation of the New Testament, 1861-1986* (2nd ed.; Oxford: Oxford University Press, 1988).

Nock, A.D., Roberts, C. & Skeat, T.C. 'The Guild of Zeus Hypsistos', *Harvard Theological Review* 29 (1936) 39-88.

Nordling, J.G. 'Onesimus Fugitivus: a Defense of the Runaway Slave Hypothesis in Philemon', *Journal for the Study of the New Testament* 41 (1991) 97-119.

North, J.A. 'Religion and Politics, from Republic to Principate', *Journal of Roman Studies* 76 (1986) 251-8.

Noy, D. *Jewish Inscriptions of Western Europe* (2 vols.; Cambridge: Cambridge University Press, 1993-1995).

Oakes, P. 'Philippians: From People to Letter', *Tyndale Bulletin* 47 (1996) 371-4.

Oakes, P. *Philippians: From People to Letter* (DPhil dissertation; Oxford: Oxford University, 1995; Cambridge: Cambridge University Press, forthcoming).

O'Brien, P.T. *Gospel and Mission in the Writings of Paul: an Exegetical and Theological Analysis* (Grand Rapids: Baker Books, 1995).

O'Brien, P.T. 'The Gospel and Godly Models in Philippians', in M.J. Wilkins & T. Paige (eds.), *Worship, Theology and Ministry in the Early Church: Essays in Honor of Ralph P. Martin* (JSNT Supplement Series, 87; Sheffield: JSOT, 1992) 273-84.

Ogilvie, R.M. *The Romans and their Gods in the Age of Augustus* (London: Chatto & Windus, 1969).

O'Neil, J.L. *The Origins and Development of Ancient Greek Democracy* (Greek Studies; Lanham: Rowman & Littlefield, 1995).

Orr, D.G.   'Roman Domestic Religion: the Evidence of the Household Shrines', *Aufstieg und Niedergang der Römischen Welt* 16.2 (1978) 1557-91.

Oster, R.E.   'Supposed Anachronism in Luke-Acts' Use of ΣΥΝΑΓΩΓΗ", *New Testament Studies* 39 (1993) 178-208.

Ovadiah, A. & Michaeli, T., 'Observations on the Origin of the Architectural Plan of Ancient Synagogues', *Journal of Jewish Studies* 38 (1987) 234-41.

Overman, J.A. & MacLennan, R.S. (eds.) *Diaspora Jews and Judaism: Essays in Honour of, and in Dialogue with, A. Thomas Kraabel* (South Florida Studies in the History of Judaism, 41; Atlanta: Scholars Press, 1992).

Parker, R.   *Athenian Religion: a History* (Oxford: Clarendon Press, 1996).

Perkins, P.   'Philippians: Theology for the Heavenly Politeuma', in J.M. Bassler (ed.), *Pauline Theology: Volume I — Thessalonians, Philippians, Galatians, Philemon* (Minneapolis: Fortress Press, 1991) 89-104.

Perkins, P.   '1 Thessalonians and Hellenistic Religious Practices', in M.P. Horgan & P.J. Kobelski (eds.), *To Touch the Text: Biblical and Related Studies in Honor of Joseph A. Fitzmyer, S.J.* (New York: Crossroad, 1989) 325-34.

Perkins, P.   'Christology, Friendship and Status: the Rhetoric of Philippians', *Society of Biblical Literature 1987 Seminar Papers* (Atlanta: Scholars Press, 1987) 509-20.

Perkins, P.   *Ministering in the Pauline Churches* (New York: Paulist Press, 1982).

Peterlin, D.   *Paul's Letter to the Philippians in the Light of Disunity in the Church* (Supplements to Novum Testamentum, 79; Leiden; New York: E.J. Brill, 1995).

Petersen, N.R.   *Rediscovering Paul: Philemon and the Sociology of Paul's Narrative World* (Philadelphia: Fortress Press, 1985).

Pilhofer, P.   *Philippi vol. 1: die Erste Christliche Gemeinde Europas* (WUNT, 87; Tübingen: J.C.B. Mohr, 1995).

Pinnock, J.   'The History of the Diaconate', in C. Hall (ed.), *The Deacon's Ministry* (Leominster: Gracewing, 1991) 9-24.

Polaski, S.H.   *Paul and the Discourse of Power* (Gender, Culture, Theory, 8; Sheffield: JSOT Press, 1999).

Pomeroy, S.B.   *Families in Classical and Hellenistic Greece: Representations and Realities* (Oxford: Clarendon Press, 1997).

Price, S.R.F.   *Rituals and Power: the Roman Imperial Cult in Asia Minor* (Cambridge: Cambridge University Press, 1984).

Rajak, T.   'Jewish Rights in the Greek Cities under Roman Rule: a New Approach', in W.S. Green (ed.), *Approaches to Ancient Judaism* (Studies in Judaism and its Greco-Roman Context, 5; Chico: Scholars Press, 1985).

Rajak, T.   'Jews and Christians in a Pagan World', in J. Neusner and E.S. Frerichs (eds.), *"To See Ourselves as Others See Us": Christians, Jews, "Others" in Late Antiquity* (Scholars Press Studies in the Humanities; Chico: Scholars Press, 1985) 247-62.

Rajak, T. & Noy, D.   '*Archisynagogoi*: Office, Title, and Social Status in the Greco-Jewish Synagogue', *Journal of Roman Studies* 83 (1993) 75-93.

Rapske, B.M.   *The Book of Acts and Paul in Roman Custody* (The Book of Acts in its First Century Setting, 3; Grand Rapids: Eerdmans, 1994).

Rapske, B.M.   'The Prisoner Paul in the Eyes of Onesimus', *New Testament Studies* 37 (1991) 187-203.

Rawson, B.   'Adult-Child Relationships in Roman Society', in B. Rawson (ed.), *Marriage, Divorce, and Children in Ancient Rome* (Oxford: Clarendon Press, 1991) 7-30.

Remus, H.   'Voluntary Association and Networks: Aelius Aristides at the Asclepieion in Pergamum', in J.S. Kloppenborg & S.G. Wilson (eds.), *Voluntary Associations in the Graeco-Roman World* (London: Routledge, 1996) 146-75.

Reynolds, J.   'Cities', in D.C. Braund (ed.), *The Administration of the Roman Empire (241 B.C. – A.D. 193)* (Exeter

Studies in History, 18; Exeter: University of Exeter, 1988) 15-51.

Rhodes, P.J.   *The Athenian Boule* (Oxford: Oxford University Press, 1985).

Rhodes, P.J. & Lewis, D.M.   *The Decrees of the Greek States* (Oxford: Clarendon Press, 1997).

Richardson, J.S.   *The Romans in Spain* (A History of Spain: Oxford: Blackwell, 1996).

Richardson, J.S.   'Imperium Romanum: Empire and the Language of Power', *Journal of Roman Studies* 81 (1991) 1-9.

Richardson, P.   'Augustan-Era Synagogues in Rome', in K.P. Donfried & P. Richardson (eds.), *Judaism and Christianity in First-Century Rome* (Grand Rapids: Eerdmans, 1998) 17-29.

Richardson, P.   'Early Synagogues as Collegia in the Diaspora and Palestine', in J.S. Kloppenborg & S.G. Wilson (eds.), *Voluntary Associations in the Graeco-Roman World* (London: Routledge, 1996) 90-109.

Richardson, P. & Heuchan, V.   'Jewish Voluntary Associations in Egypt and the Roles of Women', in J.S. Kloppenborg & S.G. Wilson (eds.), *Voluntary Associations in the Graeco-Roman World* (London: Routledge, 1996) 226-51.

Riesner, R.   'Synagogues in Jerusalem', in R. Bauckham (ed.), *The Book of Acts in its Palestinian Setting* (The Book of Acts in its First-Century Setting, 4; Grand Rapids: Eerdmans, 1995) 179-211.

Rives, J.B.   *Religion and Authority in Roman Carthage: from Augustus to Constantine* (Oxford: Clarendon Press, 1995).

Robinson, O.F.   *The Criminal Law of Ancient Rome* (London: Duckworth, 1995).

Rogers, G.M.   *The Sacred Identity of Ephesos: Foundation Myths of a Roman City* (London: Routledge, 1991).

Roos, A.G.   'De Titulo quodam latino Corinthi nuper reperto', *Mnemosyne* 58 (1930) 160-65.

Russell, R.   'The Idle in 2 Thess 3.6-12: an Eschatological or a Social Problem?', *New Testament Studies* 34 (1988) 105-19.

Rutgers, L.V.   *The Hidden Heritage of Diaspora Judaism* (Contributions to Biblical Exegesis and Theology, 20; Leuven: Peeters, 1998).

Safrai, Z.   'The Communal Functions of the Synagogue in the Land of Israel in the Rabbinic Period', in D. Urman & P.V.M. Flesher (eds.), *Ancient Synagogues: Historical Analysis and Archaeological Discovery* (Studia post-Biblica, 47; 2 vols.; Leiden: E.J. Brill, 1995) 181-204.

Saller, R.P.   *Patriarchy, Property and Death in the Roman Family* (Cambridge Studies in Population, Economy and Society in Past Time, 25; Cambridge: Cambridge University Press, 1994).

Saller, R.P.   'Corporal Punishment, Authority, and Obedience in the Roman Household', in B. Rawson (ed.), *Marriage, Divorce, and Children in Ancient Rome* (Oxford: Clarendon Press, 1991) 144-65.

Saller, R.P.   *'Familia, Domus* and the Roman Conception of the Family', *Phoenix* 38 (1984) 336-55.

Saller, R.P. & Shaw, B.D.   'Tombstones and Roman Family Relations in the Principate: Civilians, Soldiers and Slaves', *Journal of Roman Studies* 74 (1984) 124-56.

Sampley, J.P.   *Pauline Partnership in Christ: Christian Community and Commitment in Light of Roman Law* (Philadelphia: Fortress Press, 1980).

Sanders, E.P.   'Jewish Association with Gentiles and Galatians 2:11-14', in R.T. Fortna & B.R. Gaventa (eds.), *The Conversation Continues: Studies in Paul and John in Honor of J. Louis Martyn* (Nashville: Abingdon Press, 1990) 170-88.

Sandnes, K.O.   'Equality within Patriarchal Structures: Some New Testament Perspectives on the Christian Fellowship as a Brother- or Sisterhood and a Family', in H. Moxnes (ed.), *Constructing Early Christian Families: Family as Social Reality and Metaphor* (London: Routledge, 1997) 150-65.

Sandnes, K.O.   *A New Family: Conversion and Ecclesiology in the Early Church with Cross-cultural Comparisons* (Studien zur interkulturellen Geschichte des Christentums, 91; Bern: P. Lang, 1994).

Savage, T.B.   *Power through Weakness: Paul's Understanding of the Christian Ministry in 2 Corinthians* (SNTS Monograph Series, 86; Cambridge: Cambridge University Press, 1996).

Schmitt-Pantel, P. 'Collective Activities and the Political in the Greek City', in O. Murray and S. Price (eds.), *The Greek City: from Homer to Alexander* (Oxford: Clarendon Press, 1990) 199-213.

Schrage, W.   *Der erste Brief an die Korinther* (Evangelisch-katholischer Kommentar zum Neuen Testament, 7; Neukirchen-Vluyn: Neukirchener Verlag, 1991-95).

Schrage, W.   'ἀρχισυνάγωγος', *Theological Dictionary of the New Testament 7* (1971) 844-47.

Schürer, E.   *The History of the Jewish People in the Age of Jesus Christ (175 B.C. – A.D. 135)* (rev. ed.; 3 vols.; Edinburgh: T. & T. Clark, 1973-87).

Schürer, E.   *Die Gemeindeverfassung der Juden in Rom in der Kaiserzeit nach den Inschriften dargestellt, nebst 45 jüdischen Inschriften* (Leipzig: J.C. Hinrichs'sche Buchhandlung, 1879).

Schütz, J.H.   *Paul and the Anatomy of Apostolic Authority* (SNTS Monograph Series, 26; Cambridge: Cambridge University Press, 1975).

Schweizer, E.   *Church Order in the New Testament* (London: SCM Press, 1961).

Scullard, H.H.   *Festivals and Ceremonies of the Roman Republic* (London: Thames & Hudson, 1981).

Seland, T.   'Philo and the Clubs and Associations of Alexandria', in J.S. Kloppenborg & S.G. Wilson (eds.), *Voluntary Associations in the Graeco-Roman World* (London: Routledge, 1996) 110-127.

Shaw, B.D.   'The Cultural Meaning of Death: Age and Gender in the Roman Family', in D.I. Kertzer & R.P. Saller (eds.), *The Family in Italy: from Antiquity to the*

Present (New Haven: Yale University Press, 1991) 66-90.

Shaw, G.   *The Cost of Authority: Manipulation and Freedom in the New Testament* (London: SCM Press, 1983).

Simon, E.   *Die Götter der Römer* (Munich: Hirmer, 1990).

Smallwood, E.M. *The Jews under Roman Rule from Pompey to Diocletian: a Study in Political Relations* (Studies in Judaism in Late Antiquity; Leiden: E.J. Brill, 1981).

Smallwood, E.M. *Documents Illustrating the Principates of Gaius, Claudius and Nero* (Cambridge: Cambridge University Press, 1967).

Snyder, G.F.   'The Interaction of Jews with Non-Jews in Rome', in K.P. Donfried & P. Richardson (eds.), *Judaism and Christianity in First-Century Rome* (Grand Rapids: Eerdmans, 1998) 69-90.

Sordi, M.   *The Christians and the Roman Empire* (London: Routledge, 1994).

Sourvinou-Inwood, C. 'What is *Polis* Religion?', in O. Murray and S. Price (eds.), *The Greek City: From Homer to Alexander* (Oxford: Clarendon Press, 1990) 295-322.

Spawforth, A.J.S. 'Roman Corinth: the Formation of a Colonial Elite', in A.D. Rizakis (ed.), *Roman Onomastics in the Greek East: Social and Political Aspects* (Meletemata, 21; Athens: Kentron Hellenikes kai Romaikes Archaiotetos, 1996) 167-82.

Spawforth, A.J.S. 'The Achaean Federal Cult Part I: Pseudo-Julian, Letters 198', *Tyndale Bulletin* 46 (1995) 151-68.

Stambaugh, J.E.   *The Ancient Roman City* (Ancient Society and History; Baltimore: Johns Hopkins University Press, 1988).

Stambaugh, J.E.   'The Functions of Roman Temples', *Aufstieg und Niedergang der Römischen Welt* II.16.1 (1978) 554-608.

Stanley, D.M.   'Imitation in Paul's Letters: Its Significance for his Relationship to Jesus and to his own Christian Foundations', in P. Richardson and J.C. Hurd (eds.), *From Jesus to Paul: Studies in Honour of Francis Wright Beare* (Waterloo: Wilfrid Laurier University Press, 1984) 127-141.

Stowers, S.K.   'A Cult from Philadelphia: Oikos Religion or Cultic Association?', in A.J. Malherbe, F.W. Norris & J.W. Thompson (eds.), *The Early Church in its Context: Essays in Honor of Everett Ferguson* (Supplements to Novum Testamentum, 90; Leiden: Brill, 1998) 287-301.

Stowers, S.K.   'Friends and Enemies in the Politics of Heaven: Reading Theology in Philippians', in J.M. Bassler (ed.), *Pauline Theology: Volume I — Thessalonians, Philippians, Galatians, Philemon* (Minneapolis: Fortress Press, 1991) 105-21.

Stowers, S.K.   'Social Status, Public Speaking and Private Teaching: the Circumstances of Paul's Preaching Activity', *Novum Testamentum* 26 (1984) 59-82.

Strack, H.L. & Billerbeck, P. (eds.) *Kommentar zum Neuen Testament aus Talmud und Midrasch* (7 vols.; Munich: Beck, 1922-61).

Tellbe, M.   'The Sociological Factors behind Philippians 3:1-11 and the Conflict at Philippi', *Journal for the Study of the New Testament* 55 (1994) 97-121.

Tellbe, M.   *Christ and Caesar: the Letter to the Philippians in the Setting of the Roman Imperial Cult* (ThM dissertation; Vancouver: Regent College, 1993).

Theissen, G.   *The Social Setting of Pauline Christianity: Essays on Corinth* (Philadelphia: Fortress Press, 1982).

Thiselton, A.C.   *Interpreting God and the Postmodern Self: On Meaning, Manipulation, and Promise* (Edinburgh: T. & T. Clark, 1995).

Thiselton, A.C.   'Realized Eschatology at Corinth', *New Testament Studies* 24 (1978) 510-26.

Thomas, C.M.   'At Home in the City of Artemis: Religion in Ephesos in the Literary Imagination of the Roman Period', in H. Koester (ed.), *Ephesos Metropolis of Asia: an Interdisciplinary Approach to its Archaeology, Religion and Culture* (Harvard Theological Studies, 41; Valley Forge: Trinity Press International, 1995).

Trebilco, P.R.   *Jewish Communities in Asia Minor* (SNTS Monograph Series, 69; Cambridge: Cambridge University Press, 1991).

Tsafrir, Y.   'On the Source of the Architectural Design of the
                       Ancient Synagogues in Galilee: a New Appraisal',
                       in D. Urman & P.V.M. Flesher (eds.), *Ancient
                       Synagogues: Historical Analysis and Archaeological
                       Discovery* (Studia post-Biblica, 47; 2 vols.; Leiden:
                       E.J. Brill, 1995) 70-86.

Urman, D.   'The House of Assembly and the House of Study:
                       Are they one and the same?', *Journal of Jewish
                       Studies* 44 (1993) 236-57.

Urman, D. & Flesher, P.V.M. (eds.)*Ancient Synagogues: Historical
                       Analysis and Archaeological Discovery* (Studia post-
                       Biblica, 47; 2 vols.; Leiden: E.J. Brill, 1995).

Van der Horst, P.W.   *Ancient Jewish Epitaphs: an Introductory Survey
                       of a Millennium of Jewish Funerary Epigraphy (300
                       BCE – 700 CE)* (Contributions to Biblical Exegesis
                       and Theology, 2; Kampen: Kok, 1991).

Verner, D.C.   *The Household of God: the Social World of the Pastoral
                       Epistles* (Society of Biblical Literature Dissertation
                       Series, 71; Chico: Scholars Press, 1983).

Walker-Ramisch, S.   'Associations and the Damascus Document: a
                       Sociological Analysis', in J.S. Kloppenborg & S.G.
                       Wilson (eds.), *Voluntary Associations in the Graeco-
                       Roman World* (London: Routledge, 1996) 128-45.

Wallace, R. & Williams, W.   *The Three Worlds of Paul of Tarsus*
                       (London: Routledge, 1998).

Wallace-Hadrill, A.   'Family and Inheritance in the Augustan
                       Marriage-Laws', *Proceedings of the Cambridge
                       Philological Society* 207 (New Series, 27) (1981) 58-80.

Walters, J.C.   'Romans, Jews and Christians: the Impact of the
                       Romans on Jewish/Christian Relations in First-
                       Century Rome', in K.P. Donfried & P. Richardson
                       (eds.), *Judaism and Christianity in First-Century Rome*
                       (Grand Rapids: Eerdmans, 1998) 175-95.

Waltzing, J.P.   *Étude historique sur les corporations professionnelles
                       chez les Romains depuis les origines jusqu'à la chute de
                       l'Empire de l'Occident* (5 vols.; Hildesheim: Georg
                       Olms, 1970).

Wardman, A.   *Religion and Statecraft among the Romans* (London:
                       Granada, 1982).

Watson, F. 'The Two Roman Congregations: Romans 14:1-15:13', in K.P. Donfried (ed.), *The Romans Debate* (Revised & expanded ed.; Edinburgh: T. & T. Clark, 1991) 203-15.

Welborn, L.L. *Politics and Rhetoric in the Corinthian Epistles* (Macon: Mercer University Press, 1997).

West, A.B. *Corinth — Latin Inscriptions 1896-1920 Corinth: Results, viii, Part II* (Cambridge MA, 1931).

White, L.M. 'Synagogue and Society in Imperial Ostia: Archaeological and Epigraphic Evidence', *Harvard Theological Review* 90 (1997) 23-58 (also in K.P. Donfried & P. Richardson [eds.], *Judaism and Christianity in First-Century Rome* [Grand Rapids: Eerdmans, 1998] 30-63).

White, L.M. *The Social Origins of Christian Architecture: Building God's House in the Roman World: Architectural Adaptation among Pagans, Jews and Christians* (Harvard Theological Studies, 42; Valley Forge: Trinity Press International, 1996).

White, L.M. 'Visualizing the "Real" World of Acts 16: Toward Construction of a Social Index', in L.M. White & O.L. Yarbrough (eds.), *The Social World of the First Christians: Essays in Honor of Wayne A. Meeks* (Minneapolis: Fortress Press, 1995) 234-61.

White, L.M. 'Morality between Two Worlds: a Paradigm of Friendship in Philippians', in D.L. Balch, E. Ferguson & W.A. Meeks (eds.), *Greeks, Romans, and Christians: Essays in Honor of Abraham J. Malherbe* (Minneapolis: Fortress Press, 1990) 201-15.

White, L.M. 'The Delos Synagogue Revisited: Recent Fieldwork in the Graeco-Roman Diaspora', *Harvard Theological Review* 80 (1987) 133-60.

Whittaker, C.R. 'Imperialism and Culture: the Roman Initiative', in D.J. Mattingly (ed.), *Dialogues in Roman Imperialism: Power, Discourse, and Discrepant Experience in the Roman Empire* (Journal of Roman Archaeology, Supplementary Series, 23; Portsmouth, R.I.: Journal of Roman Archaeology, 1997) 143-63.

Wilken, R.L. *The Christians as the Romans Saw Them* (New Haven: Yale University Press, 1984).

Wilken, R.L.	'Collegia, Philosophical Schools, and Theology', in S. Benko & J.J. O'Rourke (eds.), *Early Church History: the Roman Empire as the Setting of Primitive Christianity* (London: Oliphants, 1971) 268-91.
Williams, C.K.	'The Refounding of Corinth: Some Roman Religious Attitudes', in S. Macready & F.H. Thompson (eds.), *Roman Architecture in the Greek World* (Occasional Paper, Society of Antiquaries of London, New Series, 10; London: Thames and Hudson, 1987) 26-37.
Williams, M.H.	'The Structure of Roman Jewry Re-considered — Were the Synagogues of Ancient Rome entirely Homogeneous?', *Zeitschrift für Papyrologie und Epigraphik* 104 (1994) 129-41.
Wilson, S.G.	'Voluntary Associations: an Overview', in J.S. Kloppenborg & S.G. Wilson (eds.), *Voluntary Associations in the Graeco-Roman World* (London: Routledge, 1996) 1-15.
Winter, B.W.	'Gallio's Exemption of Achaean Christians from the Imperial Cult', forthcoming.
Winter, B.W.	*Philo and Paul among the Sophists* (SNTS Monograph Series, 96; Cambridge: Cambridge University Press, 1997).
Winter, B.W.	'Gluttony and Immorality at Élitist Banquets: the Background to 1 Corinthians 6:12-20', *Jian Dao* 7 (1997) 55-67.
Winter, B.W.	'On Introducing Gods to Athens: an Alternative Reading of Acts 17:18-20', *Tyndale Bulletin* 47 (1996) 71-90.
Winter, B.W.	'The Achaean Federal Imperial Cult II: the Corinthian Church', *Tyndale Bulletin* 46 (1995) 169-78.
Winter, B.W.	*Seek the Welfare of the City: Christians as Benefactors and Citizens* (First Century Christians in the Graeco-Roman World; Grand Rapids: Eerdmans, 1994).
Winter, B.W.	'The Problem with "Church" for the Early Church', in D. Peterson & J. Pryor (eds.), *In the Fullness of Time: Biblical Studies in Honour of Archbishop Donald*

Winter, B.W.   'Civil Litigation in Secular Corinth and the Church:
                    the Forensic Background to 1 Corinthians 6.1-8',
                    New Testament Studies 37 (1991) 559-72.

Winter, B.W.   'Ethical and Theological Responses to Religious
                    Pluralism in Corinth — 1 Corinthians 8–10',
                    Tyndale Bulletin 41 (1990) 209-26.

Winter, B.W.   '"If a Man Does not Wish to Work...": a Cultural
                    and Historical Setting for 2 Thessalonians 3:6-16',
                    Tyndale Bulletin 40 (1989) 303-15.

Winter, B.W.   'Secular and Christian Responses to Corinthian
                    Famines', *Tyndale Bulletin* 40 (1989) 86-106.

Winter, B.W.   'The Public Honouring of Christian Benefactors:
                    Romans 13.3 and 1 Peter 2.14-15', *Journal for the
                    Study of the New Testament* 34 (1988) 87-103.

Winter, S.C.   'Paul's Letter to Philemon', *New Testament Studies*
                    33 (1987) 1-15.

Witherington, B.   *Conflict and Community in Corinth: a Socio-rhetorical
                    Commentary on 1 and 2 Corinthians* (Grand Rapids:
                    Eerdmans, 1995).

Witherington, B.   *Friendship and Finances in Philippi: the Letter of Paul
                    to the Philippians* (The New Testament in Context;
                    Valley Forge: Trinity Press International, 1994).

Witherington, B.   'Not so Idle Thoughts about *Eidolothuton*', *Tyndale
                    Bulletin* 44 (1993) 237-54.

Zanker, P.   *The Power of Images in the Age of Augustus* (Ann
                    Arbor: University of Michigan Press, 1988).

Zeitlin, S.   'The Origin of the Synagogue', in J. Gutmann (ed.),
                    *The Synagogue: Studies in Origins, Archaeology, and
                    Architecture* (The Library of Biblical Studies; New
                    York: Ktav, 1975) 14-26.

INDEX OF ANCIENT SOURCES

Tertullian
   Apologeticum
      38-39   70
      38   155
   De idololatria
      17.3   56
Thucydides
      7.77.7   13
      8.72.1   16
Valerius Maximus
      1.7.4   93
Varro
   Res rusticae
      3.2.16   63
Vergil
   Aeneid
      6.403   91
Xenophon
   Memorabilia
      1.2.35   15
      3.6.1   17

INDEX OF BIBLICAL REFERENCES

INDEX OF SUBJECTS

INDEX OF MODERN AUTHORS

Seland, T., 62, 71, 73, 156
Shaw, B.D., 84, 89
Shaw, G., 210-11
Simon, E., 97
Skeat, T.C., 63, 74
Smallwood, E.M., 75, 123
Snyder, G.F., 167
Sordi, M., 155
Sourvinou-Inwood, C., 19
Spawforth, A.J.S., 38, 42, 54
Stambaugh, J.E., 37, 38
Stanley, D.M., 224
Stegemann, E.W., 167, 190
Stowers, S.K., 162, 169
Strack, H.L., 105
Tellbe, M., 192, 193, 194, 195
Theissen, G., 67, 163, 174, 175, 184
Thiselton, A.C., 182, 211, 213, 214
Thomas, C.M., 24
Trebilco, P.R., 113, 135
Tsafrir, Y., 116
Urman, D., 121
Van der Horst, P.W., 126, 131, 132, 133
Verner, D.C., 85, 88, 89, 95, 160, 162, 164
Walker-Ramisch, S., 62, 71, 73, 76, 154
Wallace, R., 14, 24, 37, 38, 75
Wallace-Hadrill, A., 86
Walters, J.C., 167, 190
Waltzing, J.P., 60, 61, 63, 64, 70, 76
Wardman, A., 19
Watson, F., 190
Welborn, L.L., 180
West, A.B., 177

White, L.M., 108, 115, 126, 128, 130, 139, 161, 162
Whittaker, C.R., 36, 49, 57, 59
Wilken, R.L., 2, 62, 63, 154, 157
Williams, C.K., 20, 55
Williams, M.H., 114, 118, 128, 131, 132, 133, 134, 136, 140, 141
Williams, W., 14, 24, 37, 38, 75
Wilson, S.G., 62, 72, 76, 153
Winter, B.W., 13, 23, 43, 44, 53, 54, 57, 152, 153, 175, 176, 177, 179, 180, 181, 182, 183, 186, 187, 188, 189, 191, 196, 199, 200, 214, 242
Winter, S.C., 202, 203
Witherington, B., 183, 214
Zanker, P., 31, 55
Zeitlin, S., 107, 121